SEPTUAGINT:

COSMIC

GENESIS

SEPTUAGINT, VOLUME 1

SCRIPTURAL RESEARCH INSTITUTE

Published by Digital Ink Productions, 2025

COPYRIGHT

Septuagint: Cosmic Genesis

Fourth edition. September 15, 2025

Copyright © 2025 Scriptural Research Institute

ISBN: 978-1998636426

The Septuagint was translated into Greek at the Library of Alexandria between 250 and 132 BCE.

This English translation was created by the Scriptural Research Institute in 2019 through 2025, through the comparison of most published copies of Septuagint manuscripts. Additionally, the Leningrad Codex, Peshitta, Coptic, Ge'ez, and Armenian Bibles, Targums, and Dead Sea Scrolls were used for comparative analysis.

The image used for the cover is an artistic reinterpretation of "The Tower of Babel" by Joos de Momper the Younger and Frans Francken the Younger, painted sometime between 1590 and 1635. The original painting is currently located at the Royal Museums of Fine Arts of Belgium, in Brussels (Accession number: 8032).

Ebook version: ISBN 978-1998288885

Audiobook version: ISBN 978-1990289378

Hard Cover version: ISBN 978-1998636433

TABLE OF CONTENTS

TABLE OF CONTENTS

TABLE OF CONTENTS

TABLE OF CONTENTS

FORWARD

In the mid-3rd century BCE, King Ptolemy II Philadelphus of Egypt commissioned a translation of the ancient Israelite scriptures for the Library of Alexandria. This resulted in the creation of the Septuagint. The original version, published around 250 BCE, only included the Torah, also known as the Pentateuch in Greek. The Torah consists of the five books traditionally attributed to Moses, dating back to around 1500 BCE: Cosmic Genesis, Exodus, Leviticus, Numbers, and Deuteronomy.

The first of these five books was known as *Genesis Kosmou* (Γενεσις Κοσμου) in Greek, meaning "Cosmic Genesis," but as bərē'šît (בְּרֵאשִׁית) in Hebrew, which roughly translates to "In the beginning," the first few words of the book. This name is generally anglicized as *Bereshít*, and used as a reference to the versions of the book found in the Leningrad Codex and the targums. It is generally accepted that several versions existed in Aramaic and Canaanite before the translation of the Septuagint. Fragments of *Bereshít* have been found in Hebrew and Aramaic among the Dead Sea Scrolls, dated to between 300 BCE and 600 CE.

During this time, the land of Judea transitioned from the rule of the Ptolemies in Egypt to the rule of the Seleucids in Syria around 200 BCE. The Seleucids attempted to Hellenize the Judeans and effectively banned traditional Judaism. This Hellenizing activity was partially successful, leading to the

1

creation of the Sadducee faction of Judaism. However, it also led to the Maccabean Revolt in 165 BCE, which established the independent Hasmonean Kingdom of Judea in 140 BCE.

This kingdom was extremely xenophobic and governed by a priestly monarchy that wielded both state and church authority. The Hasmonean dynasty sought to conquer the entire territory that had previously been part of the Persian Province of Judea. They either expelled or exterminated the existing inhabitants based on their ethnicity. When the Edomites were conquered, they were allowed to convert to Judaism en masse as they were believed to be the descendants of Esau. However, most other ethnic groups were not accepted.

The Hasmoneans blamed the Greeks for all of Judea's issues and tried to establish an alliance with the Roman Republic. They appear to have promoted Yahweh Sabaoth in part to strengthen ties with the Romans, as Iaw (Yahweh) was pronounced very similarly to Iove (Jupiter). The Romans reacted negatively to this and expelled the Judeans from Rome in 139 BCE, as documented by Valerius Maximus:

> *"Gnaeus Cornelius Hispalus, praetor peregrinus in the year of the consulate of Marcus Popilius Laenas and Lucius Calpurnius, ordered the astrologers by an edict to leave Rome and Italy within ten days, since by a fallacious interpretation of the stars they perturbed fickle and silly minds, thereby making profit out of their lies. The same praetor compelled the Judeans, who attempted to infect the Roman custom with the cult of*

Jupiter Sabazius, to return to their homes."

During the rule of the Hasmoneans in Judea, they changed the national script from the old Canaanite script, today known as Paleo-Hebrew, to the Aramaic "block script," which is now called Hebrew. As a result, most surviving texts from the Hasmonean era and later are written in the Assyrian script, and it is uncertain to what extent the Hasmoneans edited the scriptures when they transcribed them. The scriptures left by the Hasmoneans later became the basis of the Masoretic text, which is used today by Rabbinical Jews, as well as by Catholic and Protestant Christians.

While the origin of *Cosmic Genesis / Bereshít* has been debated for millennia, it is not the most debated aspect of the book. The central theme is the relationship between humanity and something called 'ĕlōhîm (אֱלֹהִים), which the Greeks generally translated as "God" (Θεος). The Masoretic texts are mostly written in Hebrew, which is derived from Phoenician, although it also contains Aramaic words and sections; however, 'ĕlōhîm is not the word for "God" in either Phoenician or Aramaic.

In Bronze Age Ugaritic Canaanite, the word for "god" was ål (𐎛𐎍), while the word for goddess was ålh (𐎛𐎍𐎅), and ålhm (𐎛𐎍𐎅𐎎) was Canaanite for "goddesses." This confusion is manifest in various translations, where the gender in the texts shifts around elohim; however, the main source texts always agree that 'ĕlōhē is a masculine form regarding the Israelite god. This is likely because the term ål (𐤋𐤀) had become synonymous with El, the patriarch of the Canaanite pantheon by the beginning of the Iron Age, and the other gods were referred to as bȯl (ᴌᴑꟼ), meaning "lord." Therefore, the Aramaic word ȧlhȧ (𐎐𐎅𐎍𐎐), which means "god," was adopted at some point by the Israelites to denote a generic "god."

In *Names*, the Masoretic version of *Exodus*, the term 'ĕlōhē is generally used to connect texts from the time of Moses to older texts, such as the phrase "god of Abraham, god of Isaac, and god of Jacob," suggesting the Aramaic phrases were added circa 836 BCE, when the texts of Bereshít and Names were standardized under the rule of King Jehoash of Judah.

The form 'ĕlōhîm is found in the older sections of text, and is clearly a word used to denote either a singular god in some verses, or a plurality of gods in other verses. The Masoretic texts generally demark the difference between "God" and "gods" by adding "the" to the beginning of the word, rendering the plural form as hā'ĕlōhîm (הָאֱלֹהִים). This is particularly evident in Masoretic Daniel, where "lord of the gods" is rendered as 'ădōnāy hā'ĕlōhîm (אֲדֹנָי הָאֱלֹהִים) in the Aramaic sections. The origin of 'ĕlōhîm as a singular form for the Israelite god, likely dates back the translation of the older sections of text from cuneiform into the Phoenician script early in the Iron Age, plausibly in the Kingdom of Israel.

The names of the Israelite god are even more confusing in *Names* and *Exodus*, where the god identifies himself as Ōn (Ων), 'Ănā' (אֲנָא), Ånå (ܐܢܐ), and 'Ehyê (אֶהְיֶה), in the various Greek and Aramaic translations, while the Leningrad Codex contains the somewhat whimsical phrase 'ehyê 'ăšer 'ehyê (אֶהְיֶה אֲשֶׁר אֶהְיֶה), meaning "I will be what I will be."

4

Before the vowel markings that developed in the Medieval era, the Targum Jerusalem's 'Ănā' (אֲנָא) would have been Ånå (אנא), indicating there was an old Aramaic version of *Exodus* that used the name Ånå (ℵℽℵ). Ånå is not based on the Greek Ōn, as direct transliterations would be Ôn (ען) and Ôn (ܢ). The Library of Alexandra translated the Septuagint from the copies available in Egypt, indicating that the Egypto-Aramaic version of *Exodus* used the name Ôn (ℽℳ). Conversely, the Ånå (ℵℽℵ) variant is only found in texts that would have drawn from the Syro-Aramaic texts. The Peshitta is written in the Syriac form of Aramaic, and the Targum Jerusalem is written in Palestinian Aramaic. The fact that the Masoretes, who were based in Babylon, and spoke Aramaic, added the vowel markings that changed "king" Ôn (ענמלך) to "king" Ana (עֲנָמֶלֶךְ) in Masoretic Kings (Septuagint's 4th Kingdoms), supports Ana being the Syro-Aramaic pronunciation of the Samaritan and Egypto-Aramaic Ôn.

These variations of Ōn, Ånå, and 'Ehyê, as well as the singular interpretation of the word 'ĕlōhîm, can all be explained if the original phrase in the late Bronze Age text of *Names* used the name ^{deity}Éa (✳▤𒐊). Elum (✳) was the Babylonian word for "god," which was pronounced in Neo-Sumerian as ^{deity}Anu (✳𒐊𒀭). ^{deity}Éa (✳▤𒐊) was the Babylonian pronunciation of the old Akkadian name Ia (▤𒐊), the god of life and fresh water. The Canaanite version of Ia was Ym (ℽℤ), the god of the sea, therefore, transliterating ^{deity}Éa (✳▤𒐊) into the Phoenician script by the Israelites at the beginning of the Iron Age would have rendered it as

Ålhym (𐤀𐤋𐤄𐤉𐤌), the exact word found in Dead Sea Scroll 4QpaleoGen-Exod[1], which was later transliterated into Hebrew as ålhym (אלהים). This god was certainly not Ba'al Yam, the Canaanite "lord of the sea," and so the generic word ålh (𐤀𐤋𐤄) would have been used, even if it rendered a word very similar to the Phoenician word ålhm (𐤀𐤋𐤄𐤌) meaning "goddesses."

Unfortunately, the Greek translation doesn't generally distinguish between the singular and plural forms, almost always rendering the term as "the god" (o θεοσ). However, this does create some confusing concepts, such as the Egyptians worshiping the God of the Israelites instead of their own gods. In order to clarify the text, the distinction of "god" versus "gods" is imported from the Leningrad Codex, where the Hebrew reads 'ĕlōhē (אֱלֹהֵי), 'ĕlōhîm (אֱלֹהִים), or hā'ĕlōhîm (הָאֱלֹהִים), when not distinguished in the Septuagint manuscripts.

The Aramaic sections of Masoretic *Daniel* that were not translated into Hebrew maintain the term ădōnāy hā'ĕlōhîm (אֲדֹנָי הָאֱלֹהִים), meaning "Lord of the gods," while the Septuagint has "Lord the god" (Κυριον τον θεον). However, the Hebrew sections have Yəhwâ 'ĕlōhîm (יְהוָה אֱלֹהִים) where the Septuagint has "Lord the god," suggesting that the Greek version more accurately reflects the Aramaic source texts than the Hebrew translation. According to tractate *Sanhedrin* (103b) in the Talmud, this was done to repair the damage King Manasseh had done 500 years earlier when he removed the name Yahweh from the Israelite texts. However, no evidence

6

has survived from the era of Manasseh or earlier that proves the name was originally in the text, suggesting it was an attempt by the first Hasmonean High-Priest/King Simon the Zealous to create a national Judean religion with a god having a name similar to the Roman god Jove.

The name Yahweh, in the Aramaic form of Yhw (יהוֹ^) in the Judean manuscripts and Yåw (יאוֹ^) in Egyptian Israelite manuscripts, appears to have originally been transliterated into Greek in some of the books of the Septuagint, such as Leviticus. These books originated under the rule of King Josiah of Judah or later, and Yahweh was a popular god among Judeans and Israelites under Persian and Greek rule. The translators at the Library of Alexandria transliterated this name as Iaō (Ιαω) while the Old Latin translators rendered it as Iaw, both derived from the Egypto-Aramaic form of Yåw (יאוֹ^). However, under the Hasmonean Dynasty, it seems to have been added to all the books translated into Hebrew in the form of Yhwh (יהוה), creating some confusion among early Christians. This name was later accented as both Yəhōwâ (יְהוָֹה) and Yhōwâ (יְהוָֹה) in *Bereshít.* The common academic transliteration is Yahweh, which is used in this translation.

There were debates in the early Christian era about which version of the Israelite scriptures to use: the Greek, Hebrew, Samaritan, or Syriac translations. This resulted in different versions of the scriptures being used by different churches. Some versions replaced the word "Lord" with the name Iaō in the Greek texts, either in the Greek form as Iaō (Ιαω), or by copying in the Hebrew form of the name Yhwh (יהוה) or the older Phoenician form of Yhwh (𐤉𐤄𐤅𐤉), or by mocking the Hebrew with Greek letters as pipi (ΠΙΠΙ). This created a great deal of confusion among Christians, and ultimately the books of the Septuagint that had the name Iaō in them were redacted so all the books used the term "Lord" (Κύριοσ).

Most Christian translations, as well as Jewish translations, have continued to use the term "Lord" in place of the name Yahweh, due to the prohibition on using any names of God that was introduced during the Hasmonean dynasty.

There are no early surviving copies of Cosmic Genesis that contain the name Iaō (Ιαω) like some of the other books of the Septuagint. Therefore, it cannot be proven if the name was originally in Cosmic Genesis or not. However, the terms used in Cosmic Genesis are consistent with the surviving Aramaic sections of Masoretic Daniel, strongly suggesting that the Aramaic source text the Greek translators used included the term ådny hålwhym (𐡔𐡀𐡕𐡋𐡀𐡄 𐡀𐡃𐡍𐡉), and not Yåw hålwhym (𐡔𐡀𐡕𐡋𐡀𐡄 𐡉𐡀𐡅). The Aramaic term meant "Lord of the gods," but it has been interpreted in several ways within monotheistic religions, including the Jewish "powers of Yahweh" and Christian "Lord of the Trinity." As the term that survives in the Aramaic sections of Masoretic Daniel is "lord of the gods," that term is used in this translation.

The Greek terms in Cosmic Genesis are translations of known Canaanite gods, particularly El, the Canaanite father-god. El translates as "God" in Canaanite dialects, including Hebrew, and was the primary god worshiped in ancient Canaan during the era when Abraham was reported to have passed through the area. If the Greeks accurately translated the Septuagint then the term God (Θεὸς) would have been Ål (ᴌN) in the texts they translated. Similarly, "Lord of the gods" (Κύριοσ o θεοσ) would have been adny hålwhym (ᴧᴪᴧN ᴦᴧᴧᴌNᴧ), the title of El, which translates as "Father of the gods."

The Canaanite word ålhym (ᴦᴢᴧᴌᴪ) and Aramaic word ålwhym (ᴦᴧᴧᴌN) are also transcriptions of the Neo-Assyrian word elium (𒀭𒇷𒌝), which by the Iron Age meant "god," indicating that the text had previously been written in cuneiform, and was translated into Aramaic or Phoenician during the Iron Age. During the era of the Akkadian Empire, the same word was pronounced as alium (𒀀𒇷𒌝) and referred to the god ^{deity}Ilu (𒀭𒀭), the highest god and father of the other gods. His Akkadian name was derived from the word elûm (𒂊𒇻), meaning "higher," as the term was intended to convey the meaning of "highest."

During the earlier Sumerian era, Ān (𒀭) was believed to reside in the polar region of the sky, where the modern constellation of Draco is located, making him the highest in the sky, around which all the gods (stars) circled. His son was the god ^{deity}Enki (𒀭𒂗𒆠), meaning "^{deity}lord Earth," who ruled the lowest part of the sky that dipped below the edge of the world (horizon) during some months. Enki's son and Ān's grandson was ^{deity}Enlil (𒀭𒂗𒇸), who ruled the sky above the horizon that wasn't in the polar region, where the stars appear to move throughout the year.

This trinity of supreme gods was challenged in the late Sumerian era by ^{deity}Inanna (✳𝕋𝕋), a deification of the planet Venus that was apparently imported from the distant land of Aratta. The mythology of Inanna's descent into the underworld and then ascension to heaven is mirrored by the observable movement of Venus as perceived by someone who views the Earth as flat. The planet is seen setting with the sun for a week and then is below the edge of the world for a week before being seen rising with the sun for a week. It isn't clear where Aratta was; however, it was also mentioned in the Vedic texts.

In the Sumerian stories that mention Aratta, it was described as being a distant land northeast of the Zagros Mountains that was rich in lapis lazuli, indicating it was in the region of Badakhshan, in northeast modern Afghanistan and southeastern Tajikistan. Based on the archaeological evidence, the Proto-Sumerians were importing lapis lazuli from the region since the Ubaid era, generally dated to between 4900 and 4000 BCE. While Badakhshan must have been rich by the standards of the time, little beyond the mines have been found, and it isn't clear if Aratta was the name of the region or a city in the region.

During the Akkadian era, the god ^{deity}Ia (✳▦𝕀𝕀), the god of floods, replaced Enki in the Sumero-Akkadian trinity. This god was believed to have caused the seasonal floods of the Euphrates and Tigris and was blamed for the great flood, although he was also generally believed to have saved the various flood survivors in Mesopotamian mythology: the Neo-

Sumerian Ziusudra (𒍑𒍣𒌓𒅅), Old Babylonian Atra-Hasis (𒀜𒊏𒄩𒋀), and Middle Babylonian Utnapištim (𒌓𒍣). In the later Mesopotamian cultures, it became taboo to pronounce the name of Ia, as he caused rivers to flood.

During the Neo-Sumerian era, the relationship between ^{deity}Ān (𒀭𒀭), the restored ^{deity}Enki (𒀭𒂗𒆠), and ^{deity}Enlil (𒀭𒂗𒇸) became more complicated, as Enlil became the dominant god, and multiple generations of gods were added between Enki and Enlil. Massive religious reforms took place during the Neo-Sumerian era, the era when Terah, his son Abram, daughter Sarai, and grandson Lot fled Ur. Priests fleeing Ur and traveling up the Euphrates into the rebelling Amorite lands appear to be commonplace during the reforms, mirroring the story of Terah traveling to Harran.

The religious reforms during the Neo-Sumerian era resulted in all the earliest writings of Sumer and the Proto-Sumerian era being destroyed, fortunately by being used as rubble in the unfinished Ziggurat of Amar-Sin. Archaeologists rediscovered the ancient script when studying the ruins of the ziggurat. Additional caches of the old script texts have been discovered in two places, one hidden in a cave in the Babylon governate in Iraq, and another hidden in a cave in Syria. Both caches appear to have been hidden during the religious reforms of Kings Shulgi (𒀭𒁺𒄄) and Amar-Sin (𒀭𒈠𒀭𒂗𒍣), who are the kings of Ur referred to as Khodollag / Kədārəlā'ōmer and Amarphad / 'Amrāpel in Cosmic Genesis and Bereshít.

Kings Shulgi left a very negative impression on the priest-hoods of southern Iraq that lasted a long time. The *Weidner Chronicle*, which is mainly known from Neo-Assyrian and Neo-Babylonian recensions, was purportedly copied from an Old Babylonian Chronicle, reported that Shulgi "did not perform his rites to the letter," and "he defiled his purification rituals." The Middle Babylonian Chronicle of Early Kings reports he tampered with the rites, and composed "untruthful stelae" with "insolent writings" on them.

During the Old Babylonian and Old Assyrian eras, the gods Marduk and Ashur, the national gods of Babylon and Assyria, replaced Enlil as the primary god of the Mesopotamian pantheons. By the Iron Age, the word elium had come to mean "god," explaining why the Aramaic term âlhym (ל^תנLN) would have been interpreted as "god" by the Greeks.

Nevertheless, the book of *Bereshít* mentions another god called ēl Šadday (אֵל שַׁדַּי), commonly transliterated as El Shaddai, who is considered to be the god of Abraham, Isaac, and Jacob. The name El Shaddai appears 48 times in the Masoretic text, with 31 occurrences in the *Book of Job*, 6 in *Bereshít*, and once in *Names* when Moses' god introduced himself as the god of Jacob and then revealed his name as Ōn ($\Omega\nu$) in *Exodus*' version of the verse. It seems that the refer-ences to El Shaddai in *Cosmic Genesis* and the identity of Ōn in the *Names* have been edited, as there is no mention of El Shaddai in *Cosmic Genesis* or Ōn in *Names* even though the name is transliterated as Åwn (און) in other Masoretic books.

El Shaddai was the supreme god of the Amorites, whom they called Bel Šadi (𒈜 𒂊𒀭). There are references in the Torah to the Israelites during the exodus believing that their god had previously been worshiped by the Amorites, which supports this god's name being in the original texts from the era of Moses. However, that does not inherently support the name being the name of Terah's god 600 years earlier. In the Akkadian era, the precursor to Bel Shaddai was [ilu]amurru (𒀭𒈥𒈬), the personification of the west wind. The Amorites were Akkadian colonists who settled in the western lands of Mari and Ebla as the Eblaite civilization was collapsing circa 2300 BCE. The Amorites adopted an Eblaite god, which they called Bel Shaddai, and the Neo-Sumerians incorporated him into their official pantheon of gods as [an]Martu (𒀭𒈥𒈬), meaning "[deity]shovel of the sick," and En Šadi (𒈜 𒂊𒀭), which can also be interpreted as "Lord to make healthy" in Neo-Sumerian. This god was known as [ilu]Amurru (𒀭𒌋𒀀) in Old Babylonian, meaning "god of the west."

Both [an]Martu and En Šadi appear in the archaeological record during the religious reforms of King Shulgi, indicating this was a reworking of an older god. The name of the people in Syria was already documented as Åmw (𓄿𓄿𓅱𓀭) in the Egyptian Old Kingdom era and continued as the name Åmw (𓂝𓏥) in the Middle Egyptian Execration texts. Åmw was both the name of the Amorites and the Egyptian word for "fire" or "burning," which suggests the Amorite pronunciation of "Amurru" was based on the name of the Eblaite god [ilu]Rasaap (𒀭𒊏𒊓𒀊). The Eblaite culture dominated western Syria between 3000 and 2300 BCE, while the

13

Amorites became dominant starting around 2300 BCE, and ultimately rebelled from the Neo-Sumerian Empire during the religious reforms of King Shulgi circa 2050 BCE.

The name Åmw was already documented in Egyptian records before the Amorites settled there, indicating it was originally a reference to the Eblaites. ^iluRasaap (✳𐎅𐎟𐎟) was adopted by the Amorites as ^iluRašaap (✳𐎅𐎟𐎟), the Canaanites as Ršp (𐎟𐎟𐎟), and the Egyptians as Ršpw (𐎟 𐎟𐎟) during the middle Bronze Age. His name is generally rendered as Resheph today, based on Resheph (רֶשֶׁף), the Hebrew version of the name found in the Leningrad Codex. Resheph is found in many Amorite theophoric names in the ruins of Emar and Canaanite names found in the ruins of Ugarit, while Amurru is not found in any, indicating that Amurru was the Neo-Sumerian reworking of Rašaap.

A Hurrian version of the name also survives as Irašabba (𐎟𐎟𐎟𐎟), indicating that the Hurrians also worshiped him under this name, however; the name appears to be Semitic in origin. The Hurrians in Syria also knew Resheph by the title of Ablu (𐎟𐎟). This roughly translates as the Amorite and Babylonian word for "son," and is generally accepted as a shortened version of the title Aplu ^iluEllil (𐎟𐎟 ✳𐎟𐎟), an epithet of Nergal, the son of the Babylonian god Ellil, who had been known as Enlil to the Neo-Sumerians. Nergal's earliest attested name was the Old Sumerian ^anKišunug (✳𐎟𐎟𐎟), meaning "^deityLord of the City," likely a reference to the city of Kutha, where his temple was located.

However, this became ^{ilu}Girunugal (✳︎ 𒐕𒐖 𒐗𒐘) in the Akkadian era, meaning "^{deity}Lord of the Great City," interpreted as the "city of the dead," or in other words, the underworld, known as Erṣetu (𒆠) in Akkadian. The logogram used for Erṣetu (𒆠) was also the Neo-Sumerian words ki (𒆠), meaning "land," and kur (𒆠), meaning "mountain." Therefore, the mountain that Bel Shaddai was the lord of, was likely a Neo-Sumerian reference to the underworld.

The modern name of Nergal is derived from his Hebrew name Neregal (נֵרְגַל) from the Leningrad Codex, itself descended from the Old Assyrian version of his name: ^{ilu}Ner-iiglá (✳︎ 𒈤 𒄘 𒐕). The name "Neregal" does not appear in the Torah, and is only mentioned as a foreign god in the Septuagint's *4th Kingdoms* (Masoretic *Kings*), set during the Neo-Assyrian era. However, El Shaddai (אֵל שַׁדַּי) is mentioned in the Torah and the Book of Job, which include some of the oldest Israelite text set during the middle and late Bronze Age, when the Amorites were dominant and then declining in Canaan.

Like Resheph and Nergal, the Hurrian Ablu was a god of both plague and healing. He was also imported to the Neshite (Hittite) and Trojan civilizations, as the god Apaliunas (𒀭𒀊𒈛𒌋𒈾𒀸) was mentioned in a peace treaty between the civilizations in 1280 BCE. Homer reported in the Illiad that Apollōn (Απολλων) was the god that built the walls of Troy, which confirms that the Greeks did view Apaliunas as Apollo. In the Illiad, a priest of Apollo called Chryses, referred to Apollo as the "Lord of Mice" as he was believed to protect from plagues of mice, which would explain why the Pelesets tried to appease the god of King David by giving Israel statues of mice in the Septuagint's 3rd Kingdoms (Masoretic Kings).

Likewise, the Cypriots had adopted Rashef as another name for Apollo during the Bronze Age, which is documented in the Greek and Phoenician bilingual Idalion stone from circa 400 BCE, when the Greek language had supplanted the old Cypriot language, but the old script was still in use. The stone mirrored the Phoenician name Ršp Mkl (𐤋𐤊𐤌 𐤐𐤔𐤓) with the Cypriot name Apoloni toAmukoloi (𐠀𐠦𐠂𐠪𐠡𐠪𐠬𐠛), the latter meaning "Apollo of Amyclae" in Greek. Idalium was an ancient civilization in Cyprus that was neither Greek nor Phoenician. It existed from the 3rd millennium BCE until its culture was assimilated into the Phoenician and then Greek cultures during the Iron Age.

The Apollo of Amyclae mentioned in the Idalium stone was a reference to the colossal statue of Apollo in the town of Amyclae in southern Greece. The town of Amyclae was mentioned by Homer, and according to Greek legends, existed before the Dorian invasions of the Bronze Age Collapse. Archaeological evidence for the existence of the town in the Mycenaean era supports this; however, it is not clear how old the colossus was. In the myths, the Temple of Apollo in Amyclae existed before the Dorian invasion; however, this has not been proven from either early texts or archaeological evidence. If the colossus of Apollo was built during the early Classical era, then the older Cypriot name could not have been about the colossus.

FORWARD

The connection between the Greek Apollo and Canaanite Resheph is also found in the ruins of Apollonia-Arsuf (אֲפוֹלוֹנְיָה-אַרְסוּף), an ancient Judahite town on the Mediterranean coast of modern Israel named after Resheph, which the Greeks renamed Apollonia after Alexander's conquest. Apollonia-Arsuf appears to have been founded during the Persian era, around 4 kilometers north of the much older Tel Michel (תל מיכל), which dates back to the middle Bronze Age. The Mkl (𐤌𐤊𐤋) from the Idalion stone has been theoretically linked to Tel Michel, however, this is far from conclusive.

An alternate reading of Ršp Mkl (𐤓𐤔𐤐 𐤌𐤊𐤋) in the Phoenician script, but not the Greek, is a list of two gods instead of a god and an epithet. Mikal (ΜΙΚΑΛ) was an ancient Phrygian god of healing, who was later assimilated with the Israelite angel Michael in the early Christian churches in Anatolia. The Phrygians also had a god named Sabazdiōs (ΣΑΒΑΤΧΟΣ), which was later reinterpreted as Sabazios (Σαβάζιος) in the Greco-Roman era and was viewed as the Phrygian version of Sabaoth (Σαβαωθ), the god of the Israelites mentioned in several books of the Septuagint, and many Hellenistic era texts before the reforms of the Hasmonean dynasty.

The Septuagint manuscripts and Masoretic texts often differ in regards to the name or title Shaddai, suggesting that the Aramaic and Canaanite (Judahite or Samaritan) source texts they worked from differed in regards to this word. The term was omitted throughout *Cosmic Genesis*, suggesting that the earlier Aramaic translator had omitted it. However, it was

17

almost certainly in the Canaanite version the translator worked from, as it is used consistently in *Bereshít*, and is mentioned again in *Names* when Moses god's name Ōn is introduced in *Exodus*.

The confusion surrounding the term Shaddai likely arises from the different meanings of the word in Canaanite and Aramaic. By the Middle-Assyrian era, the term ^{deity}šēdu (✳ 𒁹) commonly referred to a "protective spirit" or "lesser god." By the Neo-Assyrian era, the word became šydå (𐡍𐡉𐡀𐡔) in Aramaic, meaning "demon" in the classical sense, as a type of muse or nymph. In contrast, in Canaanite, šdy (𐤔𐤃𐤉) adopted a different meaning, generally interpreted as "powerful" by the Early Classical Era. This is likely where the Greeks derived the term "omnipotent" (παντοκράτορος), which was later used in the Septuagint, where the Masoretic text generally employs the term Shaddai.

This alternate interpretation of the word šdy (𐤔𐤃𐤉) in Canaanite is likely due to the Egyptian New Kingdom era rule over Canaan. During this time, šd (𓈙𓂧𓏏𓀭) was worshiped in the region. Shed, who was often referred to as "the savior," was virtually identical to the earlier Canaanite god Resheph who was initially suppressed after the fall of the Hyksos dynasty, as well as the contemporaneous Hurrian Ablu, Neshite Apaliunas, and Greek Apoloni.

In the Masoretic Book of Job, Eliphaz referred to humanity as the "sons of Resheph" (בני־רשף) instead of the "sons of Adam," and then used Shaddai as the name of a god. This god Shaddai was explicitly listed alongside the god El in Masoretic

Job, whereas in the Septuagint's Job, they are not explicitly listed as two separate gods. The Greek translation of Shaddai in Job is consistent with most of the Septuagint, using a term that translates as "omnipotent" (παντοκράτορος), however, the name El (אל) is generally translated as a word meaning "strong" (ἰσχυρός). It is likely because the Masoretic version lists them side by side, as "god El and god Shaddai," (אל-אל ואל-שדי), which the Greek translators did not do, instead routinely dropping the second reference to a god when they were listed together.

The terms "god Shaddai" (אל-שדי) and "god El" (אל-אל) are frequently mentioned in the Masoretic version of Job, and are direct translations of the same terms in Akkadian Cuneiform: deityŠadi (✳ 𒂗 ⟠) and deityIlu (✳ ✳). A number of indicators in the Book of Job point to the origin of a shorter version of it in Sippar, earlier than the reforms of King Shulgi, before being reworked in Ammuru, and then being carried south into Egypt in the reign of King Senusret I, circa 1950 BCE. If so, the original Sumerian gods gambling on the fate of Job were likely Ān (✳) and deityEnki (✳ 𒋛 ◈), as deityŠadi (✳ 𒂗 ⟠) does not appear to date back to the era.

Like Shaddai, Resheph, and Apollo, Enki was believed to be both the cause and cure of diseases in the Old Sumerian civilization, making Bel Shaddai the logical translation in the Amorite version of Job. This suggests that the original talking thunder cloud near the end of the book was Enlil, later confusingly redacted to Yahweh. Enlil was reported in some versions of the Epic of Gilgamesh, to be the master of the monster Humbaba (𒄷𒌝𒁀𒁀), the monster that Gilgamesh killed. According to a Gilgamesh text in the Yale Babylonian Collection, Humbaba's "voice is a deluge, and his mouth is fire, his breath is death." This is similar to the description of Leviathan in Job, which describes him as breathing fire. Leviathan is descended from the ancient Canaanite word Ltn (𒇉𒈾), which was described as a sea monster. The text of Job merges the description of Leviathan with the text regarding Behemoth, some kind of land monster. The word Behemoth is out of place in the text, as it is an Egyptian word accepted as meaning "hippopotamus," yet the monster described is not a hippopotamus.

While all references to Shaddai were stripped from Cosmic Genesis at some point, either when the Greeks translated the text from Aramaic, or earlier when the Aramaic translation was made, the term must have originally been in the text, essentially where it is in Bereshít or the later references to it in Exodus and Deuteronomy make no sense, and therefore it is restored in this translation.

The absence of early references to Iaō in Cosmic Genesis also explains the absence of any names ending in -iah before the birth of Beriah, who was born in Egypt. Joseph's marriage to the daughter of the High Priest of Heliopolis (Ỉwnw in Greek, Åwn in Hebrew) after interpreting the Pharaoh's dreams suggests that he became the High Priest of Ỉȯhw, the lunar god of Heliopolis. The word ỉȯh (☽) was the Egyptian word for the moon, however, when treated as a god, it was modified to Ỉȯhw (𓇋𓂝𓎛𓇳𓏤), resulting in the two pronunciations of the name Yh (ᴎ^) and Yhw (ᴎᴎ^) found in Aramaic. The earliest depictions of Yahweh, on pottery shards found at Kuntillet Ajrud, dating to circa 800 BCE, depict Yahweh as the calf of Asherah, who was herself the personification of the starry sky, meaning Yahweh was still considered to be the moon at the time.

In this translation, the Greek term ṭeos (θεοσ) is rendered as God. The Greek term kyrios (κυριοσ) is rendered as Lord, and not replaced with the name Yahweh, which appears in the Masoretic text, as it seems to have been added to the Hebrew texts of Bereshít during the Hasmonean redaction. The Greek term kyrios o ṭeos (Κυριοσ ο θεοσ) is translated as Lord of the gods, although "Father of the gods" was likely what the source text originally used.

When the word god (θεοσ) is being used as part of a name, such as "house of god" (οικοσ Θεου), which is a Greek translation of Beit el (בֵּית אֵל), the proper name Bethel is used when referring to the town, and Baitylos is used when referring to the god. The god Bethel is mentioned in many ancient Egyptian, Canaanite, and Israelite texts from the Egyptian New Kingdom through the era of the Old Kingdoms of Samaria and Judah, although its exact nature is not clearly understood. The name Baitylos comes from Philo of Byblos' Greek translation of Sanchuniathon's *Phoenician History* and is used to differentiate the name of the god from the town named after him. Additionally, the term Bethel can be translated as "meteorite," as meteorites were believed to be parts of the god Baitylos that had fallen to Earth.

FORWARD

The Hasmonean Kingdom of Judea had a fragile alliance with the Roman Republic until General Pompey conquered Syria for the Roman Republic in 69 BCE. Pompey aimed to free Greek-speaking communities in the Middle East that had been ruled by non-Greeks after the collapse of the Seleucid Syrian Empire. He divided Judea and Edom to the east, placing Greek-speaking cities under the protection of the Roman province of Syria. Additionally, he liberated several smaller communities that had been occupied by Judea, granting them self-government. These communities included Ashdod, Yavne, Jaffa, Dora, Marissa, and Samaria.

In 37 CE, the Roman Senate appointed Herod the Great, an Edomite King, as "King of the Jews" after a series of wars weakened the Hasmonean dynasty. Herod's rule was not popular as he allowed the Romans to establish themselves in Judea. However, he did expand Judea by integrating Greek and Samaritan cities and annexing Galilee and Edom. After Herod's death, his kingdom was divided between four successors, and in 66 CE, the Romans conquered the region. An uprising in 120 CE led to the exile of the Jews from Judea, turning the region into a Greco-Roman colony. Following the exile of the Jews, the Samaritans and Christians rose in numbers after Christianity was legalized. Between 529 and 555 CE, the Samaritans revolted and were effectively annihilated by the Byzantine Empire.

The Dead Sea Scrolls, ancient documents found in the Caves in Qumran, span a significant section of Judean history. The fragments of the Torah have been found in ancient

Phoenician (also called Samaritan or Paleo-Hebrew), Hebrew, Aramaic, and Greek. The Canaanite fragments among the Dead Sea Scrolls have been particularly debated as they are believed to be the oldest. The Aramaic script, the precursor to the current Hebrew script, was adopted by some Jews during the Babylonian captivity. However, Phoenician continued to be the primary script used in Judea throughout the Babylonian, Persian, and Greek eras. Phoenician appears to have been the common script in Canaan from around 1200 BCE. Before the Bronze Age Collapse, the Akkadian Cuneiform and Ugaritic scripts were both in use in Canaan.

The terms Phoenician and Canaanite are synonymous, and the people seem to have always had two names, one of Egyptian origin and one of Akkadian. Archaeological evidence has proven that the ancient Canaanites, Samaritans, and Judahites all adopted the Canaanite script after the collapse of the Egyptian New Kingdom. However, they all used the Akkadian Cuneiform script when the New Kingdom still ruled Canaan. This has been proven by the hundreds of Amarna Letters between the Egyptian court and their subjects in Canaan in the mid-1300s BCE, including the governors of Byblos, Shechem, and Jerusalem. The earlier Akkadian source for the earliest of the Israelite books also explains the strange names of many of the early heroes and patriarchs, whose names ended in -on, instead of -el. Both the names El and Ān were spelled with the dinger (✳) in Cuneiform, meaning the original names of Aaron, Gideon, and many other early heroes likely had Canaanite names, ending with -el, and not Akkadian names, ending in -on.

FORWARD

During the rule of the Hasmoneans, the Judahite dialect of Canaanite written in the Aramaic script was adopted for religious texts, which is now known as Hebrew. However, Aramaic continued to be the primary language for secular activities. The terminology in the Septuagint suggests that the source-texts were written in Aramaic rather than Hebrew, as there are many differences in names between the two languages. For example, the name of the prophet Elijah is "Elijah" in Hebrew and "Elia" in Aramaic, which was transliterated as "Elias" in Greek. Additionally, the primary source texts used appear to have been from the Egyptian Israelite community, explaining why there are more books than the Judeans translated, and why the texts are less monotheistic, as the Egyptian Israelites continued to be polytheists long after the Judeans adopted Zoroastrianism under Persian rule.

While the reforms of Ezra restored a form of the older religion, it continued the late imperial monotheism. The religious reforms continued under the rule of the Hasmonean and Herodian dynasties, with the Hasidans, Sadducees, Pharisees, Zealots, and Sicarii each taking their turn at becoming progressively more extremist in their beliefs.

When the Samaritans refused to allow their scriptures to be changed, the Hasmoneans killed their priesthood, burned their scriptures, tore down their temples, and enslaved the entire Samaritan population. The Samaritan texts used today are generally accepted as texts created from the existing Jewish texts after they were freed by General Pompey. The Samaritans never stopped using the ancient Canaanite script, although it did evolve over time. The earliest Christians, including Jesus' apostles and disciples, considered the Samaritans to be Canaanites, as proven by Simon the Mage's other labels in early Christian works: Simon the Samaritan and Simon the Canaanite.

The modern Samaritan religion is similar to Judaism in that they have versions of the Torah and the book of Joshua; however, they do not trace their ancestry to ancient Judah, but rather, ancient Samaria, also called the Northern Kingdom of Israel. According to the Samaritans, they were the original Israelites, and the Temple of the Lord was not Solomon's Temple in Jerusalem, but rather a Temple of El in Shiloh. These "other Israelites" also contributed to the creation of the Septuagint, as the *Book of Tobit* was the story of a Samaritan who had been taken to Nineveh, the capital of the Assyrian Empire, after the Kingdom of Israel was conquered by the Assyrians. This book and several others were not considered important to Simon the Zealous and were not translated into Hebrew.

Outside of Judea, the Septuagint was the dominant form of Jewish scriptures across the Greek-speaking world, which by the time of Christ extended from the Roman Empire in the west, to the Indo-Greek Kingdom in the east. Jewish traders had established small colonies along the trade routes of the Red Sea and the Indian Ocean, reaching as far south as Eritrea, and as far east as southern India, and these Jews spoke Greek and used the Septuagint. The earliest Christians used the Septuagint exclusively, as far as the Israelite scriptures were concerned, and as a result, it is impossible to even understand the chronology of the world they described unless using the Septuagint. It is unclear why the Septuagint, Masoretic text, and Samaritan Asatir each contain a different chronology of the world. Adding the Book of Jubilees, and various variations of the Torah found within the Dead Sea Scrolls, there are no less than six ancient Israelite chronologies.

Cosmic Genesis includes an additional millennium of human history that was dropped from Bereshít in order to align the creation of the world with the beginning of the age of El, when the constellation Taurus became the marker of the northern vernal equinox, in 3760 BCE.

The Bull El was the dominant god of the Canaanite pantheon until around 1700 BCE. At that time, Attar the Goat (Aries) and Yam the Sea-Monster (Cetus) vied for control of the world beneath the sky. Both of them were eventually replaced by the god of thunder, Ba'al Hadad, in the Canaanite Ba'al Cycle. Traditional Western Christian and Jewish interpretations of the timeline within the Masoretic Text are further complicated by the so-called "missing years" of Rabbinical Time. This skips over hundreds of years of the Persian Empire in order to fit the timeline into the era since 3760 BCE. Christian chronologists have never had this problem, as Christianity developed after the astrology of Babylonian-era Judaism had been forgotten.

The earliest Christian Bibles all used the Septuagint; however, by the 4th century, some Christian scholars were discussing whether they should retranslate the Old Testament from the version the Jews were using, and some even suggested using the Samaritan version. Both suggestions were generally dismissed as heretical, as Jesus and the Apostles had quoted from the Septuagint, even though they had access to the Hebrew version then in use. This argument held in the West until the Middle Ages, when Catholic Bibles switched to the Masoretic text. In the east, Orthodox Bibles continued to use the Septuagint, as they do today. To the south, the Ethiopian Tewahedo Church continued to use the Septuagint, and across Asia, the Thomas Christians and Nestorians continued to use the Septuagint. Only in Western Europe was the later Masoretic text adopted, abandoning the more ancient Septuagint, on the assumption that the Jews had copied their texts more faithfully than the Greeks had translated them. This assumption was carried forward into the Protestant Churches that broke off from the Catholic Church, and therefore, almost all Protestant Bibles use the Masoretic text for the basis of the Old Testament.

Unfortunately, this means that the earliest Christian writing is generally confusing and ignored by Protestants and Catholics. The earliest Christians of the first and second centuries quoted books that are no longer in the Bible, and as such, their writings are not always understood. *Septuagint: Cosmic Genesis* is the first in a series of 21st century translations aimed at correcting this problem.

One of the problems with academic translations of the Septuagint is the use of unfamiliar names or terms, as the Septuagint was written in Greek, and therefore, many names are unrecognizable to modern readers who are used to Hebrew-derived names. This project uses the more commonly understood Hebrew-derived names instead of their Greek translations, such as Canaan instead of Chanaan, and Melchizedek instead of Melchisedec. Common modern names are also used instead of either Greek or Hebrew terms when geographical locations are known, such as the archaeological name Uruk instead of the Greek Orech, or the Hebrew Erech, and the archaeological term Sumer instead of Shinar or Senar. While this could be argued as not being a correct academic procedure, it does fulfill the goal of making the translation easy to read and understand.

CHAPTER 1

In the beginning, God[1] made the skies[2] and land.[3] The land was invisible and unfinished,[4] and darkness[5] covered the abyss,[6] and the air god[7] was above the water.[8]

God said, "Light be born!" and light came. God saw the light was good, and God separated the medium of light and the medium of darkness. God named the light: Day,[9] and the darkness was named: Night.[10] There was evening and there was morning, the first day.

God said, "Let there be a framework in the middle of the water and let it be a division between water and water," and it was so. God made the framework, and God divided between the water which is under the framework and the water which is above the framework. God named the framework: Shamayim,[11] and God saw that it was good, and there was evening and there was morning, the second day.

God said, "Let the water that is under the sky be collected into one meeting place, and let the dry land appear," and it was so. The water that was under the sky was collected into its meeting places, and dry land appeared. God named the dry land: Eretz,[12] and the water systems were named: Seas,[13] and God saw that it was good.

God said, "Germinate the land with plants of grass producing seed similar to its kind and according to its species, and the fruit tree producing fruit which has seed in it, according to its species on the land," and it was so.

The land sprouted the plants of grass bearing seed according to their species and according to their likeness, and the fruit trees bearing fruit whose seed is in it, according to its kind on Earth, and God saw that it was good.

There was evening and there was morning, the third day. God said, "Let there be lights in the framework of Shamayim, for shining on Earth, to separate the day and night, and let them be for signs and seasons and days and years. Let them be for light in the framework of Shamayim, to shine on Earth," and it was so.

God made the two great lights, the brighter light to rule the day, and the dimmer light to rule the night along with the stars. God placed them in the framework of Shamayim, to shine on Earth, and to regulate day and night, and to divide between the light and the darkness. God saw that it was good.

There was evening and there was morning, the fourth day. God said, "Export from the waters[14] the living minds[15] of reptiles, and winged creatures flying above the land in the framework of Shamayim," and it was so. God made the great dragon,[16] and every mind of living reptiles, which the waters brought out according to their species, and every creature that flies with wings according to its kind, and God saw that they were good. God blessed them and said, "Increase and multiply and fill the waters in the seas, and let the creatures that fly be multiplied on the land."

CHAPTER 1

There was evening and there was morning, the fifth day. God said, "Let Eretz bring out creatures of living minds according to its kind, quadrupeds and reptiles and wild animals of the land according to their species," and it was so. God made the wild animals of the land according to their species, and the livestock according to their species, and all the reptiles of the land according to their species, and God saw that they were good.

God said, "Let us make man according to our image and likeness, and let them have dominion over the fish of the sea, and over the flying creatures of the sky, and over the livestock and all the land, and over the reptiles that creep on the land."

God made man, in the image of God he made him, male and female he made them. God blessed them, saying, "Increase and multiply. You paid for the land, so conquer it. Have the fish of the seas and flying creatures of the sky, and everything and every living creature of the land."

God said, "Look I have given to you every seed-bearing plant sowing seed which is on all the land, and every tree which has in itself the fruit of seeds that are planted, for you it will be for food, and for all the wild animals of the land, and for all the flying creatures of the sky, and for every reptile creeping on the land, which has in itself the mind of life, including every green plant for food," and it was so.

CHAPTER 1

God saw all the things that had been made, and they were very good. There was evening and there was morning, the sixth day.

CHAPTER 1 NOTES

1 Papyrus 12: o T̄S (oē̄c). Translation: the god. This fragment of the Septuagint uses T̄S (ē̄c) the contracted form of ṯeos (ᴇᴏᴄ), meaning "god".

- Codex Alexandrinus: o ṯeos (oᴇᴇᴏᴄ). Translation: the god.
- Dead Sea Scroll 4QGen^g: ålhym (אֱלֹהִים)
- Dead Sea Scroll 4QGen^b: word damaged, only -m (מ-) survives. Later in chapter 1, the entire word ålhym (אֱלֹהִים) survives
- Leningrad Codex: 'ĕlōhîm (אֱלֹהִים). Translation: gods (Aramaic), goddesses (Hebrew), god (Assyrian), highest (Akkadian)
- Peshitta: ålhå (ܐܠܗܐ). Translation: god
- Targum Onkelos: Yy ("). Translation: Yahweh
- Targum Jerusalem: Yəyā (??). Translation: Yahweh
- Targum Pseudo-Jonathan: Yəyā (??). Translation: Yahweh
- Sahidic manuscripts: noute (ɴᴏʏᴛᴇ). Translation: god
- Papyrus Bohairic 2: fṫ (ϯ). Translation: God

The word ålhym also survives in whole or in part in several other Dead Sea Scrolls fragments of *Bereshít*, including 4QGen^d, 4QGen^f, and 4QGen^j from the Hasmonean Dynasty (140 to 37 BCE); 1QGen, and 4QGen^e from the Herodian Dynasty (37 BCE to 6 CE); as well as MurGen from the Wadi Muraba'at, dating to the early Roman era (6 to 135 CE). The word ålhym (𐤀𐤋𐤄𐤉𐤌) has survived in the Canaanite script in Dead Sea Scroll 4QpaleoGen-Exod^l, which includes fragments of *Bereshít* and *Names*, and is dated to the Hasmonean era (140 to 37 BCE).

The Hebrew translation uses three words for "god": 'ēl (אֵל), 'ĕlōhē (אֱלֹהֵ), and 'ĕlōhîm (אֱלֹהִים). In Bronze Age Ugaritic Canaanite, the word for "god" was âl (𐎛𐎍), while in word for goddess was was âlh (𐎛𐎍𐎅), and âlhm (𐎛𐎍𐎅𐎎) was Canaanite for "goddesses." This confusion is manifest in various translations, where the gender in the texts shift around elohim, however, the main source texts always agree that 'ĕlōhē is a masculine form in regards to the Israelite god. This is likely because the term âl (𐤋𐤀) had become synonymous with El, the patriarch of the Canaanite pantheon by the beginning of the Iron Age, and the other gods were referred to as bôl (𐤋𐤏𐤁), meaning "lord." Therefore, Aramaic word âlhâ (𐡀𐡄𐡋𐡀), which means "god," was adopts at some point by the Israelites to denote a generic "god."

The term 'ĕlōhē is generally used to connect texts from the time of Moses to older texts, such as the phrase "god of Abraham, god of Isaac, and god of Jacob," suggesting the Aramaic phrases were added circa 710 BCE, when the texts of *Bereshít* (Cosmic Genesis) and *Names* (Exodus) were standardized under the rule of King Hezekiah of Judah.

The form 'ĕlōhîm is found in the older sections of text, and is clearly a word used to denote either a singular god in some verses, or a plurality of gods in other verses. The Masoretic texts generally demark the difference between "God" and "gods" by adding "the" to the beginning of the word, rendering the plural form as hā'ĕlōhîm (הָאֱלֹהִים). This is particularly evident in Masoretic Daniel, where "lord of the gods" is rendered as 'ădōnāy hā'ĕlōhîm (אֲדֹנָי הָאֱלֹהִים) in the Aramaic sections. The origin of 'ĕlōhîm as a singular form for the Israelite god, likely dates back the translation of the older sections of text from cuneiform into the Phoenician script early in the Iron Age, plausibly in the Kingdom of Israel.

The names of the Israelite god are even more confusing in *Names* and *Exodus*, where the god identifies himself as Ōn (Ων), 'Ănā' (אֲנָא), Ånå (ܐܢܐ), 'Ehyê (אֶהְיֶה), in the various Greek and Aramaic translations, while the Leningrad Codex contains the somewhat whimsical phrase 'ehyê 'ăšer 'ehyê (אֶהְיֶה אֲשֶׁר אֶהְיֶה), meaning "I will be what I will be."

Before the vowel markings that developed in the Medieval era, the Targum Jerusalem's 'Ănā' (אֲנָא) would have been Ånå (אנא), indicating there was an old Aramaic version of Exodus that used the name Ånå (ܐܢܐ). Ånå is not based on the Greek Ōn, as direct transliterations would be Ōn (ען) and Ōn (ܥܢ). The Library of Alexandra translated the Septuagint from the copies available in Egypt, indicating that the Egypto-Aramaic version of Exodus used the name Ōn (ܥܢ). Conversely the Ånå (ܐܢܐ) variant is only found in texts that would have drawn from the Syro-Aramaic texts. The Peshitta is written in the Syriac form of Aramaic, and the Targum Jerusalem with is written in Palestinian Aramaic. The fact that the Masoretes, who were based in Babylon, and spoke Aramaic, added the vowel markings that changed "king" Ōn (ענמלך) to "king" Ana (עֲנֶמֶלֶך) in Masoretic *Kings* (Septuagint's *4th Kingdoms*), supports Ana being the Syro-Aramaic pronunciation of the Samaritan and Egypto-Aramaic Ōn.

These variations of Ōn, Ånå, and 'Ehyê, as well as the singular interpretation of the word 'ĕlōhîm can all be explained if the original phrase in the late Bronze Age text of *Names* (*Exodus*) used the name ^{deity}Éa (𒀭𒂗𒆠). Elum (𒀭) was the Babylonian word for "god," which was pronounced in Neo-Sumerian as ^{deity}Anu (𒀭𒈾). ^{deity}Éa (𒀭𒂗𒆠) was the Babylonian pronunciation of the old Akkadian name Ia (𒂍𒀀), the god of life and fresh water. The

34

Canaanite version of Ia was Ym (𐤉𐤌), the god of the sea, therefore transliterating ^{deity}Éa (✳𐎛𐎛𐎛) into the Phoenician script by Israelites at the beginning of the Iron Age would have rendered it as Ålhym (𐤉𐤌𐤋𐤀), the exact word found in Dead Sea Scroll 4QpaleoGen-Exod[1], which was later transliterated into Hebrew as ålhym (אלהים). This god was certainly not Ba'al Yam, the Canaanite "lord of the sea," and so the generic word word ålh (𐤀𐤋𐤄) would have been used, even if it rendered a word very similar to the Phoenician word ålhm (𐤌𐤋𐤀) meaning "goddesses."

Unfortunately, the Greek translation doesn't generally distinguish between the singular and plural forms, almost always rendering the term as "the god" (o θεοσ). However, this does create some confusing concepts, such as the Egyptians worshiping the God of the Israelites instead of their gods. In order the clarify the text, the distinction of "god" versus "gods" are imported from the Leningrad Codex where the Hebrew reads 'ĕlōhē (אֱלֹהֵי), 'ĕlōhîm (אֱלֹהִים), or hā'ĕlōhîm (הָאֱלֹהִים), when not distinguished in the Septuagint manuscripts.

2 Codex Alexandrinus: O̅U̅N̅O̅N̅ (O̅Y̅N̅O̅N̅). Translations: sky, universe, Ouranos (the Greek sky-god)

• Leningrad Codex: šāmayim (שָׁמַיִם). Translations: skies, Shamayim (the Canaanite sky-god)

• Peshitta: smyå (ܫܡܝܐ). Translation: sky

• Targum Onkelos: šəmayyā' (שְׁמַיָּא). Translation: sky

• Targum Pseudo-Jonathan: šəmayyā' (שְׁמַיָּא). Translation: sky

• Sahidic manuscripts: pe (ⲡⲉ). Translation: sky

• Papyrus Bohairic 2: fe (ⲫⲉ). Translation: sky

The skies (Shamayim / Ouranos) is depicted as the same type of primordial deity in the Septuagint as it was in the Greek myths and called on to witness blessings and curses, implying consciousness. The name Ouranos (Ουρανος) was derived from the Neo-Assyrian term ùruanna (𒀭𒂍𒃹𒋾𒅇), meaning "roof sky stone," which was also the Greek description of Ouranos, as the ceiling above the flat Earth. This term appears to have been absorbed into Greek as the name Ouranos during the early iron age, after the collapse of the Mycenaean civilization, as the name has not been documented in Linear-B, the script of the Mycenaeans.

The term in the Masoretic text, shamayim is the Hebrew word for "skies," however, is also the name of the ancient Semitic sky god, spelled as Šamuû (𒂊𒐼𒐊𒈠) in Old Akkadian, Šmyn (𒐼𒅆𒌋) in Ugaritic, Šmm (𐤔𐤌𐤌) in Canaanite, Smyn (𐩪𐩣𐩺𐩬) in Sabaean, and Šmyn (𐡔𐡌𐡉𐡍) in Aramaic. In Sumerian cosmology, he was ᵈᵉⁱᵗʸĀn (𒀭𒀭), the god described as creating the sky, which meant the lower sections of the sky that were closer to the ground. In Old Akkadian, the name of Ān was spelled phonetically as Šamuú (𒂊𒐼𒐊𒈠), meaning "skies," or spelled phonetically in a modified Sumerian form as Ānu (𒀭𒈠). He continued to be the same god that he had been in the Sumerian mythology, although his son ᵈᵉⁱᵗʸEnlil (𒀭𒆤) became more important, arguably the most important god.

In the later Old Babylonian era, the god Šamuú was still the sky, however, Enlil was replaced by ᵈᵉⁱᵗʸMarduk (𒀭𒀫𒌓), the sun-calf national god of Babylon. To the north in Assyria, Enlil was replaced by Anshur (𒀭𒊹), the national god "Eternal Sky" of Assyria, and Šamuú virtually disappeared. This indicates that the origin of Cosmic Genesis chapter 1 was probably in the Sumerian or Akkadian eras, before the Old Babylonian Empire.

3 Codex Alexandrinus: gē (γ‌η). Translation: land (or earth, country, soil, Ge)

CHAPTER 1

- Leningrad Codex: 'āres (אֶרֶץ). Translations: land (or earth, ground, soil, Eretz)
- Peshitta: årðå (ܐܪܥܐ). Translation: land (or earth, ground, soil, bottom)
- Targum Onkelos: 'ar'ā' (אַרְעָא). Translation: land (or earth, ground, soil, bottom)
- Targum Pseudo-Jonathan: 'ar'ā' (אַרְעָא). Translation: land (or earth, ground, soil, bottom)
- Sahidic manuscripts: kah (ⲕⲁϩ). Translation: Earth (or soil)
- Papyrus Bohairic 2: kahi (ⲕⲁϩⲓ). Translation: Earth (or soil)

The Earth (Eretz / Ge) is depicted as the same type of primordial deity in the Septuagint as she was in the Greek myths and called on to witness blessings and curses, implying consciousness. The Greek name Gē (Γη) was derived from the Sumerian logogram Ki (𒆠), meaning "land" during the Neo-Assyrian era, although the name of the Earth goddess was spelled phonetically as Ašru (𒀸𒊒) at the time, indicating that the adoption was a scientific term at first.

In early Sumerian cosmology, Ān's wife was known as ^{diety}Urash (𒀭𒅁), the goddess of barley. This term transitioned during the Sumerian civilization into a title of Ān, and Ān's wife was known as Ki (𒆠), meaning "Earth." During the Akkadian era, the goddess was known as Arṣatu (𒀀𒅕𒍢𒌈), although the name was still commonly spelled as Ki (𒆠), or shortened to Kitu (𒆠𒌈). In the later Old Babylonian era, Ānu's wife became known as Āntu (𒀭𒌈), while to the north in Assyrian she became Kishar (𒆧𒊹), the "Eternal Earth." The Akkadian name arṣatu (𒀀𒅕𒍢𒌈), meaning Earth or "land," is related to various Semitic words meaning "land," or the Earth-goddess, or both, including the Babylonian erṣetu (𒀀𒅕𒍢𒌈), Ugaritic års (𐎀𐎗𐎕), Sabaean ård

37

CHAPTER 1

(𐤄)ħ), Canaanite års (𐤀𐤓𐤑), Aramaic årq (ארק), Hebrew 'eres (אֶרֶץ), Syriac årôå (ܐܪܥܐ), Arabic åard (أَرْض), and Somali arli.

4 Codex Alexandrinus: aoratos kai akataskeuastos (ΛΟΡΑΤΟC ΚΑΙ ΑΚΑΤΑCΚΕΥΑCΤΟC). Translation: invisible (or unseen) and unfinished

• Leningrad Codex: tōhû wābōhû (תֹ֙הוּ֙ וָבֹ֔הוּ). Translations: emptiness (or nothingness) and void (or emptiness)

• Peshitta: hwt twh wbwh (ܗܘܬ ܬܘܗ ܘܒܘܗ). Translation: unformed and desolate

• Targum Onkelos: sādəyā' wərêqanyā' (צָדְיָא וְרֵיקַנְיָא). Translation: unformed and empty

• Targum Jerusalem: tahăyā' ûbahăyā' wəsādû min bənê 'ĕnāšā' wərêqanyā' mikkol bə'îr (תְּהֵיָא וּבְהֵיָא וְצָדוּ מִן בְּנֵי אֲנָשָׁא וְרֵיקַנְיָא מִכָּל בְּעִיר). Translation: delayed in creation and devoid of humans (or sons of mortal / Enosh) and empty of all animals

• Targum Pseudo-Jonathan: tahăyāy' ûbahăyāy' sadyā' mibbənê naš wərêqanyā' min kol bə'îr (תְּהֵיָא וּבְהֵיָא צָדְיָא מִבְּנֵי נַשׁ וְרֵיקַנְיָא מִן כָּל בְּעִיר). Translation: reborn (or rejuvenated, revived, resurrected) and clear devoid of humans (sons of mortal / Nosh) and empty from all animals

• Sahidic manuscripts: erof auō natsbtōtf (ⲉⲣⲟϥ ⲁⲩⲱ ⲛ̄ⲁⲧⲥⲃ̄ⲧⲱⲧϥ̄). Translation: open void and not prepared

• Papyrus Bohairic 2: erof ouohe natsobt (ⲉⲣⲟϥ ⲟⲩⲟϩⲉ ⲛⲁⲧⲥⲟⲃϯ). Translation: open void and not ready

The Greek translation assumes the two words are descriptions of the state of the world, however, in Aramaic the structure of the sentence would have read like the Greek: existing invisible and not finished. However, these terms are not the words found in the Masoretic text, which appears to be a Classical era Hebrew translation. If written in Akkadian cuneiform, the terms found in the Greek translations would have been bapálu (𒁹𒍪𒇻) and šuklulu (𒌋𒁹𒆤). The Akkadian term bapálu, meaning "unseen" or "invisible," became the Aramaic btl (ܠܛܠ), meaning "invisible," or "invalid," however, the Hebrew term bāṭal (בָּטַל) meant "cease to exist," and the related term bāṭēl (בָּטֵל) meant "void," the synonym of the term used in the Masoretic text.

The term šuklulu (𒌋𒁹𒆤), meaning "to complete" or "to perfect," became the Aramaic word šql (ܫܩܠ) meaning to "finish" or "remove," however, the Hebrew term šeqel (שֶׁקֶל), referred to a weight and a monetary unit. These two words, Invisible and not Finished, are not references to aspects of the Mesopotamian creation mythologies, but the Egyptian creation mythologies, as Amen (𓇋𓏠𓈖𓏤) and Atum (𓏏𓏠), were the two major creator gods of Egypt, whose names translate as "Invisible" and "Completer." During the Middle Kingdom era, Amen (Invisible) was the creator god of southern Egypt, while Atum (Completer) was the creator god of northern Egypt. During the Second Intermediate Period that followed, both Amen and Atum became associated with the sun, and their creation aspects diminished, suggesting the Egyptian elements were added during the Middle Kingdom or early in the Second Intermediate period, before the Canaanite Dynasty lost control of southern Egypt.

5 Codex Alexandrinus: skotos (ϲκοτοϲ). Translation: gloom (or darkness, shadow)

• Leningrad Codex: ḥōšek (חֹשֶׁךְ). Translations: darkness (in Aramaic, or evil in Hebrew)

• Peshitta: kšwkå (ܟܫܘܟܐ). Translation: darkness

• Targum Onkelos: ḥăšôkā' (חֲשׁוֹכָא). Translation: darkness

• Targum Pseudo-Jonathan: ḥăšôkā' (חֲשׁוֹכָא). Translation: darkness

- Sahidic manuscripts: kahe (ⲕⲁⲕⲉ). Translation: darkness
- Papyrus Bohairic 2: ǩaki (ⲭⲁⲕⲓ). Translation: darkness

The darkness covering the Abyss, is not a reference to Mesopotamian creation mythology, but Egyptian, as Kek (𓎡𓎡𓆇) was the embodiment of darkness that accompanied Nun, the Egyptian version of the Abyss, before the world was created. Nun and Kek were two of the best documented members of the Ogdoad, the eight gods who created the world in the Hermopolitian creation mythology.

6 Codex Alexandrinus: epanō tēs abussou (ⲉⲡⲁⲛⲱⲑⲏⲥ ⲁⲃⲩⲥⲥⲟⲩ). Translation: above (or higher, more than) the abyss

- Leningrad Codex: 'al-pənê təhôm (עַל־פְּנֵי תְהוֹם). Translations: on (or over, around, larger than, greater than) face (or interior) sea (or deep, Tiamat)

- Peshitta: ŏl åpy myå (ܥܠ ܐܦ̈ܝ ܡܝܐ). Translation: Translations: on (or over, around, larger than, greater than) face (or interior) water

- Targum Onkelos: pāraś 'al 'appê təhômā' (פְּרַשׁ עַל אַפֵּי תְהוֹמָא). Translation: spread over on (or around, larger than, greater than) face (or interior) sea (or lake)

- Targum Pseudo-Jonathan: 'al 'appê təhômā' (עַל אַפֵּי תְהוֹמָא). Translation: on (or around, larger than, greater than) face (or interior) sea (or lake)

- Sahidic manuscripts: fijm pNoun (ϩⲓϫⲙ ⲡⲚⲟⲩⲛ). Translation: upon Nun

- Papyrus Bohairic 2: fijen pNoun (ϩⲓϫⲉⲛ ⲡⲚⲟⲧⲛ). Translation: upon Nun

The abyss is a common element in most ancient middle-eastern religions. In Egyptian beliefs, the abyss was called Nun (𓏌𓏌𓏌𓈗), meaning "sky waters," and like many of the other religions, this sea was seen as being a cosmic sea, both below the Earth, and above Sky, and reaching off to infinity. The cosmic sea was an early attempt to envision what is now called outer space, assumed to be composed of freshwater.

The Sumerian name for the primordial waters was ^{deity}Nammu (✳️🔲), however, they also referred to it as abzu (🔲🔲), meaning "deep water," and zuab (🔲🔲), meaning "water deep." The Greek name abyssou may have been derived from the Sumerian term abzu, however, does not appear to have been imported to Greek thought until the early iron age, as the word is not found in the Linear-B script of the Bronze age.

The Akkadians called the Abyss tâmtu (🔲🔲🔲), which meant "lakes," however, the god that lived in it was replaced with Ia (🔲🔲), whose name is believed to be derived from the Sumerian words "praise" (🔲) and "water" (🔲). The transliteration of the word as Ia is modern, and if transliterated in Akkadian, the name would have been Sēriš Muú, meaning "praise water."

Ia replaced the earlier Sumerian god ^{deity}Enki (✳️🔲🔲), whose name translates as "God Lord Earth." During the Old Babylonian era, Ia was replaced by ^{deity}Nabu (✳️🔲), the sun-calf god's Marduk's son, and the personification of the planet Mercury in Babylonian cosmology. In Old Babylonian cosmology, the deity of the Abyss tâmtu was ^{deity}Timimat (✳️🔲🔲🔲), generally transliterated into English a Tiamat.

Both tâmtu and Tiamat are recorded in Ugaritic as thm (🔲🔲) and Thmt (🔲🔲🔲), indicating they were separate concepts in bronze age Canaan. In the book of Habakkuk, written around 612 BCE, the goddess was referred to as Təhôm (תְּהוֹם), presumably in Judahite, the precursor to Classical Hebrew which was written in the Canaanite script. By the era of Habakkuk, the Israelites had been living in Canaan for centuries, and the word yām (יָם) had replaced

CHAPTER 1

təhôm as the word meaning seas, however, Bereshít was written at least a thousand years earlier, indicating that the meaning of the word is the Akkadian "Abyss," not the seas that would be created later in the chapter.

7 Codex Alexandrinus: pneuma T̄U (ⲠⲚⲈⲨⲘⲀⲐⲨ). Translation: air (or wind, breath, spirit) god

- Leningrad Codex: rûaḥ 'ĕlōhîm (רוּחַ אֱלֹהִים). Translations: wind (or breath, spirit) god (in Assyrian, or gods in Aramaic, or goddesses in Hebrew)

- Peshitta: rwḵh dålhå (ܪܘܚܐ ܕܐܠܗܐ). Translation: wind (or life, spirit, smell) of god

- Targum Onkelos: rûḥā' min qŏdām Yəyā (רוּחָא מִן קֳדָם יְיָ). Translation: wind (or life, spirit, smell) from in front of Yahweh

- Targum Jerusalem: raḥămîn min qŏdām Yəyā hăwat mənašbā' (רַחֲמִין מִן קֳדָם יְיָ הֲוַת מְנַשְּׁבָא). Translation: wind (or life, spirit, smell) of mercy (or compassion) from in front of Yahweh quickly blew

- Targum Pseudo-Jonathan: rûaḥ raḥămîn min qŏdām Yəyā mənatbā' (רוּחַ רַחֲמִין מִן קֳדָם יְיָ מְנַתְבָא). Translation: wind (or life, spirit, smell) of mercy (or compassion) from in front of Yahweh blew

- Sahidic manuscripts: pepneuma mpnoute (ⲠⲈⲠⲚⲈⲨⲘⲀ ⲘⲠⲚⲞⲨⲦⲈ). Translation: the spirit of the god

- Papyrus Bohairic 2: ouP̄N̄A nte f̄T̄ (ⲞⲨⲠ̄Ⲛ̄Ⲁ ⲚⲦⲈ ⲫϯ). Translation: one Spirit of sky of Cross

In *Bereshít*, verse, the term rûaḥ 'ĕlōhîm (רוּחַ אֱלֹהִים) is used, which is generally translated as "Spirit of God" by Christians, and "Breath of God" by Jews. In Aramaic, the term would translate as wind gods, however, the Greeks did not translate Anemoi (Ανεμοι), meaning that they could not have interpreted the name that way in the Classical era.

42

CHAPTER 1

In the *Enuma Elish*, the Babylonian creation myth, the supreme god Marduk used the four winds to capture Tiamat, which is similar to this verse. The four winds are well documented in Old Babylonian texts as being the four seasonal winds. The oldest surviving copy of the *Enuma Elish* was discovered in the ruins of the Library of Ashurbanipal in Nineveh, dating to the Neo-Assyrian era, however, as the text is Babylonian, it is accepted as being a later Neo-Assyrian copy of an Old Babylonian text. It is also theorized by Assyriologists that the Old Babylonian version was a Babylonian version of an older Akkadian text about Ellil creating the world, as Marduk was the national god of Babylon, who took over the rule of Ellil in several Babylonian copies of older texts. In the much older Sumerian creation mythology the cosmic ocean Nammu, gave birth to the sky Ān and land Ki, who were originally united. Then they created Enlil, who separated the Ān from Ki. This is essentially identical to the Myth of Nut and Ra from Egypt, in which the sky Nut and earth Geb were originally united, until Ra separated them.

Enlil's name translates as "[deity]Lord of Líl" (✳▛▦), which generally transliterated into English as Enlil, because the concept of líl (▦) does not have a simple English translation. The Sumerians did not understand what air was, meaning that the related concepts of breath and wind were also not understood. These invisible forces were considered líl, however, as líl was also what separated the living (breathing) from the dead (not breathing), líl also meant the equivalent of the modern concepts of spirit, phantom, or ghost.

Additionally, as the unseen líl was what separated the "here" from the "there," líl was also a physical concept that would be translated today as emptiness, void, or space (but not outer space, which would have been the cosmic ocean). Both the Hebrew and Greek translations encompass some of these concepts, however, no English term comes close, as English developed after the Classical era when

43

CHAPTER 1

Hero of Alexandria documented the physics of air in his work *Pneumatica*. In English, "air," "spirit," and "space," have always been separate concepts. During the Akkadian era, the name of Enlil became Ellil (✳𒇸) in Akkadian, meaning "God of líl," which meant "wind god" in Akkadian, which appears to place the origin of Cosmic Genesis chapter 1 in the Akkadian Era. In Old Babylonian era, the Babylonian national god Marduk replaced Ellil as the creator god, and Ellil was demoted to a secondary sky god. During the subsequent Middle Babylonian era, the Assyrian god Ashur replaced entirely Ellil by 1300 BCE.

The replacement of Enlil with Marduk and Assur appears to be related to the way the Semitic interpretation the word líl (𒇸) shifted after the decline of the Sumerian language, as it was a near homonym of līla (𒆠𒀀), meaning "night." During the Old Babylonian era, the meaning of the concept of líl shifted from "wind-spirit," to "night-demon," making Ellil the "god of demons." This may have influenced the development of Moabite god El Shadyin, also meaning "god of demons." El Shadayin is generally accepted as the Moabite counterpart of the Israelite El Shady, however, šdyn (𐤔𐤃𐤉𐤍) specifically meant "demons," in Canaanite, while šdy (𐤔𐤃𐤉) only meant "powerful."

The Israelite El Shady only became the "demonic god" after Aramaic became dominant in southern Canaan due to the meaning of šydå (ܫܝܕܐ) in Aramaic. The two gods did probably share a common origin, as Enlíl's (Ellil's) son in Sumerian and Akkadian religion was Nergal, who by the Middle Babylonian era was viewed as the Mesopotamian version of Resheph. By the era that the Aramaic translation of Cosmic Genesis was made, the god Ellil was forgotten, within Canaan, explaining why the name was translated as rwkǎ ǎlhym (ܪܘܚܐ ܐܠܗܝܢ), meaning "wind god." The modern Hebrew translation of Enlil continues to be ǎdwn hrwǩ (אדון הרוח), meaning "Lord of the wind/spirit."

44

CHAPTER 1

8 Codex Alexandrinus: udatos (ΥΔΑΤΟC). Translation: water (or rain, freshwater)

• Septuagint 122: údatōn (ꙁⷣⷪ ⲧ𝖎̆). Translation: water (or rain, freshwater)

• Leningrad Codex: pənê hammāyim (פְּנֵי הַמָּיִם). Translation: face (or interior, speak) the waters

• Peshitta: åpy myå (ܐ̄ܦ̈ܝ ܡ̈ܝܐ). Translations: surface (or face, region) water

• Targum Onkelos: 'appê mayyā' (אַפֵּי מַיָּא). Translation: surface (or face, region) water

• Targum Jerusalem: 'appê mayyā' (אַפֵּי מַיָּא). Translation: surface (or face, region) water

• Targum Pseudo-Jonathan: 'anpê maya' (אַנְפֵּי מַיָּא). Translation: my face of water

• Sahidic manuscripts: moou (ⲘⲞⲞⲨ). Translation: water

• Papyrus Bohairic 2: mōou (ⲙⲱⲟⲩ). Translation: water

The pairing of Ellil with the "waters," which will later create life, indicates that "waters" or "face of waters" was being used as a translation for Ia (𒂍𒀀). In Akkadian creation mythology, after Ellil separated the sky from the land, the god Ia created live. Ia's name is derived from the Sumerian words I (𒂍), meaning both "praise" and "come from," and A (𒀀), meaning "water." The transliteration of the name as "Ia" is modern, and if pronounced in Akkadian, the name would have been Ṣēriš Muú. It is also possible that the name was Akkadian, or a Sumerian name spelled phonetically, as it has not been documented earlier than the Akkadian era.

9 Papyrus 12: ēmeran (ⲎⲘⲉⲣⲀⲚ). Translation: Hemera (or day).

• Septuagint manuscript 228: éméran o ēn uperanō tou stereōmatos (ἡμέραν ο ⲱ ὑπέρανω το ϛϛⲟⳝⲙⲁⲧⲟⲥ). Translation:

45

CHAPTER 1

Hemera (or day) the which (or who) above the framework (or firmament, foundation)

- Leningrad Codex: yôm (יֹום). Translation: day, daylight
- Peshitta: åymmå (ܐܝܡܡܐ). Translations: daytime
- Targum Onkelos: yəmāmā' (יְמָמָא). Translation: daytime
- Targum Pseudo-Jonathan: yəmāmā' (יְמָמָא). Translation: daytime

The Greek translation used the name Hemera, the name of a goddess that personified the daytime in Greek philosophy. According to the Greek philosopher Hesiod circa 700 BCE, she was the daughter of Erebus (Darkness) and Nyx (Night), along with her brother Aether (Brightness), differing somewhat from this interpretation, which has Hemera and Nyx as siblings, or at least counterparts. The generations of these primordial gods were not agreed upon in the Classical era. Around 475 BCE, the Greek poet Bacchylides, recorded that Hermera was the daughter of Nyx and Chronus (Time). Her Roman equivalent was Dies (Day), who the Roman mythographer Hyginus circa (10 CE), was the daughter of Chaos and Caligo (Mist), and the sister of Nox (Night), Erebus and Aether. None of the primordial gods of Greece appear to have been worshiped earlier than the iron age as their names do not appear in the bronze age Mycenaean Linear-B script, suggesting that the idea of them was imported from Canaan after the bronze age collapse, circa 1200 BCE.

The Masoretic term was not a direct transliteration of the Canaanite word ym (𐤉𐤌), or Aramaic ywma (𐡀𐡌𐡅𐡉), but a separate classical era pronunciation, similar to the Arabic word yawm (يَوْم) and Sabaean word ywm (𐩺𐩥𐩣), indicating it was a Hasmonean substitution for an older term. The bronze age Ugaritic word ym (𐎊𐎎) was spelled the same as the later Phoenician Canaanite term, confirming the Masoretic and Arabic spelling were a later development in the Classical era.

46

CHAPTER 1

The earlier Old Akkadian phonetically spelling was Úmuum (𒌝𒈬𒌝) although it was also written with the Sumerian logogram UD (𒌓). The logogram UD (𒌓) was used to denote several related concepts in the earlier Sumerian language. In the form of the word ud (𒌓), it meant day, heat, fever, or summer. In the form of the word zalag (variously written as 𒌓 or 𒍣), meant pure, bright, or shine. In the form of barbar (𒌓𒌓), it meant "white." When combined with the dinger it became ^{deity}Utu (𒀭𒌓), the sun god, however, the sun was created later in the chapter. While Utu was one of the major gods of the Sumerian pantheon, and his Akkadian counterpart Shamash was one of the major gods of the Akkadian pantheon, Night, was not.

This section of text seems to be a reference to the Egyptian Myth of Nut and Ra, in which Ra (Day) separated the Nut (Night-sky) from Geb (Earth) creating the world. The Myth of Nut and Ra was popular in the Middle Kingdom. If this verse was inspired by the Myth of Nut and Ra, it must have been before the New Kingdom era, as Ra had become the supreme god in northern Egypt, and would not have been treated a mere personification of the day be that era.

10 Papyrus 12: nukta (ⲚⲨⲔⲦⲀ). Translation: Nyx (or night)

- Leningrad Codex: lāyəlâ (לַיְלָה). Translation: night
- Peshitta: llyå (ܠܠܝܐ). Translations: night
- Targum Onkelos: lêləyā' (לְילְיָא). Translation: night
- Targum Pseudo-Jonathan: lêləyā' (לְילְיָא). Translation: night

The Greek translation used the accusative singular of the name Nyx, the name of a goddess that personified the night in Greek philosophy. According to the Greek philosopher Hesiod circa 700 BCE, she was the daughter of Chaos, along with her brother Erebus

47

(Darkness). Nyx and Erebus were then the parents of Aether (Brightness) and Hemera (Day).

None of the primordial gods of Greece appear to have been worshiped earlier than the iron age as their names do not appear in the bronze age Mycenaean Linear-B script, suggesting that the idea of them was imported from Canaan after the bronze age collapse. The word in the Masoretic text, lāyəlâ (לַיְלָה), which means "night" in Hebrew, is essentially the same in all recorded Semitic languages.

It was līlumz (𒈗𒄿𒈨𒐉) in Old Akkadian, līla (𒈗𒌇) in Ebliate, ll (𐎍𐎍) in Ugaritic, ll (𐤋𐤋) in Phoenician, lly (𐩡𐩡𐩺) in Sabaean, lylyå (𐡋𐡋𐡋) in Aramaic, and layla (لَيْلَة) in Arabic, Nevertheless, Night did not play a role in the creation mythology of Mesopotamia, suggesting that this verse was adopted from the Myth of Nut and Ra in the Myth of Nut and Ra, Ra (Day) separated the Nut (Night sky) from Geb (Earth) creating the world.

This mirrors the events described in this section of text, however, unlike the rest of the text, does not appear in Mesopotamian creation mythologies. The Sumerian language, the word for night was g̃ig (𒈪), however, there was no known god named Gig, and there is no known mention of g̃ig being part of the Sumerian creation mythology. Conversely, the name Nut, the Egyptian goddess of the night sky, is documented in the bronze age form of Akkadian used in Canaan and Egypt during the New Kingdom era, as Niā (𒉌𒊒), and later in the early iron age as Nå (𐤍𐤅) in Canaanite, either of which may have influenced the Greek goddess Nyx (Νυξ).

---

11 Codex Alexandrinus: stereōma OUNON (ⲥⲧⲉⲣⲉⲱⲙⲁ ⲞⲨⲚⲞⲚ). Translation: framework (or foundation) Ouranos (or vaulted sky)

• Leningrad Codex: rāqîa' šāmāyim (רְקִיעַ שָׁמָיִם). Translations: framework Shamayim

CHAPTER 1

- Peshitta: rqyåå šmyå (ܪܩܝܥܐ ܫܡܝܐ). Translation: space (or opening, thickness) sky
- Targum Onkelos: rəqî'ā' šəmayyā' (רְקִיעָא שְׁמַיָּא). Translation: space (or opening, thickness) sky
- Targum Pseudo-Jonathan: rəqî'ā' šəmayā' (רְקִיעָא שְׁמַיָא). Translation: space (or opening, thickness) sky

The framework or firmament of the skies was a reference to the metal sky above the flat earth in the Babylonian cosmology. The name Ouranos (Ουρανος) was derived from the Neo-Assyrian cuneiform term ùruanna (𒀭𒌷𒀭𒈾), meaning "roof sky stone," which was also the Greek interpretation of Ouranos, as the ceiling above the flat Earth. This term was subsequently absorbed into Greek as the name Ouranos during the Greek Dark Age, after the collapse of the Mycenaean civilization, as the name has not been documented in Linear-B, the script of the Mycenaeans. The Hebrew name is essentially the same as the Old Akkadian name Šamuû (𒊮𒄖), Ugaritic Šmyn (𐎌𐎎𐎊𐎐), Canaanite Šmm (𐤔𐤌𐤌), Sabaean Smyn (𐩪𐩣𐩺𐩬), and Aramaic Šmyn (𐡔𐡌𐡉𐡍), all meaning "skies." As this chapter appears to have originated in cuneiform, the Hebrew name is imported from the Masoretic text.

12 Codex Alexandrinus: gē (ΓΗ). Translation: land (or earth, country, soil, Ge)
- Leningrad Codex: 'eres (אֶרֶץ). Translations: Eretz (or land, dirt, country)
- Peshitta: åråå (ܐܪܥܐ). Translation: land (or soil)
- Targum Onkelos: 'ar'ā' (אַרְעָא). Translation: land (or soil)
- Targum Pseudo-Jonathan: 'ar'ā' (אַרְעָא). Translation: land (or soil)

The Greek name Ge (Γη) was probably derived from the Sumerian term Ki (𒆠), meaning "Earth," which is not been documented in Linear-B, the script of the Mycenaean era Greeks, and was therefore most likely introduced by Phoenician or Neo-Assyrian traders during the early iron age. The Hebrew name 'eres (אֶרֶץ), meaning earth or land, is essentially the same in many Semitic languages, including the Akkadian Arsatu (𒅈𒍝𒌈𒌝), which was also spelled with the Sumerian logogram Ki (𒆠), Ugaritic års (𒁹), Canaanite års (𐤀𐤓𐤑), Neo-Babylonian Ersetum (𒅕𒍢𒌈), Sabaean ård (𐩱𐩧𐩳), and Aramaic årq (ארק).

The Egyptian version of was Geb (𓅬𓃀), who was created when Ra (Day) separated him from Nut (Night-sky) in the Myth of Nut and Ra, or by the creator god Shu (Dryness) in the Heliopolite creation mythology. As the Israelites didn't worship the Greek gods, the name is imported from the Masoretic text.

13 Codex Alexandrinus: talassas (ΘΑΛΑϹϹΑϹ). Translation: seas (or Thalassas)

• Leningrad Codex: yammîm (יַמִּים). Translations: seas

• Peshitta: ymmå (ܝܡܡܐ). Translation: seas

• Targum Onkelos: yammê (יַמְמֵי). Translation: Yam (or sea)

• Targum Pseudo-Jonathan: yammê (יַמְמֵי). Translation: Yam (or sea)

The Greek term is the name of a primordial Greek spirit of the sea, and accepted as the Laconian variant of the word "seas." In the Attican and Koine dialects, the name was Talattē (Θαλαττη), which the Hellenistic Babylonian writer Berossus used as the Greek translation of the name Tiamat. Conversely, the Hebrew translation uses the plural form, meaning "seas."

The Old Akkadian name could only have been tâmtu (𒋾𒀀𒄠𒌈), meaning "lake" or "sea," however, during the Old Babylonian era, term became deityTiamat (𒀭𒋾𒊩𒆳). Tiamat was the goddess that replaced Ia in the Abyss, meaning that by the early iron age, when the Canaanite translation was been made, the term would have needed to be replaced with the Canaanite word for "seas."

14 Codex Alexandrinus: exagagetō ta udata erpeta (Є�ᲐᲒᲐᲠᲔᲦᲬᲝ ᲦᲐᲧᲫᲐᲦᲐᲔᲠᲘᲔᲦᲐ). Translation: export from the water reptiles

• Septuagint manuscript 346: exagetō ta údata erpeta (ἐξαγέτω τὰ ὕδατα ἑρπετά). Translation: lead out of the water reptiles.

• Leningrad Codex: yišrəṣû hammayim šereṣ (יִשְׁרְצוּ הַמַּ֫יִם שֶׁ֫רֶץ). Translations: will swarm the waters swarms

• Peshitta: nrkšwn myâ rkšâ (ܢܪܟܫܘܢ ܡܝܐ ܪܟܫܐ). Translation: will flow from water insects (or reptiles)

• Targum Onkelos: yirḥăšûn mayyā' rəḥēš (יְרְחֲשׁוּן מַיָּא רְחֵשׁ). Translation: will crawl from water insects (or reptiles, vermin)

• Targum Pseudo-Jonathan: yərahăšûn rəqāqê môy rəhēš (יְרְחֲשׁוּן רְקָקֵי מוֹי רְחֵישׁ). Translation: will crawl from swamp water insects (or reptiles, vermin)

• Papyrus Bohairic 2: maremmōou taouo ebol nhanjatbe (ⲙⲁⲣⲉⲙⲙⲱⲟⲩ ⲧⲁⲟⲩⲟ ⲉⲃⲟⲗ ⲛ̄ⲏⲁⲛⲭⲁⲧⲃⲉ). Translation: from the water send out the snakes (or worms)

• Lycopolitan manuscript 200: maremmou teuo ebol nhenjatfe (ⲙⲁⲣⲉⲙⲙⲟⲩ ⲧⲉⲩⲟ ⲉⲃⲟⲗ ⲛ̄ⲏⲉⲛⲭⲁⲧϥⲉ). Translation: from the water send out the snakes (or worms)

• Sahidic manuscript 2020: maremmoou tauo ebol nhenjatfe (ⲙⲁⲣⲉⲙ̄ⲙⲟⲟⲩ ⲧⲁⲩⲟ ⲉⲃⲟⲗ ⲛ̄ⲏⲉⲛⲭⲁⲧϥⲉ). Translation: from the water send out the snakes (or worms)

15 Codex Alexandrinus: šukōn zōsōn (ϯⲩⲭⲱⲛⲍⲱⲥⲱⲛ). Translation: minds (or personalities, psyches) living

- Leningrad Codex: nepeš hayyâ (נֶפֶשׁ חַיָּה). Translations: minds (or lives, souls, persons) of animals
- Peshitta: npšå ǩytå (ܢܦܫܐ ܚܝܬܐ). Translation: breath (or psyche) living
- Targum Onkelos: napšā' ḥaytā' (נַפְשָׁא חַיְתָא). Translation: breath (or psyche) living
- Targum Pseudo-Jonathan: napšat biryāytā' (נַפְשַׁת בְּרִייָתָא). Translation: breath (or psyche) creatures
- Papyrus Bohairic 2: nem hansuke euonž (ⲚⲈⲘ ⲀⲚⲰⲨⲬⲎ ⲈⲦⲞⲚⳅ). Translation: with face of soul who live
- Lycopolitan manuscript 200: msuke euonh (ⲘⲨⲮⲬⲎ ⲈⲨⲞⲚⲌ). Translation: the soul of that live
- Sahidic manuscript 2020: msuke euonh (ⲘⲯⲨⲬⲎ ⲈⲨⲞⲚⲌ). Translation: the soul of that live

This is generally used only in relation to humans and messengers who have a more developed mind. Some Christian, Islamic, and Druze groups take this as a reference to another world before God made Adam. According to the Islamic historian Al-Tabari in the 9th century CE, this was the time when the Jinn (Genies) rebelled against Allah, and the Hinn fought on the side of the angels under the leadership of Iblis (possibly Satan before his rebellion) against the Jinn.

The Hinn are not described in the Quran, and some view them as the reptiles referenced in *Cosmic Genesis*, chapter 1. Those that accept the idea of an entire civilization between the 5th and 6th days of creation do not accept the idea of a literal 24 hour day, but an eon of time, which the Hebrew word "yom" can also be interpreted as.

16 Codex Alexandrinus: kētē ta megala (ⲔⲎⲦⲎ ⲦⲀ ⲘⲈⲄⲀⲖⲀ). Translation: Cetus the Great

- Dead Sea Scroll 4QGen^d: tnynym- (-תנינם). Only the first word survives. Translation: dragons.
- Dead Sea Scroll 4QGen^b: tnynm hgdlym (תנינם הגדלים). Translation: dragons the great (in Hebrew, or twisted in Aramaic).
- Leningrad Codex: tannînim haggədōlîm (תַּנִּינִם הַגְּדֹלִים). Translation: crocodiles (or dragons) the great (in Hebrew, or twisted in Aramaic)
- Peshitta: tnynâ rwrbâ (ܬܢܝܢܐ ܪܘܪܒܐ). Translation: dragon (or sea serpent, monster, serpent, Satan, Draco) lord
- Targum Onkelos: tannînayyā' rabrəbayyā' (תַּנִּינַיָּא רַבְרְבַיָּא). Translation: dragon (or sea serpent, monster, serpent, Draco) great-master
- Targum Pseudo-Jonathan: tanînayā' rabrəbayā' yat liwyātān ûbar zûgêh dəmit'attədîn ləyôm nehĕmātā' (תַּנִינַיָא רַבְרְבַיָא יַת לִוְיָתָן וּבַר זוּגֵיה דְמִתְעַתְּדִין לְיוֹם נֶחֱמָתָא). Translation: dragon (or sea serpent, monster, serpent, Draco) great-master, he leviathan, and his partner (or wife) which are prepared for the day of consolation
- Papyrus Bohairic 2: ništ nkētos (ⲛⲓϣϯ ⲛ̄ⲕⲏⲧⲟⲥ). Translation: Great the sea monster (or fish, whale)
- Sahidic manuscript 2020: noh nkētos (ⲛⲟϭ ⲛ̄ⲕⲏⲧⲟⲥ). Translation: Great the sea monster (or fish, whale)

The Greek term is generally translated as "whale," however, the Cetus was a legendary monster in Æthiopia in the legend of Perseus, which was also referenced in the Books of Psalms and Job. In Greek mythology, Cetus was killed by the demigod Perseus, who, like the seventh sage Lu-Nanna, was part human and part god, suggesting the Greek and Neo-Akkadian stories had a common origin. Perseus was the legendary founder of the Mycenaean civilization, which would place the origin of the story in the 1600s BCE, however, thus far no evidence of the name Perseus has been found in the Liner-B script from the era, and so he is widely believed to have been a fictional character developed later in the iron age.

The translators of the Peshitta and Targums interpreted the term the same as the Greek translators. In the early 2nd century Targum Onkelos, the term was similar to the Greek, indicating that the earlier Aramaic source texts for the Septuagint probably read quite similar. Like the Septuagint's interpretation, Onkelos can be interpreted either as a "great-master monster," or as a constellation, however, Onkelos uses the Aramaic name for Draco, instead of the name for Cetus. The 4th century Peshitta reads the same way, however, by the forth century, the term had shifted within Christian Aramaic, and now referred to the Lord Satan, meaning the verse had become about the creation of Satan.

The Canaanite word tannin (╾╍╍ / תַּנִּין / 𐤕𐤍𐤕) and Aramaic word tnynå (ܢܝܢܐ / ܬܢܝܢܐ) are both accepted by linguists as being derived from the Akkadian word danninu (𒁕𒀭𒉌𒉡), meaning "underworld." This suggests the original text was about God creating everything between the sky-waters (υδατα) above the framework (στερεωμα) of the sky (ουρανον), and the underworld (𒁕𒀭𒉌𒉡). The transition of the term danninu in Canaanite from "underworld" to "serpent" or "crocodile," took place during the Hyksos dynasty, indicating that the original version of Bereshít must have been written during the Egyptian Canaanite Dynasty or earlier.

CHAPTER 2

The heavens and Earth were finished, and the whole world of them. God finished on the sixth[1] day the works which he made, and he ceased on the seventh day from all his works which he made. God blessed the seventh day and sanctified it because on it he completed his work, which God started in the beginning.

This is the book of the descendants of Shamayim and Eretz, when it took place, in the day in which God made the sky and land, and every plant of the field before it was on land, and all the grass of the field before it sprang up, for God had not rained on the land,[2] and there was not a man to cultivate it. But there rose a fountain out of the land and watered the whole surface of Eretz. God formed the man of the dust of Eretz and breathed on his face the breath of life, and the man became a living mind.

Lord the god planted a paradise[3] to the east, in Eden,[4] and placed there the man that he had formed.

God also made to sprout up out of the land every tree beautiful to see and good for food, and the tree of life in the middle of paradise, and the tree of learning that which is to be known of good and evil. A river proceeded out of Eden to water paradise, where it divided itself into four heads. The name of the one is Pison[5] which winds through the whole land of Euilat,[6] where there is gold. The gold of that land is good, and there is also carbuncle and emerald. The name of the second river is Karun,[7] which winds through all of Khuzestan.[8] The third river is Tigris,[9] this is the one that flows out past the Assyrians. The fourth river is the Euphrates.[10]

Lord the god[11] took the man that he had formed, and placed him in paradise, to cultivate and keep it. Lord the god ordered Adam,[12] "From every tree in paradise you may eat, but from the tree of the knowledge of good and evil, you will not eat, or in whichever day you eat of it, you will die the death."

Lord the god said, "It is not good that the man should be alone, let us make for him a helper according to him."

God formed even more out of Eretz, all the wild animals of the field and all the birds of the sky, and he brought them to Adam, to see what he would call them, and whatever Adam called any living mind, that was the name of it. Adam called names of all the livestock and all the birds of the sky, and all the wild animals of the field, but for Adam, there was not found a helper like himself.

God brought a trance on Adam, and he slept, and he took one of his ribs and filled up the flesh. God built the rib which he took from Adam into a woman, and brought her to Adam. Adam said, "This now is bone out of my bones, and flesh of my flesh. She will be called wife because she was taken out of her husband." Therefore will a man leave his father and his mother and will be cemented to his wife, and the two will be one flesh.

CHAPTER 2 NOTES

1 Codex Alexandrinus: ektē (ⲉⲕⲧⲏ). Translation: sixth

- Leningrad Codex: šəbîî (שְׁבִיעִי). Translation: seventh

- Peshitta: šttå (ܫܬܐ). Translation: sixth

- Samaritan Torah: šyšy (ﬡﬤﬡﬤﬡ). Translation: sixth

- Targum Onkelos: šəbî'ā'â (שְׁבִיעָאה). Translation: seventh

- Targum Pseudo-Jonathan: šəbî'ā'â (שְׁבִיעָאה). Translation: seventh

- Sahidic manuscripts: sašf (ⲥⲁϣϥ). Translation: seven

- Papyrus Bohairic 2: šašf (ϣⲁϣϥ). Translation: seven

- Lycopolitan manuscript 200: sašf (ⲥⲁϣϥ). Translation: seven

2 Papyrus Oxyrhynchus 1007: ou gar ebrexen ƵƵ epi tēn gēn (ⲞⲨⲄⲀⲢⲈⲂⲢⲈⲊⲈⲚⲌⲌⲈⲠⲒⲦⲎⲚⲅⲎⲚ). Translation: not since drenched Yahweh on the land.

Papyrus Oxyrhynchus 1007 is unusual in that it appears to include an attempt to write the Phoenician letters ƵƵ as a substitute for the word "God." The papyrus dates to the 3rd century CE; however, it is likely a copy of a kaige revision from the 1st century BCE. The copies of the Septuagint that imported the name written in the Aramaic or Phoenician scripts are referred to as kaige revisions, and appear to have originated in Herodian Judea in the 1st century BCE. This variant text shows that the name Yahweh was still being substituted for Elohim at the time. The same variation is found in the Targum Onkelos from the early 2nd century; however, it is not clear if the deviation dates to the early 2nd century, as the targum was edited in Babylonia during the 4th or 5th century.

- Codex Alexandrinus: ou gar ebrexen o T̄S epi tēn gēn (ⲞⲨⲄⲀⲢ ⲈⲂⲢⲈⲊⲈⲚ Ⲟ Ⲟ̄Ⲥ̄ ⲈⲠⲒ ⲦⲎⲚ ⲅⲎⲚ). Translation: not since drenched the god on the land

CHAPTER 2

- Septuagint manuscript 17: ou gar ebrexen Kurios o Ṯeos epi tēn gēn (ου ᵏ κ ϬυβϬϟϛϲαι ιυβιος ο θϬοϲ Ϭπι Ϝϳ γιω). Translation: not since drenched Lord the God on the land.

- Septuagint manuscript 72: ou gar ebreǩen o ṯeos epi tēs gēs (ου ᵏ κ ϬυβϬχαι ο θϬοϲ Ϭπι Ϛϙ γιλϲ). Translation: not since drenched the God on the world.

- Septuagint manuscript 75: ou gar ebreǩen o ṯeos epi tēn gēn (ου ᵏ κ ϬυβϬχαι ο θϬοϲ Ϭπι Ϝϳ γιω). Translation: not since rained the God on the land.

- Septuagint manuscript 509: ou gar ebrexen epi tēn gēn o ṯeos (ου ᵏ κ ϬυβϬϟϛϲαι Ϭπι Ϝϳ γιω ο θϬοϲ). Translation: not since drenched on the land the God

- Leningrad Codex: kî lō' himtîr Yǝhōwâ 'ĕlōhîm 'al-hā'āres (כִּי לֹא הִמְטִיר יְהוָה אֱלֹהִים עַל־הָאָרֶץ). Translation: because not the rain Yahweh elohim on the Earth

- Peshitta: mṭl dlâ âǩt mryâ âlhâ mṭrâ ôl âyp ârôâ (ܡܛܠ ܕܠܐ ܐܚܬ ܡܪܝܐ ܐܠܗܐ ܡܛܪܐ ܥܠ ܐܦ ܐܪܥܐ). Translation: roof of everything your master (or lord) god rain on surface (or region) land

- Targum Onkelos: lā' 'āhît mitrā' yǝyā 'ĕlōhîm 'al 'ar'ā (לָא אֲחִית מִטְרָא יְיָ אֱלֹהִים עַל אַרְעָא). Translation: not your rain Yahweh elohim (or gods) on land (or region)

- Targum Pseudo-Jonathan: lā' 'imtar yǝyā 'ĕlhîm 'al 'ar'ā (לָא אַמְטַר יְיָ אֱלֹהִים עַל אַרְעָא). Translation: not your rain Yahweh gods on land (or region)

3 Codex Alexandrinus: paradison (ΠΑΡΑΔΕΙϹΟΝ). Translation: walled garden

- Leningrad Codex: gan (גָּן). Translation: garden

- Peshitta: prdyśâ (ܦܪܕܝܣܐ). Translation: paradise, walled garden

- Targum Onkelos: gînǝtā' (גִּינְתָא). Translation: garden

- Targum Jerusalem: gintā' (גִּנְתָא). Translation: garden
- Targum Pseudo-Jonathan: gînûnîtā' (גִּינוּנִיתָא). Translation: pleasure garden
  - Sahidic manuscripts: paradisos (ⲡⲁⲣⲁⲁⲓⲥⲟⲥ). Translation: garden
  - Papyrus Bohairic 2: paradisos (ⲡⲁⲣⲁⲁⲓⲥⲟⲥ). Translation: garden

The Greek word paradise is ultimately derived from the Avestan pairi.daēza (𐬞𐬀𐬌𐬭𐬌⸱𐬛𐬀𐬉𐬰𐬀), meaning "walled enclosure." It was adopted into Neo-Babylonian as pardēsu (𒉺𒅋𒀧𒋢), Old Persian Cuneiform as paradayadam (𐎱𐎼𐎭𐎹𐎭𐎶), Aramaic as prdyså (פרדיסא), and Greek as paradeisos (παράδεισος). The Hebrew term gan (גָּן) is a continuation of the Sumerian word gan (𒃷) which meant "cultivated field." The logogram was also used in Akkadian to mean "field," however, the Old Akkadian pronunciation was eqel (𒀱), and the later Neo-Assyrian and Neo-Babylonian pronunciation was eqlum (𒀳𒇴 / 𒀳𒈝). The Semitic term is also found in Sabaean as ḥql (𐩢𐩤𐩡), Aramaic as ḵqlā (חקלא), Arabic as ḥaql (حَقْل), and Ge'ez as ḥäqəl (ሐቀል), as well as the Central Atlas Tamazight akal (ⴰⴽⴰⵍ).

The term gan is not generally found in Afro-Asiatic languages, and the Hebrew word appears to be a legacy of the word surviving in the Bereshít. While it may have been written in Akkadian cuneiform as the logogram 𒃷, it could not have been written in Aramaic without being translated into another tern such as "field" (חקלא) or "paradise" (פרדיסא). The existence of the word in Bereshít suggests that the book originated in the Neo-Sumerian Empire, when phonetic spelling of Sumerian terms was common in Akkadian cuneiform.

4 Codex Alexandrinus: Edem (ⲉⲁⲉⲙ)
- Leningrad Codex: 'Ēden (עֵדֶן)

CHAPTER 2

- Peshitta: Ôdn (ܥܕܢ)
- Targum Onkelos: 'Ēden (עֵדֶן)
- Targum Jerusalem: 'Ēden (עֵדֶן)
- Targum Pseudo-Jonathan: 'Ēden (עֵדֶן)
- Sahidic manuscripts: Edem (ⲈⲆⲈⲘ)
- Papyrus Bohairic 2: Edem (ⲈⲆⲈⲘ)

Most scholars agree this is a transliteration of the Akkadian word edinu (𒂔) meaning "plain," itself derived from the Sumerian word edin (𒂔) also meaning "plain" or "steppe." In Sumerian and Akkadian the word referred to the plains of southern Iraq.

In the Sumerian creation stories, humans were first made in edin, suggesting this secondary creation narrative in chapter 2 was also part of the text since before the Israelites entered Egypt during the Middle Kingdom era.

5 Codex Alexandrinus: Feisōn (ⲪⲈⲓⲤⲰⲚ)
- Septuagint manuscript 127: Fusōn (ⲪⲩⲤⲰⲚ)
- Septuagint manuscript 75: Fēsōn (ⲪⲏⲤⲰⲚ)
- Septuagint manuscript 19: Feisōn (ⲪⲇⲤⲰⲚ)
- Septuagint manuscript 246: Fisōn (ⲪⲓⲤⲰⲚ)
- Leningrad Codex: Pîšôn (פִּישׁוֹן)
- Peshitta: Pyšwn (ܦܝܫܘܢ)
- Targum Onkelos: Pîšôn (פִּישׁוֹן)
- Targum Pseudo-Jonathan: Pîšôn (פִּישׁוֹן)
- Papyrus Bohairic 2: Fisōn (ⲪⲓⲤⲰⲚ)
- Sahidic manuscript 2020: Fison (ⲪⲓⲤⲟⲚ)

There has been speculation regarding the location of this river for over 2000 years. In the 1st century CE, the Jewish historian Flavius Josephus identified it as the Ganges in India, in his Antiquities of the Jews. The 4th century Cave of Treasures identified it as being the Indus River in Pakistan. In the 11th century CE, the Rabbi Shlomo Yitzchaki (Rashi) identified it as the Nile.

It has also variously been identified as the Rohni in Georgia, the Aras in the Armenian highlands, and the Amu Darya in Central Asia. Most of these locations have been suggested based on older commentaries from Jewish and Israelite communities spread across the old Persian Empire. Rashi's theory ultimately derived from Egyptian-Israelite commentary regarding the name Pak̆namounis (Παχναμουνίς), a major city in the Sebennytos district of the Nile Delta, through which one of the major tributaries of the Nile flowed in ancient times. The city was also the capital of Egypt during the 30th Dynasty (380 to 343 BCE). The name Pak̆namounis seems to have originated in the Libyan 23rd Dynasty of Egypt, between 837 and 728 BCE. It is composed of the words Pak̆n and aman (oⲤoⳊ), meaning "Pak̆n River" in Libyan languages. However, the Egyptian translators transliterated the name as Fison (Ⲫⲓⲥⲟⲛ) or Fisōn (Ⲫⲓⲥⲱⲛ), not Pak̆n (Ⲡⲁⲭⲛ), indicating that they did not view it as Rashi did.

The dominant theory today is that it was a reference to the dried river bed of a major river that once flowed across the Arabian Peninsula from the mountains near Medina to the old Iraqi wetlands, where the Euphrates, Tigris, and Karun Rivers merge. Part of this river still flows seasonally today as the Wadi al-Batin (وادي الباطن) in northeast Saudi Arabia, Kuwait, and Iraq. The Wadi al-Batin is the final section of the much longer Wadi al-Rummah dry river valley that runs across the peninsula, but is today disconnected from the Wadi al-Batin by sand dunes that have covered a section of the former river valley.

When the river still flowed, it was an estimated 1,200 km (750 mi) long, and connected a number of now dried lakes in the interior of the Arabian peninsula. It is unclear when the river last flowed its full length, but some estimates place it at 8000 BCE. The wadi that runs out of the mountains near Medina still floods approximately three times a century. In 1838, the wadi overflowed and created a 520 km² (200 mile²) lake that lasted for 2 years.

If this name originated in Sumerian, like several other terms in *Cosmic Genesis* and *Bereshít*, then the name was probably not a name, but a description of the dried out river bed. In Sumerian, the term pronounced as pí sún (𒉿𒊺), would mean "it is destroyed." This supports the identification of the Pison as being the dried out riverbed of the al-Rummah when the oldest form of the text was written, with the flowing river being a distant memory from an age before the great flood.

6 Codex Alexandrinus: Euilat (ⲉⲩⲉⲓⲗⲁⲧ)

- Septuagint manuscript 707: Euilato (Ευιλατο)
- Septuagint manuscript 18: Ebitat (ευιτατ)
- Septuagint manuscript 121: Euēlat (Ευλ λατ)
- Septuagint manuscript 75: Ebilat (Ευιλατ)
- Septuagint manuscript 82: Euēlattōn (Ευλ λαττῶ)
- Septuagint manuscript 246: Euilat (Ευιλατ)
- Leningrad Codex: Hăwîlâ (חֲוִילָה)
- Peshitta: Ǩwylā (ܟܘܝܠܐ)
- Targum Onkelos: Hăwîlâ (חֲוִילָה)
- Targum Pseudo-Jonathan: Hînədiqê (הִינְדְקִי). Translation: India
- Papyrus Bohairic 2: Euialat (Ⲉⲧⲓⲁⲗⲁⲧ)
- Sahidic manuscript 2020: Eueilat (Ⲉⲩⲉⲓⲗⲁⲧ)

According to the author of the Cave of Treasures, attributed to Ephrem the Syrian in the 4th century CE, this was Hend, the ancient name of the Sindh province of Pakistan. Few modern scholars accept this interpretation. Based on the identification of the Pishon River as the Wadi al-Rummah, and the land of Euilat / Hăwîlâ having gold, this would have been the Mahd adh Dhahab (مَهد الذَهـب), meaning "cradle of gold," near modern Medina, in Saudi Arabia. The region is believed to have still been connected to Sumer via a series of wadis along the Wadi al-Rummah and Wadi al-Batin as late as 3000 BCE, and was the site of extensive gold mines at the time. It is still the site of significant gold mines, which appear to have been in constant production since ancient times.

The two names in the Hebrew and Greek translations may support this claim, if accepted as beginning in Sumerian, like many of the other terms in this section of text. As the Greek is based on an Aramaic transliteration, and the Hebrew is based on a Canaanite transliteration, the differences can be accounted for by two alternate transliterations from cuneiform.

The Greek transliteration is missing the first sound in the Hebrew transliteration, the H (ח), which could be accounted for by the original word beginning with a KI (𒆠), meaning "land" as it could have been interpreted as a repetitive term once translated into another language. Many Akkadian geographical terms included a the term "land" (𒆠), including "land Sumer" (𒆠𒂗𒄀) and "land Akkad" (𒆠𒀝). The final sound in the word is also different, however, can be accounted for by different transliterations of the A (𒀀) logogram.

In Sumerian A (𒀀) was pronounced as A, while in Akkadian and later Semitic languages, it was pronounced as ET (or ED). The A / ET logogram meant several related concepts involving labor, wages, and military forces. Based on the common Greek and Hebrew spelling of the rest of the word, it appears the Sumerian term would have been ᵏⁱÉuila (𒆠𒂍𒈗𒀀), meaning "land Estate of the lord of the porter-laborers." This description of the land supports the idea that the pí sún (𒀀𒉌𒋛) river was already reduced to being a series of wadis running from the Cradle of Gold to the wetlands of Sumer.

7 Codex Alexandrinus: Gēōn (ΓΗⲱΝ)

- Septuagint manuscript 15: Geōn (Γ𝟨ⲟⲟⲛ)
- Septuagint manuscript 392: Gēsōn (ΓⳞⲋⲉⲛ)
- Septuagint manuscript 730: Gaiōn (Γⲁⲓⲟⲟⲛ)
- Septuagint manuscript 19: Geiōn (Γⲇⲟⲟⲛ)
- Leningrad Codex: Gîḥôn (גִּיחֹון)
- Peshitta: Gyk̆wn (ܓܝܚܘܢ)
- Targum Onkelos: Gîḥōn (גִּיחֹון)
- Targum Pseudo-Jonathan: Gîḥōn (גִּיחֹון)
- Papyrus Bohairic 2: Geōn (Ⳝⲉⲱⲛ)
- Sahidic manuscript 2020: Geōn (Γⲉⲱⲛ)

This river's location is debated, as the Greek identification of it flowing through Æthiopia suggests it is the Nile. In modern Sudan (Classical Æthiopia) and Ethiopia (ancient Punt) it has generally been interpreted as the Blue Nile (Abay), which was known as Gʷäzam (ጐዛም) in the earliest records from the region.

The dominant view outside of Northeast Africa, is that it was the Karun River, which flows through Khuzestan province in southwestern Iran. Identifying the Gichon as the Karun is based on the identification of Kush in the Masoretic text as the Khuz instead of the Kingdom of Kush. If the name Gēōn / Gîḥōn is derived from the Sumerian name, the original name was probably [id]Geana (𒀀𒀭𒆠𒀀𒈾), meaning "[river]flowing in rocks," similar to the Sumerian name for the Tigris: [id]Idigna (𒀀𒁇𒄀𒈾), meaning "[river]flowing rough," and the Sumerian name for the Euphrates: [id]Buranun (𒀀𒁓𒉣𒈾), meaning "[river]Copper source."

CHAPTER 2

The Euphrates was the source of the copper for the Sumerian civilization, and the Tigris is a rough fast-flowing river, while the Karun flowed down through the Zagros Mountains into plains of Khuzestan before flowing into the old Sumerian wetlands in Iraq.

As the location of "Kush" is confirmed as being in Khuzestan in the genealogy of nations, the modern name Karun in used as a translation for the Gēōn / Gîhōn.

8 Codex Alexandrinus: gēn Aitiopias (ΓΗΝΑΙΘΙΟΠΙΑC).
Translation: land Æthiopia (or Sudan, Kush)

• Septuagint manuscript 392: gēn Aitiōpias (γῆν Αιθιοπιᾶc).
Translation: land Æthiopia (or Sudan, Kush)

• Septuagint manuscript 319: gēn Aitiōpian (γῆν Αιθιοπιδν).
Translation: land Æthiopians (or Sudanese, Kushites)

• Septuagint manuscript 75: gēn Etiopias (γῆν Εθιοπιᾶc).
Translation: land Æthiopia (or Sudan, Kush)

• Leningrad Codex: 'eres Kûš (כּוּשׁ אֶרֶץ). Translation: land Kush (or Sudan)

• Peshitta: årōå dkwš (ܟܘܫ ܐܪܥܐ). Translation: land of Kush (or Sudan)

• Targum Onkelos: 'ar'ā' dəkûš (דְכוּשׁ אַרְעָא). Translation: land of Kush (or Sudan)

• Targum Pseudo-Jonathan: 'ar'ā' dəkûš (דְכוּשׁ אַרְעָא). Translation: land of Kush (or Sudan)

• Papyrus Bohairic 2: epkahi tērf nniehauš (ⲉⲡⲕⲁϩⲓ ⲧⲏⲣϥ ⲛⲛⲓⲉϭⲁⲧⲩ). Translation: from the whole land of Kushites

• Sahidic manuscript 2020: epkah tērf nnehooše (ⲉⲡⲕⲁϩ ⲧⲏⲣϥ ⲛ̄ⲛⲉϭⲟⲟϣⲉ). Translation: from the whole land of Kushites

The Greek term Æthiopia did not refer to the lands of the modern nation of Ethiopia, but the kingdom of Kush in modern Sudan.

CHAPTER 2

Æthiopia was also sometimes used for the region of southern India where darker skinned people's lived.

The translators of the Septuagint interpreted the name in Cosmic Genesis as referring to the land of Kush, south of Egypt, however, this may have been done for political reasons, as the Ptolemies had plans to conquer Kush early in their dynasty. Exploratory expeditions were sent, into modern Sudan, and at one point followed the Nile and Black Nile (Atbarah-Tekezé) into the highlands of Punt (northern Eritrea). The majority of the Kushite civilization had been relocated farther south after the Persian invasion, and the Greeks ultimately decided not to attempt the invasion.

The dominant theory about what this word means outside of Northeast Africa, is that is refers to Khuzestan province in southwest Iran. The region does not appear to have been known as "Khuze land," until the 9th century CE when it became Khuzestan, named after the Khuz people that lived there.

The term Khuz was applied to the dark skinned decedents of the Elamites that originally inhabited the region from at least the Neo-Assyrian era onward. Multiple Classical and Medieval sources suggest or claim that "Khuze" was the Elamite pronunciation of the Greek Uxi (Yξι) and Old Persian Uvaja (⟨𐎢⟩-𐎺-𐎩), both referring to the region later called Khuzestan, however, the earlier Elamite name of Elam before the Persians settled in the region was Haltamti (𒄬𒆷𒁴𒋾), and therefore modern scholars question this claim. The more probable origin of the name Khuz for the dark skinned descendants of the Elamites, was the Neo-Assyrian kusaaa (𒆪𒊭𒀀𒀀) and Neo-Babylonian word kuúšu (𒆪𒊭𒋳), which both referred to dark skinned people of any origin.

As the term would have been the same in both Aramaic and Hebrew, the Greek translation would have been the first translation to explicitly indicate the land of Æthiopia in modern Sudan. Later in the genealogy of nations, the author of that section of text, who was most likely the original Aramaic translator, uses the name Kush for the name of the people who lived in Sumer, confirming that is was Khuzestan being referred. As 'eres Kûš (ארץ כוש) means "Khuze land," the modern name is used.

9 Codex Alexandrinus: Tigris (Τιγρις). Translation: Tigris
• Septuagint manuscript 55: Tigreis (Τιγρϵις)
• Septuagint manuscript 319: Tigrēs (Τιγρης)
• Septuagint manuscript 54: Tugris (Τυγρις)
• Leningrad Codex: hidDeqel (חִדֶּקֶל). Translation: Tigris
• Peshitta: Dqlt (ܕܩܠܬ). Translation: Tigris
• Targum Onkelos: təlîtā'â Dîgəlat (תְּלִיתָאָה דִיגְלַת). Translation: royal Tigris
• Targum Pseudo-Jonathan: Dîgəlat (דִיגְלַת). Translation: Tigris
• Papyrus Bohairic 2: Jikris (Ϫⲓⲕⲣⲓⲥ)
• Sahidic manuscript 2020: Tekris (Ⲧⲉⲕⲣⲓⲥ)

Both the Greek and Hebrew names are ultimately derived from the Sumerian name of the Tigris River: idIdigna (𒀀𒇋𒂵𒃼), via the Akkadian Cuneiform name: Idiglat (𒀀𒇋𒂵𒃼). The Aramaic name was adopted from the Akkadian name as Dyglt (𐡃𐡉𐡂𐡋𐡕), which was adopted by the Persians as Tigrā (𐎫𐎡𐎥𐎼𐎠), which was in turn transliterated into Greek as Tígris (Τιγρις). The Hebrew name appears to be a direct transliteration of the Akkadian name. The reference to the Tigris as "royal" in the Targum Onkelos, may have use a copy of the Aramaic translation made during the reign of King Hezekiah, when the Tigris river was the most important river in the Neo-Assyrian Empire.

CHAPTER 2

10 Codex Alexandrinus: Eufratēs (ⲉⲩⲫⲣⲁⲧⲏⲥ). Translation: Euphrates

- Septuagint manuscript 707: Efratēs (Ε$ρα$^)
- Septuagint manuscript 56: Eufrátēs outos o megas potamos (Ευ$Δ$^ ουτοc ο μ$γα$c ποτ$Δ$μοc). Translation: Euphrates other the great river

- Leningrad Codex: Pərāt (פְּרָת). Translation: Euphrates
- Peshitta: prt (ܦܪܬ). Translation: Euphrates
- Targum Onkelos: Pərāt (פְּרָת). Translation: Euphrates
- Targum Pseudo-Jonathan: Pərāt (פְּרָת). Translation: Euphrates
- Papyrus Bohairic 2: Eupratēs (ⲉⲧⲡⲣⲁⲏⲥ). Translation: Euphrates
- Sahidic manuscript 2020: Eufratēs (ⲉⲩⲫⲣⲁⲧⲏⲥ). Translation: Euphrates

Both the Greek and Hebrew names are ultimately descended from the Sumerian name of the Euphrates river: [id]Buranun (𒀀𒇉𒄯𒌝), via the Akkadian name Purattu (𒀀𒇉𒄯𒌝). The Aramaic name was adopted from the Akkadian name as Prt (פרת), which was later adopted into Hebrew as Pərāt (פְּרָת). The Akkadian name was also adopted as the Elamite Úipratuiš (𒈨𒇽𒅗𒍨𒂊), which was adopted into Persian as [h]Ufrātuš (𒅀𒆠𒌋𒄑𒅔𒊏), and then into Greek as Eufratēs (Ευφρατης). The extended text in Septuagint manuscript 56 appears to be a note added by an Egyptian scribe.

11 Codex Alexandrinus: KS o ṬS (ⲕⲥ ⲟ ⲑⲥ). Translation: Lord the god

- Leningrad Codex: Yəhōwâ 'ĕlōhîm (יְהוָה אֱלֹהִים). Translation: Yahweh elohim
- Peshitta: mryå ålhå (ܡܪܝܐ ܐܠܗܐ). Translation: master (or lord) God

68

CHAPTER 2

- Targum Onkelos: Yəyā 'ĕlōhîm (יְיָ אֱלֹהִים). Translation: Yahweh elohim

- Targum Jerusalem: Yəyā 'ĕlhîm (יְיָ אֱלֹהִים). Translation: Yahweh gods

- Targum Jonathan: Yəyā 'ĕlhîm (יְיָ אֱלֹהִים). Translation: Yahweh gods

- Papyrus Bohairic 2: ouohe aphs f̄t (ογοϩε ⲁⲡ̄ⲟ̄ⲥ ⲫ̄ϯ). Translation: shepherd (or scorpion) lord God

- Sahidic manuscript 2020: apjoeis pnoute (ⲁⲡϫⲟⲉⲓⲥ ⲡⲛⲟⲩⲧⲉ). Translation: the owner the god

The Aramaic sections of Masoretic Daniel that were not translated into Hebrew maintain the term ădōnāy hā'ĕlōhîm (אֲדֹנָי הָאֱלֹהִים), meaning the "Lord of the gods" where the Septuagint has "Lord the god" (Κυριον τον θεον). As most books of the Septuagint were translated from Aramaic texts, the Aramaic text almost certainly used the term ădōnāy hā'ĕlōhîm where the Septuagint has "Lord the god." The name Yahweh appears to have been added to most of the books in the Masoretic text when the texts were translated to Hebrew during the Hasmonean Dynasty of Judea, between 140 and 37 BCE.

According to the Talmud, this was to repair the damage King Manasseh had done 600 years earlier when he removed the name Yahweh from the Israelite Texts, however, no evidence has survived from the era of Manasseh or earlier that proves the name was originally in the text, suggesting it was an attempt by the first Hasmonean High-Priest / King Simon the Zealous to create a national Judean religion with a god having a name similar to the god Jove.

The name Yahweh, in the Aramaic form of Yhw (יהו^) does appear to have originally been in some of the books of the Septuagint, such as Leviticus, which originated under the rule of

69

King Josiah or later, and Yahweh was a popular god among Judeans and Israelites under Persian and Greek rule. The translators at the Library of Alexandria transliterated this name as Iaō (Ιαω) in the books it was originally in, however, under the Hasmonean Dynasty it seems to have been added to all the books translated into Hebrew, creating some confusion among early Christians.

There were debates in the early Christian era about which version of the Israelite scriptures to use, the Greek, Hebrew, Samaritan, or Syriac translations, resulting in different versions of the scriptures being used by different churches. Some versions replaced the name Lord with Iaō in the Greek texts, either in the Greek form as Ιαω, or by copying in the Hebrew form of the name Yhwh (יהוה) or the older Phoenician form of Yhwh (𐤉𐤄𐤅𐤄), or by mocking the Hebrew with Greek letters as ΠΙΠΙ. This created a great deal of confusion among Christians, and ultimately the books of the Septuagint that had the name Iaō in them were redacted so all the books used the term Lord (Κυριος). Most Christian translations, as well as Jewish translations, have continued to use the term "Lord" in place of the name Yahweh, due to the prohibition on using any names of God that was introduced during the Hasmonean dynasty.

There are no early surviving copies of Cosmic Genesis which have the name Iaō (Ιαω) in them, like some of the other books of the Septuagint, and therefore it cannot be proven if the name was in Cosmic Genesis or not. Nevertheless, the terms used in Cosmic Genesis are consistent with the surviving Aramaic sections of Masoretic Daniel, indicating the Aramaic source text the Greek translators used included the term "lord of the gods," not "Yahweh gods."

12 Codex Alexandrinus: Adam (ⲀⲆⲀⲘ)

- Leningrad Codex: hā'ādām (הָאָדָם). Translation: the man (or earth, soil, light brown, red)

- Peshitta: lådm (ܠܐܕܡ). Translation: the man

- Targum Onkelos: 'ādām (אָדָם). Translation: Adam (or man)

- Targum Pseudo-Jonathan: 'ādām (אָדָם). Translation: Adam (or man)

- Papyrus Bohairic 2: rōmi (ⲣⲱⲙⲓ). Translation: human (or man)

- Sahidic manuscript 2020: rōme (ⲣⲱⲙⲉ). Translation: human (or man)

CHAPTER 3

The two were naked, both Adam and his wife, and neither were exalted. The serpent[1] was the wisest[2] of all the beasts on the land, which the Lord the god[3] made, and the serpent asked the woman, "Has God said, 'Don't eat of every tree in paradise?'"

The woman said to the serpent, "We may eat of the fruit of the trees of paradise, but of the fruit of the tree which is in the middle of paradise, God said, 'You will not eat of it, neither will you touch it, in case you die.'"

The serpent said to the woman, "You will not die the death. For God knew that in whatever day you should eat of it your eyes would be opened, and you would be like the gods,[4] knowing good and evil."

The woman saw that the tree was good for food and that it was pleasant to the eyes to look at and beautiful to contemplate, and she took its fruit and ate, and she gave to her husband also, and they ate. The eyes of both were opened, and they perceived that they were naked, and they sewed fig leaves together and made themselves aprons to go round them. They heard the voice of the Lord the god walking in Paradise in the afternoon, and both Adam and his wife hid from the face of the Lord the god in the middle of the trees of Paradise. Lord the god called Adam and said to him, "Adam, where are you?"

CHAPTER 3

He answered him, "I heard your voice walking in paradise, and I was afraid because I am naked and I was hiding."

The reply was, "Did they tell you that you were naked? Did only one of them eat from the tree? Did you eat?"

Adam answered, "The woman that was given me, she gave me of the tree and I ate."

Lord the god asked the woman, "What did you do?"

The woman answered, "The serpent deceived me and I ate."

Lord the god said to the serpent, "Because you have done this you are cursed more than all livestock and all the animals of the land, on your breast and belly you will go, and you will eat earth all the days of your life. I will put enmity between you and the woman and between your descendants and her descendants, he will keep watch against your head, and you will keep watch against his heel."

To the woman said, "Greatly multiply your regrets and your sighs. In sorrow, you will give birth to children. To your man, you will turn, and he will dominate you."

To Adam he said, "Because you have listened to the voice of your wife, and eaten of the tree which I told you I alone would eat from, cursed is the ground in your labors, in regret will you eat all the days of your life. Thorns and thistles will it bring forth to you, and you will eat the plant of the field. In the sweat of your face will you eat your bread until you return to Eretz out of which you were taken, for dirt you are and to dirt you will return."

Adam called the name of his wife Life,[5] that is, the mother of all living. Lord the god made for Adam and his wife garments of skin and clothed them. God said, "Look, Adam has become as one of us, knowing good and evil, Now if he stretches out his hand, and takes from the tree of life and eats, he will live forever."

So Lord the god sent him out of paradise to cultivate the ground out of which he was taken. He threw out Adam and caused him to live outside paradise, and placed the cherubs[6] and flaming broadsword that circles to guard the path to the tree of life.[7]

CHAPTER 3 NOTES

1 Codex Alexandrinus: ofis (ⲟⲫⲓⲥ). Translation: snake

• Leningrad Codex: nāḥāš (נָחָשׁ). Translation: snake

• Peshitta: k̆wyå (ܚܘܝܐ). Translation: snake

• Targum Onkelos: ḥiwyā' (חִוְיָא). Translation: snake

• Targum Pseudo-Jonathan: ḥiwyā' (חִוְיָא). Translation: snake

• Papyrus Bohairic 2 (later in the chapter): hof (ϩⲟϥ). Translation: snake (or worm)

• Sahidic manuscript 2020 (later in the chapter): hof (ϩⲟϥ). Translation: snake (or worm)

2 Codex Alexandrinus: fronimōtatos (ⲫⲣⲟⲛⲓⲙⲱⲧⲁⲧⲟⲥ). Translation: wisest (or prudentist, most well behaved)

- Cotton Genesis: fronimōteros (ϕΡΟΝΙΜѠΤΕΡΟC). Translation: sane (or the most "in one's right mind")
- Septuagint manuscript 56: fronēmōteros (ϕⴲⳑμοοτꝗοc). Translation: moralist (or with the greatest conscience)
- Leningrad Codex: 'ārûm (עָרוּם). Translation: naked
- Peshitta: ȯrym (ܥܪܝܡ). Translation: ruggedest (or roughest)
- Targum Onkelos: ḥakkîm (חַכִּים). Translation: wise
- Targum Pseudo-Jonathan: ḥakkîm (חַכִּים). Translation: wise

This conflicting reference to the snake being the wisest, or most naked creature in the garden, has led to some different translations. It is often assumed that the original reference was the exalted serpent Mušmaḱḱū (𒈲𒈣𒆅) from Sumerian mythology, resulting in some bibles translating the snake in this verse as "most exalted." The term 'ārûm (עָרוּם) is essentially the same word as the Akkadian erium (𒅤𒈠) and Arabic ȯuryān (عُزيِان). In the case of the Akkadian word, it also meant "low" and "poor," making the Akkadian description of the snake the "lowest" among the creatures, which does seem to fit the narrative better that "nakedest" or "wisest."

3 Codex Alexandrinus: K̄S o T̄S (K̄CоӨC). Translation: lord the god
- Leningrad Codex: Yəhōwâ 'ĕlōhîm (יְהֹוָה אֱלֹהִים). Translation: Yahweh god (in Assyrian, or gods in Aramaic, goddesses in Hebrew)
- Peshitta: mryå ålhym (ܡܪܝܐ ܐܠܗܝܡ). Translation: master (or lord) gods
- Targum Onkelos: Yəyā 'ĕlōhîm (יְיָ אֱלֹהִים). Translation: Yahweh gods (or god in Neo-Assyrian, goddesses in Hebrew)

CHAPTER 3

• Targum Pseudo-Jonathan: Yəyā 'ĕlôhîm (יְיָ אֱלֹהִים). Translation: Yahweh elohim (or god in Assyrian, or gods in Aramaic, goddesses in Hebrew

4 Codex Alexandrinus: ṯeoi (ⲐⲈⲞⲒ). Translation: gods
• Leningrad Codex: 'lōhîm (אֱלֹהִים). Translation: goddesses (or gods in Aramaic)
• Peshitta: âlhå (ܐܠܗܐ). Translation: God
• Targum Onkelos: kərabrəbîn (כְּרַבְרְבִין). Translation: cherub masters
• Targum Pseudo-Jonathan: mal'ākîn rabrəbîn (מַלְאָכִין רַבְרְבִין). Translation: messenger (or angel) great-masters
• Sahidic manuscripts: noute (ⲚⲞⲨⲦⲈ). Translation: god
• Papyrus Bohairic 2: nout (ⲚⲞⲨϯ). Translation: god

5 Codex Alexandrinus: Zōē (ⲌⲰⲎ). Translations: life (or spirit)
• Septuagint manuscript 400: Zōēn (Ζωην). Translation: alive
• Leningrad Codex: ḥawwâ (חַוָּה). Translation: farm
• Peshitta: ḵwå (ܚܘܐ). Translation: life (or Ophiuchus)
• Targum Onkelos: ḥawwâ (חַוָּה). Translation: life (or Ophiuchus)
• Targum Pseudo-Jonathan: ḥawâ (חַוָה). Translation: life (or Ophiuchus)
• Papyrus Bohairic 2: Zōē (Ⲍⲱⲏ). Translation: Zoe
• Sahidic manuscript 2210: Zōē (Ⲍⲱⲏ). Translation: Zoe

The name Zōē and Ḥawwâ are both direct translations of the name Ḵwh (חוה), meaning "living." In other verses the Greeks transliterated the name as Eua (Ευα), which was translated into Latin as Eve. The Assyrian Christians believe that Eve's real name was Ǩwå (ܟܘ), which was corrupted into Eua by the Greeks when they translated the Septuagint.

The woman called "Life," made from Adam's rib, is undoubtedly related to the story from Enki and Ninhursag in which a goddess called ^{deity}Ninti (𒀭𒀺𒋾 / 𒀭𒊩𒌆𒋾) meaning "Lady Life" is made from the god Enki's rib. Enki translates as "Lord Earth," while ådm (𐤀𐤃𐤌 / 𐎀𐎄𐎎) means "earth" in Canaanite suggesting that the original story was about Enki and Ninti. Both Enki and Ninti were documented in Old Sumerian texts; however, the oldest surviving copy of *Enki and Ninhursag* dates to the late Neo-Sumerian era. While there are obvious parallels to the Adam and Eve story, *Enki and Ninhursag* includes a number of other gods being created from Enki's body parts, suggesting it was created in the Neo-Sumerian reforms when the Enki-Ninki ancestors of Enlil were added to the pantheon. The Enki and Ninti story that would have been carried out of the Neo-Sumerian Empire by the rebel priests appears to have been much simpler than the story found in *Enki and Ninhursag*; however, there are also parallels between the *Enki and Ninhursag* narrative and the Osiris and Isis mythology, which had already been established in Egypt. This suggests that the longer narrative might have been carried back into Iraq by descendants of the priests who fled the reforms and settled in Egypt.

Although significant in the late Neo-Sumerian *Enki and Ninhursag*, Ninti generally disappeared from Mesopotamian literature during the following Old Babylonian era. Assyriologists generally view Ninti as the precursor to Ereshkigal, the goddess of the underworld who appeared during the Neo-Sumerian era and became more significant during the Old Babylonian era. Like Nergal, Ereshkigal's major temple was in Kutha and was probably built by King Shulgi, like the major temple of Nergal.

As Zōē (Ζωη), Ḥawwâ (חַוָּה), Ḱwh (תוה), and ^{deity}Ninti (✳🝫𓏤 / ✳𒉈𒋾) are all versions of the name "Life," that name is used as a direct translation for Zōē. In places where the Greeks transcribed the name as Eua (Ευα), it is transliterated in the common English "Eve."

6 Codex Alexandrinus: ḱeroubin (ⲭⲉⲣⲟⲩⲃⲓⲛ)

- Septuagint manuscript 17: ḱeroubein (χϐουμϟν)
- Septuagint manuscript 55: ḱeroubeim (χϐουμϟμ)
- Septuagint manuscript 75: ḱairoubēm (χαιϱουμϧμ)
- Septuagint manuscript 664: ḱerobim (χϐουμμ)
- Leningrad Codex: kərūbîm (כְּרֻבִים). Translation: cherubs (or griffins)
- Peshitta: krwbå (ܟܪܘܒܐ). Translation: cherubs (or plow, plowman)
- Targum Onkelos: kərûbayyā' (כְּרוּבַיָּא). Translation: cherubs (or plow, plowman)
- Targum Jerusalem: kərôbayā' (כְּרוֹבַיָּא). Translation: cherubs (or plow, plowman)
- Targum Pseudo-Jonathan: kərûbayā' (כְּרוּבַיָּא). Translation: cherubs (or plow, plowman)
- Papyrus Bohairic 2: ḱeroubin (ⲭⲉⲣⲟⲩⲃⲓⲛ)
- Sahidic manuscript 2210: ḱeroubein (ⲭⲉⲣⲟⲩⲃⲉⲓⲛ)
- Sahidic manuscripts 16L: ḱeroubin (ⲭⲉⲣⲟⲩⲃⲓ̈ⲛ)

The word "cherub" (ܟܪܘܒܐ / כרוב / 𐤊𐤓𐤁 / 𐎋𐎗𐎁) was the Semitic term for the mythical creature generally called a "griffin" today. The oldest form is recorded in the Akkadian word karibu (𒅗𒊒𒁍), meaning "one who blesses." Based on the archaeological record of Canaan, it appears that during the late Bronze Age, the "cherub" was depicted as a sphinx. During the Iron Age, the

Assyrian karubu (𒀀𒇯𒐈𒑏) iconography was adopted by the Israelites. The term "cherub" appears to have been used as a substitute for śārāp (שָׂרָף) after King Hezekiah or King Manasseh's reforms to the Torah in the early 8th century BCE. Isaiah called Nəhuštān (נְחֻשְׁתָּן) a seraph when he visited the temple in the late 9th century BCE, before it was destroyed at the beginning of the 8th century BCE. Nəhuštān was the name or title of the Bronze Serpent statue that Moses made in Numbers, chapter 21. This suggests that the original "cherubs" on the Ark of the Testimony were seraphs or wadjets. Typically, wadjets were depicted in pairs in older Egyptian literature. During the Middle Bronze Age, paintings and carvings of Egyptian sacred barks, which the Ark of the Testimony was modeled on, were almost always depicted with wadjets. They became less common in the Late Bronze Age, when Amen became the dominant god, and sphinx statues became more common as "guardian gods."

In this verse, it seems apparent that the original Akkadian cuneiform text would have read girtablilû (𒄈𒋰𒇷𒇻), as the guardians of the abode of Ān (Heaven) in the Old Babylonian era and earlier were the girtablilû. These creatures are generally called the scorpion-men in modern literature, and were depicted as being scorpion-human chimeras, however, the guardians of Ān were specifically a male and a female girtablilû in the *Epic of Gilgamesh*. They were replaced early in the Middle Babylonian era by two ancient Sumerian gods, Dumuzid and ⁿⁿNingishzida.

The idea that the scorpion men were the guardians of the sky most likely originated during the Neo-Sumerian era, when Scorpio and Orion were the constellations that rose and set with the sun during the winter solstice. Orion was known as ᵐᵘˡSipazianna (𒀯 𒋢𒅆𒑖𒀭𒈾), meaning "ˢᵗᵃʳˢShepherd in the Sky," while Scorpio was known as ᵐᵘˡGirtab (𒀯 𒄈𒋰), meaning "ˢᵗᵃʳˢScorpion."As the mythical king Dumuzid was also known as "the shepherd" it makes sense that his name replaced Sipazianna by the Middle Babylonian era. By the Middle Babylonian era, ᵐᵘˡSipazianna and ᵐᵘˡGirtab were no longer the constellations that rose and set with the sun at the winter solstice, and so the symbolism would have been lost, and they became mytho-fictional characters in *Adapa and the South Wind*.

Unfortunately, if there was a Proto-Sumerian version of the guardians of the sky, it has not survived to the present. Nevertheless, there is a parallel type of being, which may have predated the Neo-Sumerian Scorpion men, muškigīr (𒀭𒈬𒇥𒁇), which translates as "snake with dagger." The Akkadians later interpreted this as muškuššu (𒀭𒈬𒁇), meaning "snake with fire." This serpent with a dagger or a fire was depicted as a scaly animal with arms and legs like a lion's legs, talons like an eagle, a long neck and tail, two bovine horns on its head, and a serpentine tongue. All of these traits seem similar to the descriptions of cherubs from the various Israelite texts, which were described as having features of lions, bulls, serpents, eagles, and humans. Therefore, it is plausible that the original "cherubs" in this text were muškigīrs. Furthermore, it also suggests the snake in the garden was a muškigīr.

The concept of a Neo-Assyrian karābu (𒅗𒊏𒁍) would have been anachronistic before the early Iron Age. In this verse, girtablilû may be a more accurate translation, however, was probably no longer understood in the era when the Israelites left Egypt, as even the Babylonians were no longer commonly using the term.

7 Berlin Genesis: floginēn tēn romfaian strefomenēn fulassein tēn odon   tou   xulou   tēs   zōēs   (ΦΛΟΓΙΝΗΝ   ΤΗΝ   ΡΟΜΦΑΙΑΝ

ⲤⲦⲢⲈⲪⲞⲘⲈⲚⲎⲚ ⲪⲨⲀⲀⲤⲤⲈⲒⲚ ⲦⲎⲚ ⲞⲆⲞⲚ ⲦⲞⲨ ⳩ⲨⲀⲞⲨ ⲦⲎⲤ ⲌⲰⲎⲤ).
Translation: the flaming (or fiery) that circles (or crowns, honors, twists, writhes) broadsword to guard (or protect, defend) the threshold (or road, path) the timber (or wood, log, stick, tree) the life.

• Codex Alexandrinus: floginēn romfaian tēn strefomenēn fulassein tēn odon tou xulou tēs zōēs (ⲪⲀⲞⲄⲒⲚⲎⲚ ⲢⲞⲘⲪⲀⲒⲀⲚ ⲦⲎⲚ ⲤⲦⲢⲈⲪⲞⲘⲈⲚⲎⲚ ⲪⲨⲀⲀⲤⲤⲈⲒⲚ ⲦⲎⲚ ⲞⲆⲞⲚ ⲦⲞⲨ ⳩ⲨⲀⲞⲨ ⲦⲎⲤ ⲌⲰⲎⲤ). Translation: the flaming (or fiery) broadsword that circles (or crowns, honors, twists, writhes) to guard (or protect, defend) the threshold (or road, path) the timber (or wood, log, stick, tree) the life.

• Septuagint manuscript 55: flogínēn romfaían meta strefoménēn fulássein tēn odon tou xúlou tēs zōēs (𝆑ⲟⲅ𝆑ⲛⲗⲱ ⲉⲟⲙ𝆑ⲁ𝆑ⲇⲟⲛⲩ μⲅⲧⲁ ⲥⲣ𝆑ⲱⲟⲙⲗⲩⲗⲱ 𝆑ⲩⲗⲁⲛⲛⲟⲥⲟⲇⲛ 𝆑 ⲟⲁ⊕ ⲧⲟⲟ ⳩𝆑ⲟⲩ 𝆑ᵉ Ⲍⲟⲟⲗⲥ). Translation: the flaming (or fiery) broadsword with circles (or crowns, honors, twists, writhes) to guard (or protect, defend) the threshold (or road, path) the timber (or wood, log, stick, tree) the life.

• Septuagint manuscript 121: flogínēn romfaían fulássein tēn odon tou xúlou tēs zōēs (𝆑ⲟⲅ𝆑ⲛⲗⲱ ⲉⲟⲙ𝆑ⲁ𝆑ⲇⲟⲛⲩ 𝆑ⲩⲗⲁⲛⲛⲟⲥⲟⲇⲛ 𝆑 ⲟⲁ⊕ ⲧⲟⲟ ⳩𝆑ⲟⲩ 𝆑ᵉ Ⲍⲟⲟⲗⲥ). Translation: the flaming (or fiery) broadsword to guard (or protect, defend) the threshold (or road, path) the timber (or wood, log, stick, tree) the life.

• Septuagint manuscript 130: flogínēn romfaían tēn strefoménēn fulássein tou xúlou tēs zōēs (𝆑ⲟⲅ𝆑ⲛⲗⲱ ⲉⲟⲙ𝆑ⲁ𝆑ⲇⲟⲛⲩ 𝆑 ⲥⲣ𝆑ⲱⲟⲙⲧⲛⲗⲱ𝆑ⲩⲗⲁⲛⲛⲟⲥⲟⲇⲛ ⲧⲟⲟ ⳩𝆑ⲟⲩ 𝆑ᵉ Ⲍⲟⲟⲗⲥ). Translation: the flaming (or fiery) broadsword that circles (or crowns, honors, twists, writhes) to guard (or protect, defend) timber (or wood, log, stick, tree) the life.

• Leningrad Codex: lahaṭ haḥereb hammithappeket lišmōr 'et-derek 'ēṣ haḥayyîm (לַהַט הַחֶרֶב הַמִּתְהַפֶּ֫כֶת לִשְׁמֹר אֶת־דֶּרֶךְ עֵץ הַחַיִּים).

Translation: blazing (or enchanted, incandescence, flashing) the sword (or plow, many, a lot, increase) surrounding (or encircling) to guard (defend, protect) the road (or path, way) tree (or wood) the life (or living)

• Peshitta: wšnnå dǩrbå dmtpkå lmṯr åwrǩå dåylnå dǩyå (ܟܘܪܐܘ ܘܗܢ ܟܠܝܐܗ ܟܘܝܐܘܟ ܠܠܡܬ ܟܘܦܟܘܗ :ܟܘܝܚ ܗܢ). Translation: hated (or fanged, jagged) the desert (or desolate, barren, sword) surrounding protecting (or guarding) way (or path, journey, road) to tree of live (or Eve)

• Targum Onkelos: yāt šǝnan ḥarbā' dǝmithappǝkā' lǝmîtar yāt 'ôraḥ 'îlan ḥayyāy' (יָת שְׁנַן חַרְבָּא דְּמִתְהַפְּכָא לְמִיטָר יָת אוֹרַח אִילָן חַיָּא). Translation: hated (or fanged, jagged) desert (or desolate, barren, sword) surrounding protecting (or guarding) the way (or path, journey, road) to tree of live (or Eve)

• Papyrus Bohairic 2: tsēfe nsate eskōte auō eshareh etehiē mpšēn mpōnh (ϫⲥϩϥⲉ ⲛ̄ⲥⲁϫⲉ ⲉⲥⲕⲱϫⲉ ⲁⲧⲱ ⲉⲥϩⲁⲣⲉϩ ⲉϫⲉϩⲓⲏ ⲙ̄ⲡϣⲏⲛ ⲙ̄ⲡⲱⲛ̄ϩ). Translation: the sword (or knife) of fire circling (or spinning, orbiting) and guarding the path to the tree of the life

• Sahidic manuscript 2210: tsēfe nsate eskōte eareh etehiē mpšēn mpōnf (ⲧⲥⲏϥⲉ ⲛ̄ⲥⲁⲧⲉ ⲉⲥⲕⲱⲧⲉ ⲉⲁⲣⲉϩ ⲉⲧⲉϩⲓⲏ ⲙ̄ⲡϣⲏⲛ ⲙ̄ⲡⲱⲛ̄ϩ). Translation: the sword (or knife) of fire circling (or spinning, orbiting) to guard (or watch) the path to the tree of the life

• Sahidic manuscript 16L: tsēfe nsate eskōte eareh etehiē mpšēn mpōnf (ⲧⲥⲏϥⲉ ⲛ̄ⲥⲁⲧⲉ ⲉⲥⲕⲱⲧⲉ ⲁⲩⲱ ⲉⲥϩⲁⲣⲉϩ ⲉⲧⲉϩⲓⲏ ⲙ̄ⲡϣⲏⲛ ⲙ̄ⲡⲱⲛ̄ϩ). Translation: the sword (or knife) of fire circling (or spinning, orbiting) and guarding (or studying) near the path to the tree of life

Both the Greek and Hebrew translations read essentially the same, indicating that the Aramaic source text must have read more-or-less identical to the Masoretic version. While the "fiery sword circling" interpretation is valid in Hebrew, the Aramaic words don't mean exactly the same thing. This appears to be Aramaic translations of names of the guardians of Ān from Middle Babylonian beliefs. In the Middle Babylonian text Adapa and the South Wind, the two guardians were Dumuzid and Ningishzida which appear to be the same two guardians as those listed here. Lht hk̆rb hmthpkt (להט החרב המתהפכת) which is generally translated loosely as "fiery the sword circling" in Hebrew, is Aramaic for "magnificent cherub that returned from death," which would be a reference to Dumuzid, the god that returned from the land of the dead each vernal equinox during the Babylonian Akitu festival.

The name in the Masoretic text is an Aramaic translation of his title [an]Dag̃al riabu-ušum anna (𒀭𒆤𒂍𒂠𒀭𒉺), meaning "[deity]vast (𒀭𒆤) returning (𒂍) dragon (𒂠) from sky-stone (𒀭𒉺)." The word anna (𒀭𒈾), which was the Sumerian word for "metal," was a combination of the words an (𒀭), meaning "god," "star," and "sky," and na (𒈾), meaning "stone." The word generally meant "metal," however, also referred to the metal-sky above the world in Babylonian cosmology, interpreted as the framework of Shamayim in the Septuagint.

Therefore, this title of Dumuzid is generally interpreted as describing his return from the land of the dead / sky, each spring. The other guardian of the entrance to the sky in *Adapa and the South Wind*, was [an]Ningishzida (𒀭𒊩𒌇𒍣𒁕), whose name translates as "[deity]Lord (𒀭𒊩𒌇) to (𒁕) the tree (𒍣) of life (𒌇)," which is virtually identical to the Masoretic "guardian the path tree of life" (לשמר את דרך עץ החיים). The oldest surviving fragments of Adapa and the South Wind, have been found in El Amarna Egypt, and generally dated to the 1300s BCE. The text remained important for centuries, as a copy has been recovered from the Library of Ashurbanipal, dating to the 600s BCE. As *Cosmic Genesis* lists both the "cherubs" and the two guardians, it suggests that the text originated before Dumuzid and Ningishzida became the guardians of Ān in the early Middle Babylonian era, and their names were added later, if so, the original version of the text would have probably been written prior to 1595 BCE.

CHAPTER 4

Adam knew Eve his wife, and she conceived and gave birth to Cain[1] saying, "I have made a man through God."

She later carried his brother Abel.[2] Abel was a shepherd, while Cain was a worker of the ground. It was so, later, that Cain made a sacrifice to the Lord from the fruits of the land. Abel also brought from the firstborn of his sheep and of his lambs, and God looked on Abel and his gifts, but Cain and his sacrifices he did not consider, and Cain was very sad and became depressed. Lord the god said to Cain, "Why have you become very sad? Why have you become depressed? Haven't you sinned if you have brought it rightly, but incorrectly divided it? Be calm. He will submit to you, and you will rule over him."

Cain said to Abel his brother, "Let us go out into the plain," and while they were in the plain Cain attacked Abel his brother and killed him.

Lord the god asked Cain, "Where is Abel your brother?"

He answered, "I don't know, am I my brother's keeper?"

The Lord asked, "What have you done? The voice of your brother's blood cries out to me from Eretz. Now you are cursed on Eretz who has opened her mouth to receive your brother's blood from your hand. When you till the land, it will not continue to give its strength to you. You will be groaning and trembling on the land."

Cain said to the Lord the god, "My crime is too great for me to be forgiven. If you throw me out today from the face of Eretz, then I will be hidden from your presence, and I will be groaning and trembling on the land. Then it will be that anyone that finds me will kill me."

Lord the god said to him, "Not so, anyone who kills Cain will pay seven penalties," and the Lord the god set a mark on Cain that no one that found him might kill him.

Cain left the presence of God and lived in the land of Nod[3] near Eden. Cain knew his wife, and having conceived she carried Enoch.[4] Enoch built a city and he named the city after the name of his son.[5] To Enoch was born Gaidad,[6] and Gaidad fathered Mehujael,[7] and Mehujael fathered Methuselah,[8] and Methuselah fathered Lamech.[9] Lamech for himself had two wives, the name of the one was Adah[10] and the name of the second Zillah.[11] Adah carried Jabal,[12] he was the father of those that live in tents, feeding livestock. The name of his brother was Jubal,[13] he was who invented the lute and harp. Zillah carried Thobel,[14] he was a smith, a manufacturer both of brass and iron, and Thobel's sister was Naamah.[15] Lamech said to his wives, Adah and Zillah, "Hear my voice, you wives of Lamech, consider my words because I have killed a man to my sadness and a youth to my pain. Because vengeance has been exacted seven times on Cain's behalf, on Lamech's it will be seventy times seven."

CHAPTER 4

Adam knew Eve his wife, and she conceived and carried a son, and called his name Seth,[16] saying, "For God has raised for me another seed instead of Abel, who Cain killed." Seth had a son, and he called his name Enosh,[17] as he had faith to call on the name of the Lord the god.

CHAPTER 4 NOTES

1 Codex Alexandrinus: Kain (ⲔⲀⲒⲚ)

• Leningrad Codex: Qayin (קַיִן). Translation: craftsman, metal-smiths

• Peshitta: Qån (ܩܐܝܢ)

• Targum Onkelos: Qayin (קַיִן)

• Targum Jerusalem: Qayin (קַיִן)

• Targum Pseudo-Jonathan: Qayin (קַיִן)

• Papyrus Bohairic 2: Kain (Ⲕⲁⲓⲛ)

• Sahidic manuscript 2210: Kain (Ⲕⲁⲓⲛ)

The story of Cain and Abel is generally accepted in academic studies as being based on the Old Akkadian Debate Between Sheep and Grain, in which the god Ellil created the grain god Ashnan and cattle goddess Lahar who then debate which is the better food for the gods. Tablet 14005 at the University of Pennsylvania Museum of Archaeology and Anthropology is generally viewed as the earliest version of the debate, at only 61 lines long, and in it Ellil did not crate them instead it was the gods Enki and Ia. The tablet is an Old Babylonian copy of an older poem, believed to date to the Sumerian era, however, in either the Akkadian or Neo-Sumerian eras, Ia, the god of the sacred waters, was added to the poem. As Ia is generally viewed as being the replacement of Enki, the surviving version of the poem likely dates to the transitional period between the Sumerian and Akkadian civilizations.

It seems likely that the Ashnan and Lahar story was integrated into the earliest version of Cosmic Genesis near the beginning of the Hyksos dynasty, as the roles of Ashnan and Lahar mirror the roles of Setekh and Heru-ur in Old Egyptian beliefs, as the older brothers of Osiris (pre-Hyksos Seth), with Setekh ultimately killing Heru-ur. Both the brothers in the story have names that appear to have originated in Akkadian cuneiform, however, neither are similar to Ashnan and Lahar, suggesting an Old Akkadian language translation was carried into Egypt. Additionally, as the female Lahar was transitioned to being the male Abel, it supports an Old Akkadian translation, as their would have been no cultural need to change the god's sex either Sumer or Egypt. Kain/Qayin (Καιν / קַיִן) appears to be a transliteration of the Akkadian word qanû (𒄑𒅆𒔿𒈨), meaning "reeds," which was also the Ugaritic word qn (𐎖𐎐), meaning "reed," or "cane." This interpretation has existed since the Second Temple era, as it was included in the Apocalypse of Moses, which while it only survives in Greek, must have originated in a Semitic language or the reference makes no sense.

Abel / Hābel (Αβελ / הֶבֶל) is a transliteration of aplu (𒀀𒄖), pronounced as ablu in Amorite and Hurrian, meaning "son." Aplu was a common term applied to the sons of the various father-gods in Mesopotamian religions. In this case, it was likely spelled the older Sumerian and early Akkadian way eduru (𒂃), which was also pronounced as aplu/ablu, however, meant "heir," meaning that the reason for Cain's killing of Abel, was because Abel was the chosen heir in the Old Akkadian translation, and Cain was jealous. Qyn (קין) was also the name of the people who Moses forbade the Israelites from killing when they left Egypt, often translated as Kenites, and who he married his daughter to.

CHAPTER 4

Joshua also allowed them to leave the cities he besieged before killing everyone else in the cities, however, they disappeared from the Israelite story as soon as Egypt took control of Canaan during Joshua's time, suggesting they were a group of people living under Hyksos rule. Again, this melding of Sumerian and Old Egyptian mythology could only have taken place earlier than the Hyksos dynasty, as during the Hyksos dynasty Setekh replaced Osiris, and by the new Kingdom Heru-ur had been forgotten.

Furthermore, the gateway to Ān, which the guardians Dumuzid and [an]Ningishzida protected in *Adapa and the South Wind* is also the Káānraki (𒆍𒀭𒊏𒆠) that the city of Babylon was named after. Káānraki translates as approximately "Gateway from Sky to Earth" in Neo-Sumerian, but was pronounced as Bābilim in Akkadian. The city of Babylon was founded near the ancient city of Kutha during the Neo-Sumerian era and quickly became a major religious center as it was reported to be where the gods had originally entered the realm of Earth. These gods appeared through a gateway, or portal, that opened between the realm of the gods and the realm of humans. This belief was also carried into Egypt during the later Second Intermediate Period, resulting in a second Bābilim being identified in northern Egypt, near the city of Iunu, later called Heliopolis.

While Cosmic Genesis and Bereshít mention the "path" (ὁδον) and "the road" (אֶת־דֶּרֶךְ), which may be interpreted as connecting to another world, it is easier to read this as simply a path leading back to the garden, suggesting that the Káānraki was a Neo-Sumerian reworking of this story, which would then make the Adam and Eve story, as Enki and Ninti, older than the founding of Babylon. However, by the Classical era, many commentaries on the "pathway" between Eden and Earth supported the idea that Eden was on another world above the sky. It was believed the Euphrates, Tigris, Nile (believed to be the Gēōn / Gîhôn), and Indus River

CHAPTER 4

(believed to be the Pheisōn / Pîšôn) all flowed out of Eden, and fell to Earth landing in tall mountains.

2 Codex Alexandrinus: Abel (ⲀⲂⲈⲖ)

- Leningrad Codex: hābel (הֶבֶל). Translation: breath, vapor

- Peshitta: hbyl (ܗܒܝܠ)

- Targum Onkelos: Hābel (הֶבֶל)

- Targum Jerusalem: Hebel (הֶבֶל)

- Targum Pseudo-Jonathan: Hebel (הֶבֶל)

- Papyrus Bohairic 2: Abel (ⲀⲂⲉⲗ)

- Sahidic manuscript 2210: Abel (ⲀⲂⲈⲖ)

3 Codex Alexandrinus: Naid (ⲚⲀⲓⲆ)

- Septuagint manuscript 120: Aid (ⲀⲓⲆ)

- Septuagint manuscript 500: Gaid (ⲅⲀⲓⲆ)

- Septuagint manuscript 72: Nain (ⲚⲀⲓⲛ)

- Septuagint manuscript 59: Naina (ⲚⲀⲓⲛⲀ)

- Leningrad Codex: nôd (נוֹד). Translation: wandering

- Peshitta: nwd (ܢܘܕ). Translation: wandering

- Targum Onkelos: bə'ar'ā' gālê ûmiṭṭaltal (בְּאַרְעָא גָּלֵי וּמְטַלְטַל). Translation: in land of grass and wandering

- Targum Jerusalem: 'ar'ā' gəlê ûməṭaltēl (אַרְעָא גָּלֵי וּמְטַלְטֵל). Translation: land of grass and wandering

- Targum Pseudo-Jonathan: 'ar'ā' ṭiltôl gālûtêh (אַרְעָא טִלְטוֹל גָּלוּתֵיה). Translation: land of wandering exile

- Sahidic manuscript 2037: Naeid (ⲚⲀⲉⲓⲆ)

This term was probably a mistranslation of NA ID (𒈾 𒁳), meaning river rocks, suggesting one of the tributaries to the Iraqi wetlands (Eden/edin). This translation is supported by the story of

CHAPTER 4

Cain's life found in the Ge'ez book of 1st Maccabees, which reports that Cain settled in the land of qifaz (ቄፋዝ), a transliteration of the Greek word kēfas (κηφᾶς), itself a transliteration of the Aramaic word kypå (כיפא), meaning "rock," or "stone." The story is reported to be drawn from the lost Oral Torah, and the text includes several Aramaic words transliterated into Ge'ez via a Greek intermediary translation, that supports its pre-Christian origin.

There is no precise dating for the genealogy of Cain, unlike the genealogy of Seth. As Seth was listed as born after Cain killed Abel, and Adam was recorded as 205 year old at the time, this would have to predate that. Based on the radiocarbon dating of the flood sediment from the flood or series off floods that engulfed Sumer in approximately 2900 BCE, and the Septuagint's dating of the events between the birth of Seth and the flood, Seth should have been born in 4912 BCE, and Adam therefore would have been created 230 years earlier, in 5142 BCE, meaning Cain's moving to "Nod," should have happened during that era. Nevertheless, it is worth noting that the earliest surviving structures in Eridu are estimated to have been built around 5300 BCE.

4 Codex Alexandrinus: Enŏǩ (ⲉⲚⲱ̄x)

- Septuagint manuscript 15: Enōs (Ⲉⲛⲟⲟⲥ)
- Leningrad Codex: Hănôk (חֲנוֹךְ)
- Peshitta: Ǩnwk (ܚܢܘܟ)
- Targum Onkelos: Hănôk (חֲנוֹךְ)
- Targum Pseudo-Jonathan: Hănôk (חֲנוֹךְ)
- Sahidic manuscript 2037: Enŏǩ (Ⲉⲛⲱx)
- Bohairic manuscripts: Enōs (Ⲉⲛⲱⲥ)

If read as a series of metaphors regarding temples and cities, wherein "Enoch's son" Irad was the city of Eridu, Enŏǩ / Hănôk

93

probably started as a reference to the temple of Enki in Eridu, which likely predated the city itself. This temple was known as É-Abzu (▦⊏◁▦) in Akkadian, and É-Engura (▦◪⦀) in Neo-Sumerian, however, its pre-flood Sumerian name is believed to have been Eugtum (▦▩▨), which was mentioned in some Emegir Sumerian texts as being the temple of Enki in Uruk. Sumerian had several dialects, however, the main dialect during the post-flood era, was Emegir, meaning "native tongue," which was primarily used for business and politics. The other main dialect, was Emesal, the "fine tongue," which was generally used in religious songs and the speeches of the goddesses in religious texts.

As the earliest names of many later Sumero-Akkadian gods include the Sumerian title "Lady" (▽▯), it is generally accepted that most of the early Sumerian deities were goddesses who were later masculinized as the Akkadian culture became dominant. Therefore, Emesal is often viewed as being the older dialect, likely the dominant dialect from the Uruk period when writing was first being developed by the Sumerians. If so, this name "Enoch" may be derived from the Emesal dialect, as the Emegir name of the Temple of Enki: Eugtum (▦▩▨), would have been pronounced as Ekanagir (▦▨⛬▨▽) in Emesal. If this is a reference to the founding of the Temple of Enki in Eridu, based on the archaeological evidence, it should have been around 5300 BCE.

5 The structure of the sentence in Hebrew does not make it clear if Cain named the city after his son Enoch, or if Enoch named the city after his son Gaidad / Irad. While the Greek text structures the sentence almost the same way, it is clear from context that the Greek translator believed that the city was named after Enoch, however, the Aramaic verse would have read almost exactly the same as the Hebrew, laving the underlying question of the city's name.

CHAPTER 4

Nevertheless, Eridu (𒉣𒆠), was the first city of Sumer according to the Sumerian king lists, and its foundation was a mound of rocks (𒆠 𒉺𒂍), in the mouth of the Ephrates River, which flowed into the Iraqi wetlands (Eden/edin) indicating that this was the city being referenced. Additionally, the presence of possible Sumerian kings names in the genealogy of Cain supports this section of text originated as an explanation for the pre-flood Sumerian civilization. Therefore, this translation follows the interpretation that the city was named after Gaidad / Irad / Eridu, and not Enoch.

6 Codex Alexandrinus: Gaidad (ⲅⲁⲓⲇⲁⲇ)

- Septuagint manuscript 426 Gairad (Γαιραδ)
- Septuagint manuscript 422 Kaidad (Καιδαδ)
- Septuagint manuscript 414: Gaiddan (Γαιδδαν)
- Leningrad Codex: ʿÎrād (עִירָד)
- Peshitta: Ŏydr (ܥܝܕܪ)
- Targum Onkelos: ʿÎrād (עִירָד)
- Targum Pseudo-Jonathan: ʿÎrād (עִירָד)
- Sahidic manuscript 2037: Gaidad (ⲅⲁⲓⲇⲁⲇ)

This appears to be a reference to the foundation of Eridu (𒉣𒆠). It is unclear when the settlement became a town, however, settlement in the area is documented as early as 5400 BCE. The earliest sections of the Temple of Enki appear to have been built around 5300 BCE. Based on the increase in buildings in the region around 4500 BCE, it is likely there was a central government of some kind, suggesting that is the era being referenced.

7 Berlin Genesis: Maiēl (ⲙⲁⲓⲏⲗ)

- Cotton Genesis: Maouia (ⲙⲁⲟⲩⲓⲁ)
- Septuagint manuscript 509: Maouiēl (Μλοωηλ)

- Septuagint manuscript 15: Maleleēl (ⲘⲀⲖⳐⳐⲖⲗⲀ)
- Septuagint manuscript 121: Maleēl (ⲘⲀⲖⳐⲖⲗⲀ)
- Septuagint manuscript 392: Maiouia (ⲘⲁⳝⲟⲱⲀ)
- Septuagint manuscript 16: Meēl (ⲘⳐⲖⲗ Ⲗ)
- Septuagint manuscript 120: Maouiaēl (ⲘⲀⲟⲱⲀⲖⲗ Ⲗ)
- Septuagint manuscript 134: Mauiēl (ⲘⲀⲱⲖⲗ Ⲗ)
- Septuagint manuscript 370: Maliēl (Ⲙⲁⲗⳝ ⲟⲁⳝⲗ)
- Septuagint manuscript 129: Maouēl (ⲘⲀⲟⲩⲖⲗ Ⲗ)
- Leningrad Codex: Məhûyā'ēl (מְחוּיָאֵל)
- Peshitta: Mhwȧyl (ܡܚܘܐܝܠ)
- Targum Onkelos: Məhûyā'ēl (מְחוּיָאֵל)
- Targum Pseudo-Jonathan: Məhûyā'ēl (מְחוּיָאֵל)
- Sahidic manuscript 2037: Maiēl (ⲘⲀⲏⲖ)
- Bohairic manuscripts: Meouia (ⳙⲉⲟⲧⲓⲀ)

This may be a transliteration of the name [en]Menluan (𒆠𒈗𒀭𒌓 / 𒌷𒈗𒂍𒀭), meaning [lord]Crown-sheep-god, and generally interpreted as something like "Prince of the sheep of god." Məhûyā'ēl has no intrinsic meaning in Hebrew, however, the end of the name is el (אֵל), which is a translation of Ān (𒀭), as well as the Egyptian nṯr (𓊹), all of which translate as "god." Ān (𒀭) and nṯrt (𓊹𓏏), both also translate as "goddess."

Based on the surviving Hebrew translation, this name was probably rendered as mhyt[nṯrt] (𓏏𓇌𓏤𓅓) in Middle Egyptian, meaning Mehit[goddess]. In the Middle Kingdom, mhyt was both the name of the north wind, and an ancient Egyptian and Nubian war goddess generally referred to today as Mehit (Egyptian) and Menhit (Nubian). It is also possible that the name was spelled as [nṯr]mhyt (𓊹𓏏𓇌𓏤𓅓), however, this is unlikely as the north wind was not viewed as a god in Egypt.

CHAPTER 4

The common modern Egyptological name Mehit is derived from the Old Egyptian pronunciation, however, the pronunciation had shifted to m'ḥiːiy' by the Middle Kingdom, m'ḥeːʹə by the New Kingdom, and mə'ḥeːʹ by the era the Aramaic language genealogy of nations was added to Cosmic Genesis. While the Middle Kingdom pronunciation seems almost identical, a New Kingdom translation of this name is also possible.

In Sumerian pre-flood mytho-history, Lord Menluan, was the king who captured the kingship from Eridu, and carried it to Bad-tibira (𒁷𒁮𒌷𒁉𒊏𒆠), the fortress of the smiths. While it is not clear if or when this happened, based on the archaeology, Eridu went into decline around 4000 BCE, and was almost abandoned by 3800 BCE. This is generally associated with the change of the course of the Euphrates, and the resulting rise of Uruk, not the rise of Bad-tibira. As the city of Uruk appears to have been under the control of the Sethite genealogy, this appears to be a genealogy of a rival bloodline claiming descent from a common ancestor.

8 Codex Alexandrinus: Maṯousala (ΜΑΘΟΥϹΑΛΑ)

- Septuagint manuscript 121: Maṯousaēl (Μαθουϲαλλ)
- Septuagint manuscript 16: Maṯousaēla (Μαθουϲαλλα)
- Leningrad Codex: Məṯûšā'ēl (מְתוּשָׁאֵל)
- Peshitta: Mtwšyl (ܡܬܘܫܝܠ)
- Targum Onkelos: Məṯûšā'ēl (מְתוּשָׁאֵל)
- Targum Pseudo-Jonathan: Məṯûšā'ēl (מְתוּשָׁאֵל)
- Sahidic manuscript 2037: Maṯousala (Μαθογϲαλα)

The Septuagint refers to this person by the same name as the later Methuselah from the Masoretic text, suggesting that both names were Methuselah in the Aramaic version, however, the Hebrew translation is different.

The Hebrew name may be a transliteration of the name
^{en}Mengalan (🐾🗺️⏚✳️ / 𒈗𒀭✳️), meaning ^{lord}Crown-great-god,
and generally interpreted as something like "Prince of the great
god." Metusha'el has no intrinsic meaning in Hebrew, however, the
end of the name is el (אֵל), which is a translation of ān (✳️), as well as
the Egyptian ntr (𓊹), all of which translate as "god."

Based on the surviving Hebrew translation, this name was
probably rendered as mîtw ^{ntr}såh (𓈖𓐍 𓊹𓋴𓄿𓎸) in Middle
Egyptian, meaning "Likeness of ^{god}Såh." Såh was the Old Kingdom's
supreme father god of the sky, and therefore, the Egyptian parallel
of Ān (✳️). By the Middle Kingdom he was no longer actively
worshiped, however, was known from the ancient texts, and
therefore would have made an appropriate reference to the much
earlier era of the old kings of Sumer. In Sumerian pre-flood mytho-
history, Lord Mengalan, was the king who ruled Bad-tibira, the
fortress of the smiths, after Lord Menluan.

9 Codex Alexandrinus: Lameǩ (ⲗⲁⲙⲉⲭ)

- Leningrad Codex: Lāmek (לֶמֶךְ)
- Peshitta: Lmk (ܠܡܟ)
- Targum Onkelos: Lāmek (לֶמֶךְ)
- Targum Pseudo-Jonathan: Lāmek (לֶמֶךְ)
- Sahidic manuscript 2037: Lameǩ (ⲗⲁⲙⲉⲭ)

Like the previous names on this list, Lamech appears to be a
reference to the pre-flood kings of Bad-Tibira; in this case the third
king Dumuzid (the shepherd). Dumuzid was deified as the god
Tammuz, explaining why the name would have been redacted.
Additionally, another famous King of Uruk also bore the name,
although the existence of the second King Dumuzid (the fisherman)
has been questioned by some Assyriologists, who view him as an
addition made to the king lists during the Neo-Sumerian era, in

order to nationalize Dumuzid / Tammuz. This redaction would have probably taken place sometime around 2100 BCE, when King Utu-hengal established the independent kingdom of Sumer and Akkad, which was then based in Uruk.

His seven-year reign is estimated to have been somewhere between 2119 and 2048 BCE by various Assyriologists, around the time the texts would have been carried to Harran by Terah. Remku (𓂋𓅓𓎡𓅱) is the Egyptian word for "fisher," confirming that this was a reference to Dumuzid, however, also claiming that the earlier Dumuzid was a fisher, and not a shepherd, which is consistent with narrative, in which his son Iōbēl / Yābāl was the first shepherd.

If "Remku" was transliterated into the Middle Egyptian hieratic, it would have probably been rendered as Rîmkw (𓂋𓇋𓅓𓎡𓅱), which would have been pronounced as "Lîmkw" by someone speaking with a Fayyumic dialect. The Fayyumic dialect was spoken in the Faiyum Oasis, as well as the region of the Nile where the canal that carried water into the Faiyum Oasis connected to the Nile. In this region was the Egyptian city of Nn-nswt (𓎛𓎛 𓏤 𓊖), from which the dialect was likely derived. The name is commonly anglicized as Henen-Nesut, and was one of the capitals of Egypt during the First Intermediate Period, specifically during the 9th and 10th dynasties.

The dialect is believed to have become dominant in the Faiyum Oasis during the 12th dynasty, when the Faiyum basin was flooded with Nile flood water diverted via a canal, turning the oasis into a lake the size of Lake Superior in North America. During this era, the Faiyum was colonized by Egyptians and refugees from the rebellion in Amorite-controlled Syria and Canaan. There are other words in Hebrew in the Torah that are based on the Fayyumic dialect of Egyptian, such as 'Ămālēq (עֲמָלֵק), which was based on âmw-rqî / âmw-lqî (𓄿𓄿𓃀𓏤𓈎𓅱). This indicates that the Israelites were part of the Canaanite and Amorite population of the Fayyum during the Middle Kingdom and Second Intermediate Period. After the Israelites left Egypt, Lîmkw would have been transliterated as Lameku (𓀁𓃾𓏤𓊖) in cuneiform during the New Kingdom era, which would have subsequently been translated into Lmk (𐤋𐤌𐤊) during the Iron Age.

10 Codex Alexandrinus: Ada (ⲀⲆⲀ)
- Septuagint manuscript 131: Adda (Ⲁⲇⲇⲁ)
- Septuagint manuscript 246: Adad (Ⲁⲇⲁⲇ)
- Septuagint manuscript 314: Adada (Ⲁⲇⲁⲇⲁ)
- Leningrad Codex: 'ādâ (עָדָ֑ה). Translation: dawn (or ornament)
- Peshitta: ǩdâ (ܟܕܐ). Translation: dawn (or ornament)
- Targum Onkelos: 'ādâ (עָדָה). Translation: dawn (or ornament)
- Targum Pseudo-Jonathan: 'ādâ (עָדָה). Translation: dawn (or ornament)
- Sahidic manuscript 2037: Adda (ⲁⲇⲇⲁ)

The two wives of Lameǩ, which can be read as "Dawn" and "Evening," appear to be a references to ^{deity}Inanna (𒀭𒈹 / 𒀭𒈹), the wife of Dumuzid (the shepherd), in her form as the planet Venus. Multiple texts dating to the Sumerian era confirm that she was viewed as being the planet Venus, both in the dawn, and in the evening, as the Sumerians were one of the few cultures to realized Venus was both the morning star and the evening star. The movement of Inanna in Inanna's Descent to the Underworld is generally accepted by Assyriologists as a description of Venus" setting after sunset, followed by its rising before the sun seven days later.

CHAPTER 4

11 Codex Alexandrinus: Sella (ⲥⲉⲗⲗⲁ)

- Septuagint manuscript 392: Sela (Σⱸⲗ)
- Septuagint manuscript 125: Sala (Σⲁⲗⲁ)
- Leningrad Codex: ṣillâ (צִלָּה). Translation: grill (or roast)
- Peshitta: slå (ܨܠܐ). Translation: descend (or go down, incline)
- Targum Onkelos: ṣillâ (צְלָה). Translation: descend (or go down, incline)
- Targum Pseudo-Jonathan: ṣilâ (צְלָה). Translation: descend (or go down, incline)
- Sahidic manuscript 2037: Slla (Ⲥⲗⲗⲁ)

The Hebrew word is generally not viewed as reflecting the meaning of the word. In the 11th century CE, Rabbi Shlomo Yitzchaki (Rashi), reported that the original meaning was sēl (צֵל), meaning "shadow," which is generally accepted by Jews, Christians, and non-religious academics. The older Akkadian cuneiform name would have therefore been Ṣillu (𒄑𒆠𒂊), also meaning "shadow," however, the original Sumerian term would have been ĝissu (𒄑𒈪), which can mean "shadow," "shade," "protection," "darkening," or "evening."

The two wives of Lamek, which can be read as "Dawn" and "Evening," appear to be a references to [deity]Inanna (𒀭𒈹), the wife of Dumuzid (the shepherd), in her form as the planet Venus. Multiple texts dating to the Sumerian era confirm that she was viewed as being the planet Venus, both in the dawn, and in the evening, as the Sumerians were one of the few cultures to realized Venus was both the morning star and the evening star. The movement of Inanna in Inanna's Descent to the Underworld is generally accepted by Assyriologists as a description of Venus" setting after sunset, followed by its rising before the sun seven days later.

12 Codex Alexandrinus: Iōbel (ⲓⲱⲃⲉⲗ)

- Septuagint manuscript 509: Iōbēd (ⲓⲟⲟⲩⲗⲇ)
- Septuagint manuscript 15: Iōbēl (ⲓⲟⲟⲩⲗ λ)
- Septuagint manuscript 120: Iōabel (ⲓⲟⲟⲇⲩⲅ)
- Septuagint manuscript 426: Iōbal (ⲓⲟⲟⲩⲇλ)
- Septuagint manuscript 414: Ôbel (ⲱⲩⲅ)
- Leningrad Codex: Yābāl (יָבָל)
- Peshitta: Ybl (ܝܒܠ)
- Targum Onkelos: Yābāl (יְבָל)
- Sahidic manuscript 2037: Iōbēl (ⲓⲱⲃⲏⲗ)

Both this name and the following name Ioubal / Yûbāl appear to have originated as a transliteration of É-Áblua (𒂍𒃷𒌋𒈣 / 𒂍𒀸𒂖𒐖), the name of the temple of the moon god Nanna in Urum. While not as old as Eridu, Urum was one of the oldest Sumerian cities, dating back to the Ubaid period, generally dated to 6500-3800 BCE. The temple of Nanna is generally accepted as the large "Painted Temple," around which the city was built.

The name É-Áblua (𒂍𒀸𒂖𒐖), translates as approximately "Temple of cow's and sheep's father," supporting this being the temple of the "father of those that live in tents, feeding livestock." If these names were originally Sumerian, the original text must have also been Sumerian or Neo-Sumerian, indicating a date of earlier than 1900 BCE. The reference to the temples instead of the cities built around them also indicates the text probably dates back to earlier than the Akkadian era, earlier than 2334 BCE.

13 Codex Alexandrinus: Ioubal (ⲓⲟⲩⲃⲁⲗ)

- Septuagint manuscript 75 Ioubad (ⲓⲟⲩⲩⲇⲇ)
- Septuagint manuscript 130: Iōbal (ⲓⲟⲟⲩⲇλ)
- Septuagint manuscript 72: Iobal (ⲓⲟⲩⲇλ)

- Leningrad Codex: Yûbāl (יוּבָל)
- Peshitta: Ywbl (ܝܘܒܠ)
- Targum Onkelos: Yûbāl (יוּבָל)
- Targum Pseudo-Jonathan: Yābāl (יְבָל)
- Sahidic manuscripts: Iōbal (Ⲓⲱⲃⲁⲗ)

Both this name and the previous name Iōbel / Yābāl appear to have originated as a transliteration of É-Áblua (𒂍𒀊𒇉 / 𒂍𒀊𒇉), the name of the temple of the moon god Nanna in Urum. The temple of Nanna is generally accepted as the large "Painted Temple," around which the city of Urum was built. A very similar "White Temple," of Nanna was built in Ur in the same era. The name of the "White Temple," was É-Kišnugãl (𒂍𒆜 / 𒂍𒆜), the meaning of which is debated, as it has no obvious meaning. Based on the rest of the description of this "Ioubal," It is likely that the translator misread the Sumerian name as É-Inugãl (𒂍𒆜 / 𒂍𒆜), meaning "Temple of stringed instruments that exists," While not as old as Eridu, Ur was one of the oldest Sumerian cities, dating back to the Ubaid period, generally dated to 6500-3800 BCE.

14 Berlin Genesis: Ṭobel (ⲑⲟⲃⲉⲗ)
- Septuagint manuscript 392: Ṭōbel (Θωυϭλ)
- Septuagint manuscript 426: Ṭoubal (Θουυλλ)
- Leningrad Codex: tûbal qayin (תּוּבַל קַיִן). Translation: abominable smiths
- Peshitta: Twbqlyn (ܬܘܒܩܠܝܢ)
- Targum Onkelos: Tûbal qayin (תּוּבַל קַיִן)
- Targum Pseudo-Jonathan: Tûbāl qayin (תּוּבָל קַיִן)
- Sahidic manuscript 2037: Ṭōbel (Ⲑⲱⲃⲉⲗ)

CHAPTER 4

The addition of "Qayin" (Cain) in the Masoretic text was likely added to distinguish it from the kingdom, of Tabal (𒋰𒁄), in southern modern Turkey during the Neo-Assyrian era. Tabal was subjugated by Assyria in 713 BCE, suggesting the scribal note was no longer relevant when the Aramaic translation of Cosmic Genesis was made, some time between 715 and 706 BCE, and therefore not included in the Aramaic text that the Greeks later translated. Based on this "Ṭobel / Tûbal" being described as "a smith, a manufacturer both of brass and iron," it seems clear that this was a mistranslation of tibira (𒌈𒋞 / 𒁷𒊬𒁉𒊏), the Sumerian word for "smiths." Bad-Tibiraᵏⁱ (𒂦𒌈𒋞𒆠 / 𒁁𒀜𒁷𒊬𒁉𒊏𒆠) was a major center for metal working in Sumer, and the city where Menluan, Mengalan, and Dumuzid (the shepherd) were king according to the Sumerian king lists.

There were several ways that "tibira" could have been transliterated into Egyptian, however, all of them would have resulted in the R sound being replaced by an L sound when transliterated back into Canaanite, if the translator knew the Fayyumic dialect of Egyptian.

15 Berlin Genesis: Noemma (ⲚⲞⲈⲘⲘⲀ)

• Codex Alexandrinus: Noema (ⲚⲞⲈⲘⲀ)

• Septuagint manuscript 121: Noeman (Νοέμαν)

• Septuagint manuscript 343: Nosma (Νοσμα)

• Septuagint manuscript 246: Neeman (Νέεμαν)

• Septuagint manuscript 799: Noemman (Νοέμμαν)

• Septuagint manuscript 53: Noemam (Νοέμαμ)

• Leningrad Codex: Na'ămâ (נַעֲמָה). Translation: loveliness

• Peshitta: nŏmå (ܢܥܡܐ). Translation: ostrich

• Targum Onkelos: Na'ămâ (נַעֲמָה)

- Targum Pseudo-Jonathan: Na'ămâ (נַעֲמָה)
- Sahidic manuscript 2037: Noemma (Ⲛⲟⲉⲙⲙⲁ)

Assuming that Ṯobel / Tûbal Qayin was Bar-Tibira, and this is a reference to a sister city, it is almost certainly Umma^{ki} (𒌦𒈠𒆠 / 𒌑𒈠𒆠), a city approximately 30 kilometers north of Bad-tibira. The origin of the N sound at the beginning of the Greek and Hebrew names likely dates back to the original Middle Egyptian translation, as GIŠ (𒄑 / 𒄑) was used to spell many disparate words that may have been adopted from other languages, including the word for chariot, spelled logographically as gišgigir (𒄑𒈕), and phonetically as narkabtum (𒈾𒅕𒅗𒁍𒌈), and the word for plum, spelled logographically as giškib (𒄑𒊺), and phonetically as šaluruum (𒊭𒇻𒊒𒌝). Umma was one of the Sumerian cities of the Early Dynastic Period (2900-2300 BCE), however, it has not been proven to predate the Sumerian flood of 2900 BCE.

16 Codex Alexandrinus: Sēṯ (Ⲥⲏⲑ)
- Leningrad Codex: Šēt (שֵׁת). Translation: compensation (or placed, appointed)
- Peshitta: Šyt (ܫܝܬ)
- Targum Onkelos: Šēt (שֵׁת)
- Targum Pseudo-Jonathan: Šēt (שֵׁת)
- Sahidic manuscript 2037: Sēt (Ⲥⲏⲑ)

The name is most likely derived from the older Egyptian god Setekh (𒀭𒈤), which was also transliterated as Sēṯ (Σηθ) in ancient Greek, and Sēt (Ⲥⲏⲧ) in Coptic, resulting in the other two common English names: Seth and Set. The oldest archaeological reference to Setekh is currently dated to the Amratian culture of pre-dynastic Egypt, generally dated to between 3790 and 3500 BCE. Setekh was widely worshiped by Canaanites during the rule of the Hyksos dynasty, which ended around 1550 BCE.

At the time, he was viewed as the Egyptian version of the Amorite god Rašaap (𒀭𒈦𒉺), later known as Ršp (𒀭𒊕𒉺) in Ugaritic Canaanite, and Shed (𓈙𓂧𓏏) in the New Kingdom Egyptian dialect spoken in Canaan. In the Masoretic Book of Job, Eliphaz referred to humanity as the "sons of Resheph" (בני-רשף) instead of the "sons of Adam," and then used Šdy (שדי) as the name of his god, indicating that Shaddai was the iron age name of Resheph among the Israelites. The modern academic name of the god is Resheph, based on the later Hebrew word meaning "plague," or "fever."

In the Eblaite texts, generally dated to the 3rd millennium BCE, Rašaap's wife was the Amorite earth goddess Adamma, who continued to be worshiped by Hurrians, and was mentioned as the name of the earth goddess of the Israelites in Masoretic Numbers. Resheph's Babylonian counterpart was the war god Nergal, who was also married to the earth goddess [deity]Ereshkigal (𒀭𒊩𒆗𒃲), and associated with sunset during the Old Babylonian era.

This indicates that Resheph was the Amorite version of Baal Shalim, the Canaanite god of the sunset, who was also married to Asherah, a Canaanite goddess of the earth and fertility during the bronze age, whose sacred oak trees were used as important grave markers. If the origin of the name "Seth" in this verse was a Middle Egyptian translation of an older Akkadian text, it must have taken place before the fall of the Hyksos dynasty, or the name would have been updated to Shed, and then Shaddai.

Nergal's father was generally viewed as being Ellil, however, in the Old Babylonian Myth of Nergal and Ereshkigal, he referred to Ia (𒂍𒀀) as his father. Ia was the Old Akkadian replacement of the older Sumerian god Enki, whose name meant "Earth Lord," suggesting that the origin of this genealogy was a Sumerian text about Ān (God), Enki (Adam/land), and Nergal (Seth), before being updated during the Hyksos dynasty. Assuming such a Sumerian text existed, it would have been heretical by the standards of the Neo-Sumerian era onward. Nevertheless, Setekh was nothing like Nergal or Resheph before the Hyksos dynasty, suggesting that Setekh was a Hyksos era replacement of another god. Based on Jacob's dream later in Cosmic Genesis, it was almost certainly Osiris, who also ascended to the sky on a ladder in Egyptian mythology.

During the Hyksos dynasty, the worship of Osiris was suppressed in favor of Setekh / Resheph, explaining why he would have been redacted. The original Middle Egyptian translation of this genealogy, would therefore, have read Atum (creator), Geb (Adam / land), and Osiris, who was then replaced with Setekh (Seth) under Hyksos rule. Like Resheph and Nergal, Osiris was associated with death and rebirth, and prayed to to protect from plague-demons. This translation of Nergal as Osiris could only have happened earlier than the Hyksos dynasty, as the substitution of Setekh could only have happened during the Hyksos dynasty, meaning the latest the Egyptian translation could have been made was the Canaanite (14th) dynasty.

If read as a continuation of the city states of pre-flood Sumer, "Seth" (Setekh, Resheph, Nergal) would have been a reference to Gudua, the home of Nergal's original temple. The Sumerian name of Nergal had been ^{deity}Kišunu (✳🏹𓐝), meaning "god of Gudua," a city in central modern Iraq that was later called Kutha. By the Old Akkadian era, his name had shifted to ^{deity}Kišurugal (✳🦬🔺🗝), meaning "god lord of the great city," a reference to the city of the dead. In Sumerian beliefs, the capital city of the underworld was Ganzir, however, in Akkadian beliefs the name was Kutha, adopted from the Akkadian name of Gudua, where Nergal's original temple had been built.

In the Neo-Sumerian era, the era of Abraham and Amar-Sin, an alternate form of name appeared in Ur: ^{deity}Kišabgal (✳🏺⟫⟬⊏┤⊟├), meaning "god of all the great water," which appears to be related to the transition of the "Earth Lord" Enki, to the "Sacred Waters" Ia. This suggests that the unstated reason Terah left Ur, was due to religious reforms involving Enki / Ia and Nergal.

The Neo-Sumerian religious reforms involving Nergal appear to have been initiated by King Shulgi of Ur, who rebuilt the temple of Nergal in Kutha. He was the father of Amar-Sin, and ruled for 48 years, confirming that whatever the reason, Terah would have left Ur during his reign if Amarphal/Amrapal was Amar-Sin. See the note regarding Amarphal the King of Sumer for more information. The name later became ^{deity}Gìrunuggal (✳🏺⟫⊏┤⊟├) during the Old Babylonian era, and then ^{deity}Ugur (✳⟨⊟) during the Middle Babylonian era, which remained the Cuneiform spelling until the Greco-Roman era. However, the older pronunciation appears to have continued, at some point loosing the GÌR (🏺⟫), ending with the Aramaic transliteration of Nrgl (𐡋𐡓𐡂𐡋) during the Neo-Assyrian era.

Like the other Sumerian cities mentioned in the pre-flood genealogy, Gudua was a major religious center in pre-flood Sumer. The flooding of the city was extensive, and while the temple reopened, it appears that most of the city was not rebuilt after the great Sumerian flood of 2900 BCE. Based on the archaeology done at the site, most of the city remained in ruins until King Shulgi began rebuilding it sometime between 2094 and 1982 BCE, explaining how it became to be called the "city of the dead." It is not clear when it was founded, but like most ancient Sumerian cities, probably began with the temple.

Based on the Old Babylonian *Cuthean Legend of Naram-Sin*, which likely originated in Old Akkadian during the reign of the Akkadian king Naram-Sin, Kutha (Gudua) already existed before the time of ^{en}Merkar, the founder of Uruk. While the Cuthean Legend of Naram-Sin is regarded as fiction, it does nevertheless reflect the fact that the Akkadians viewed Kutha as older than Uruk, meaning it also dated to the Ubaid era, like the other Sumerian cities listed in the pre-flood genealogy. The date given in the following chapter, suggests that the temple of ^{deity}Kišunu was founded 205 years before the first king of Eridu ruled in 4707 BCE, which would make the founding date approximately 4912 BCE. During the era, the region is known to have been occupied, however, no remains of a temple have been found to date.

17 Codex Alexandrinus: Enōs (ⲉⲛⲱⲥ)

- Septuagint manuscript 128: Enōk̆ (Ɛνⲟⲟχ)
- Septuagint manuscript 130: Enos (Ɛνⲟⲥ)
- Leningrad Codex: 'ĕnôš (אֱנוֹשׁ). Translation: mortal (or human)
- Peshitta: ånwš (ܐܢܘܫ). Translation: human
- Targum Onkelos: 'ĕnôš (אֱנוֹשׁ). Translation: human
- Targum Jerusalem: 'ĕnôš (אֱנוֹשׁ). Translation: human
- Targum Pseudo-Jonathan: 'ĕnôš (אֱנוֹשׁ). Translation: human
- Sahidic manuscript 2037: Enōs (ⲉⲛⲱⲥ)

The term Ånwš (אנוש) is generally viewed as being the Aramaic word ånwš (ܐܢܘܫ), imported into Hebrew, as it was the common Aramaic word for "human," and not generally used in Hebrew, other than sections of the Torah and Tanakh (Christian Old Testament) that are thought to have originated in Aramaic. This may be the work of the editor in the time of Hezekiah, however, it may simply be the relic of the Sumerian term Lugal (𒈗), meaning "king," transliterated via its Akkadian pronunciation of Kaniš. If so, the text appears to have once stated that the first king, presumably of Eridu, was in power 190 years before there was a

CHAPTER 4

Lord of the Land in 4517 BCE, which would have been in 4707 BCE. According to archaeologists, Eridu was the only recognizable town in Sumer. It is unknown how it was governed, however, if governed like later towns and cities, there would have been either a lugal (king), or an ensi (governor).

CHAPTER 5

This is the book of the generation of men in the day in which God made Adam, in the image of God he made him. He made them male and female, and blessed them, and he called their name Adam, in the day in which he made them.

Adam lived two hundred and thirty years and fathered a son in his own form, and in his own image, and he called his name Seth. The days of Adam, which he lived after his fathering Seth, were seven hundred years, and he fathered sons and daughters. All the days of Adam that he lived were nine hundred and thirty years, and he died.

Seth lived two hundred and five years, and then fathered Enos. Seth lived after his fathering Enos, seven hundred and seven years, and he fathered sons and daughters. All the days of Seth were nine hundred and twelve years, and he died.

Enos lived a hundred and ninety years and fathered Kenan.[1] Enos lived after his fathering Kenan, seven hundred and fifteen years, and he fathered sons and daughters. All the days of Enos were nine hundred and five years, and he died.

Kenan lived a hundred and seventy years, and he fathered Mahalalel.[2] Kenan lived after his fathering Mahalalel, seven hundred and forty years, and he fathered sons and daughters. All the days of Kenan were nine hundred and ten years, and he died.

CHAPTER 5

Mahalalel lived a hundred and sixty-five years, and he fathered Jared.[3] Mahalalel lived after his fathering Jared, seven hundred and thirty years, and he fathered sons and daughters. All the days of Mahalalel were eight hundred ninety-five years, and he died.

Jared lived a hundred and sixty-two years and fathered Enoch,[4] and Jared lived after his fathering Enoch, eight hundred years, and he fathered sons and daughters. All the days of Jared were nine hundred and sixty-two years, and he died.

Enoch lived a hundred and sixty-five years and became the father of Methuselah.[5] Enoch traveled with the gods[6] after his fathering Methuselah for two hundred years, and he fathered sons and daughters. All the days of Enoch were three hundred and sixty-five years. Enoch was very pleasing to God and was not found, because God transformed him.

Methuselah lived a hundred and sixty-seven[7] years and fathered Lamech.[8] Methuselah lived after his fathering Lamech eight hundred-two years and fathered sons and daughters. All the days of Methuselah which he lived, were nine hundred and sixty-nine years, and he died.

Lamech lived a hundred and eighty-eight years and fathered a son. He called his name Noah,[9] saying, "This one will cause us to cease from our works, and from the difficulties of our hands, and from Eretz, which the Lord the god has cursed." Lamech lived after his fathering Noah, five hundred and sixty-five years, and fathered sons and daughters. All the days of Lamech were seven hundred and fifty-three years, and he died.

CHAPTER 5 NOTES

1 Codex Alexandrinus: Kainan (ⲔⲀⲒⲚⲀⲚ)

• Leningrad Codex: qênān (קֵינָן). Translation: to nest

• Peshitta: Qynn (ܩܝܢ)

• Targum Onkelos: Qênān (קֵינָן)

• Targum Pseudo-Jonathan: Qênān (קֵינָן)

• Sahidic manuscript 2037: Kainan (ⲔⲀⲒⲚⲀⲚ)

This name appears to be a transliteration of kinin (𒂗𒆠), meaning "lord (or lady) of the land," suggesting an era when there was a single leader of Sumer. The date provided is 170 years before something happen at 4347 BCE, making it 4517 BCE. During the era, there was only the one city in Sumer according to archaeologists, Eridu, as all other settlements were not much more than villages, and there for there probably was a single "Lord of Sumer."

2 Codex Alexandrinus: Maleleēl (ⲘⲀⲖⲈⲖⲈⲎⲖ)

• Septuagint manuscript 108: Meleleēl (Μελελεὴλ)

• Leningrad Codex: Mahălal'ēl (מַהֲלַלְאֵל). Translation: glorifying El (or God)

• Peshitta: Mhllåyl (ܡܗܠܠܐܝܠ)

• Targum Onkelos: Mahălal'ēl (מַהֲלַלְאֵל)

• Targum Pseudo-Jonathan: Mahălal'ēl (מַהֲלַלְאֵל)

• Sahidic manuscripts: Maleleēl (ⲘⲀⲖⲈⲖⲈⲎⲖ)

CHAPTER 5

This appears to be a translation of ^{en}Mendurān (𒀭𒌆𒀭𒀫 / 𒀭𒌆𒀭𒀫), meaning approximately "^{lord}Crowning Ān (or Ilu, deity)." Lord Mendurān was the pre-flood king of Sippar according to the Sumerian king lists. Sippar^{ki} (𒍝𒅎𒌷𒆠) was a pre-flood Sumerian city dating back to at least the Uruk Period, generally dated to 4000 to 3100 BCE. There is no evidence that the city existed earlier than the Uruk period, however, this verse would seem to be implying that Lord Mendurān of Sippar was born 165 years before Uruk was unified in 4182 BCE, or at least doing something in Sippar at the time, which would have been in 4347 BCE.

Lord Mendurān is generally viewed as fictional by Assyriologists, however, appears to have been viewed as import in ancient times, as he is one of only eight pre-flood kings mentioned on the Sumerian king lists. He was the only king of Sippar mentioned in the Sumerian king lists, either before or after the flood, suggesting that something important happened in Sippar in the pre-flood era. According to the Classical Babylonian era scholar Berossus, Ziusudra (Ξίσουθρος) built a library in the Sippar before the flood. No evidence of proto-Cuneiform writing has been found in Sippar, however, proto-Cuneiform writing has been found in Khafajah around 50 kilometers northeast of Sippar, indicating that writing was known in the region before the flood.

The city of Sippar was built around the É-Nunāna^{ki} (𒂍𒉣𒀫𒆠), the temple of Utu the sun god, however, it is unclear when it was built. Tens of thousands of Neo-Babylonian clay tablets were found in ruins of the É-Nunāna, suggesting it was used as a library in the Neo-Babylonian era. If it was used as a library in the Uruk period, all the older tablets must have been removed in ancient times. As Ziusudra was associated with the city of Shuruppak, which was in southern Sumer, near Uruk and Isin, while Sippar and Khafajah were in the north, in modern Baghdad governate, if there was a library in the region that survived the flood, it was probably built

CHAPTER 5

by someone else, and long before they learned there was a flood coming down the river.

3 Codex Alexandrinus: Iared (ιλϝεδ)

- Septuagint manuscript 509: Iaret (ιαϝότ)
- Septuagint manuscript 120: Iaret̲ (ιλϝόθ)
- Leningrad Codex: Yāred (יֶרֶד). Translation: to descend
- Peshitta: Yrd (ܝܪܕ)
- Targum Onkelos: Yāred (יֶרֶד)
- Targum Pseudo-Jonathan: Yered (יֶרֶד)
- Sahidic manuscript 2037: Iaret̲ (Ιλϝεθ)

Over the centuries, many Rabbis and Biblical scholars have suggested that Iared / Yared (Ιαρεδ / יֶרֶד) and Gaidad / Irad (Γαιδαδ / עִירָד) from the genealogy of Cain were corruptions of the same original name, which would then indicated the city of Eridu was being referenced.

Nevertheless, based on the story, and following reference to what appears to have started as references to the É-Ānki and the É-Ānna in Uruk, the simplest explanation for the origin of the word would be scribal error which altered Uruk to Yared. Uruk was spelled using the letters UNU (𒌷) and UNUG (𒀕), in Sumero-Akkadian cuneiform, which could have been misread as URU AD (𒌷𒀜). In Middle Babylonian cuneiform, used during the New Kingdom era, the spelling was still URU UNUG (𒌷𒀕) which still could have been misread as URU AD (𒌷𒀜). If the text had have been transcribed correctly throughout the bronze age, and URU UNUG was transcribed correctly into the Phoenician script as Yrg (𐤉𐤓𐤂), it still could have been easily misread as Yrd (𐤉𐤓𐤃). If this began as a reference to Uruk, being founded 162 years before the Ānu Ziggurat (É-Ānki) was built in 4020 BCE, that would place the

115

foundation of Uruk in 4182 BCE. Based on the archaeology, the region where Uruk later existed was inhabited since at least 5000 BCE, however, in approximately 4200 BCE, two smaller Ubaid era settlements merged to from Uruk.

4 Greek: Enŏk (ενωx)

- Septuagint manuscript 15: Ainŏk (Αινωχ)
- Leningrad Codex: Hănôk (חֲנוֹךְ). Translation: dedicated
- Peshitta: Ǩnwk (ܚܢܘܟ)
- Targum Onkelos: Hănôk (חֲנוֹךְ)
- Targum Jerusalem: Hănôk (חֲנוֹךְ)
- Targum Pseudo-Jonathan: Hănôk (חֲנוֹךְ)
- Sahidic manuscript 2037: Enŏk (Ενωx)

This is the second reference to an Enŏk / Hănôk in the pre-flood genealogy, the first being the son of Cain. See the note regarding Enoch the son of Cain in chapter 4. While this could be another reference to the temple of Enki in Eridu, the settling of this section of text appears to be in Uruk, suggesting this was originally about the É-Ānki (𒂍𒀭𒆠), the Temple of Ān and Ki in Uruk, where Inanna (Venus) was worshiped as the one who could return both from the sky and the underworld. To some degree, this parallel's the later legend of Enoch in the Enochian literature, in which he traveled to the sky (Ān), and never died, becoming trapped in the Earth (Ki), like most mortals do.

Assuming this verse began as a reference to the É-Ānki being built 165 years before the É-Ānna 3855 BCE, that would date its foundation to 4020 BCE, which is the same era that Assyrologists believe the Ānu Ziggurat was built. The Ānu Ziggurat was a large dirt mound that rose above the rest of the city of Uruk believed to have been built circa 4000 BCE. It is generally believed to have originally been dedicated to Ān before Inanna became dominant, and the É-Ānna was built. As writing appears in the archaeological record after Inanna rose to prominence, it cannot be proven that the Ānu Ziggurat was the É-Ānki, however, it is generally accepted by Assyriologists that it was.

5 Greek: Maṭousala (ΜΑΘΟΥCΑΛΑ)

- Septuagint manuscript 551:Maṭousalan (ΜάθουϚαλϖ)
- Leningrad Codex: Məṯûšālaḥ (מְתוּשֶׁלַח)
- Peshitta: Mtwšlk̆ (ܡܬܘܫܠܟ)
- Targum Onkelos: Məṯûšālaḥ (מְתוּשֶׁלַח)
- Targum Jerusalem: Məṯûšelaḥ (מְתוּשֶׁלַח)
- Targum Pseudo-Jonathan: Məṯûšālaḥ (מְתוּשֶׁלַח)
- Sahidic manuscript 2037: Maṭousala (ΜΑΘΟΥCΑΛΑ)

There have been many attempts to decipher the meaning of the Hebrew version of the name. The beginning of the name is "death" (מת), however, the rest could be interpreted as "sending" or "using daggers." Based on the story of Methuselah, the longest living human, it probably originated in the Old Babylonian mâtusalàù (𒁹𒈨𒌓𒋛𒆷), meaning "to cheat death."

This translation probably appeared in the New Kingdom era, when the text was translated into Canaanite using Middle Babylonian Cuneiform. Due to the differences between the Egyptian and Canaanite use of the sounds L and R, if it was a transliteration of an Egyptian name, it would have been mtsörö (𓌷𓏤𓋴𓅱𓏏𓏤), meaning "death ascended place." "Ascended place" is also an accepted translations of the name of the É-Ānna (𒂍𒀭𒈾), the temple of Ianna in Uruk. This temple was near the older Ānu Ziggurat, where Ān (𒀭) was worshiped before the rise of the cult of Inanna. This suggests that the original Middle Egyptian translation referred to it as the "ascended place" of mwt (🦅⌒𓏤), not mt (🦅⌒𓏤). If so, there must have been an intermediary phonetic translation before the Middle Babylonian translation, possibly in the Hyksos era proto-Sinaitic script, which would have rendered both words as mwt (✝=〰).

The É-Ānna was the major religious center of Uruk, both before and after the flood. Based on the archaeological record, Uruk was itself the cultural center of pre-flood Sumer for an estimated 900 years, which Assyriologists refer to as the Uruk period. The period is estimated to have begun around 4000 BCE and continued until 3100 BCE, during which the Sumerians developed their pictographic proto-cuneiform script, although the script appears to have mainly been used in Uruk before the Jemdet Nasr period (3100-2900 BCE), when it spread to Niru.

If this statement was originally about the É-Ānna in Uruk, it appears to be stating that the É-Ānna was built 167 years before Dumuzid (the fisherman), was born in 3688 BCE, which would have been 3855 BCE. Based on the current archaeological evidence, while Uruk appears to have existed since 5000 BCE, the É-Ānna district is believed to have been built between 3800 and 3400 BCE, over an older Ubaid era (5500–3900 BCE) temple. This suggests that the origin of this "genealogy" may have started interfering, as records of a priesthood of Ān who relocated to Niru when the É-Ānna was taken over by the priests of Inanna.

6 Codex Alexandrinus: euērestēsen de Enŏk tō ţeō (ⲉⲩⲏⲣⲉⲥⲧⲏⲥⲉⲛⲁⲉⲉⲛⲱⲭⲧⲱⲑⲉⲱ). Translation: very pleasing was Enoch to the gods

• Codex Coislinianus: euērestēsen de Enŏk tō ţeō ezēse Enŏk (ⲉⲩⲏⲣⲉⲥⲧⲏⲥⲉⲛⲁⲉⲉⲛⲱⲭⲧⲱⲑⲉⲱⲉⲍⲏⲥⲉⲉⲛⲱⲭ). Translation: very pleasing was Enoch to the gods lived Enoch

CHAPTER 5

- Septuagint manuscript 15: euērestēsen de Ainŏk̆ tō ṯeō Ainŏk̆ (ⲋⲩⲗⲫⲋⲟⲧⲗⲟⲋⲛ ⲇⲋ ⲁⲓⲛⲟⲟⲭ ⲧⲟⲟ ⲑⲋⲟⲟ ⲁⲓⲛⲟⲟⲭ). Translation: very pleasing was Ainokh the gods of Ainokh

- Septuagint manuscript 55: euērestēsen de Enŏk̆ ton ṮN ezēse Enŏk̆ (ⲋⲩⲗⲫⲋⲟⲧⲗⲟⲋⲛ ⲇⲋ ⲉⲛⲟⲟⲭ ⲧⲟⲛ ⲑⲛ ⲋⲍⲗⲟⲋ ⲉⲛⲟⲟⲭ). Translation: very pleasing was Enoch to the god lived Enoch

- Septuagint manuscript 73: ézēse de Enŏk̆ (ⲋⲍⲗⲟⲋ ⲇⲋ ⲉⲛⲟⲟⲭ). Translation: lived did Enoch

- Septuagint manuscript 130: euērestēsen de tō ṯeō Enŏk̆ (ⲋⲩⲗⲫⲋⲟⲧⲗⲟⲋⲛ ⲇⲋ ⲧⲟⲟ ⲑⲋⲟⲟ ⲉⲛⲟⲟⲭ). Translation: very pleasing was the god of Enoch

- Septuagint manuscript 376: euērestēsen de Enŏk̆ tō KŌ (ⲋⲩⲗⲫⲋⲟⲧⲗⲟⲋⲛ ⲇⲋ ⲉⲛⲟⲟⲭ ⲧⲟⲟ ⲕⲱ). Translation: very pleasing was Enoch to the Lord (or lords)

- Septuagint manuscript 458: ézēse Enŏk̆ tō ṯeō kai ouk̆ ēurisketo (ⲋⲍⲗⲟⲋ ⲉⲛⲟⲟⲭ ⲧⲟⲟ ⲑⲋⲟⲟ ⲕⲁⲓ ⲟⲩⲭ ⲗⲩⲫⲓⲟⲗⲋⲧⲟ). Translation: lived Enoch the god and not discovered

- Septuagint manuscript 509: ézēse Enŏk̆ (ⲋⲍⲗⲟⲋ ⲉⲛⲟⲟⲭ). Translation: lived Enoch

- Leningrad Codex: yithallēk Hănôk 'et-hā'ĕlōhîm (יִתְהַלֵּ֣ךְ חֲנוֹךְ֮ אֶת־הָֽאֱלֹהִ֒ים). Translation: he departed (or traveled) Enoch with the gods

- Peshitta: k̆dyrh Ǩnwk ôm âlhå tltmåå šnå (ܫܢܝ̈ܢ ܡܐܬ̈ܝܢ ܘܬܠܬ ܐܠܗܐ ܥܡ ܚܢܘܟ ܟܕܝܪܗ). Translation: wandered Enoch with gods for 300 years

- Targum Onkelos: hallîk Hănôk bədaḥaltā' daYyā (הַלִּיךְ חֲנוֹךְ בְּדַחַלְתָּא דַיְיָ). Translation: walked Enoch in fear of the Yahweh

- Targum Pseudo-Jonathan: pəlaḥ Hănôk biqšôt qŏdām Yəyā (פְּלַח חֲנוֹךְ בִּקְשׁוֹט קֳדָם יְיָ). Translation: labored Enoch with decorations in front of Yahweh

CHAPTER 5

- Sahidic manuscript 2307: aEnōǩ de ranaf mpnoute (ⲁⲈⲛⲱⲝ Ⲁⲉ ⲠⲀⲚⲀϥ Ⲙ̄ⲠⲚⲞⲨⲦⲉ). Translation: preformed Enoch then 100 equal parts for the god

The story of Enoch is similar to the Neo-Sumerian mythical king Lord Menduranki (𒈗𒆠𒀭𒈨𒌍𒀭), who was taken to the sky and taught by the gods Shamash and Adad.

7 Berlin Genesis: etē ekaton exēkonta epta (ⲉⲦⲎ ⲉⲕⲀⲦⲞⲚ ⲉⲜⲎⲕⲞⲚⲦⲀ ⲉⲦⲦⲀ). Translation: years hundred and sixty-seven (167)

- Codex Alexandrinus: ekaton kai ogdoēkonta epta (ⲉⲕⲀⲦⲞⲚⲕⲀⲒ ⲞⲄⲀⲞⲎⲕⲞⲚⲦⲀ ⲉⲦⲦⲀ). Translation: hundred and eighty-seven (187)

- Cotton Genesis: epta kai ogdoēkonta kai ekaton etē (ⲉⲦⲦⲀⲕⲀⲒ ⲞⲄⲀⲞⲎⲕⲞⲚⲦⲀ ⲕⲀⲒ ⲉⲕⲀⲦⲞⲚ ⲉⲦⲎ). Translation: seven and eighty and hundred (187)

- Septuagint manuscript 127: ekaton kai ebdomēkonta epta etē (ϭⲕⲁⲧ⊕ ⳑⲁⳑ ϭⲩⲀⲟⳙⳑⳑ⊕ⲧⲀ ϭⲡ̄Ⲁ ϭⲧⳑ). Translation: hundred and eighty-seven (177)

- Septuagint manuscript 527: ekaton kai exēkonta pente etē (ϭⲕⲁⲧ⊕ ⳑⲁⳑ ϭⵅⲣⳑ⊕ⲧⲀ πⲱⲧϭ ϭⲧⳑ). Translation: hundred and sixty-five (165)

- Leningrad Codex: šeba' ûšəmōnîm šānâ ûmə'at šānâ (שֶׁבַע וּשְׁמֹנִים שָׁנָה וּמְאַת שָׁנָה). Translation: seven and eighty years and hundred (187)

- Peshitta: måå wtmnåyn wšbȯ šnyn (ܡܐܐ ܘܬܡܢܝܢ ܘܫܒܥ ܫܢܝܢ). Translation: hundred and eighty and seven (187)

- Targum Onkelos: mə'â wətamnîn ûšəba' šənîn (מְאָה וְתַמְנִין וּשְׁבַע שְׁנִין). Translation: century (or one hundred) and eighty and seven (187)

CHAPTER 5

- Targum Pseudo-Jonathan: mə'â ûtəmānîn ûšəba' šənîn (מְאָה וּתְמָנִין וּשְׁבַע שְׁנִין). Translation: century (or one hundred) and eighty and seven (187) years

- Sahidic manuscript 2037: nše setē nrompe (ⲛ̄ϣⲉ ⲥⲉⲧⲏ ⲛ̄ⲣⲟⲙⲡⲉ). Translation: one century sixty the eight of years (168)

8 Codex Alexandrinus: Lameǩ (ⲗⲁⲙⲉⲝ)

- Leningrad Codex: Lāmek (לֶמֶךְ)

- Peshitta: Lmk (ܠܡܟ)

- Targum Onkelos: Lāmek (לְמֶךְ)

- Targum Jerusalem: Lāmek (לְמֶךְ)

- Targum Pseudo-Jonathan: Lāmek (לְמֶךְ)

- Sahidic manuscript 2037: Lameǩ (ⲗⲁⲙⲉⲝ)

Lamech was previously mentioned in the genealogy of Cain, and based on the generations from Adam to Noah, however, these two Lamechs should not have lived at the same time. As the first Lamech appears to be a reference to Dumuzid (the shepherd), this may be a reference to the second Dumuzid (the fishermen), who is estimated to have lived in the Jamdet Nasr period if he existed.

While he is generally viewed as being a later addition during the Neo-Sumerian era, he was is listed as living in Uruk, and base on the era in this text, if Dumuzid (the fisherman) lived 188 years before the foundation of Niru in 3500 BCE, this would mean he was born circa 3688 BCE. Based on the archaeological evidence, during the era, Uruk was the dominant Sumerian city. The era is known by Assyriologists as the Uruk period, a period spanning 4000 to 3100 BCE. During the era, the pictographic proto-cuneiform script was developed, however, does note appear to have been used much outside of Uruk until the following Jamdet Nasr period, when it was widely used in Niru.

9 Codex Alexandrinus: Nōe (ⲛⲱⲉ)

- Leningrad Codex: nōaḥ (נֹחַ). Translation: rest

- Peshitta: nwk̆ (ܢܘܚ). Translation: quiet (or calm, rest)

- Targum Onkelos: nōaḥ (נֹחַ). Translation: quiet (or calm, rest)

- Targum Jerusalem: Naḥ (נַח)

- Targum Pseudo-Jonathan: Naḥ (נַח)

- Sahidic manuscript 2037: Nōhe (ⲛⲱϩⲉ)

It is generally accepted by academics that the Noah narrative is based on the Sumerian flood survivor stories of Ziusudra, Utnapishtim, and Atra-Hasis. The oldest surviving copy of these stories is found in the Old Babylonian Epic of Ziusudra, which tells a tale similar to the Noah narrative, in which King Ziusudra (𒍣𒌓𒋤𒁺𒊏) was warned of an oncoming storm by Enki, the Sumerian precursor to the Akkadian Ia, which is accepted as evidence that it was originally a Sumerian story that had been translated into Old Babylonian. In the story, Ziusurda was told to build a large boat, in which he and others survived the storm and flood that followed, ultimately washing up in Dilmun.

Ziusudra, or Zin-Suddu, is recorded as the son of the last king of the city of Shuruppak before the flood in Tablet WB 62 of the Sumerian king lists, the oldest surviving versions of the king lists. The king lists almost all date to the Old Babylonian era, however, Tablet WB 62, also known as the Weld-Blundell prism, has been dated to the earlier Neo-Sumerian era, year 11 of King Sin-Magir of Isin, who is estimated to have reigned sometime around 1800 BCE. There is an older version of the king list from the reign of King Shulgi of Ur, the Neo-Sumerian king of Ur who would have been the king when Terah left Ur in the chronology where Shulgi's son Amar-Sin or Ur was "King Amarpl of Sumer" who took Terah's nephew Lot captive. The version of the king list from Shulgi's reign is known as the USKL, and does not include the pre-flood kings or the kings of cities other than where Shulgi's ancestors lived. This indicates that the king lists were massively expanded during the Neo-Sumerian era, but that that expansion does not appear to have begun until after Terah left Ur. If so, the pre-flood records in this section of text would be older than the surviving pre-flood king lists. The earliest surviving reference to Ziusudra, is found in the Sumerian Instructions of Shuruppak, which is dated to circa 2600 BCE, however, it is not clear that he was viewed as the flood survivor from the Instructions. The flood deposits that covered Shur*ppak, and most of southern Iraq, have been radiocarbon dated to approximately 2900 BCE, however, there are debates about whether it was one massive flood, or a series of floods.

During the Old Babylonian era, Neo-Sumerian poems about Bilgamesh were combined and expanded into the Epic of Gilgamesh. In the Epic, Utnapishtim (𒌓𒍣) was the ancient survivor of the flood, whom the gods had granted immortality. The older Neo-Sumerian poems do not mention Utnapishtim, and he is believed to have been an Old Babylonian addition to Gilgamesh, likely based on Ziusudra. Like Ziusudra, Utnapishtim was told of the coming flood by Enki, and built a giant wooden box to survive, known as the Preserver of Life. He took in animals, plants, and various craftsmen to help him rebuild after the flood. Unlike Ziusudra's flood, this one was described as covering all of the land, and Utnapishtim's Preserver of Life ended up at Mount Nisir, theorized to be Pir Omar Gudrun in Iraqi Kurdistan. It is not entirely clear if it was simply built on Mount Nisir, or built elsewhere and washed up on Mount Nisir. If the presence of Enki is taken as a reference to a prophet of Enki, a metaphor, or simply a fictional addition, it is possible that these originated in two separate flood survivor stories.

The oldest surviving copy of the Epic of Atra-Hasis (𒀜𒊏𒄩𒋛𒅀) also dates to the Old Babylonian era, to the reign of King Ammi-

Saduqa in the 1600s BCE. Unlike Ziusudra and Utnapishtim, in the Epic of Atra-Hasis, the Ia was the god who warned Atra-Hasis of the coming flood, although had to do it behind the other gods' backs as they did not want to get involved in Ellil's plan to destroy humanity with a flood. Like Ziusudra, Atra-Hasis builds a large boat, and survives a river flood, ending up in Dilmun, suggesting that Atra-Hasis is an Akkadian or Old Babylonian reworking of Ziusudra. The author of Atra-Hasis also appears to have read Utnapishtim, as when Ellil accuses Ia of interfering, he defends his actions by claiming he "preserved life," a reference to Utnapishtim's Preserver of Life.

All of the surviving stories date to after the time that Terah would have left Ur, early in the Neo-Sumerian Empire, however, the presence of Ziusudra in the Instructions of Shuruppak and the Weld-Blundell prism strongly suggest that the original name of the flood survivor hero was Ziusudra (or Zin-Suddu), assuming all the stories share a common origin. The name of Noah may suggest there was more than one survivor epic, as Noah's name appears to be based on the name of Niru ($\mathbb{p}{\triangleright}\Sigma$), the ancient Akkadian name of Jemdet Nasr. Given the northern location, and the similarity to Utnapishtim's story and the final resting place of the giant box, in the mountains north of Sumer, it is plausible that Utnapishtim was the king of Niru. Assuming Noah was originally a reference to the city-state known in Akkadian records as Niru ($\mathbb{p}{\triangleright}\Sigma$), then this is a reference to the last major era of pre-flood Sumerian civilization, the Jemdet Nasr period, generally dated to 3100 to 2900 BCE. If this is a reference to Niru being 600 years old when the flood happened, the implication is that the text was reporting that Niru was founded around 3500 BCE. Uruk era seal have been found at the site dated to circa 3350 BCE, however, so date it is not proven there was a city there circa 3500 BCE.

CHAPTER 5

The era, like the earlier Uruk period, is considered to have been literate, a many tablets have been found with a pictographic script on them known as proto-cuneiform, and therefore, there could have been records of the pre-flood era passed on. The Middle Egyptian translator appears to have transcribed the name as nỏĩ (⚏ ⚐), meaning "boat traveler." If this stared as the story of Utnapishtim of Niru, some variant must have been carried out of Ur by Terah circa 2075 BCE.

CHAPTER 6

Noah was five hundred years old, and he fathered three sons, Shem,[1] Ham,[2] and Japheth.[3] It happened when humans began to be numerous on the land, and daughters were born to them, that the sons of God[4] saw the daughters of humans, that they were beautiful, and took for themselves wives, all whom they chose.

Lord the god said, "My Spirit will certainly not remain among these men forever, because they are flesh, but their days will be a hundred and twenty years."

Now the Gigantes[5] were in the land in those days, and after that, when the sons of God used to go into the daughters of humans, they carried children for them, and those were the ancient Gigantes, the men of infamy. Lord the god, having seen that the wicked actions of men were multiplied in the land and that everyone in his heart was intently brooding over evil continually, then God regretted that he had made man on the land, and he pondered it deeply.

God said, "I will blot out man, whom I have made, from the surface of the Earth, including, men and livestock, and reptiles and flying creatures of the sky, for I have thought that I have made them."

But Noah found favor before the Lord the god. These are the generations of Noah. Noah was an honest man. Being perfect in his generation, Noah was very pleasing to God.

CHAPTER 6

Noah fathered three sons, Shem, Ham, and Japheth. But Eretz was corrupted before God, and the land was filled with iniquity. Lord the god saw Eretz, and she was corrupted because all flesh had corrupted its way on the land.

Lord the god said to Noah, "The time of every man has come before me because the land has been filled with iniquity by them, and I will destroy them and Eretz. Therefore, make for yourself an box[6] of square timber, you will make the box in nests, and you will pitch it within and without with pitch. You will make the box like this: three hundred cubits[7] will be the length of the box, and fifty cubits will be the breadth, and thirty cubits will be the height of it."

"You will narrow the box while building it, and in a cubit above you will finish it, and the door of the box you will make out of its side. Make it with lower, second, and third levels. I bring a flood of water onto the land, to destroy all flesh in which has the breath of life under the sky, and whatever things are on the land will die. I will establish my covenant with you, and you will enter into the box with your sons and your wife, and your sons' wives with you."

"Of all livestock and all reptiles and all wild animals, even of all flesh, you will bring by two, two of all, into the box, that you may feed them with yourself: male and female they will be. Of all winged birds according to their species, and all livestock according to their species, and of all reptiles creeping on the land according to their species, pairs of all will come to you, male and female to be fed by you. And you will take for yourself of all kinds of food that you eat, and you will gather them for yourself, and it will be for you and them to eat."

Noah did all things that the Lord the god commanded him.

CHAPTER 6 NOTES

1 Codex Alexandrinus: Sēm (ϲΗΜ)

- Septuagint manuscript 319: Sim (Σιμ)
- Septuagint manuscript 129: Sēṯ (Σῃθ)
- Leningrad Codex: Šēm (שֵׁם). Translation: name
- Peshitta: Šym (ܫܝܡ)
- Targum Onkelos: Šēm (שֵׁם)
- Targum Pseudo-Jonathan: Šēm (שֵׁם)

Based on the later genealogy of nations, this probably started as a reference to the Šimašgi (𒋾𒈦𒄀) dynasty in Elam. The location of the land of Šimašgi isn't clear today, but is believed to have been in the interior of modern Iran. It was part of the country of Elam, so it was presumably in southern Iran. Shem was reported to be an ancestor of Elam and Eber, likely a reference to the early Elamite king Iabarati (𒅀𒁀𒊏𒋾), later spelled as Ebarti (𒂊𒁀𒅕𒋾). Iabarati was the founder of an Elamite noble household in the Gutian era, which Terah appears to have been descended from.

2 Codex Alexandrinus: Ǩaf (ΧΑΦ)

- Septuagint manuscript 31: Ǩam (ΧΑΜ)
- Leningrad Codex: hām (חָם). Translation: hot
- Peshitta: Ǩm (ܚܡ)
- Targum Onkelos: Ḥām (חָם)

CHAPTER 6

- Targum Pseudo-Jonathan: Ḥām (חָם)

3 Codex Alexandrinus: Iafet (ιΑϕεΘ)
- Leningrad Codex: Yāpet (יֶפֶת)
- Peshitta: Ypt (ܝܦܬ)
- Targum Onkelos: Yāpet (יֶפֶת)
- Targum Pseudo-Jonathan: Yāpet (יֶפֶת)

Iafeṯ / Yāpet has been considered a Canaanite variant on Iapetos (Ιαπετος) since at least the Classical Era, as recorded by Josephus in the 1st century CE. Iapetus was the Titan who created humans in Greek mythology.

4 Berlin Genesis: huioe tou T̄U̅ (ΥΙΟΙΤΟΥΘΥ). Translation: sons of the god
- Codex Alexandrinus: aŋgeloi tou T̄U̅ (ΑΓΓΕΛΟΙΤΟΥΘΥ). Translation: messengers of the God
- Leningrad Codex: bənê-hā'ĕlōhîm (בְנֵי־הָאֱלֹהִים). Translation: sons of the elohim
- Peshitta Manuscript 5b1: br ålwhym (ܒܪ ܐܠܘܗܝܡ). Translation: sons (or followers, disciples) of gods (or elohim)
- Peshitta Manuscript 7a1: br dynå (ܒܪ ܕܝܢܐ). Translation: sons (or followers, disciples) of the judges (or justice, law, rule, judgment)
- Targum Onkelos: bənê rabrəbayyā' (בְנֵי רַבְרְבַיָּא). Translation: sons (or followers, disciples) of great-leaders
- Targum Pseudo-Jonathan: bənê rabrəbayā' (בְנֵי רַבְרְבַיָּא). Translation: sons (or followers, disciples) of great-leaders.

The Greek translators interpreted these beings as either the sons, or messengers of God, while the Masoretic text calls them the sons of the elohim. They were called 'äyärän (ዐይራን) meaning "watchers" or "guardians" in the Books of Enoch, and Grigori (ႢႰႨႢႭႰႨ) in

130

the Secrets of Enoch, likely transliterated from the Greek egeírō (εγείρω) meaning "awaken." Given the similarity of the stories and the connections to Mount Hermon, they were likely based on the older Akkadian Igigi (𒂊𒆠𒇀𒂊𒆠), a group of lesser gods that rebelled against the ruling ^{an}Anuna (𒀭𒉪𒆤).

The name ^{an}Anuna translates as "sons of ^{deity}Ān / sky" in Akkadian, suggesting that term was ^{an}Anuna in Cuneiform, and the following mention of the Gigantes were the Igigi who rebelled against them. The ^{an}Anuna were a group of ruling gods, conceptually similar to the Olympian gods of Greek mythology. Significant members of this group of gods include Enki, the "lord of earth," and Enlil, the "lord of air/spirit," and Nergal, the god of the dead. They were also called the ^{an}Anunakene (𒀭𒉪𒆤𒈨𒌷), more commonly transliterated into English as Anunnaki, as they were described as being the "children of Ān (the sky god) on Ki (the Earth)."

The variation found in Peshitta Manuscripts 7a1, from the 7th century, is curious, as the text deviates from both the Septuagint and Masoretic text. It is possible that 7a1 represents an alternate Aramaic interpretation of ålwhym, in which the term referred to a group of "judging gods." If so, this would indicate that the Aramaic word ålwhym also specifically referred to the ^{an}Anuna, who were described as the judging gods in the Epic of Gilgamesh, which is itself believed to have originated during the Neo-Sumerian Empire, circa 2100 BCE.

In the Enûma Eliš, generally dated to the Old Babylonian empire between 1894 and 1595 BCE, 900 ^{an}Anunakene are mentioned, 300 in the sky, and 600 in the underworld, suggesting they originated in a Sumerian of Akkadian star-catalog, which became deified during the Gutian dynasty, or the Neo-Sumerian Empire. If so, then the "followers of the ⁿᵃAnuna," probably originated in a reference to an astrological religion.

5 Codex Alexandrinus: gigantes (ᴦⲓⲅⲁⲚⲦⲉⲥ). Translation: Gigantes

• Leningrad Codex: nəpilîm (נְפִלִ֑ים). Translation: fallen

• Peshitta: gnbrå (ܓܢܒܪܐ). Translation: strong men (or giants, heroes, Orion)

• Targum Onkelos: gibbārayyā' (גִּבָּרַיָּא). Translation: husbands (or men)

• Targum Pseudo-Jonathan: Šamḥazā'ê wə'Ûzî'ēl hînûn nəpîlîn min šəmayā' (שַׁמְחֲזָאֵי וְעֻזִיאֵל הִינוּן נְפִילִין מִן שְׁמַיָא). Translation: Samyaza and Uziel those fallen (or giants, Orions, guardians) from the sky

While most Christian translations of both the Septuagint and the Masoretic text translate this word as "giant," neither the Greek nor Hebrew terms mean "giant." The Hebrew term is accepted as meaning "fallen," and, the term is likely related to the Aramaic name for the Orion constellation, Npylyå (ࠊࠋࠌ). The term nəpilîm (נְפִלִ֑ים) likely originated as a description of the Orionid meteor shower that happens each year, between October 2 and November 7, as the Earth passes through the debris left by Halley's Comet. Peaks of 70 meteors a minute have been recorded, and these meteors fall from the region of the sky where Orion's upstretched arm is located.

The region of the sky where the constellations Orion and Lepus are located was known as the asterism Såh (𓊨𓇳𓀭𓊛) in the religion of the Egyptian Old Kingdom, which represented Såh, the father of the gods. The Sumerian version of Såh was ⁿᵃĀn (𒀭𒀭), who was also the father of the gods, and represented by the stars of Orion. The name Greek name Ōriōn (Ωριων) is derived from the

Babylonian name úru Ān (𒌷𒀭), meaning "Light of Ān," and the asterism was believed to represent the god Ān. This term was subsequently absorbed into Greek as the name Orion during the Greek Dark Age, after the collapse of the Mycenaean civilization, as the name has not been documented in the Linear-B script.

As the Greeks neither translated nor transliterated the term Nephilim, it is unlikely it was in the Aramaic text they translated, suggesting whatever term they found in the text was either conceptually or phonetically similar to the Greek Gígas (Γίγας).

A more detailed version of this story appears in the Books of Enoch, where the term was translated into Ge'ez as 'äyärän (ዐየራን) meaning "watchers" or "guardians". A similar term, egeírō (εγείρω) meaning "awaken," appears to have been used in the Greek translation of *Secrets of Enoch*, which was later transliterated into Old Slavonic as Grigori (Григори). This indicates the original term was likely something that meant "watcher" and sounded like Gígas, and given the connections to Mount Hermon, the Orion constellation, and thereby the god Ān, and his children the [an]Anuna (𒀭𒀀𒉣𒈾), the original term in the Cuneiform text was almost certainly Igigi (𒉌𒄀𒄀). The Igigi were described as being a group of lesser gods that rebelled against the rule of the god Anuna, which translates as "sons of the [deity]Ān / sky," and their name was the homophone of the Akkadian word igigi (𒄿𒄀𒄀) meaning to "observe and measure."

---

6 Codex Alexandrinus: kibōton (ΚΙΒѠΤΟΝ). Translation: box (or ark)

- Leningrad Codex: tēbâ (תֵּבָה). Translation: box (or ark)

- Peshitta: qbwtå (ܩܒܘܬܐ). Translation: container (or cistern, sepulcher)

- Targum Onkelos: tēbôtā' (תֵּבוֹתָא). Translation: chest (or box, ark)

CHAPTER 6

- Targum Pseudo-Jonathan: tēbôtā' (תֵּיבוֹתָא). Translation: chest (or box, ark)

- Sahidic manuscript 16L: kibōtos (ⲕⲓⲃⲱⲧⲟⲥ). Translation: box (or chest, ark)

Both the Hebrew and Armenian terms are accepted as being translations of the Aramaic word tybwtå (תֵּיבוּתָא), meaning "sarcophagus," "coffin," or "box." The Greek word kibōton (κιβωτον), meaning "coffin," or "box" was also derived from the Aramaic term, and was originally spelled as tibōtos (τιβωτος). The Peshitta uses a term that appears to be a Syrianized version of the Greek kibōton (κιβωτον), while the Targum Onkelos skips the opening consonant, and only renders the second half of the word.

The word has been recognized as being derived from the Egyptian word ḏbåt (�), meaning "sarcophagus," since the classical era, which has resulted in many strange translations. If the word originated in Old Akkadian or Neo-Sumerian, the Egyptian term "sarcophagus" was probably used as a proper name, and not a description, as the Old Akkadian and Neo-Sumerian flood survivor was described as surviving in a house-barge named the "preserver of life," which is approximately what ḏbåt (�) means.

7 Codex Alexandrinus: pēkeōn (ⲡⲏⲭⲉⲱⲛ). Translation: cubits

- Septuagint manuscript 319: pēkōn (πηχων)

- Leningrad Codex: 'ammâ (אַמָּה). Translation: cubits

- Peshitta: åmyn (ܐܡܝܢ). Translation unclear. It appears to be an Aramaic plural of the Hebrew term for "cubit." It is identical to the term used in the Targum Onkelos, suggesting the Peshitta was partially translated from the Onkelos, or that the term was used in an earlier Aramaic translation.

- Targum Onkelos: 'ammîn (אַמִּין). Translation: unclear. It appears to be an Aramaic plural of the Hebrew term for "cubit."

134

CHAPTER 6

• Targum Pseudo-Jonathan: qôlîn (קוֹלִין). Translation unclear. The word translates as "compartments," "prisons," "light materials," or "lenient rulings." It may be an Aramaic form of the Greek word kōlon (κωλον), which in this context would translated as "arm," as a cubit (πηχεων / אַמָּה) was viewed as being the length of a fore-arm and hand.

• Oxyrhynchite manuscript 201: mehe (ⲙⲉϩⲉ). Translation: forearms (or cubits)

• Sahidic manuscript 16L: mahe (ⲙⲁϩⲉ). Translation: forearms (or cubits)

The length of the cubit changed between cultures and through time. When the Septuagint was translated into Greek, the Greek cubit was approximately 46 cm (18 inches), while the Judean cubit is believed to have been around 51 cm (21 inches).

CHAPTER 7

Lord the god said to Noah, "Enter, you and all your house, into the box, as I have seen that you are righteous in this generation. Of the clean livestock take in sevens, male and female, and of the unclean livestock pairs male and female. Of clean flying creatures of the sky sevens, males and females, and of all unclean flying creatures pairs of male and female, to maintain their descendants on all the land. For after seven days I will bring rain on the land, for forty days and forty nights, and I will blot out every descendant I have made, from the face of all of Eretz."

Noah did all things, whatever the Lord the god commanded him. Noah was six hundred years old when the flood of water was on the land. Then, Noah and his sons and his wife, and his sons' wives with him, went into the box, because of the water of the flood. Of clean flying creatures and unclean flying creatures, and clean livestock and unclean livestock, and of all things that creep on the land, pairs went to Noah into the box, male and female, as God commanded Noah.

It happened after the seven days that the flood of water came over the land. In the six hundredth year of the life of Noah, in the second month, on the twenty-seventh day of the month, on that day all the fountains of the abyss were broken up, and the cataracts of the sky were opened. The rain fell on the land for forty days and forty nights. On that very day,

CHAPTER 7

Noah, Shem, Ham, and Japheth, the sons of Noah, and the wife of Noah, and the three wives of his sons, entered into the box. All the wild animals according to their species, and all livestock according to their species, and every reptile moving on the land according to its species, and every flying bird according to its species, went to Noah, and in the box, in pairs, male and female of all flesh in which is the breath of life. They that entered went in male and female of all flesh, as God commanded Noah, and the Lord the god shut the box outside of him.

The flood was on the land forty days and forty nights, and the water surged greatly and lifted the box up, and it was carried up off of the land. The water conquered and flooded greatly over the land, and the box was carried on the water. The water conquered greatly over Eretz, and covered all the high mountains which were under the sky. The water was raised up fifteen cubits high, and it covered all the high mountains. All the flesh died that moved on the land, of flying creatures and livestock, and wild animals, and every reptile moving on the land, and every man. All things which have the breath of life, and whatever was on the dry land died. God blotted out every offspring which was on the face of Eretz, both man and animal, and reptiles, and birds of the sky, and they were blotted out from the land, and Noah was left alone with those in the box. The water was raised above the land for a hundred and fifty days.

CHAPTER 8

God remembered Noah, and all the wild animals, and all the livestock, and all the birds, and all the reptiles that crawl, and all that were with him in the box, and God brought a wind on Eretz, and the water stopped. The fountains of the deep were closed up, and the flood-gates of the sky and the rains from the sky were stopped. The water subsided and ran off the land, and after a hundred and fifty days the water was lowered, and the box rested in the seventh month, on the twenty-seventh day of the month, in the mountains of Ararat.[1]

The water continued to decrease until the tenth month. In the tenth month, on the first day of the month, the heads of the mountains were seen. It happened after forty days, that Noah opened the window of the box which he had made. He sent out the raven to see if the water had ceased, and it went out and did not return until the water was dried from off the land. He sent the dove after it to see if the water had ceased from off the land. The dove not having found rest for her feet, returned to him into the box, because the water was on all the face of Eretz, and he reached out his hand and took her, and brought her into the box. Having waited another seven days, he again sent forth the dove from the box. The dove returned to him in the evening, and had a leaf of olive, a sprig in her mouth, Noah knew that the water had ceased from off the

139

land. Having waited another seven days, he again sent forth the dove, and she did not return to him again.

It happened in the six hundred and first year of the life of Noah, in the first month, on the first day of the month, the water subsided from off the land, Noah opened the covering of the box which he had made, and he saw that the water had subsided from the face of Eretz. In the second month, the land had dried, on the twenty-seventh day of the month. Lord the god said to Noah, "Come out from the box, you and your wife and your sons, and your sons' wives with you, and all the wild animals, as many as are with you, and all flesh both of birds and animals, and every reptile moving on the land, bring out with you, and increase yourselves and multiply on the land."

Noah came out, and his wife and his sons, and his sons' wives with him. All the wild animals and all the livestock and every bird, and every reptile creeping on the land according to their species came out out of the box. Noah built an altar to God, and took of all clean animals, and all clean birds, and offered a whole burnt offering on the altar. Lord the god smelled a smell of sweetness, and the Lord the god having considered, said, "I will not again curse Eretz because of the actions of men, because the imagination of man is intently bent on evil things from his youth, I will not, therefore, again strike all living flesh as I have done. All the days of Eretz, seed and harvest, cold and heat, summer and spring, will not cease by day or night."

CHAPTER 8

CHAPTER 8 NOTES

1 Codex Alexandrinus: Ararat (ⲀⲣⲀⲣⲀⲧ)

• Leningrad Codex: 'Ărārāt (אֲרָרַט)

• Peshitta: Qrdw (ܩܪܕܘ). Translation: Corduene (or Kurdistan)

• Targum Onkelos: Qardû (קַרְדּוּ). Translation: Corduene (or Kurdistan)

• Targum Pseudo-Jonathan: ṭawwrê dəQadrôn šûm ṭawwrā' had Qardanyā' wəšûm ṭawwrā' had 'Armînəyā' (טַוְורֵי דְקַדְרוֹן שׁוּם טַוְורָא חַד קַרְדָנְיָא וְשׁוּם טַוְורָא חַד אַרְמִינְיָא). Translation: mountain of Qadron – one indicated a mountain in Corduene (or Kurdistan) and one indicated a mountain in Armenia

• Sahidic manuscripts: Barat (Ⲃⲁⲣⲁⲧ)

The Peshitta and Targum Onkelos use the substitute term Corduene (ܩܪܕܘ / קַרְדּוּ), an ancient reference to Kurdistan, in the region of modern northern Iraq and southeastern Turkey. Corduene was mentioned in Greek sources in the 6th century BCE as Gordi (Γορδι), a region in the Persian Empire north of the old Assyrian homeland, but south of Urartu. They were recorded as the Kardouǩoi (Καρδουχοι), a tribe living north of the Tigris River and in revolt against the Persian Empire circa 400 BCE. Between 290 and 278 BCE, the Babylonian historian Berossus wrote the *Babyloniaca*, which reported that the Babylonian flood survivor Xisthros' ship landed in Corduene. In the 1st century CE, the Jewish historian Josephus reported that the box of Noah was still visible in Karṛon (Καρρον), which is generally accepted as being a reference to Corduene. The Targum Jerusalem includes a scribal note that reports the sources used by the scribe differed, one indicating Cordune, and the other indicating Armenia.

The Hebrew and Greek name is probably older than the Aramaic name, as the Kurds were not recorded in the region until after the

CHAPTER 8

fall of the Neo-Assyrian Empire. Ararat is accepted as a Hebrew variation of ᵏᵘʳUrartu (𒆳𒌑𒊏𒅈𒌇), the name of Armenia during the Neo-Babylonian Empire. Bilingual texts from the Persian empire confirm that ᵏᵘʳUrartu (𒆳𒌑𒊏𒅈𒌇) and Armina (𒅈𒈪𒈾) were the same country. The presence of the name Ararat in *Cosmic Genesis* suggests that the early Aramaic text the Greeks translated included the name, however, it does not survive in the Targums or Peshitta.

CHAPTER 9

God blessed Noah and his sons, and said to them, "Increase and multiply, and fill the land and have dominion over it. The dread and the fear of you will be in all the wild animals of the land, all the birds of the sky, and all things moving on the land, and all the fish of the sea, I have placed them under your hands. And every reptile which is living will be meat for you, I have given all things to you like the green plants. But flesh with the blood of life you will not eat. For your lifeblood I will require from the hand of all wild animals, and I will require the life of man at the hand of his brother man. He that sheds man's blood, because of that blood will his own be shed, for in the image of God I made man. Increase and multiply, and fill the land, and have dominion over it."

God spoke to Noah, and to his sons with him, saying, "Look I establish my covenant with you, and with your descendants after you, and with every living mind with you, of birds and of animals, and with all the wild animals of the land, all that came out of the box. I will establish my covenant with you and all flesh will not again die by the water of the flood, and there will never again be a flood of water to destroy all the land."

Lord the god said to Noah, "This is the sign of the covenant which I set between me and you, and between every living creature which is with you for perpetual generations. I set my bow in the cloud, and it will be for a sign of the covenant between me and Eretz. It will be when I gather clouds on Eretz, that my bow will be seen in the cloud. I will remember my covenant, which is between me and you, and between every living mind in all flesh, and there will no longer be water for a deluge to blot out all flesh. And my bow will be in the cloud, and I will look to remember the everlasting covenant between me and Eretz, and between every living mind in all flesh, which is on the land."

God said to Noah, "This is the sign of the covenant, which I have made between me and between all flesh, which is on the land."

Now the sons of Noah which came out of the box, were Shem, Ham, and Japheth. Ham was the father of Canaan. These three are the sons of Noah, from these, were men scattered over all the land. Noah began to be a vintner, and he planted a vineyard. He drank of the wine, and was drunk, and was naked in his house. Ham the father of Canaan saw the nakedness of his father, and he went out and told his two brothers outside. Shem and Japheth having taken a garment put it on both their backs and went backward, and covered the nakedness of their father, and their face was turned away, and they didn't see the nakedness of their father. Noah recovered from the wine and knew all that his younger son had done to him. He said, "Cursed be the servant Canaan, a slave will he be to his brothers."

He said, "Blessed be the Lord the god for Shem, Canaan will be his slave. May God make room for Japheth, and let

CHAPTER 9

him live in the habitations of Shem, and let Canaan be his servant."

Noah lived after the flood for three hundred and fifty years. All the days of Noah were nine hundred and fifty years, and he died.

CHAPTER 10

Now, these are the generations of the sons of Noah, Shem, Ham, Japheth, and sons were born to them after the flood.

The descendants of Japheth were Cimmeria,[1] Magi,[2] Medes,[3] Ion,[4] (Alashiya),[5] Tabal,[6] Mushki,[7] and Troy.[8]

The descendants of Cimmeria were Ashkenaz,[9] Ripat,[10] and Togarmah.[11]

The descendants of Ion were Alashiya, Tartessos,[12] the Cypriots,[13] and the Rhodians.[14] From these, were the islands of the nations divided in their land, each according to his tongue, in their tribes and their nations.

The descendants of Ham were Khuz,[15] Egypt,[16] Put,[17] and Canaan.

The descendants of Khuz were the Sabaeans,[18] Havilah,[19] Shabwat,[20] the Ramanites,[21] and Sabtecha.[22] The descendants of the Ramanites were Sheba,[23] and Dedan.[24]

Khuz fathered Eridu,[25] who became great on the Earth.[26] (He was a strong hunter against the Lord of the gods, and therefore they say, "Like Eridu's Lord Alulim.")[27]

The beginning of his kingdom was Eridu,[28] Uruk,[29] Akkad,[30] and Kish[31] in the land of Sumer.[32] From that land came Ashur,[33] who built Nineveh, and the cities of Rehoboth, Kalhu, and Resen, between Nineveh and Kalhu.[34] (This is the great city.)

Egypt fathered the Lydians,[35] the Upper Egyptians,[36] the Libyans,[37] the Lower Egyptians,[38] the Nubians,[39] the people of the land of Kush[40] (where the Pelesets[41] came from), and the Minoans.[42] Canaan fathered Sidon his firstborn, and the Cypriots,[43] Jebusites, Amorites, Girgashites, Mitanni,[44] Arkites, Sinites, Arvadites, Zemarites, Hamathites, and after these tribes of Canaanites were dispersed. The boundaries of the Canaanites were from Sidon until one approaches Gerar and Gaza, until one comes to Sodom and Gomorrah, Adama and Bet Rabim, as far as Lasha. Those were the sons of Ham, in their tribes according to their tongues, in their countries, and their languages.

To Shem children were also born, the father of all the sons of Eber,[45] the brother of Japheth the elder.

The sons of Shem were Elam,[46] Ashur, Arphaxad, Lud, Aram, (and Cainan).[47]

The sons of Aram were Huz, Hul, Gater, and Mash.

Arphaxad fathered (Cainan, and Cainan fathered)[48] Salah, and Salah fathered Eber. To Eber were born two sons, the name of the one was Peleg, because in his days the land was divided, and the name of his brother Joktan.

Joktan fathered Almodad, Saleth, Hazarmaveth, Jerah, Hadoram, Aibel, Diklah, Eval, Abimael, Sheba, Ophir, Havilah, and Jobab. All these were the sons of Joktan. Their dwelling was from Mesha until one comes to Sephar, a mountain of the east. Those were the sons of Shem in their tribes, according to their tongues, in their countries, and in their nations.

CHAPTER 10

Those are the tribes of the sons of Noah, according to their generations, according to their nations. From them were the islands of the nations scattered over the land after the flood.

CHAPTER 10 NOTES

1 Codex Alexandrinus: Gamer (ΓΑΜΕΡ)
- Septuagint manuscript 56: Gaber (Γαϐ)
- Septuagint manuscript 376: Gomer (Γομϐ)
- Septuagint manuscript 53: Gomor (Γομοϐ)
- Leningrad Codex: Gōmer (גֹּמֶר)
- Peshitta: Gmr (ܓܡܪ)
- Targum Onkelos: Gōmer (גּוֹמֶר)
- Targum Jerusalem: Gōmer (גּוֹמֶר)
- Targum Pseudo-Jonathan: Gōmer (גּוֹמֶר)
- Old Armenian manuscripts: Gamirk' (Գամիրք)

This term was widely debated for over 1500 years, until the deciphering of Akkadian cuneiform in the past century. In the 1st century, the Jewish historian Josephus claimed the Gomer were the Galatians, which would make them Gauls, as the Galatians were Gauls who emigrated to Anatolia in the 3rd century BCE. In the early 3rd century, the Christian theologian Hippolytus of Rome reported that Gomer was the ancient Cappadocian civilization near where the Galatians settled. Near the end of the 4th century, the Christian scholar Jerome claimed that Gomer were the Celts, likely a reinterpretation of Josephus.

Around the same time, the Jewish Bereshít Rabbah was composed, in which Rabbi Samuel ben Ammi claimed Gomer was Germania. After cuneiform was deciphered, and the Assyrian annals were studied, it became clear that Gomer was a reference to the ᵏᵘʳGimirrāya (𒆳𒄀𒅎𒅕𒊑𒅀), who the Greeks knew as the Kimmerios (Κιμμεριος), and the Armenians knew as the Gamirk' (Գամիրք). The Cimmerians were an ancient Indo-Iranian tribe that lived north of the Black Sea in modern Ukraine and southern Russia. They were driven south out of Europe into Anatolia and settled in the region of Cappadocia.

2 Codex Alexandrinus: Magōg (Μᴀⲅⲱⲅ)
- Septuagint manuscript 707: Mgōn (Μγⲱⲟɴ)
- Septuagint manuscript 246: Magōṯ (Μᴧγⲱⲟθ)
- Septuagint manuscript 77: Magōn (Μᴧγⲟⲟɴ)
- Septuagint manuscript 53: Mak̆ōn (Μᴧχⲟⲟɴ)
- Leningrad Codex: Māgôg (מָגֹוג)
- Peshitta: Mgwg (ܡܓܘܓ)
- Targum Onkelos: Māgôg (מָגֹוג)
- Targum Jerusalem: 'Aprîqê wəGarmanyā' (אַפְרִיקֵי וְגָרְמַנְיָא). Translation: Africa and Germany. The Roman province of Africa was roughly the same region as modern Tunisia, which was occupied by the Germanic Vandal tribe in 439, and survived as a North African Germanic state until 554, when Vandal Africa was conquered by the Byzantine empire. The listing of these two regions suggest the list was composed during the era. The identification of Germanic tribes as the Magog was common in the late Classical era, later replaced by the Mongols in the medieval era.
- Targum Pseudo-Jonathan: Māgôg (מָגֹוג)

The meaning of Magog has been disputed since the Greco-Roman era, as the term is used in Israelite texts referring to both a tribe and a group of priests or sorcerers. This usage is identical to the use of the term Magos (Μαγος) in Greek literature from the era, which was both the name of a Medo-Persian tribe, and a priestly caste. The Greek term is based the name Mguš (𒈦𒄖𒍑) used in Persian cuneiform during the Achaemenid Empire, however, the earlier Persian spelling in Elamite cuneiform was Makuuka (𒈠𒆪𒌑𒅗). The archaic pronunciation may have been maintained in the Israelite texts in order to avoid seeming rebellious during the Medo-Persian era when the Magi were the official priesthood of the Median and Persian monarchs.

3 Codex Alexandrinus: Madai (ΜΑΔΑΙ)
- Septuagint manuscript 509: Malai (ΜΑλΑγ)
- Septuagint manuscript 55: Amada (ΑμαδΑ)
- Septuagint manuscript 135: Madaim (ΜΔΔΑγμ)
- Septuagint manuscript 392: Amadai (ΑμαΔαγ)
- Septuagint manuscript 319: Made (ΜΔΔϚ)
- Septuagint manuscript 129: Mamalai (ΜΔμαλαγ)
- Septuagint manuscript 56: Madaē (ΜΔδαλ)
- Septuagint manuscript 79: Madaeia (ΜΔδαϨΔ)
- Septuagint manuscript 246: Madan (ΜΔδαν)
- Septuagint manuscript 77: Madain (ΜΔΔαγν)
- Septuagint manuscript 569: Madim (ΜΔΔιμ)
- Septuagint manuscript 761:Madiam (ΜΔΔιΔμ)
- Septuagint manuscript 53: Madam (ΜΔδαμ)
- Septuagint manuscript 31: Maidi (ΜαγΔι)
- Septuagint manuscript 376: Mōdai (ΜωΔΔι)
- Leningrad Codex: Māday (מָדַי). Translation: Medes
- Peshitta: Mdy (ܡܕܝ)
- Targum Onkelos: Māday (מָדַי)
- Targum Jerusalem: Māday (מָדַי). Translation: Medes
- Targum Pseudo-Jonathan: Māday (מָדַי). Translation: Medes
- Sahidic manuscripts: Amaǩa (ΑΜΑΧΑ)

4 Codex Alexandrinus: Iōuan (ΙΩΥΑΝ).
- Cotton Genesis: Iōouam (ΙΩΟΥΑΜ)

151

- Septuagint manuscript 15: Iōouan (ιοοουλ̄ρ)
- Septuagint manuscript 17: Iōuian (ιοοωλρ)
- Septuagint manuscript 730: Auan (ᴧυλρ)
- Septuagint manuscript 426: Iouōan (ιουοολρ)
- Septuagint manuscript 500: Aunan (ᴧωλρ)
- Septuagint manuscript 75: Iōgan (ιοογαΝ)
- Septuagint manuscript 413: Uiōuian (Υιοοωλρ)
- Septuagint manuscript 71: Iōan (ιοολρ)
- Septuagint manuscript 76: Iouan (ιουλρ)
- Septuagint manuscript 108: Iōunan (ιοοωλρ)
- Septuagint manuscript 527: Ian (ιλρ)
- Septuagint manuscript 53: Iōban (ιοουλρ)
- Septuagint manuscript 59: Iōian (ιοολρ)
- Leningrad Codex: Yāwān (יָוָן)
- Peshitta: Ywn (ܝܘܢ)
- Targum Onkelos: Yāwān (יָוָן)
- Targum Jerusalem: Miqdônəyā' (מְקְדוֹנְיָא). Translation:
Macedonia
- Targum Pseudo-Jonathan: Yāwān (יָוָן)
- Bohairic manuscripts: Iōban (Ιωβᴀɴ)

The Hebrew term is a transliteration of the early Aramaic name Ywn (𐡉𐡅𐡍), and Neo-Assyrian name Iauna (𒅀𒌑𒈾), both meaning "Ion." The Neo-Assyrian and Aramaic words are accepted as being transliterations of the archaic Greek Iawōn (Ιαϝων), the name of a Greek patriarch who the Ionian Greek tribes were believed to descend from. Ionian Greeks primarily lived in Ionia, a region of western Anatolia. The term was in common use during the era of the Neo-Assyrian empire for "Greeks" when pluralized into Ywnyn (𐡉𐡅𐡍𐡉𐡍), which was adopted into Late Egyptian as the word Wynn (𓇌𓏲𓈖𓈖), meaning "Greek," which continued to be used in Coptic in the Classical era as Ouainin (Ογᴀιɴιɴ) and Ouenin

152

(Oyeinin). As both the Greek and Hebrew transliterations are ultimately derived from a term that has a more commonly spelling in English, the more common name Ion is used.

5 Septuagint manuscript 961: Elisa (ελεικα)
- Codex Alexandrinus: Elisa (ελικα)
- Septuagint manuscript 15: Lisa (λισα)
- Septuagint manuscript 730: Elissa (Ελισσα)
- Septuagint manuscript 120: Elisan (Ελισαν)
- Septuagint manuscript 75: Elisae (Ελισαι)
- Septuagint manuscript 82: Elusa (Ελυσα)
- Septuagint manuscript 107: Elēsa (Ελησα)
- Septuagint manuscript 527: Elka (Ελκα)
- Septuagint manuscript 376: Inesan (ινεσαν)
- Leningrad Codex (in the later reference to the son of Yāwān): 'Ĕlîšâ (אֱלִישָׁה)
- Peshitta (in the later reference to the son of Ywn): Ålyšå (ܐܠܝܫܐ)
- Targum Onkelos (in the later reference to the son of Yāwān): 'Ĕlîšâ (אֱלִישָׁה)
- Targum Jerusalem (in the later reference to the son of Yāwān): 'Ĕlîšâ (אֱלִישָׁה)
- Targum Pseudo-Jonathan (in the later reference to the son of Yāwān): 'Ĕlîšâ (אֱלִישָׁה)

Elisa / 'Ĕlîšâ is not mentioned in the Leningrad Codex, Peshitta, or targums at this point, only in the following list of the sons of Iōyan / Ywn. The Kingdom of Alashiya was mentioned in many texts from the late bronze age. Based on chemical analysis of the clay tablets sent from Alashiya to other kingdoms during the bronze age, is believed to have been in southern Cyprus, spanning the region where the cities of Kalabasós (Καλαβασός) and Alassa (Ἀλασσα) are located today. The name of Alassa is probably descended from

Alashiya. During the bronze age, the Egyptian court corresponded with the civilization using the Akkadian cuneiform script, in which it was known as Alašiia (𒀀𒆷�𒅀), which is probably the closest to its native pronunciation. The Mycenaean Greeks of the era recorded the name as Arasijo (𐀀𐀭𐀯𐀍), while the Ugaritic Canaanites recorded the name as Ålṭy (𐎀𐎍𐎘𐎊).

6 Codex Alexandrinus: Ṭobel (ⲐⲞⲂⲈⲀ)
- Septuagint manuscript 319: Ṭōbel (Θωυℓ)
- Septuagint manuscript 376: Ṭoubel (Θουυℓ)
- Leningrad Codex: Tūbāl (תֻּבָל)
- Peshitta: Twbyl (ܬܘܒܝܠ)
- Targum Onkelos: Tûbāl (תּוּבָל)
- Targum Jerusalem: Yētānəyā' (יְתָנְיָא)
- Targum Pseudo-Jonathan: Tûbāl (תּוּבָל)

Tabal was an early iron age kingdom in southeast Anatolia. It was conquered by the Neo-Assyrian Empire in 713 BCE, around the time the genealogy of nations was added, after entering into an anti-Assyrian alliance with the Mushki and the city of Carchemish.

7 Septuagint manuscript 961: Mosek̆ (ⲘⲞⲤⲈⲬ)
- Codex Alexandrinus: Mosok̆ (ⲘⲞⳝⲞⲬ)
- Septuagint manuscript 319: Mosōk̆ (Μοⳝεχ)
- Septuagint manuscript 54: Masōk̆ (Μᾳⳝεχ)
- Septuagint manuscript 74: Misok̆ (Μισοχ)
- Septuagint manuscript 106: Masok̆ (Μᾳσοχ)
- Septuagint manuscript 53: Mesok̆ (Μόσοχ)
- Leningrad Codex: Mešek (מֶשֶׁךְ)
- Peshitta: Mšk (ܡܫܟ)
- Targum Onkelos: Mešek (מֶשֶׁךְ)
- Targum Jerusalem: 'Ănasyā' (אֲנַסְיָא)

- Targum Pseudo-Jonathan: Mešek (מֶשֶׁךְ)
- Bohairic manuscript: Moško (Uocxo)

The Muški (𒈉𒅖𒆠) were recorded in Hittite and Assyrian records as invading northeast Anatolia during the bronze age collapse, however, they were repulsed, and initially settled in the region of modern Georgia. Later the tribe divided into two tribes, and one migrated to Cilicia, settling around Tabal. In the era of the Neo-Assyrian Empire, they were recorded in the annals of Urartu as the Muškini (�𒀀𒅖𒆠𒉌), while the Greeks later called them the Moškoi (Μοσχοι). Josephus identified the Mosok as the Moškoi in the 1st century, which is generally accepted today, however, was heavily debated during the Medieval era, with European scholars identifying Mosok with variety of locations, including France, Britain, and Moscow.

8 Septuagint manuscript 961: Ṭeiras (ⲐⲈⲒⲢⲀⳆ)
- Codex Atheniensis: Ṭiras (ⲐⲓⲣⲁⳆ)
- Septuagint manuscript 17: Ṭēras (ⲐⲏⲣⲁⳆ)
- Septuagint manuscript 53: Ṭēras kai Ṭarsēs (ⲐⲏⲣⲁⳆ ⲕⲁⲓ ⲐⲁⲣⲟⲏⳆ). Translation: Thera (or Santorini) and Tharsis
  - Leningrad Codex: Tîrās (תִּירָס)
  - Peshitta: Tyrs (ܬܝܪܣ)
  - Targum Onkelos: Tîrās (תִּירָס)
  - Targum Jerusalem: Tarqê (תִּרְקֵי)
  - Targum Pseudo-Jonathan: Tîrās (תִּירָס)

The location of Ṭeiras / Tîrās has been debated for millennia. In the Second Temple Era Book of Jubilees, the descendants of Tîrās had four large lands in the sea, possibly a reference to the Etruscans, who controlled the Tyrrhenian (Etruscan) Sea before the rise of the Carthaginian, Greek, and Roman empires, as the Tyrrhenian Sea is surrounded by Sicily, Sardinia, Corsica, and the Italian peninsula.

CHAPTER 10

In the first century CE, Josephus claimed Ṭeiras was the ancestor of the Thracians in the Balkan Peninsula. In the Talmud's Yoma tractate Ṭeiras is identified as the ancestors of the Persians, however, this may simply be a conflation with the early dynastic Persian king Teispes (𒈜𒍝𒅖𒉿𒄑). In the medieval Jewish Yosippon, Tîrās was identified as the ancestor of the Kievan Rus. Since the deciphering of Egyptian hieroglyphs, the dominant theory turned to them being the Turšå (𓍿𓂋𓅱𓈙𓀀), generally anglicized as Teresh, one of the sea peoples who attacked Egypt during the bronze age collapse.

The Teresh are often identified with the "Tyrrhenians," however, according to Strabo, Tyrrhenian was simply the Greek name of the Etruscans. The Etruscans called themselves the Rassena (ᴐNNᴇꙄᴐꟼ), and the name "Etruscan" was ultimately derived from the early Greek name for them Tursēnoi (Τυρσηνοι), essentially meaning "tower people," as their cities were built on hills. This means that any identification of the Rassena and Teresh, based on the later Greek term Tursēnoi, is entirely anachronistic. If any of the sea peoples were the Rassena, they were likely the Wåšåšå (𓅱𓈙𓈙𓈙), generally anglicized as Weshesh, as the Egyptians had difficulty transliterating foreign words that involved the R sound. Since the deciphering of Akkadian cuneiform, and then the Neshite (Hittite) language in the past century, an alternate interpretation of the Teresh has emerged, as the Neshites referred to their neighbors to the northwest as Taruiša (𒋫𒊒𒄿𒊭).

A similar term for the people from the region has been found in Mycenaean Linear-B as Toroja (𐀵𐀫𐀊). As this is the same location as the later Greek legends about Troía (Τροία), commonly referred to as Troy. As the names are clearly similar, Taruiša and Toroja are viewed as alternative ways of writing Troy. Given that the other locations in this list are mostly in Anatolia, the Aegean, or the Black

Sea, and Tyrs (תירס) appears to be a transliteration of Taruiša (𒋫𒊒𒄿𒊭), the name Troy is used in this translation.

9 Berlin Genesis: Aškanas (ⲁⲥⲭⲁⲛⲁⲥ)
- Septuagint manuscript 961: Aškenez (ⲁⲥⲭⲉⲛⲉⲍ)
- Codex Alexandrinus: Aškanaz (ⲁⲥⲭⲁⲛⲁⲍ)
- Septuagint manuscript 57: Aškana (Ασχανὰ)
- Septuagint manuscript 58: Aškanaza (Ασχανὰζὰ)
- Septuagint manuscript 343: Aškanez (Ασχανόζ)
- Septuagint manuscript 426: Aškalez (Ασχαλόζ)
- Septuagint manuscript 72: Kanax (Χανὰξ)
- Septuagint manuscript 569: Akanaz (Αχανὰζ)
- Leningrad Codex: 'Aškănaz (אַשְׁכְּנַז)
- Peshitta: Åšknz (ܐܫܟܢܙ)
- Targum Onkelos: 'Aškənaz (אַשְׁכְּנַז)
- Targum Jerusalem: 'Asyā' (אַסְיָא). Translation: Asia
- Targum Pseudo-Jonathan: 'Aškənaz (אַשְׁכְּנַז)
- Bohairic manuscripts: Aškanas (ⲁⲥⲭⲁⲛⲁⲥ)

The earliest records of the Aschanaz date to the Neo-Assyrian era, when the Cimmerians invaded the Urartu, and were repulsed by the Áškuzai (𒀸𒄖𒍝𒀀𒀀), which Armenian historians have accepted as the earliest reference their ancestors arriving in Urartu. As the Armenians were established in the region by the beginning of the Persian era, this interpretation does seem likely, however, the Urartians continued to be the dominant culture until the Neo-Babylonian era.

The report regarding the Cimmerian (𒋛-𒅖𒊏𒄿𒅎) invasion of Urartu was from the reign of Sargon II, and along with other reports show a series of invasionary migrations of the Cimmerians as the Scythians pushed them south through the trans-Caucus into the Armenian Highlands and northern Anatolia. These reports are

dated to between 720 and 714 BCE, during the early years of
Sargon II, which, combined with the subsequent scribal note about
Kalhu being the capital city, indicate that the genealogies of nations
was likely added between 720 and 705 BCE.

10 Cotton Genesis: Erifaṯ (ⲉⲣⲓⲫⲁⲑ).
- Septuagint manuscript 407: Rifaṯ (Ριϸⲁθ)
- Septuagint manuscript 15: Erifat (Εϸιϸⲁⲧ)
- Septuagint manuscript 17: Rifaṯ (Ρϥϸⲁθ)
- Septuagint manuscript 58: Rifta (Ριϸθⲁ)
- Septuagint manuscript 370: Rifag (Ριϸⲁγ)
- Septuagint manuscript 82: Rifat (Ριϸⲁⲧ)
- Septuagint manuscript 343: Rifṯan (Ριϸθⲁⲫ)
- Septuagint manuscript 458: Rēfaṯ (Ρⲗϸⲁθ)
- Leningrad Codex: Rîpat (רִיפַת)
- Peshitta: Dypr (ܪܝܦܕ)
- Targum Onkelos: Rîpat (רִיפַת)
- Bohairic manuscripts: Rifat (Ριⲑⲁⲧ)

11 Codex Alexandrinus: Ṯergama (ⲑⲉⲣⲅⲁⲙⲁ)
- Septuagint manuscript 407: Ṯorgama (Θοϸγⲁμⲁ)
- Septuagint manuscript 426: Ṯōrgama (Θωϸγⲁμⲁ)
- Septuagint manuscript 343: Ṯorgaman (Θοϸγⲁμⲁν)
- Septuagint manuscript 458: Ṯogarma (Θογϸμⲁ)
- Septuagint manuscript 527: Orgomaṯ (Οϸγⲟμⲁθ)
- Leningrad Codex: Tōgarmâ (תֹגַרְמָה)
- Peshitta: Twgrmå (ܬܘܓܪܡܐ)
- Targum Onkelos: Tôgarmâ (תּוֹגַרְמָה)
- Targum Jerusalem: Barbərî'â (בַּרְבְּרִיאָה). Translation: Algeria (or
Eritrea, Bavaria). The term is Greek and was applied to several
regions around the periphery of Greek civilization.

CHAPTER 10

- Targum Pseudo-Jonathan: Tôgarmā' (תּוֹגַרְמָא)

12 Septuagint manuscript 961: Ṭarseis (ΘΑΡϹΕΙϹ)
- Codex Alexandrinus: Ṭarseis (ΘΑΡϹΙϹ)
- Cotton Genesis: Ṭarsēs (ΘΑΡϹΗϹ)
- Septuagint manuscript 426: Ṭareis (Θαρϛⲥ)
- Leningrad Codex: Taršîš (תַרְשִׁישׁ)
- Peshitta: Tršyš (ܬܪܫܝܫ)
- Targum Onkelos: Taršîš (תַרְשִׁישׁ)
- Targum Jerusalem: 'Alastārəsôm (אֲלַסְטָרְסוֹם). This appears to be a corruption of the 'Alas wəTarsas (אֲלָס וְטַרְסַס) found in the Targum Pseudo-Jonathan, suggesting that Alas was in additional targums, as the Targum Jerusalem is generally viewed as older than Targum Pseudo-Jonathan, and the Targum Pseudo-Jonathan includes what appears to be quotes from the Targum Jerusalem.
- Targum Pseudo-Jonathan: 'Alas wəTarsas (אֲלָס וְטַרְסַס).

Translation: Alas and Tarsas

This civilization was also recorded in the Neo-Assyrian records of Esarhaddon as Tarsisi (𒋼𒅕𒋆𒋆), where it was used as a metaphor for the most distant known land. It was also recorded as Tršš (𐤕𐤓𐤔𐤔), on the Phoenician language Nora Stone discovered in Sardinia, which is also believed to date to the era. It was later known as Tartēssos (Ταρτησσος) in Greek myths, however, was no longer viewed as being a known land that people sailed to. In the 4th century BCE, Aristotle identified Tartēssos as being on the Atlantic coast of Iberia. Around the same time, the Greek geographer and explorer Pytheas reported that the civilization once existed on the Baetis River, the modern Guadalquivir River in southwest Spain.

While the location of the civilization has been debated for thousands of years, it is commonly accepted as being the "Tartessian" culture of southwest Iberia. During the 1900s, extensive remains of a bronze age civilization were discovered by archaeologists working ins southwest Spain and southern Portugal. This civilization existed between approximately 1900 and 700 BCE. It controlled extensive mines in southwest Iberia, which produced both metals and gemstones, and it also appears to have traded extensively with both the Phoenicians and Celts. The script used by the Tartessians was similar to the Greek script, which may have been why they were included in this list of nations.

13 Codex Alexandrinus: Kētioi (ΚΗΤΙΟΙ).

• Cotton Genesis: Ǩeuoṯaieim Kitioi (ΧΕΥΟΘΑΙΕΙΜΚΙΤΙΟΙ)
Translation: Kheuothaieim Citians

• Septuagint manuscript 135: Ǩetieim Kuprioi (Χϭʰιԁμ Κυѡρɪϴ).
Translation: Chetiim Cypriots

• Septuagint manuscript 57: Kittioi (Κιτʰιϴ)

• Septuagint manuscript 58: Ǩeṯṯeim kai Kítioi (Χϭϴϴԁμ ʰαι Κíʰιϴ).
Translation: Ǩeṯṯeim and Citians

• Septuagint manuscript 343: Ǩeṯeim (Χϭϴԁμ)

• Septuagint manuscript 458: Kitios (Κíʰιος)

• Septuagint manuscript 54: Ǩeṯṯieim (Χϭϴʰιԁμ)

• Septuagint manuscript 71: Kutioi (Κυʰιϴ)

• Septuagint manuscript 107: Kotēoi (Κοτʰϴ)

• Septuagint manuscript 106: Ǩeuoṯieim (Χϭυοϴʰιԁμ)

• Septuagint manuscript 527: Kēstioi (Κʰςιϴ)

• Septuagint manuscript 44: Ǩeuoṯēieim (Χϭυοϴʰιԁμ)

• Septuagint manuscript 376: Kiteoi (Κιτϭϴ)

• Leningrad Codex: Kittîm (כִּתִּים). Translation: Cypriots

• Peshitta: ktym (ܟܬܝܡ). Translation: Cypriots

• Targum Onkelos: Kittîm (כִּתִּים). Translation: Cypriots

• Targum Pseudo-Jonathan: 'Akazyā' (אֲכַזְיָא)

The various manuscripts of the Septuagint contain a number of variations at this point, some including a Greek transliteration of the

Aramaic word Ktym (*ך^קy*), others including a translation as "Citians," and some including both. Only one known Greek manuscript separates them with an "and" (και), Septuagint manuscript 58 from the 11th century, however, that variation must have been in wide use in Egypt during the medieval era, as it is the variation that was translated into Ge'ez, the classical language of Ethiopia.

Kt (*+y*) and Kty (*^קy*) were the Canaanite and Aramaic names of Cyprus during the Neo-Assyrian and Neo-Babylonian era, based on the name of the ancient Cypriot city-state, subsequently known as Cition (Κίτιον) in Greek. The name was recorded as Kåtjåy (𓈖𓏤𓊃𓈙) in Egyptian records from the New Kingdom Era in the late Bronze Age, and appears to have survived the bronze age collapse better than most states. According to Josephus in the 1st century CE, Kytm was originally a place Cyprus, however, the term appears to have come to mean all Greeks, or even all non-Semitic Mediterranean peoples in the Judahite dialect of Canaanite by the 7th century BCE, which appears to be the intended usage here. In this verse, as the name "Citians" is being used to clarify the various transliterations of "Cyprus" it is treated as a Greek scribal note.

14 Berlin Genesis: Roaioi (ροΛιοι). This appears to be a simple scribal error of "Rhodians" (ροΔιοι)

• Codex Alexandrinus: Rodioi (ροΔιοι). Translation: Rhodians.

• Septuagint manuscript 319: Rōdioi (ΡωΔιοι). Translation: Rhodians

  • Leningrad Codex: Dōdānîm (דֹּדָנִים)

  • Peshitta: Dwdnym (ܗܘܕܢܡ)

  • Targum Onkelos: Dōdānîm (דֹּדָנִים)

  • Targum Jerusalem: Dôdanyā' (דֹּודָנְיָא)

  • Targum Pseudo-Jonathan: Dôrədanyā' (דֹּורְדָנְיָא)

CHAPTER 10

The Greek translation does not correspond to the Hebrew and Aramaic translations in this verse. The Greek Rodioi referred to people from the island of Rhódos (Ῥόδος), while the Hebrew Dodanim was a plural of Dōdōnē (Δωδώνη). There were two Dodonas in Greece, one in Epirus, and the other in Thessaly near Mount Olympus. Both were oracle sites of Zeus.

The difference between the names was almost certainly already in the Aramaic text the Greek translated, as the same deviation is also found in Masoretic book *Dibrê Hayyāmîm,* which renders the name as Rôdānîm (רוֹדָנִים), mirrored in 1st Paralipomenon by Rodioi (Ροδιοι). The letters representing D and R are almost identical in both Phoenician (𐤃 and 𐤓) and Aramaic (ד and ר), and therefore the error could have originated in either script, however, as the Greek translation uses the name Rhodians in both places, the error was likely made when the genealogy of nations was added to the Torah between 612 and 607 BCE.

15 Codex Alexandrinus: Ǩous (ⲭⲟⲩⲥ)
• Leningrad Codex: Kûš (כּוּשׁ)
• Peshitta: Kwš (ܟܘܫ)
• Targum Onkelos: Kûš (כּוּשׁ)
• Targum Pseudo-Jonathan: Kûš (כּוּשׁ)

The Septuagint generally uses the name "Æthiopia" where the Masoretic text uses "Kush," however, as it is interpreted here as the name of a patriarch, as transliterated directly, confirming that the old Aramaic text did use the same name as the Hebrew and Syriac translations. In the context of the genealogy of nations, this "Kush," who is the father of the Southern Semites, well as Eridu, can only be interpreted as the Sumerians, who are otherwise conspicuously absent from the genealogy of nations.

According to Assyriologists, the Elamites were the ethnolinguistic group most closely related to the Sumerians, and therefore, like the

162

Southern Semites and Elamite, the Sumerians were probably dark skinned, which was called kusaaa (𒆸𒊩𒌦) in Assyrian. This reference to the Sumerians as "Ǩous" confirms that the Gēōn / Gîhôn River in chapter 2 was the Karun River that flows through Khuzistan. Therefore, the name Khuz used as a translation for "Ǩous."

16 Codex Alexandrinus: Mesrain (ⲘⲈⲤⲢⲀⲓⲚ)
- Cotton Genesis: Mestraim (ⲘⲈⲤⲦⲢⲀⲓⲘ)
- Septuagint manuscript 15: Mestrem (Μέςβόμ)
- Septuagint manuscript 17: Mesraeim (Μέσρα̣ δμ)
- Septuagint manuscript 318: Mesraim (Μέσβαιμ)
- Septuagint manuscript 319: Mesraēm (Μέσρα̣λμ)
- Septuagint manuscript 14: Mesaraim (Μέσσαραιμ)
- Septuagint manuscript 25: Messaraim (Μέσσσαραιμ)
- Septuagint manuscript 343: Metraim (Μέτβαιμ)
- Septuagint manuscript 79: Messaraein (ΜέσσσαρΔδν)
- Septuagint manuscript 82: Mestreim (Μέςβδμ)
- Septuagint manuscript 408: Messaraeim (ΜέσσσαρΔδμ)
- Septuagint manuscript 54: Mestraeim (Μέςρα̣ δμ)
- Septuagint manuscript 71: Mesorem (Μέσσοβόμ)
- Septuagint manuscript 74: Mesrai (Μέσβαι)
- Septuagint manuscript 108: Mesaraeim (ΜέσσαρΔδμ)
- Septuagint manuscript 376: Misraeim (Μισρα̣ δμ)
- Leningrad Codex: Miṣrayim (מִצְרַיִם). Translation: Egypt (or Egyptians)
- Peshitta: Mṣrym (ܡܨ̇ܪܝܢ). Translation: Egyptians
- Targum Onkelos: Miṣrayim (מִצְרַיִם). Translation: Egyptians
- Targum Pseudo-Jonathan: Miṣrayim (מִצְרַיִם). Translation: Egyptians
- Bohairic manuscripts: Nestrem (ⲚⲈⲤⲦⲢⲉⲙ)

CHAPTER 10

The Canaanite form of the words meaning "Egypt," and "Egyptian," were both spelled as plural forms of Mṣr, as there were two lands of Egypt, Upper and Lower Egypt. The plural form was used in Ugaritic as Mṣrm (𐎎𐎕𐎗𐎎), Phoenician as Mṣrm (𐤌𐤑𐤓𐤌), Aramaic as Mṣryn (𐡌𐡑𐡓𐡍), and Hebrew as Mṣrym (מצרים). The origin of the name "Mṣr" isn't clear, however, it was used as a singular form in Akkadian as Muṣur (𒈬𒋩), and later East Semitic languages as Miesri (𒈪𒅖𒊑), and continues to be a singular form in Arabic as Miṣr (مِصْر). In the names comprising the genealogy of nations, there are the names of mythical patriarchs, countries, and tribes, and therefore it is not clear if the original list referred "Egypt," or "Egyptians," or if a mythical patriarch was actually being referred to.

If the Egyptians had a mythical patriarch they all descended from, his name has not survived, however, given the Egyptians' view of their country's early history, when it was ruled by the gods and demigods, a mythical patriarch seems unlikely. It is possible the author was thinking of Menes (𓏠𓈖) the quasi-mythical founder of Egypt.

The Egyptians had legends of Menes, however, to date no clear evidence has been found confirming his existence. It is theorized the legends of Menes may have been based on early dynastic king Narmer, who is known from the archaeological record, but not the king lists, and if so, it is plausible that Muṣur is also a corruption of his name. If so, it probably started as the Sumerians transliterating Når-mer (𓆤) as Amar-mu (𒀫𒈬), and the Akkadians reversing the logograms to Mu-amar (𒈬𒀫), as they did with some other names. As the Sumerian AMAR (𒀫 / 𒀫) logogram was commonly pronounced as SUR in Akkadian, it would have resulted in the name Mu-sur. While the Greeks may have interpreted the name as a literal patriarch, the genealogy of nations appears to be more figurative, attempting to explain which nations descended from

which other nations, and so the name "Egypt" is imported from the
Masoretic text.

17 Codex Alexandrinus: Foud (ϕoⲨⲁ)
- Cotton Genesis: Fouṯ (ϕoⲨⲉ)
- Septuagint manuscript 319: Fout (ϕoⲨⲧ)
- Septuagint manuscript 57: Ǩoud (ⲭoⲨⲁ)
- Septuagint manuscript 120: Foul (ϕoⲨλ)
- Septuagint manuscript 426: Four (ϕoⲨβ̧)
- Septuagint manuscript 551: Fōoud (ϕoⲟⲟⲨⲁ)
- Leningrad Codex: Pût (פּוּט)
- Peshitta: Pwt (ܦܘܛ)
- Targum Onkelos: Pût (פוט)
- Targum Pseudo-Jonathan: Pût (פוט)

The Pådw (𐎛 𐎝𐎨) were a Libyan tribe recorded in Egyptian
records of the 22nd dynasty, who appear to have lived in Cyrene
before the Greeks colonized the region in 631 BCE. The annals of
Nebuchadnezzar II report that in 567 BCE, the Greeks from Putu,
called the Putu Iáaman (𒉺𒌓𒅀𒀀𒈠𒀭) in Neo-Babylonian, were
fighting in the Egyptian army. The Canaanites appear to have been
trading with the Pådw for centuries before the Greeks established a
colony in Cyrene, and so the name Pwt (𐤕𐤅𐤐) appears to have been
applied to the entire Libyan (Berber) population of northern Africa.
When the Persians later conquered Egypt, Cyrene joined the
Persian Empire, and they integrated Cyrene as the Satrapy of
Putāya (𐏐𐎢𐎫𐎠𐎹).

18 Codex Alexandrinus: Saba (ⲥⲁⲃⲁ)
- Septuagint manuscript 370: Sabaṭa (Σαυαθα)
- Septuagint manuscript 77: Saua (Σαυα)
- Septuagint manuscript 761: Saban (Σαυαν)

- Leningrad Codex: Səbā' (סְבָא)
- Peshitta: Šbå (ܣܒܐ)
- Targum Onkelos: Səbā' (סְבָא)
- Targum Pseudo-Jonathan: Səbā' (סְבָא)

This reference, along with the Sabata / Sabtâ (Σαβατα / סַבְתָּה) and Sebekata / Sabtəkā' (Σεβεκαθα / סַבְתְּכָא), appear to be references to Sabaean tribes of southern Arabia. Based on them all being descends of Kush, it appears the other Sabaean tribes were not viewed as being descendants of Saba at the time. Sbâ (ሰባ), generally anglicized as Saba, was a kingdom in modern western Yemen, based out of its capital of Mryb (ማእረብ). Based on the archaeological evidence, the Sabaeans formed a small kingdom around Mryb circa 1200 BCE, and by 800 BCE ruled western Yemen.

19 Codex Alexandrinus: Euila (ΕΥΙΛΑ)
- Cotton Genesis: Euilat (ΕΥΙΛΑΤ)
- Septuagint manuscript 15: Euilat (ΕυϊλΑτ)
- Septuagint manuscript 344: Euila (ΕυϊλΑ)
- Septuagint manuscript 131: Leuilat (ΛϊυϊλΑτ)
- Septuagint manuscript 739: Leeuilat (ΛϊϊυϊλΑτ)
- Septuagint manuscript 120: Euēlat (Ευλ̄ λΑτ)
- Septuagint manuscript 128: Leuilat (ΛϊυϊλΑτ)
- Septuagint manuscript 77: Leuitat (ΛϊυϊτΑτ)
- Leningrad Codex: Hăwîlâ (חֲוִילָה)
- Peshitta: Ǩwylå (ܟܘܝܠܐ)
- Targum Onkelos: Hăwîlâ (חֲוִילָה)
- Targum Pseudo-Jonathan: Hăwîlâ (חֲוִילָה)
- Bohairic manuscripts: Euilat (ΕⲦΙⲖⲀⲦ)

Based on the geographical description in chapter 2, this appears to be the Cradle of Gold, near modern Medina, in Saudi Arabia. For more information, see the note on Euilat in chapter 2.

20 Septuagint manuscript 961: Sabata (ᴄᴀʙᴀᴛᴀ)

- Codex Alexandrinus: Sabaṭa (ᴄᴀʙᴀⵙᴀ)
- Septuagint manuscript 730: Basa (ʙⴷⵛ)
- Septuagint manuscript 319: Sababaṭa (ᴤⴷuⴷuⴷθⴷ)
- Septuagint manuscript 370: Sabasa (ᴤⴷuⴷⵛ)
- Septuagint manuscript 346: Sabbaṭa (ᴤⴷuuⴷθⴷ)
- Septuagint manuscript 108: Sabaṭat (ᴤⴷuⴷθⴷᴛ)
- Septuagint manuscript 551: Sauaṭa (ᴤⴷuⴷθⴷ)
- Leningrad Codex: Sabtâ (סַבְתָּה)
- Peshitta: Sbtâ (ܣܒܬܐ)
- Targum Onkelos: Sabtâ (סַבְתָה)
- Targum Pseudo-Jonathan: sabtā (סַבְתָּ)

This is probably a reference to a kingdom based out of Šbwt (𐩲𐩨𐩩), in central modern Yemen. The root terms Sb (𐩨𐩲) and Šb (𐩪𐩨) were used by most of the tribes of southern Arabia, making identification of the specific land difficult, however, the 1st century CE guide to the Indian Ocean known as the *Periplus of the Erythraean Sea*, a major trading center named Sabbaṭa (Σαββαθα) was recorded as being in the interior of modern Yemen. This is the name used in Septuagint manuscript 346, and virtually identical to the spelling in the Codex Alexandrinus and Septuagint manuscript 319, indicating at least some of the classical and medieval scribes viewed this as a reference to Šbwt.

Pliny the Elder's Natural History, written at approximately the same time, called the city Sabota (Σαβοτα), and claimed it was the capital city of the Adramitae Sabaean tribes, which is considered to be the origin of the regional name Hadhramaut (حَضْرَمَوْت) for modern eastern Yemen.

The ruins of Šbwt, generally anglicized to Shabwat or Shabwa, have been studied by archaeologists in the past century, and were not inhabited by the similarly named Sabaeans to the west, but a different South Semitic people. Sabaean and Hadramitic writing

167

CHAPTER 10

have been found in the remains of the city, but mostly Hadramitic. Based on the archaeological evidence, the city of Shabwat existed from the 1300s BCE until the 200s CE.

21 Codex Alexandrinus: Reŋǩma (ρεϲxма)
- Septuagint manuscript 318: Regma (Ρόγμα)
- Septuagint manuscript 707: Ragma (Ρλγμα)
- Septuagint manuscript 730: Rekma (Ρόϗμα)
- Septuagint manuscript 400: Resma (Ρόσμα)
- Leningrad Codex: ra'mah (רַעְמָה)
- Peshitta: rômâ (ܪܥܡܐ)
- Targum Onkelos: ra'mah (רַעְמָה)
- Targum Pseudo-Jonathan: ra'ama (רַעֲמָא)

This location is somewhat debated, however, generally accepted as a reference to the Ramanitēs (Ραμανίτης) tribe, who Pliny the Elder later recorded in the first century CE, as living in the region of modern UAE. Around the same time, Strabo referred to them as the Rammanites (Ραμμανίτες) in his *Geographica*.

22 Septuagint manuscript 961: Sebekata (ϲεϐεκλΘλ)
- Codex Alexandrinus: Sabakata (ϲλϐλκλΘλ)
- Septuagint manuscript 15: Sebakata (Σόυλϗαθλ)
- Septuagint manuscript 730: Sakabata (Σλϗαυλθλ)
- Septuagint manuscript 129: Sabaikata (Σλυαγϗαθλ)
- Septuagint manuscript 56: Sabekatas (Σλυόϗαθλϲ)
- Septuagint manuscript 79: Sauakata (Σλυλϗαθλ)
- Septuagint manuscript 458: Sararata (Σαραρλθλ)
- Septuagint manuscript 108: Seabakata (Σόλυλϗαθλ)
- Septuagint manuscript 551: Sabata (Σλυλθλ)
- Septuagint manuscript 527: Sakakata (Σλϗαϗαθλ)
- Septuagint manuscript 53: Sabakatas (Σλυλϗαθλϲ)
- Septuagint manuscript 31: Sabataka (Σλυλθλϗα)

- Septuagint manuscript 122: Kaṯa (Κἀθλ)
- Leningrad Codex: Sabtəkā' (סַבְתְּכָא)
- Peshitta: Sbtkå (ܣܒܬܟܐ)
- Targum Onkelos: Sabtəkā' (סַבְתְּכָא)
- Targum Pseudo-Jonathan: Sabtəkā' (סַבְתְּכָא)
- Bohairic manuscripts: Sabaṯaha (Ϭⲁⲃⲁⲑⲁⳃⲁ)

This may be the same location later recorded as Saḵalítēs (Σαχαλίτης), in the first century CE guide to the Indian Ocean known as the *Periplus of the Erythraean Sea*. The exact location of Saḵalítēs is debated as different Classical era authors placed it either east or west of Suagros, another trading port generally accepted as being in the region of Dhofar, Oman. In Claudius Ptolemaeus' 2ⁿᵈ century *Geography*, it was simply known as Saḵlē (Σαχλη), and placed to the east of Suagros, in the bay where islands of Kurya Murya lay, which is also in Dhofar.

23 Codex Alexandrinus: Saba (ⲥⲁⲃⲁ)

- Septuagint manuscript 509: Saban (Σλυἀψ)
- Septuagint manuscript 707: Saba Ṯauderetader (Σλυλ Ϲλυⲁⳃϭθλⲁⳃ)
- Septuagint manuscript 730: Saba Regma (Σλυλ Ρϭγμα)
- Septuagint manuscript 79: Sauan (Σλυἀψ)
- Septuagint manuscript 458: Sebai (Σϭuⲁⲓ)
- Septuagint manuscript 72: Saba kai Massabaemassada (Σλυλ ⲕⲁⲓ ΜλσϹⲁuⲁϭμⲁσϹⲁⳃⲁ). Translation: Saba and Massabaemassada
- Leningrad Codex: šəbā' (שְׁבָא)
- Peshitta: Šbå (ܫܒܐ)
- Targum Onkelos: Šəbā' (שְׁבָא)
- Targum Pseudo-Jonathan: Šəbā' (שְׁבָא)

This is a reference to the city that the queen who visited Solomon came from, however, it is not clear from the context where it was.

Saba, and most of the southern coast of Arabia appears to have been established. The following reference to Dedan, along the incense roads from the southern coast to Canaan, suggests that this Sheba may likewise have been somewhere along the interior roads of Arabia, possibly in the Asir Mountains in the southwest, north of the kingdom of Saba, but south of Dedan.

24 Codex Alexandrinus: Dadan (ᴅᴀᴅᴀɴ)
- Septuagint manuscript 15: Oudadan (Ουδαδαν)
- Septuagint manuscript 17: Ioudadan (ιουδαδαν)
- Septuagint manuscript 121: Daidan (Δαιδαν)
- Septuagint manuscript 135: Ioudas (ιουδας)
- Septuagint manuscript 707: Dedan (Δεδαν)
- Septuagint manuscript 18: Daithan (Δαιθαν)
- Septuagint manuscript 134: Ioudiadan (ιουδιαδαν)
- Septuagint manuscript 370: Ioudiadam (ιουδιαδαμ)
- Septuagint manuscript 82: Idadan (ιδαδαν)
- Septuagint manuscript 72: Dethan (Δεθαν)
- Septuagint manuscript 74: Ioudiada (ιουδιαδα)
- Septuagint manuscript 107: Iouddan (ιουδδαν)
- Septuagint manuscript 527: Daddan (Δαδδαν)
- Septuagint manuscript 53: Daidam (Δαιδαμ)
- Leningrad Codex: Dədān (דְּדָן)
- Peshitta: Drn (ܕܪܢ)
- Targum Jerusalem: Bābel (בָּבֶל). Translation: Babylon
- Targum Pseudo-Jonathan: Pûnətôs (פונטוס). Translation: Pontus
- Targum Onkelos: Dədān (דְדָן)

Dedan was the name of a kingdom in the Hijaz mountains of modern Saudi Arabia during the 7ᵗʰ and 8ᵗʰ centuries BCE.

25 Codex Alexandrinus: Nebrōd (ⲚⲈⲂⲢⲰⲆ)

- Septuagint manuscript 509: Nebrōn (Ⲛⲟⲩⲣⲱⲛ)
- Septuagint manuscript 128: Ebrōṯ (Ⲉⲩⲣⲱⲑ)
- Septuagint manuscript 75: Nebrōṯ (Ⲛⲟⲩⲣⲱⲑ)
- Septuagint manuscript 79: Neurōd (Ⲛⲟⲩⲣⲱⲇ)
- Septuagint manuscript 376: Ebrōdō (Ⲉⲩⲣⲱⲇⲱ)
- Leningrad Codex: Nimrōd (נִמְרֹד)
- Peshitta: Nmrwd (ܢܡܪܘܕ)
- Targum Onkelos: Nimrōd (נִמְרֹד)
- Targum Jerusalem: Nimrôd (נִמְרוֹד)
- Targum Pseudo-Jonathan: Nimrôd (נִמְרוֹד)
- Sahidic manuscript 2212 (later in the verse): Nebrōd (Ⲛⲉⲃⲣⲱⲇ)

Based on the description of this "patriarch," it has to be a reference to the original Sumerian city of Eridu, which was spelled as Nun^{ki} (𒉣𒆠) in Sumerian. Nun^{ki} can be variously interpreted as "noble place," or "ruling place," or, more relevantly "first place."

The Akkadians pronounced Nin^{ki} as Eridu, which may have also been the later Sumerian nickname of Nun^{ki} as the Sumerian word for "copper" was urudu (𒍐), and the city's primary industry was working the copper from the trade on the Euphrates. The copper trade in Eridu was so important to the Sumerian civilization that the Sumerian name of the Euphrates was ^{id}Buranun (𒀀𒌓𒁕𒉣𒆠), believed to mean "source of copper." In this section of text, it appears the author misunderstood a cuneiform text about Eridu, which had the name both written as Nun^{ki} (𒉣𒆠) and then spelled phonetically as Eridu^{ki} (𒂍𒇻𒄭𒆠). This would have been necessary after the rise of the Old Babylonian Empire, as the name "great place" (𒉣𒆠) was appropriated by Babylon. This also explains why Babylon (Βαβυλων / בָּבֶל) is listed as being in Sumer, as Nun^{ki} by itself meant "Babylon" by the time the Aramaic translation was made.

Transliterated directly into Aramaic, the name Nun[ki] Eridu[ki] (⌗⟨⊜ 𒂊𒆠⌐⟨⊜) is Nnrd (ꠤ꠨꠨), as there was no E (𒂊) in Aramaic or Phoenician, and the KI (⊜) would not have been transliterated. This can itself by transliterated into Greek as Nebrōd by misreading the second Aramaic N (ꠤ), as the similarly shaped Aramaic B (ꠅ), or into Hebrew as Nmrd, by misreading the second N (ꠅ) in the Phoenician script as a similarly shaped M (ꠅ). As all historical sources agree that the Septuagint was translated from Aramaic, while the Hebrew translation that later served as the source for the Masoretic text was translated from older Judahite texts written in the Phoenician script, this seems a probable explanation for the differences between the Greek and Hebrew names. As this "patriarch" has to have originally been Eridu, the name "Nimrod" is corrected back to "Eridu."

26 Codex Alexandrinus: gigas epi tēs gēs (ΓΙΓΑΣΕΠΙΤΗΣΓΗΣ). Translation: Gígas on the earth (or land)

• Leningrad Codex: gibbōr bā'āres (גִּבֹּר בָּאָרֶץ). Translation: powerful (or strong) on earth (or land)

• Peshitta: gnbrå bårδå (ܓܲܢܒܪܵܐ ܒܐܲܪܥܵܐ).Translation: strong man (or giant, hero, Orion) on earth (or land, soil)

• Targum Onkelos: gibbar taqqîp bə'ar'ā' (גְּבַר תַּקִּיף בְּאַרְעָא). Translation: powerful (or strong) attacker on earth (or land, soil)

• Targum Jerusalem: gibbôr bəsayydā' bəhet'â (גְּבוֹר בְּצַיְידָא בְּחֶטְאָה). Translation: powerful (or strong) in hunting of sinners

• Targum Pseudo-Jonathan: gibbar mərôdā' (גְּבַר מְרוֹדָא). Translation: powerful (or strong) rebel (or mutineer)

• Sahidic manuscript 2212: pgigas pherēh mpemto (ⲡⲅⲓⲅⲁⲥ ⲛ̄ⲃⲉⲣⲏϭ ⲙ̄ⲡⲉⲙⲧⲟ). Translation: the giant hunter in sky and depths

In Greek mythology, the Gigantes were an ancient tribe of people or demigods who challenged the rule of the gods. The Greek

172

translators appear to have interpreted this story as being much the same, using the word gigas essentially as "apostate." The Masoretic version is quite different, as it indicates the Aramaic term would have been gbrå (גברא), meaning "husband," "owner," or "ruler." This means the term translated from the Akkadian cuneiform precursor text would have been lugal (𒈗), also meaning "lord," "master," or "king."

According to various king lists recovered from archaeological digs in Iraq, Eridu was the original "capital city" of Sumer, before a great flood destroyed all the cities of Sumer. Based on the archaeological evidence uncovered to date, the city was founded around 5400 BCE, and reached a peak around 3000 BCE. It later went into decline and was almost abandoned by 2000 BCE, when King Amar-Sin of Ur began a massive reconstruction of the city, culminating in the unfinished Ziggurat of Amar-Sin. Therefore, the era when Eridu would have dominated Mesopotamia, would have probably been around 3000 BCE.

27 Codex Alexandrinus: kunēgos enantion KU (ΚΥΝΗΓΟC ΕΝΑΝΤΙΟΝΚῩ). Translation: hunter opposing (or against) Lord

• Septuagint manuscript 15: kunēgos enanti Kuriou (κωληγος ανδμ]τ Κυρϕου). Translation: hunter before Lord

• Septuagint manuscript 125: kunēgos gígas enantíon Kuríou tou teou (κωληγος γιγας ανδμτϕϴ Κυρϕου τϖ θϭου). Translation: hunter of Gígas opposing (or against) Lord the god

• Septuagint manuscript 58: kunēgos enantíon Kuríou tou teou (κωληγος ανδμτιϴ Κυρϕου τϖ θϭου). Translation: hunter against Lord the god

• Leningrad Codex: gibbôr ṣayid lipnê Yəhōwâ (גִּבֹּר צַיִד לִפְנֵי יְהוָֹה). Translation: powerful (or strong) hunter in front of Yahweh

• Peshitta: nkšyrtnå qdm mryå (ܣܬܝܪܬܢܐ ܩܕܡ ܡܪܝܐ). Translation: divine inheritor before the master

• Targum Onkelos: gibbar taqqîp qŏdām Yəyā (גְּבַר תַּקִּיף קֳדָם יְיָ). Translation: powerful (or strong) attacker before Yahweh

• Targum Jerusalem: gibbôr bəṣayydā' bəhet'â qādām Yəyā (גְבוֹר בְּצָיְידָא בְחֶטְאָה קֳדָם יְיָ). Translation: powerful (or strong) in hunting of sinners before Yahweh

• Targum Pseudo-Jonathan: gibbar bəṣêdā' ûmərôdā' qŏdām Yəyā (גְבַר בְּצֵידָא וּמְרוֹדָא קֳדָם יְיָ). Translation: powerful (or strong) in hunting and sinning before Yahweh

• Sahidic manuscript 2212: ebol mpjoeis pnoute (ⲉⲃⲟⲗ Ⲙⲡ̄ⲭⲟⲉⲓⲥ ⲡⲛⲟⲩⲧⲉ). Translation: before the master the god

The original Aramaic writer of the genealogy of nations appears to be attempting to explain the name of the first king in of Eridu: ensi Alulim (𒂗𒉌 𒀀𒇻𒇴). Ensi (𒂗𒉌) was the Sumerian word for "lord" or "governor," while Alulim (𒀀𒇻𒇴) was composed of the logograms meaning "strong" (𒀉), "animal" (𒄠), and "look for" (𒌋), resulting in this strange scribal note.

28 Codex Alexandrinus: Babulōn (ΒΑΒΥΛΩΝ). Translation: Babylon

• Septuagint manuscript 73: Babulō (βαβυλω)

• Leningrad Codex: Bābel (בָּבֶל). Translation: Babylon

• Peshitta: Bbl (ܒܒܠ). Translation: Babylon

• Targum Onkelos: Bābel (בְּבֶל). Translation: Babylon

• Targum Jerusalem: Bābel (בְּבֶל). Translation: Babylon

• Targum Pseudo-Jonathan: Bābel rabbətî (בְּבֶל רַבְּתִי). Translation: Babylon the Great

• Sahidic manuscript 2212: Babulōn (Ⲃⲁⲃⲩⲗⲱⲛ). Translation: Babylon

CHAPTER 10

As this could not have been the later city of Babylon, which was not in Sumer, it must be assumed this is another reference to Eridu, which was also spelled as Nun^ki (𒉣𒆠) in Akkadian cuneiform. For more information on Eridu see the previous note in this chapter.

29 Cotton Genesis: Orek (ⲟⲣⲉⲭ)

- Septuagint manuscript 707: Orak (Οραχ)
- Septuagint manuscript 75: Ṭoubek (Θουϐϰχ)
- Septuagint manuscript 129: Oreki (Οϐϰυ)
- Septuagint manuscript 426: Ōred (ωϐϰⲁ)
- Septuagint manuscript 82: Ōrek (ωϐϰχ)
- Septuagint manuscript 458: Ṭobel (Θουϐλ)
- Septuagint manuscript 527: Ōrk (ωϐχ)
- Septuagint manuscript 376: Erek (Εϐϰχ)
- Leningrad Codex: 'Erek (אֶרֶךְ)
- Peshitta: Årk (ܐܪܟ)
- Targum Onkelos: 'Erek (אֶרֶךְ)
- Targum Jerusalem: Hădās (הֲדָס)
- Targum Pseudo-Jonathan: Hădās (הֲדָס)
- Sahidic manuscript 2212: Orek (ⲟⲣⲉⲭ)

This name is generally accepted as referring to the ancient Sumerian city of Unug (𒀉), using the Old Akkadian name of Uruk (𒌷𒀕).

30 Codex Alexandrinus: Arkad (ⲁⲣⲭⲁⲇ)

- Cotton Genesis: Akad (ⲁⲭⲁⲇ)
- Septuagint manuscript 76: Arka (ⲁϐⲭⲁ).
- Septuagint manuscript 761: Akaṯ (ⲁⲭⲁⲑ)
- Septuagint manuscript 31: Arkaṯ (ⲁϐⲭⲁⲑ)
- Septuagint manuscript 376: Arkamas (ⲁϐⲕⲁⲙⲁⲥ)
- Leningrad Codex: 'Akkad (אַכַּד)

CHAPTER 10

- Peshitta: Åkd (ܐܟܕ)
- Targum Onkelos: 'Akkad (אַכַּד)
- Targum Jerusalem: Nəsîbîn (נְצִיבִין)
- Targum Pseudo-Jonathan: Nəsîbîn (נְצִיבִין)
- Sahidic manuscript 2212: Arǩad (ⲀⲢⲬⲀⲀ)

Akkad[ki] (𒀀𒂵𒀉) was the capital of the Akkadian Empire which ruled Mesopotamia for a few centuries before the rise of the Neo-Sumerian Empire.

31 Codex Alexandrinus: Ǩalannē (ΧΑΛΑΝΝΗ)
- Septuagint manuscript 509: Galanni (ΓΑΛΑΝΝΙ)
- Septuagint manuscript 55: Ǩallanē (ΧΑΛΛΑΝΗ)
- Septuagint manuscript 135: Ǩalannei (ΧΑΛΑΝΝΔ)
- Septuagint manuscript 707: Ǩalnan (ΧΑΛΝΑΝ)
- Septuagint manuscript 319: Ǩalanēn (ΧΑΛΑΝΗΝ)
- Septuagint manuscript 58: Galannē (ΓΑΛΑΝΝΗ)
- Septuagint manuscript 78: Ǩalanē (ΧΑΛΑΝΗ)
- Septuagint manuscript 527: Ǩalanē (ΧΑΛΑΝΗ)
- Septuagint manuscript 376: Ǩalan (ΧΑΛΑΝ)
- Leningrad Codex: Kalnê (כַלְנֵה)
- Peshitta: Klyå (ܟܠܝܐ)
- Targum Onkelos: Kalnê (כַלְנֵה)
- Targum Jerusalem: Qitîsəpôn (קְטִיסְפוֹן). Translation: Ctesiphon
- Targum Pseudo-Jonathan: Qitîsəpôn (קְטִיסְפוֹן). Translation: Ctesiphon
- Sahidic manuscript 2212: Ǩalannē (ⲬⲀⲗⲀⲚⲚⲎ)

The location of Kalnê has been debated for thousands of years. The name is not known among the cities of Sumer, and therefore many, mostly anachronistic locations have been suggested. The 4th century CE Christian scholars Eusebius of Caesarea and of Stridon both identified Kalnê as Ctesiphon, near modern Baghdad, however

176

Ctesiphon wasn't founded until the 120s BCE, which was not only after the genealogy of nations was added to Cosmic Genesis, but after both the Greek and Hebrew translations had been made. In the Talmud (Yoma 10a) Kalnê is identified as being Nûpar Nînəpî (נוּפַּר נִינְפִי), which has been interpreted by some as a reference to the ancient Sumerian city of Nippur^ki (𒉌𒂗𒆠).

The word is accepted by some Christian groups as being a corruption of the Hebrew word kūllānû (כֻּלָּנוּ), meaning "everything," meaning the sentence would have once read "The beginning of his kingdom was Eridu, Uruk, Akkad, and everything in the land of Sumer." Unfortunately, the "Hebrew corruption" is also in the Greek translation, which was made from an Aramaic text. The equivalent term in Aramaic was klnå (ܢܠܟ), which is not the word found in the Masoretic text, and the word that was transliterated as Kalnê appears to be based on kalnêh (כַלְנֵה), not klnå (ܢܠܟ) or kūllānû (כֻּלָּנוּ). If the word in the Aramaic text was the same word retained in the Masoretic text, then it was almost certainly a transliteration of kalûma (𒆗𒈠), also meaning "everything."

Kalûma (𒆗𒈠), was the phonetic spelling of Kish (𒆧), one oldest and most famous ancient Sumerian cities. Kish is the Sumerian pronunciation of the city's name, however, it would have been pronounced as Kalûma in later Semitic cultures, therefore the more common Sumerian-derived English name of Kish is used.

32 Codex Alexandrinus: Sennaar (ϲєννααρ)
- Septuagint manuscript 120: Ennaar (Ɛννλαρ)
- Septuagint manuscript 121: Senaar (Σϲνλαρ)
- Septuagint manuscript 129: Seinnaar (Σⲇⲛⲛλαρ)
- Septuagint manuscript 75: Sernnaar (Σⴆⲛⲛλαρ)
- Septuagint manuscript 343: Senar (Σϲναρ)
- Septuagint manuscript 376: Naar (Nλαρ)

- Septuagint manuscript 53: Seenar (Σϵ́ϵναρ)
- Septuagint manuscript 527: Senaan (Σανϵ́αϵν)
- Leningrad Codex: Šin'ār (שִׁנְעָר)
- Peshitta: Snôr (ܣܢܥܪ)
- Targum Onkelos: Bābel (בָּבֶל)
- Sahidic manuscript 2212: Senaar (ⲤⲈⲚⲀⲀⲢ)
- Bohairic manuscripts: Senaar (ⲤⲈⲚⲀⲀⲢ)

33 Codex Alexandrinus: Assour (ⲀⲤⲤⲞⲨⲢ)

- Septuagint manuscript 17: Nassour (Νασσουϵ́)
- Septuagint manuscript 127: Asour (Ασουϵ́)
- Septuagint manuscript 400: Naassour (Νααϵσσουϵ́)
- Leningrad Codex: Aššûr (אַשּׁוּר). Translation: Assyria, Ashur
- Peshitta: Åtwryå (ܐܬܘܪܝܐ). Translation: Assyrians
- Targum Onkelos: 'Ătûrā'â (אֲתוּרָאָה). Translation: Assyrians
- Targum Jerusalem: 'Ătôrayāy' (אֲתוֹרְיָיא)
- Targum Pseudo-Jonathan: 'Attûr (אַתּוּר). Translation: Assyria
- Sahidic manuscript 2212: Assour (ⲀⲤⲤⲞⲨⲢ)
- Old Armenian manuscripts: Asowr (Ասուր). Translation: Ashur

Aššur (𒀭𒊹) was the national god of Assyria, normally anglicized as Ashur, while Aššur^{ki} (𒌷𒀸𒋩) was the original capital city of Assyria, normally anglicized as Assur. Unfortunately, both of these names were spelled the same in Aramaic, and other less complicated scripts, resulting this verse being rendered differently in Hebrew versus Greek. The Greek states that Ashur came from Sumer, and built the Assyrian cities, while the Hebrew does not specify who did it, implying it was the "Nimrod" of the previous verse who went to Assur and built the cities of Assyria. However, later in the chapter Ashur is identified as being a Semite, not a Khuzite, which seems to confirm the Greek reading, that the

CHAPTER 10

Semite Assur had been living in the Khuzite cities before traveling north and founding Assyria.

Assyrian historical records do not record the city of Assur being founded by someone called Ashur, instead recording that the ancestors of the Assyrians original lived in tents, and later settled in a Hurrian city called Baltil, which later became Assur after the Assyrians became dominant. Therefore, if the genealogy of nations was originally written by an Assyrian, it was probably not a genealogy that claimed all people sprang from one small family, but a list of nations that had colonized the world in ancient times, which the Aramaic author simplified for some reason.

34 Cotton Genesis: Ǩalaǩ (ⲭⲗⲗⲗⲭ)
- Septuagint manuscript 509: Ǩalek (ⲭⲗⲗϭⲩ)
- Septuagint manuscript 75: Malaǩ (ⲙⲗⲗⲗⲭ)
- Septuagint manuscript 313: Ǩalam (ⲭⲗⲗⲗⲙ)
- Septuagint manuscript 615: Ǩalan (ⲭⲗⲗⲗⲱ)
- Septuagint manuscript 82: Ǩalak (ⲭⲗⲗⲗⲩ)
- Septuagint manuscript 54: Ǩaleǩ (ⲭⲗⲗϭⲭ)
- Septuagint manuscript 72: Ǩallak (ⲭⲗⲗⲗⲗⲩ)
- Septuagint manuscript 59: Ǩalaak (ⲭⲗⲗⲗⲗⲩ)
- Septuagint manuscript 44: Ǩalaǩaǩ (ⲭⲗⲗⲗⲭⲗⲭ)
- Leningrad Codex: Kālaḥ (כֶּ֖לַח)
- Peshitta: Klǩ (ܟܠܟ)
- Targum Onkelos: Kālaḥ (כָּלַח)
- Targum Jerusalem: Ḥaryayt (חַרְיַית)
- Targum Pseudo-Jonathan: Ḥaryayt (חַרְיַית)
- Sahidic manuscript 2212: Kalaǩ (ⲕⲗⲗⲁⲭ)
- Bohairic manuscripts: Ǩalaḥ (ⲭⲗⲗⲁϭ)

The name is generally normalized as Kalhu in modern English, and is accepted as the city which once stood where the ruins of

179

Nimrud lay today. The name Nimrud (النمرود / ܢܡܪܘܕ), was commonly applied to the ruins during the early late Classical era by Syriac Christians, based on the story of "Nimrod" building a great city somewhere in the region, and was later adopted by the Muslims. The ruins continue to be known by both names in most languages.

The following scribal note about Kalhu being the great city, is generally accepted as a reference to it being the capital of the Assyrian Empire, which places the origin of the scribal note between circa 864 BCE and 706 BCE. In approximately 864 BCE, King Ashurbanipal II inaugurated Kalhu as the new capital of the Neo-Assyrian Empire, after approximately 15 years of rebuilding the large but dilapidated ancient city. It was the first time the capital of the Assyrians was moved from Assur in recorded history.

The capital was later moved to Dur Sharrukin by Sargon II in approximately 706 BCE. Many biblical scholars accept this era as being when the genealogy of the nations was added to Cosmic Genesis, as the tribes listed are all recognizable from the era of the Neo-Assyrian Empire, including the Medes, Lydians, and Greeks, at the edge of the known world.

35 Codex Alexandrinus: Loudiim (ΛΟΥΔΙΙΜ)
- Septuagint manuscript 407: Loudieim (Λουδιдμ)
- Septuagint manuscript 15: Doudieim (Δουδιдμ)
- Septuagint manuscript 135: Loulieim (Λουλιдμ)
- Septuagint manuscript 707: Loidieim (ΛΘΔιдμ)
- Septuagint manuscript 319: Aoudieim (Λουδιдμ)
- Septuagint manuscript 426: Ouléd (Ουλλλ)
- Septuagint manuscript 343: Loudiēm (Λουдιλμ)
- Septuagint manuscript 82: Doulieim (Δουλιдμ)
- Septuagint manuscript 376: Loudiōm (Λουдι∞μ)
- Leningrad Codex: Lûdîm (לוּדִים). Translation: Lydians

- Peshitta: Lwdym (ܠܘܕܝܡ). Translation: Lydians
- Targum Onkelos: Lûdā'ê (לוּדָאֵי)
- Targum Jerusalem: Maryôtā'ê (מַרְיוֹטָאֵי)
- Targum Pseudo-Jonathan: Gîwawtā'ê (גִּיוַוטָאֵי)
- Sahidic manuscript 2212: Loutēim (ⲖⲞⲨⲦⲎⲒⲘ)

The Hebrew term certainly means "Lydians," however, the Greeks appear to have not been sure about the translation, as they did not translated the well known name as Ludikos (Λυδικος). Lydia was an ancient kingdom in western Anatolia which became wealthy and powerful during the early iron age. It is plausible that the Assyrians viewed the Lydians as being an Egyptian colony, as both they had originally used a hieroglyphic script, like most ancient Anatolian cultures. There is no evidence that Egypt ever exerted any political control over Lydia, however, there certainly would have been a great deal of trade between the cultures.

Due to the improbability of Egypt colonizing western Anatolia, it is often suggested that this was a transcription error of "Libyans" (לובים), which could have easily happened in either Aramaic, by reading a B (ﬧ) as a D (ﬣ), or in Phoenician, by reading a B (𐤁) as a D (𐤃). However, the scribe added a note later in the sentence stating that the Pelesets came from the region of the Kaslōniim / Kasluchim, which seems to confirm that the scribe interpreted this location as being in Anatolia.

Additionally, the Caphtorites / Kaftorim are generally accepted as being either the Minoans or an Anatolian people, and they are mentioned in the same list of Egyptian colonies. Like the Lydians, the Minoans originally used a hieroglyphic script, suggesting that the Assyrians viewed all the hieroglyphic writing civilizations as coming from Egypt.

36 Codex Alexandrinus: Ainemetieim (ⲀⲒⲚⲈⲘⲈⲦⲒⲈⲒⲘ)
- Septuagint manuscript 407: Enemetieim (Ενϭμϭ]ᴧϥμ)

- Septuagint manuscript 509: Enemetiein (Ⲉⲛⳓⲙⳓⲕⲇⲛ)
- Septuagint manuscript 15: Nemetieim (Ⲛⳓⲙⳓⲕⲇⲙ)
- Septuagint manuscript 17: Enemitieim (Ⲉⲛⳓⲙⲕⲇⲙ)
- Septuagint manuscript 55: Enaimitieim (Ⲉⲛⲁⲩⲙⲕⲇⲙ)
- Septuagint manuscript 135: Enematieim (Ⲉⲛⳓⲙⲁⲕⲇⲙ)
- Septuagint manuscript 318: Enaimitiein (Ⲉⲛⲁⲩⲙⲕⲇⲛ)
- Septuagint manuscript 392: Ainemitieim (Ⲁⲓⲛⳓⲙⲕⲇⲙ)
- Septuagint manuscript 319: Enilieim (Ⲉⲛⲓⲗⲓⲇⲙ)
- Septuagint manuscript 16: Nematieim (Ⲛⳓⲙⲁⲕⲇⲙ)
- Septuagint manuscript 120: Ainemitiein (Ⲁⲓⲛⳓⲙⲕⲇⲛ)
- Septuagint manuscript 343: Enemētieim (Ⲉⲛⳓⲙⲗⲕⲇⲙ)
- Septuagint manuscript 426: Senemieim (Ⲥⲁⲛⳓⲙⲇⲙ)
- Septuagint manuscript 56: Enetieim (Ⲉⲛⳓⲕⲇⲙ)
- Septuagint manuscript 79: Enaimatieim (Ⲉⲛⲁⲩⲙⲁⲕⲇⲙ)
- Septuagint manuscript 82: Enimieim (Ⲉⲛⲓⲙⲇⲙ)
- Septuagint manuscript 799: Anepitiēm (Ⲁⲛⳓⲡⲓⲕⲗⲙ)
- Septuagint manuscript 46: Enaimetieim (Ⲉⲛⲁⲩⲙⳓⲕⲇⲙ)
- Septuagint manuscript 108: Aineiamieim (Ⲁⲓⲛⲇⲁⲙⲇⲙ)
- Septuagint manuscript 376: Enestisō (Ⲉⲛⳓⲥⲓⲱ)
- Leningrad Codex: 'Ănāmîm (עֲנָמִים)
- Peshitta: Yŏbym (ܝܚܒܡ)
- Targum Onkelos: 'Ănāmā'ê (עֲנָמָאֵי)
- Targum Jerusalem: Pantəpôlîtā'ê (פְּנְטְפּוֹלִיטָאֵי)
- Targum Pseudo-Jonathan: Martiyôtā'ê (מְרְטִיוֹטָאֵי)
- Sahidic manuscript 2212: Enemitiem (Ⲉⲛⲉⲙⲓⲧⲓⲉⲓⲙ)
- Bohairic manuscripts: Midiim (ⲙⲓⲇⲓⲓⲩ)

This appears to be a reference to Upper Egyptians using a Semitic plural of the Egyptian name ǩn mnw (𓈖𓏌𓏤𓏤𓐍), later known as Ǩemmis (Χέμμις) in Greek, Ǩmim (Ϩⲙⲓⲙ) in Akhmimic Coptic, Šmim (Ϣⲙⲓⲛ) in Bohairic Coptic, and Akhmim (أخميم) in Arabic. Akhmim was a major city in Upper Egypt, and the source of the Akhmimic dialect of ancient Egyptian. Upper Egypt was the region

182

north of Aswan, and south of Memphis, which had once been the heartland of Egypt, however, in the era the genealogy of nations was added to Cosmic Genesis, was viewed as being one of Egypt's children, which is mirrored in mirrored in the Greek records from the era, which claimed that Egyptian civilization began in Æthiopia (Kush), and colonized Upper and Lower Egypt.

37 Codex Alexandrinus: Labiim (ⲗⲁⲃⲓⲓⲙ)
- Septuagint manuscript 407: Labieim (ⲗⲁⲩⲓϥⲙ)
- Septuagint manuscript 17: Labiem (ⲗⲁⲩⲓϭϥ)
- Septuagint manuscript 392: Abieim (ⲁⲩⲓϥⲙ)
- Septuagint manuscript 18: Labiein (ⲗⲁⲩⲓϥⲛ)
- Septuagint manuscript 343: Elabieim (Ⲉⲗⲁⲩⲓϥⲙ)
- Septuagint manuscript 56: Neftalieim (Ⲛϭϧⲑⲗⲓϥⲙ)
- Septuagint manuscript 82: Lamiein (ⲗⲁⲙϥⲛ)
- Septuagint manuscript 54: Dabieim (ⲁⲩⲓϥⲙ)
- Septuagint manuscript 799: Labiēm (ⲗⲁⲩⲓⲗⲙ)
- Septuagint manuscript 107: Damieim (ⲁ ⲁⲙϥⲙ)
- Septuagint manuscript 664: Neftaleim (Ⲛϭϧⲑⲗϥⲙ)
- Septuagint manuscript 31: Labeim (ⲗⲁⲩϥⲙ)
- Leningrad Codex: Ləhābîm (לְהָבִים)
- Peshitta: Lhbym (ܠܗܒܝܡ)
- Targum Onkelos: Ləhābā'ê (לְהָבָאֵי)
- Targum Jerusalem: Lôsətā'ay (לוֹסְטָאֵי)
- Targum Pseudo-Jonathan: Lîwawqā'ê (לִיוַוקָאֵי)
- Sahidic manuscript 2212: Baleeim (Ⲃⲁⲗⲉⲉⲓⲙ)

This is generally accepted as a reference to Libyans, via the Egyptian word Libu (𓃭𓃀𓈎𓅱). The term had been used in Egypt for hundreds of years by the time the genealogy of nations was added to the text, however, it is not clear how it would have been spelled in Assyrian or early Aramaic.

CHAPTER 10

In the Classical era, the Neo-Aramaic Syriac spelling of Libya was Lwbå (ܠܘܒܐ), however, this would have been influenced by Greek. In the Neo-Assyrian era, the Egyptian term referred to the Libyan (Berber) peoples of North Africa west of the Nile. This included Put, which was mentioned separately earlier, suggesting that only the inland Libyans of the oases were being referred to.

It is equally possible that more distant Libyans were being referred to, as Libyans (Berber) tribes were reported living right across North Africa, from Sudan to Morocco.

38 Codex Alexandrinus: Neftaliim (Νεφθαλιιμ)

- Cotton Genesis: Neftadieim (Νεφθαδιειμ)
- Septuagint manuscript 509: Neftaleim (Νεφθαλdμ)
- Septuagint manuscript 56: Labieim (Λαβιdμ)
- Septuagint manuscript 15: Neftabieim (Νεφθαβιdμ)
- Septuagint manuscript 318: Naiftabieim (Ναιφθαβιdμ)
- Septuagint manuscript 707: Natalieim (Ναθαλιdμ)
- Septuagint manuscript 58: Nefabieim (Νεφαβιdμ)
- Septuagint manuscript 129: Neftalēm (Νεφθαλλημ)
- Septuagint manuscript 134: Neftalim (Νεφθαλιμ)
- Septuagint manuscript 75: Meftabieim (Μεφθαβιdμ)
- Septuagint manuscript 458: Meftabieim (Μεφθαριdμ)
- Septuagint manuscript 53: Ladibieim (Λαδιβιdμ)
- Septuagint manuscript 54: Neftamieim (Νεφθαμιdμ)
- Septuagint manuscript 72: Neutalieim (Νευθαλιdμ)
- Septuagint manuscript 376: Neftalseim (Νεφθαλσdμ)
- Septuagint manuscript 664: Ladieimbieim (Λαδιdμμιdμ)
- Leningrad Codex: Naptuhîm (נַפְתֻּחִים)
- Peshitta: Yptwǩym (ܢܦܬܘܟܝܡ)
- Targum Onkelos: Naptûhā'ê (נַפְתּוּחָאֵי)
- Targum Pseudo-Jonathan: Pantaskînā'ê (פַּנְטַסְכִּינָאֵי)

184

- Sahidic manuscript 2212: Baleeim (Ⲃⲁⲗⲉⲉⲓⲙ)
- Bohairic manuscripts: Saftabiim (Ⲥⲁⲫⲑⲁⲃⲓⲓⲩ)

The Hebrew name appears to be a reference to Lower Egyptians, using the name Nefertem (𓄤𓏏𓐠, transliteration: nfr tm, or nfl tm in the Fayyumic dialect). Nefertem was a god mainly worshiped in Memphis, and believed to be the son of Ptah, the god the city was named after. During the era when Kush ruled Egypt, Memphis was the northern capital of the Kingdom of Kush, while Napata in modern Sudan, was the southern capital. The Memphitic dialect of Egyptian dominated Lower Egypt, ultimately giving rise to the Bohairic dialect of Coptic. It appears that the author of the genealogy of nations, or an Assyrian predecessor, interpreted Nefertem as the founding patriarch of Memphis, however, there is no evidence the Egyptians viewed him that way.

39 Berlin Genesis: Patrosonniei (ⲡⲁⲧⲣⲟⲥⲟⲛⲛⲓⲉⲓ)
- Septuagint manuscript 961: Patrosonieim (ⲡⲁⲧⲣⲟⲥⲟⲛⲓⲉⲓⲙ)
- Codex Alexandrinus: Patrosōniim (ⲡⲁⲧⲣⲟⲥⲱⲛⲓⲉⲓⲙ)
- Septuagint manuscript 509: Patrosonoeim (ⲡⲁⲧⲣⲟⲥⲟⲑⲟⲟ̄ⲓⲙ)
- Septuagint manuscript 17: Patrossonieim (ⲡⲁⲧⲣⲟⲥⲥⲟ̄ⲓⲙ)
- Septuagint manuscript 707: Patrosoneim (ⲡⲁⲧⲣⲟⲥⲟ̄ⲙ)
- Septuagint manuscript 730: Patronōsieim (ⲡⲁⲧⲣⲟ̄ⲟⲟⲥⲓⲙ)
- Septuagint manuscript 58: Prosonieim (ⲡⲣⲟⲥⲟ̄ⲓⲙ)
- Septuagint manuscript 128: Paprosson (ⲡⲁⲡⲣⲟⲥⲟ̄)
- Septuagint manuscript 129: Patrosōnoeim (ⲡⲁⲧⲣⲟ Ⲟⲩⲛⲟⲙ)
- Septuagint manuscript 313: Patrossonim (ⲡⲁⲧⲣⲟⲥⲟ̄ⲓⲙ)
- Septuagint manuscript 458: Patrōsōnieim (ⲡⲁⲧⲣⲱ Ⲟⲩⲛⲓⲙ)
- Septuagint manuscript 799: Patrosōniēm (ⲡⲁⲧⲣⲟ Ⲟⲩⲛⲓⲗⲩⲙ)
- Septuagint manuscript 53: Patrosōeim (ⲡⲁⲧⲣⲟ Ⲟⲩⲙ)
- Septuagint manuscript 46: Patrōsōniim (ⲡⲁⲧⲣⲱ Ⲟⲩⲛⲓⲓⲙ)
- Septuagint manuscript 54: Patrosthōnieim (ⲡⲁⲧⲣⲟⲑⲟⲟⲛⲓⲙ)
- Septuagint manuscript 74: Patrosōniim (ⲡⲁⲧⲣⲟ Ⲟⲩⲛⲓⲓⲙ)

CHAPTER 10

- Septuagint manuscript 376: Pathrouseim (ⲡⲁⲑⲣ ⲟⲩ ϥμ)
- Septuagint manuscript 664: Patronoeim (ⲡⲁⲧⲣⲫⲟϥμ)
- Leningrad Codex: Patrusîm (פַּתְרֻסִים)
- Peshitta: Ptrwsym (ܦܬܪܘܣܝܡ)
- Targum Onkelos: Patrûsā'ê (פַּתְרוּסָאֵי)
- Targum Jerusalem: Pîlôsā'ê (פִּילוֹסָאֵי)
- Targum Pseudo-Jonathan: Nasyôtā'ê (נְסִיוֹטָאֵי)
- Sahidic manuscript 2212: Patrosōnieim (Ⲡⲁⲧⲣⲟⲥⲱⲛⲓⲉⲓⲙ)
- Bohairic manuscripts: Patrosomiim (Ⲡⲁⲧⲣⲟⲥⲟⲙⲓⲓⲙ)

This is term referred to the people of southernmost Egypt, which the Assyrians called Patúrisi (𒉺𒌅𒊑𒋛) in the Annals of Esarhaddon. The name was adopted from the Demotic Egyptian name På-tårsy (𓊖/𓇌𓂋𓇥), meaning "southern land." This region was northern Nubia during the Old Kingdom era, and although colonized by Egyptians appears to have remained mainly Nubian until the recent past. The Persians and Greeks both referred to the region as variations of "Nubia" or "Kush." The modern English equivalent to Ptrsym (פתרסים) would be Aswani, as the region is administered by the Aswan governate, however, the term Nubia appears to be more historically accurate.

40 Codex Alexandrinus: Ǩasmōn (ⲭⲁⲥⲙⲱⲛ)
- Septuagint manuscript 407: Ǩaslōnieim (ⲭⲁⲥⲗⲟⲟⲛⲓϥμ)
- Septuagint manuscript 509: Ǩaloeim (ⲭⲁⲗⲟϥμ)
- Septuagint manuscript 135: Ǩaslon (ⲭⲁⲥⲟⲃⲛ)
- Septuagint manuscript 318: Ǩalōniem (ⲭⲁⲗⲟⲟⲛⲓϭμ)
- Septuagint manuscript 17: Ǩasdon (ⲭⲁⲥⲁⲫ)
- Septuagint manuscript 346: Ǩasaon (ⲭⲁⳊⲁⲫ)
- Septuagint manuscript 128: Ǩalōrieim (ⲭⲁⲗⲟⲟⲃⲓϥμ)
- Septuagint manuscript 56: Ǩalon (ⲭⲁⲃⲛ)
- Septuagint manuscript 79: Ǩaslorieim (ⲭⲁⲥⲟⲃⲃⲓϥμ)

- Septuagint manuscript 82: Ǩallōn (ҳᴧᴧⲱⲟ𝑁)
- Septuagint manuscript 130: Ǩalōn (ҳᴧᴧⲟⲟ𝑁)
- Septuagint manuscript 46: Ǩalōniim (ҳᴧᴧⲟⲟ𝑁ιιμ)
- Septuagint manuscript 74: Ǩaslōniim (ҳᴧσᴧⲟⲟ𝑁ιιμ)
- Septuagint manuscript 54: Ǩailōn (ҳⲁ/ᴧⲟⲟ𝑁)
- Septuagint manuscript 72: Kanieim (Ҝⲇⲡιɖμ)
- Septuagint manuscript 376: Ǩaslōm (ҳᴧσᴧⲟⲟμ)
- Septuagint manuscript 799: Ǩasloniēm (ҳᴧσ/ⲃ𝑁ιℓμ)
- Septuagint manuscript 106: Ǩelon (ҳℓℊ⊕)
- Septuagint manuscript 664: Ǩalonoeim (ҳᴧ/ⲃ𝑁oɖμ)
- Septuagint manuscript 31: Ǩasmon (ҳᴧσμ⊕)
- Leningrad Codex: Kasluhîm (בְּסְלֻחִים)
- Peshitta: Kslwǩym (ܟܣܠܘܟܝܡ)
- Targum Onkelos: Patrûsā'ê (פְּתְרוּסָאֵי)
- Targum Jerusalem: Pənatsaknā'ê (פְּנַטְסַכְנָאֵי)
- Targum Pseudo-Jonathan: Pantəpôlôtā'ê (פְּנְטְפוֹלוֹטָאֵי)
- Sahidic manuscript 2212: Ǩaslōnieim (Ⲭⲁⲥⲗⲱⲛⲓⲉⲓⲙ)

This location is widely debated as there are no known references to the land earlier than the Greco-Roman era mention of a land of Kasluǩet on the Temple of Kom Ombo in Aswan, and that dates to a century after *Cosmic Genesis* was translated into Greek. In Josephus' 1st century CE Jewish Antiquities, he mentioned that the Haslōniim were an ancient Nubian people who were destroyed during Thutmose II's wars in Kush, circa 1500 BCE.

However, this would be a reference to the destruction of Kerma, the first Kushite capital. If so, the Kasluhîm were the Kushites themselves. This view appears to have been repeated in the Bereshít Rabbah a few of centuries later, which referred to Kasluchim as Pekusim (פְּקוּסִים), which would be a transliteration of the Demotic Egyptian på-Kåsh (𐤃𐤕𐤉), meaning "land of Kush," in the Hebrew plural form, and therefore the "land of the Kushites." The probable origin of the word "Kasluhîm" was the Assyrian ᵏᵘʳKasi āliūtum (𒆳𒂊𒇷𒌓 𒄠𒄭𒈨), meaning "land of Kush's citizens," a reference to the ethnic Kushites, as opposed to the rest of the Egyptians.

While this may have been what the earlier Assyrian author of the genealogy of nations was referring to, this interpretation is impossible if the "father" "Egypt / Mitzrayim" is interpreted as Kush, which the Aramaic author has clearly done. The scribal note added, which claims the Pelesets originated in this land, means it was clearly not identified as Kush by the Aramaic author. The Pelesets were a Mediterranean or Anatolian people and not an African people, based on both the Egyptian records of their invasion, and the archaeological evidence. In this case, the author appears to have confused the term with the similar name ᵏᵘʳKaskatum (𒆳𒁔𒂊𒇷𒈨), commonly translated into English as Kaskians.

The Kaskians lived in Anatolia north of the Lydians, in the region where the Palaa (𒉿𒆷𒀀) had lived before migrating away at the end of the bronze age. It is believed that the Kaskians may have pushed the Palaa out of their homeland, however, another interpretation is that they simply migrated into the region after the Palaa abandoned it. In any event, the scribal note indicating the homeland of the Pelesets indicates that the Aramaic author believed the reference was to the Kaskians. Nevertheless, the Kaskians were an Indo-European people who would have been included with the decedents of Gomer, and cannot be interpreted as being an Egyptian colony by any interpretation of the term, therefore, the term is interpreted via the Assyrian meaning in this translation.

41 Codex Alexandrinus: Fulistieim (ϕΥΛΙϹΤΙΕΙΜ)
• Septuagint manuscript 392: Fulēstieim (Φυλησιdμ)
• Septuagint manuscript 72: Filistieim (Φιλισιdμ)

CHAPTER 10

- Septuagint manuscript 376: Filisṯēeim (Φιλιϑῃδμ)
- Septuagint manuscript 799: Filistiēm (Φιλιϛιῃμ)
- Leningrad Codex: Pəlištîm (פְּרִשְׁתִּים). Translation: Philistines (or Palestinians, Pelesets)
  - Peshitta: Plštyå (ܦܠܫܬܝܐ)
  - Targum Onkelos: Pəlištā'ê (פְּלִשְׁתָּאֵי)
  - Targum Jerusalem: Pəlîšətā'ê (פְּלִישְׁתָּאֵי)
  - Targum Pseudo-Jonathan: Pəlîšətā'ê (פְּלִישְׁתָּאֵי)
- Sahidic manuscript 2212: Fulēstieim (ϥⲩⲗⲏⲥⲧⲓⲉⲓⲙ)

The Pelesets were an ancient people based in the region of the modern Gaza Strip of the Palestinian Territories. The earliest surviving mention of them is from the reliefs of the Temple of Ramses III at Medinet Habu in Egypt that dates back to some time between 1186 and 1155 BCE, in which they were called Pwlåsåti (𓊪𓏌𓊪𓈗𓏏𓇌). They were also known in Middle Babylonian as the ᵏᵘʳPalastu (𒆳𒉺𒆷𒀸𒌓). It is unclear where they came from, however, one theory is that they were the Pala, a Luwian people from the Black Sea coast of Anatolia.

The region was an independent country called Palaa (𒉺𒆷𒀀) in the Neshite (Hittite) records from the 1600s BCE, however, have become part of the Neshites Empire by the 1500s BCE. Around the time the Pelesets invaded Canaan, the Pala were driven from their homeland by the neighboring Kaskians from northeast Anatolia, which supports the connection between the groups, however, it has yet to be proven conclusively.

The presence of the Pelesets in Southern Canaan during the time of Abraham and Isaac is anachronistic, and therefore this section of text, describing the origin of the Semitic tribes, found in both the Septuagint and the Masoretic text, likely dates to the original Phoenician translation in the early Iron Age.

CHAPTER 10

42 Berlin Genesis: Kaftōr (ⲕⲁⲫⲟⲱⲣ)

- Septuagint manuscript 961: Kaftorieim (ⲕⲁⲫⲟⲟⲣⲓⲉⲓⲙ)
- Codex Alexandrinus: Kaft (ⲭⲁⲫⲟ)
- Septuagint manuscript 318: Kaftoriein (ⲭⲁ𝄢ⲑⲟⲣⲓⲇⲛ)
- Septuagint manuscript 56: Kaftar (ⲕⲁ𝄢ⲑⲁⲣ)
- Septuagint manuscript 134: Kaftoriim (ⲕⲁ𝄢ⲑⲟⲣⲓⲓⲙ)
- Septuagint manuscript 370: Kauft (ⲕⲁⲩ𝄢ⲑ)
- Septuagint manuscript 799: Kaftoriēm (ⲕⲁ𝄢ⲑⲟⲣⲓⲗⲙ)
- Septuagint manuscript 458: Kalaftonieim (ⲭⲁⲗⲁ𝄢ⲑⲟ℗ⲓⲇⲙ)
- Septuagint manuscript 376: Kamftōreim (ⲕⲁⲙ𝄢ⲑⲟⲟⲣⲇⲙ)
- Septuagint manuscript 107: Kamftōr (ⲕⲁⲙ𝄢ⲑⲟⲟⲣ)
- Septuagint manuscript 56: Kaftar (ⲭⲁ𝄢ⲑⲁⲣ)
- Septuagint manuscript 31: Gaft (ⲅⲁ𝄢ⲑ)
- Septuagint manuscript 44: Kamfōr (ⲕⲁⲙ𝄢ⲟⲟⲣ)
- Leningrad Codex: Kaptōrîm (כַּפְתֹּרִים). Translation: Caphtorites
- Peshitta: Qpwdqyå (ܩܦܘܕܩܝܐ). Translation: Cappadocians
- Targum Onkelos: Qappûtəqā'ê (קַפּוּטְקָאֵי). Translation: Cappadocians
- Targum Jerusalem: Qappûtəqā'ê (קַפּוּטְקָאֵי). Translation: Cappadocians
- Targum Pseudo-Jonathan: Qappûdəqā'ê (קַפּוּדְקָאֵי). Translation: Cappadocians
- Sahidic manuscript 2212: Kaftorieim (Ⲕⲁⲫⲟⲟⲣⲓⲉⲓⲙ)

Caphtor was mentioned in several surviving ancient texts from the 2nd millennium BCE, including the Mari Tablets, dated to circa 1770 BCE, Thutmose III's *Hymn of Victory*, from circa 1450 BCE, and the *Ras Sharma Texts* from Ugarit, dated to circa 1340 BCE. Cosmic Genesis refers to Caphtor as a son of Mizraim (Egypt), which implies a colony of Egypt, while the Ras Sharma Texts uses the name Caphtor as the name of the home of the Canaanite god Kothar-wa-Khasis, which is believed to be the Canaanite version of the Egyptian god Ptah.

CHAPTER 10

The location of Caphtor was already long lost and debated by the time the Septuagint was translated at the Library of Alexandria, which supports the antiquity of *Cosmic Genesis.* At the time, Greek translators believed it was in Cappadocia, which was the translation used in the Septuagint's *Deuteronomy.* Cappadocia was in central modern Turkey, however, the Egyptian records that mention Kftyw (⊇🖎⅏), list it as being a port city, and Cappadocia was an inland nation. This identification of Caphtor with Cappadocia is based on its location in Thutmose III's biography, from circa 1450 BCE, which placed Caphtor as Thutmose's northernmost conquest, and his Empire had conquered all of Canaan, and extended to the border of Cappadocia. Jewish scholars have traditionally rejected Cappadocia as the location of Caphtor. In the 1st century CE, the Jewish historian and general Josephus wrote in his Antiquities of the Jews, that the Caphtorites were an Egyptian people whose city was destroyed in a war with the Æthopians (Kushites) and migrated to Philistia (the modern Gaza Strip).

Other Jewish sources, such as Maimonides, in the 12th century CE, have placed Caphtor in the Nile Delta. Early Christians accepted the Greek identification of Caphtor as Cappadocia, and Cappadocia was the translation of Caphtor that Jerome chose for the Vulgate in the 4th century. Modern scholars have debated the issue, with many locations suggested, including Cicilia (southern Turkey), Cyprus, Crete, or some other island in the Aegean Sea. Currently, the academic view is that either Cicilia or Crete are the most likely locations of Caphtor, however, the archaeological evidence from Crete shows that some major force burnt almost every town in Crete during the life of Thutmose III, which his biography claims he did to Caphtor, and therefore, the terms Crete and Minoan are used in this translation.

CHAPTER 10

43 Berlin Genesis: Ǩetein (ⲭⲉⲧⲉⲓⲛ)
- Septuagint manuscript 961: Ǩettieim (ⲭⲉⲧⲧⲓⲉⲓⲙ)
- Septuagint manuscript 407: Ǩettaion (ⲭⲟⲧⲧⲁⲓⲱ)
- Septuagint manuscript 18: Ǩaitt (ⲭⲁⲓⲧ)
- Septuagint manuscript 129: Ǩettaiōn (ⲭⲟⲧⲧⲁⲓⲱⲛ)
- Septuagint manuscript 458: Gett (ⲅⲟⲧ)
- Septuagint manuscript 550: Ǩetaion (ⲭⲟⲧⲁⲓⲱ)
- Leningrad Codex: Hēt (חֵת). Translation: Cyprus
- Peshitta: Ǩytyå (ܟܬܝܐ). Translation: Cypriots
- Targum Onkelos: Hēt (חֵת). Translation: Cyprus
- Targum Pseudo-Jonathan: Hēt (חֵת). Translation: Cyprus
- Sahidic manuscript 2212: Ǩettaios (ⲭⲉⲧⲧⲁⲓⲟⲥ)

This term has created a great deal of confusion since the misidentification of the ruins of the Neshites as being "Hittite" in the 1800s. The modern archaeological name "Hittite," is not derived from an ancient name for the culture applied by themselves, or anyone else, but rather adopted from the biblical reference to a then-unknown civilization somewhere in the region. There was an ancient culture in the region called the Hattians, however, they were conquered by the Nesites before 1700 BCE, and subsequently disappeared from the historic records.

The name was applied to culture today referred to as "Hittites," before the "Hittite" language had been translated, and is incorrect. Since 1906, excavations at Boğazköy, the ancient "Hittite" capital Hattusa have uncovered more than 10,000 "Hittite" texts, including the royal achieve. The actual name of the "Hittite" language and people was Nešili (𒉌𒅖𒇷), which is now rendered in some academic literate as Nesite or Neshite. As early as the mid-1800s some scholars disputed the identification of the Nesites as the Biblical Hittites, including the Orientalist Max Müller, who was one of many claiming the Biblical Hittites were ancient Greeks or some other Mediterranean people.

CHAPTER 10

Later in the Septuagint's translation of the Maccabees, the similar term Kettiim (Χεττιιμ) as a reference to all Greek-speaking lands, and therefore the Biblical Hittites were likely the Minoans or the Achaean Greeks. In the 1st century CE, the Jewish historian Josephus reported that Kethima was the name of Cyprus in Aramaic, and the Kettim were the descendants of Noah's grandson Kethimus, who had settled on Cyprus. Josephus reported that the name was preserved in the Greek name of the town Kítion (Κίτιον). Most historians view it as more likely that the Aramaic name was derived from the city-state of Kítion, which was known as Kâtjây (𓈎𓏏𓇌𓈉) in Egyptian records from the New Kingdom Era in the late Bronze Age, and Kt (𐤊𐤕) or Kty (𐤊𐤕𐤉) in Phoenician records from the early Iron Age. While this may be the origin of the term, by the era of the Neo-Assyrian era, the term must have also referred to other Greek islands, as both the prophets Isaiah and Ezekiel used the term "Islands of Kittim." As the term referred to people from Cyprus in Aramaic, the translations of "Cypriots" is used.

44 Septuagint manuscript 407: Euaion (ΕΥΑΙΟΝ)
- Septuagint manuscript 318: Neuaion (Νⴇⲩⲁⲓⲱ)
- Septuagint manuscript 107: Ebaion (Εⲩⲁⲓⲱ)
- Leningrad Codex: Hiwwî (חִוִּי)
- Peshitta: Ǩwylå (ܚܘܝܠܐ)
- Targum Onkelos: Ḥăwîlâ (חֲוִילָה)
- Targum Jerusalem: Tərîppôlā'ê (טְרִיפּוֹלָאֵי)
- Targum Pseudo-Jonathan: Hiwā'ê (חִוָּאֵי)
- Sahidic manuscript 2212: Euhaios (Εⲩ̅ⲁⲓⲟⲥ)

The Hebrew term Hiwwî (חִוִּי) is used interchangeably with the term Hōrî (חֹרִי) throughout the Israelite texts. Hōrî is accepted as referring to the Hurrians, which the Egyptians called Ǩårw

(𓐍𓄿𓂋𓏤𓏭𓀀), and the Babylonians called Ǩuurri (𒆪𒌋𒌨𒊑). The Hurrians were one of the oldest cultures in the Middle East, however, became largely a slave culture within the Akkadian and Old Babylonian empires. Under the Mitanni empire, they rose to a position of wealth, and formed the noble caste. The Greek transliteration of this term was Ǩorr̥aious (Χορραιους), which, like the Hebrew term, was used interchangeably in the texts with Euaion (Ευαιον) / Ḥiwwî (חִוִּי), although that term generally applied to the rules and priests.

The ultimate origin of the terms Euaion (Ευαιον) and Ḥiwwî (חִוִּי), both appear to be the cuneiform word Éan (𒂍𒀭), meaning temple or sacred. In the Amarna Letters, which date to the 1330s BCE, the term Éan (𒂍𒀭) was the name of a people, who appear to be the Mitanni, or a group within the Mitanni. A similar correlation between the terms is found in the Septuagint's 1st Paralipomenon and Masoretic *Divrei-hay Yamim*, where the Greek translation uses Baiṯani (Βαιθανι), however, the Hebrew uses the term Mitnî (מִתְנִי). This term also refers to a group of people, meaning the underlying Edomite text the Greeks translated would have been "people of the House of Ån (𐤁𐤉𐤕𐤀𐤍), a direct Canaanite translation of É Ān (𒂍𒀭).

While Mitnî was the transliteration used in the Edomite text that formed the basis of the Hebrew translation of Divrei-hayYamim, it was replaced with Ḥiwwî (חִוִּי) in the Judahite texts, which served as the basis of most of the Masoretic texts. This likely originated in a Judahite copy of the text, after the Aramaic translation had been made, where an N (𐡍) was replaced with a W (𐡅). The Aramaic translation would have already been made in the time of King Manasseh, were the term was transliterated as Hyån (𐡇𐡉𐡀𐡍), itself a transliteration of the early Canaanite Hyån (𐤇𐤉𐤀𐤍).

The term Ebaion (Εβαιον), which is found as a substitute for Euaion (Ευαιον) in some copies of the Septuagint for term, must

CHAPTER 10

have originated in an intentional alteration to the text, as there are no similar letters for B (ב / ﬞ / 𐤁) and Y (י / � / 𐤉) in the Semitic alphabets the text was previously in. This probable origin was an Ebionite translation in the 1st century CE. The Ebionites were an early Judeo-Christian sect based in Judea before the First Jewish-Roman war. Many fled east to Mesopotamia with the Mandeans and other smaller Judahite religious groups, while others fled south into Arabia. The Arabian Ebionites are generally viewed as shaping the Islamic view of the prophet Jesus (عِيسَى).

45 Septuagint manuscript 407: Eber (Ɛυϭϸ)
- Septuagint manuscript 509: Ebor (Ɛυoϸ)
- Septuagint manuscript 707: Eben (Ɛυϭɴ)
- Leningrad Codex: 'Ēber (עֵבֶר)
- Targum Onkelos: 'Ēber (עֵבֶר)
- Targum Pseudo-Jonathan: 'Îbərā'ê (עִיבְרָאֵי). Translation: Hebrews

Given the connection to both Shem and Elam, the original name was likely a cuneiform spelling of Iabarati (𒊭𒀀𒋡𒁉), the mythical ancestor of the Shimashki dynasty of Elam. It isn't clear when he lived; however, it was likely during the Gutian period of circa 2154 to 2119 BCE. The same name was later spelled as Ebarti (𒀹𒋡𒁉) during the reign of Ebarat I, and Ebarada (𒀹𒋡𒁕) during the reign of Ebarat II. All three of these names were spelled as Ebarada (𒁹𒁕𒇷𒁕) in Akkadian Cuneiform. As the final sound TI (𒁉) or later DA (𒁕 / 𒁕) was an honorific meaning "father," the actual name was Iabara, Ebar, or Ebara. Ebarat I was a latter peer of the Neo-Sumerian king Shulgi, during the Shimashki dynasty of Elam. Ebarat II was the founder of the Sukkalmah dynasty of Elam, which defeated the Neo-Sumerians near the beginning of the 2nd millennium BCE, in alliance with the Amorites.

The older name, beginning with IA ($\forall\Diamond$) indicates that the Elamite royal family was worshiping the Akkadian god Ia during the Gutian era. The transition of the spelling of the name to E ($\maltese$) indicates that the Elamites were generally synchronized with the Neo-Sumerian religious reforms, as E (𒂊) was the word meaning "canal," while IA (�𒄿) was the god of "sacred water."

46 Septuagint manuscript 833: Alam (ᴀλᴀμ)
- Septuagint manuscript 407: Ailam (ᴀιλᴀμ)
- Septuagint manuscript 509: Ailad (ᴀιλᴀᴅ)
- Septuagint manuscript 15: Elam (ℇλᴀμ)
- Septuagint manuscript 128: Eleim (ℇλɖμ)
- Septuagint manuscript 82: Iaelam (ιɑ/λᴀμ)
- Septuagint manuscript 130: Mailam (Mɑ/λᴀμ)
- Septuagint manuscript 551: Ailēm (ᴀιλʮμ)
- Septuagint manuscript 59: Kelam (ĸℓɟᴀμ)
- Leningrad Codex: 'Êlām (עֵילָ֔ם). Translation: Elam
- Peshitta: Åylm (ܥܝܠܡ)
- Targum Onkelos: 'Êlām (עֵילָם)
- Targum Pseudo-Jonathan: 'Êlām (עֵילָם)
- Bohairic manuscripts: Elam (Ⲉⲗⲁⲙ)
- Old Armenian manuscripts: Ḥewatsin (Խուզաղու). Translation: Khuzestan

Elam being listed as a Semitic nation is strange, as the Elamite language was not a Semitic language. This suggests that the author was not classifying them as Semitic based on their spoken language, but their written script, which was a derivative of Akkadian cuneiform. There were several scripts used in Elam, and Akkadian cuneiform was adopted sometime before 2500 BCE. It was simplified to Elamite cuneiform in the 1st millennium BCE, parallel to the development of Neo-Assyrian and Neo-Babylonian cuneiform. Akkadian cuneiform was used in parallel to Linear

196

CHAPTER 10

Elamite before the development of Elamite cuneiform. Linear Elamite may have developed from Proto-Elamite, which was in use around the same time that Proto-Sumerian was used in Iraq. The Elamites being listed as a Semitic nation also confirms that the author was not referring to them as the Khuzites, who founded the cities of Sumer, even though in later centuries their descendants became known as Khuze.

47 Codex Alexandrinus: Kainan (ΚΑΙΝΑΝ)
- Septuagint manuscript 135: Kainam (Καῐναμ)
- Septuagint manuscript 72: Kaiēl (Καιηλ)
- Ge'ez manuscripts: Ça'änamə (ቃአናም)

The Cainan are not mentioned in this verse of Bereshít, but are mentioned a couple of verses later, where they also appear in Cosmic Genesis. They are later mentioned in both versions of Exodus / Names, and Moses married his daughter to one of them. Joshua was also reported to have allowed them to leave the cities that the Israelites were besieging before killing everyone else in the city, suggesting they were viewed as important in the era right after the exodus.

The Hebrew word qênî (קֵינִי) translates as "blacksmiths" and was likely an alternate to the term 'ănāq (עֲנָק), which was almost certainly a transliteration of the Amorite name ānak (𒀭𒉺𒂖), meaning "tin." The Amorite word ānakum (𒀭𒉺𒂖𒈥) translates as "metalworkers," suggesting that qyny (𐤒𐤉𐤍𐤉) was the early Iron Age translation of ānakum (𒀭𒉺𒂖𒈥), while ānak (𒀭𒉺𒂖) was transliterated directly as ånq (𐤏𐤍𐤒).

The Anakites were a tribe of people also referred to in the books of *Deuteronomy*, *Joshua*, and *Judges*. According to the *Book of Judges*, they lived in Hebron. Egyptian execration texts from the Middle Kingdom Era record a group of Canaanites in the region called the Ånq (𓂝𓈖𓈎) who are generally considered to be the same people. This term was also adopted by the Mycenaean Greeks as wakana (𐀷𐀙𐀏), meaning "lord." In the Iron Age, this evolved into the Dorian Greek wanax (ϝαναξ), meaning "king," and later into the Koine Greek anax (αναξ), meaning "lord." The Greek digamma (ϝ) was used in the early Iron Age for words adopted from Semitic languages to represent the W (ו / 𐤅) vowel, but later dropped from Greek in favor of the ō (ω) or o (o), which were natural vowels in Greek. The Semitic word was also adopted into Cypriot as wanakse (𐠷𐠙𐠊𐠭) and Old Phrygian as vanaktei (φανακτει), both meaning "lord."

Anax (Αναξ) was also the name of the legendary king of Anaktoria (Ανακτορια), a Bronze Age kingdom in southeast Anatolia. While the archaeological evidence of the civilization exists, the only surviving records are via Greek interpretations of Minoan stories of the culture. Wanax was likely the title of the leader, and not his name, and Anakt oria (Ανακτ ορια) simply translates as "Anax's boundaries."

The land of Anaktoria was later conquered by the legendary Minoan warrior Miletus, who renamed the city of Anaktoria to Miletus (Μίλητος). This may simply be a Greek legend about the Minoanization of the region in the Middle Bronze Age, as there was also a plant in the region called Miletus. In the late Bronze Age, the region was known as Mirati (𐀖𐀨�) in Greek, and Millawanda (𒈫𒆷𒉿𒀭𒁕) in Neshite. The archaeological evidence supports the culture going through a rapid Minoanization starting around 1900 BCE, so the legend of a Minoan conquering the region may be accurate. The older "Wanaxian" culture appears in the archaeological record only a century earlier, around 2000 BCE, and appears to have been an Amorite colony.

It is unclear why Cainan would have been removed from the Hebrew translation; however, it appears that at one point they were generally redacted from the Israelite texts, as while initially being important, virtually no mention of them survives in the texts. This redaction found in the Masoretic text suggests they were still being redacted as late as the time of King Josiah, circa 625 BCE, who would have probably been responsible for the original translation of the genealogy of nations into Judahite when he published his authorized version of the Torah.

48 Like the previous mention of Kainan (ᴋᴀɪɴᴀɴ), this one is missing from the genealogy of Noah.

CHAPTER 11

In all the land was one language, and there was one language for all. It happened as they moved from the east, they found a plain in the land of Sumer, and they lived there. A man said to his neighbor, "Come, let us make bricks and bake them with fire."

The brick was for them like stone, and their mortar was bitumen. They said, "Come, let us build for ourselves a city and tower, whose top will be in the sky, and let us make a name for ourselves before we are scattered across the face of all the land."

The Lord came down to see the city and the tower, which the sons of men built. The Lord said, "Look, there are one people, and one language for all, and they have begun to do this. Now nothing will stop them, in anything that they may have decided to do. Come, let's go down and confuse their language, that they may not understand each one the voice of his neighbor."

The Lord scattered them from there over the face of all the land, and they stopped building the city and the tower. (On this account, its name was called Confusion,[1] because the Lord confused the languages of all the land there, and the Lord scattered them on the surface of all the land from there.)

These are the generations of Shem: and Shem was a hundred years old when he fathered Arphaxad, the second year after the flood. Shem lived, after he had fathered Arphaxad, five hundred years, and fathered sons and daughters, and died. Arphaxad lived a hundred and thirty-five years and fathered Cainan. Arphaxad lived after he had fathered Cainan, four hundred years, and fathered sons and daughters, and died.

Cainan lived a hundred and thirty years and fathered Salah, and Cainan lived after he had fathered Salah, three hundred and thirty years, and fathered sons and daughters, and died. Salah lived a hundred and thirty years and fathered Eber. Salah lived after he had fathered Eber, three hundred and thirty years, and fathered sons and daughters, and died.

Eber lived a hundred and thirty-four years and fathered Peleg. Eber lived after he had fathered Peleg two hundred and seventy years, and fathered sons and daughters, and died.

Peleg lived a hundred and thirty years and fathered Reu. Peleg lived after he had fathered Reu, two hundred and nine years, and fathered sons and daughters, and died.

And Reu lived a hundred and thirty-two years and fathered Serug. And Reu lived after he had fathered Serug, two hundred and seven years, and fathered sons and daughters, and died.

Serug lived a hundred and thirty years and fathered Nahor. Serug lived after he had fathered Nahor, two hundred years, and fathered sons and daughters, and died.

Nahor lived a hundred and seventy-nine years and fathered Terah. Nahor lived after he had fathered Terah, a hundred and twenty-five years, and fathered sons and daughters, and he died. And Terah lived seventy years and fathered Abram, Nahor, and Harran. These are the generations of Terah.

Terah fathered Abram, Nahor, and Harran. Harran fathered Lot. Harran died in the presence of Terah his father, in the land in which he was born, in the country of the Chaldeans. Abram and Nahor took for themselves wives, and the name of the wife of Abram was Sarai, and the name of the wife of Nahor, Milcah, daughter of Harran, and he was the father of Milcah, the father of Iscah. Sarai was barren and did not bear children. And Terah took Abram his son, and Lot the son Harran, the son of his son, and Sarai his daughter-in-law, the wife of Abram his son, and led them out of the land of the Chaldeans, to go into the land of Canaan, and they came as far as Harran, and he lived there. All the days of Terah in the land of Harran were two hundred and five years, and Terah died in Harran.

CHAPTER 11 NOTES

1 Codex Alexandrinus: sunḱusis (ⲥⲨⲅⲭⲨⲥⲓⲥ). Translation: revolt (or confounding, disturbing, overthrow)
- Leningrad Codex: Bābel (בָּבֶל). Translation: Babylon
- Peshitta: Bbl (ܒܒܠ). Translation: Babylon (or Babylonia)
- Targum Onkelos: Bābel (בָּבֶל). Translation: Babylon (or Babylonia)
- Sahidic manuscript 2037: jōōre (ⲭⲱⲱⲣⲉ). Translation: disperse (or strong, powerful)

CHAPTER 11

- Old Armenian manuscripts: bawił (բաւիղ). Translation: labyrinth

- Ge'ez manuscripts: Babilonə (ባቢሎን)

As this could not have been the later city of Babylon, which was not in Sumer, it must be assumed this is another reference to Eridu, which was also spelled as Nun[ki] (𒉣𒆠) in Akkadian cuneiform. For more information on Eridu see the note in chapter 10. The in the text for the explanation of the name of "Babylon" does not make sense, as the name translates as "gateway of god" in Semitic languages. It suggests that the explanation of the meaning of the name was already in the cuneiform text that the genealogy of nations was translated from, and interpreted the city of Nun[ki] as the "first place" (𒉣𒆠). The tower in question was probably Amar-Sin's unfinished ziggurat, from circa 2000 BCE.

When he began building the ziggurat, Ur controlled most of the world they knew of, including most of modern Iraq, and Syria, and a large section of Iran. After Amar-Sin's early death, work on the ziggurat appears to been halted while his heir Shu-Sin dealt with a rebellion in Syria. After his death just seven years into his reign, possibly fighting in southern Canaan, Ur's power was weakened, and his heir Ibbi-Sin fought a long series of revolts among the Amorites and Elamtes, before finally being conquered by Elam.

As a result, work never resumed on Ziggurat of Amar-Sin. The building of the ziggurat would have been controversial at the time, as it was built on top of an ancient temple complex dedicated to Enki / Ia. The 18 ancient temples appear to have remained in use even after most of Eridu was abandoned, suggesting that one of the reasons the ziggurat was not completed after Amar-Sin's death was due to local outrage in Eridu, which Shu-Sin didn't also want to rebel, like the Amorites in Syria.

CHAPTER 11

2 Codex Alexandrinus: Ṭara (ӨⲀⲢⲀ)
- LXX 961: Ṭarra (ӨⲀⲢⲢⲀ)
- LXX 319: Ṭaran (ӨⲀβⲀⲛ)
- Leningrad Codex: Teraḥ (תֶּרַח)
- Targum Onkelos: Teraḥ (תֶּרַח)
- Targum Pseudo-Jonathan: Teraḥ (תֶּרַח)
- Sahidic manuscript 2069: Ṭara (ӨⲀⲢⲀ)
- Bohairic manuscripts: Ṭarra (ӨⲀⲢⲢⲀ)

3 LXX 911: Abran (ⲀⲃⲢⲀⲛ)
- Codex Alexandrinus: Abram (ⲀⲃⲢⲀⲙ)
- LXX 135: Abraam (ⲀⲩβⲀⲁⲙ)
- LXX 319: Nakŏr (ⲛⲀχ∞β)
- LXX 343: Autam (Ⲁⲩⲧⲁⲙ)
- Leningrad Codex: 'Abrām (אַבְרָם)
- Targum Onkelos: 'Abrām (אַבְרָם)
- Targum Pseudo-Jonathan: 'Abrām (אַבְרָם)
- Sahidic manuscript 2037: Abram (ⲀⲃⲢⲀⲙ)

This name is recorded in Elbaite Cuneiform as Ibrium (𒉈𒂍𒈾𒈨) from the 3rd millennium on wards.

4 LXX 961: Arṛon (ⲀⲢⲢⲀⲛ)
- Codex Alexandrinus: Nakŏr (ⲛⲀⲭⲱⲢ)
- LXX 707: Akŏr (Ⲁχ∞β)
- Leningrad Codex: Nāḥôr (נָחֹור)
- Targum Onkelos: Nāḥôr (נָחֹור)
- Targum Pseudo-Jonathan: Nāḥôr (נָחֹור)
- Sahidic manuscript 2037: Akŏr (ⲀⲭⲱⲢ)
- Ge'ez manuscripts: Arəran (�አርⳄ)

CHAPTER 11

This name likely originated in the Elamite name Našur (!◈θ / ◈-𝕎), which was one of the names used among the descendants of Iabarati.

5 Codex Alexandrinus: Arran (ⲀⲢⲢⲀⲚ)

• LXX 246: Aran (Ⲁⲣⲁⲛ)

• LXX 18: Arram (Ⲁⲣⲣⲁⲙ)

• LXX 72: Aram (Ⲁⲣⲁⲙ)

• LXX 130: Arran kai Arran egénnēse ton Lōt (Ⲁⲣⲣⲁⲛ ⲕⲁⲓ Ⲁⲣⲣⲁⲛ ⲉ̄ⲅⲁⲛⲛⲗⲟⲥ̄ⲧⲟⲛ ⲗⲟⲟⲧ). Translation: Arran and Arran fathered the Lot

• LXX 799: Sarran (Σⲁⲣⲣⲁⲛ)

• Leningrad Codex: Hārān (הָרָן)

• Targum Onkelos: Hārān (הָרָן)

• Targum Pseudo-Jonathan: Hārān (הָרָן)

• Sahidic manuscript 2037: Arran (ⲁⲣⲣⲁⲛ)

This name likely originated in the Elamite name Hutran (⊗!◈⊗), which was one of the names used among the descendants of Iabarati.

CHAPTER 12

The Lord said to Abram, "Go out of your land and away from your families, and out of the house of your father, and come into the land which I will show you. I will make you a great nation, and I will bless you and magnify your name, and you will be blessed. I will bless those that bless you, and curse those that curse you, and in you will all the tribes of the land be blessed."

Abram went as the Lord told him, and Lot departed with him, and Abram was seventy-five years old when he went out of Harran. Abram took Sarai his wife, and Lot the son of his brother, and all their possessions, as many as they had got, and every mind which they had gotten in Harran, and they left to go to the land of Canaan. Abram traversed the land lengthwise as far as the place Shechem,[1] to the high oak, and the Canaanites then inhabited the land.

The Lord appeared to Abram and said to him, "I will give this land to your descendants."

Abram built an altar there to the Lord who appeared to him. He departed there to the mountain east of the House of El,[2] and there he pitched his tent with the Temple of El to the west and the government office[3] to the east, and there he built an altar to the Lord, and called on the name of the Lord. Abram departed and went and camped in the wilderness.

CHAPTER 12

There was a famine in the land, and Abram went down to Egypt to stay there because the famine prevailed in the land. It happened when Abram drew near to enter into Egypt, Abram said to Sarai his wife, "I know that you are a beautiful woman. It will come to pass then that when the Egyptians will see you, they will say, "This is his wife," and they will kill me, and they will keep you alive. Say, therefore, "I am his sister," that it may be well with me on account of you, and my mind will live because of you."

It happened when Abram entered into Egypt, the Egyptians saw his wife, that she was very beautiful, and when the officials of Pharaoh[4] saw her they praised her to Pharaoh and brought her into the house of Pharaoh. They treated Abram well on her account, and he had sheep, calves, donkeys, menservants, women-servants, mules, and camels. God afflicted Pharaoh with great and severe afflictions, and also his house, because of Sarai, Abram's wife. Pharaoh having called Abram, said, "What is this you have done to me, that you did not tell me that she was your wife? Why did you say, 'She is my sister?' and I took her as a wife for myself? Now, look! Your wife is before you, take her and go quickly away."

Pharaoh gave orders to men concerning Abram, to join in sending him away, and his wife, and all that he had, and also Lot with him.

CHAPTER 12

CHAPTER 12 NOTES

1 Codex Alexandrinus: Sŭkem (ⲤⲨⲬⲈⲘ)

- Septuagint manuscript 343: Sunkem (Σωχόμ)

- Septuagint manuscript 31: Sēkem (Σ𝚑χόμ)

- Leningrad Codex: Šəkem (שְׁכֶם)

- Peshitta: Škym (ܫܟܡ)

- Targum Onkelos: Šəkem (שְׁכֶם)

- Sahidic manuscript 2148: Sekēm (ⲤⲈⲬⲎⲘ)

Shechem was an ancient city at the foot of Mount Gerizim, on the outskirts of modern Nablus in the northern Palestinian West Bank. It was mentioned in the Elba Tablets from the 3rd millennium BCE, and continuously inhabited until 67 CE when it was destroyed during the First Jewish-Roman War.

2 Codex Alexandrinus: Baitēl (ⲂⲀⲒⲐⲎⲖ)

- Septuagint manuscript 343: Betēl (Βϵθ𝚑λ)

- Septuagint manuscript 130: Kaitēl (Κα/θ𝚑λ)

- Leningrad Codex: bêt-ēl (בֵּית־אֵל). Translation: house (or temple) of El (or god)

- Peshitta: byt åyl (ܒܝܬ ܐܝܠ). Translation: house (or temple) of El (or god)

- Targum Onkelos: bêt-ēl (בֵּית־אֵל). Translation: house (or temple) of El (or god)

- Targum Pseudo-Jonathan: bêt ēl (בֵּית אֵל). Translation: house (or temple) of El (or god)

- Sahidic manuscript 2148: Baitēl (ⲂⲀⲒⲐⲎⲖ)

The term Bethel meant several things in ancient Canaan. The term translates as "house of god," which can be translated as either

CHAPTER 12

"Temple of God (or El)" or "sky." Bethel was worshiped as a god by the ancient Canaanites, the brother of El and Dagon according to Sanchuniathon, who referred to him as Baitylos, which is the name used in this translation when the god is denoted. The term can also be translated as "meteorite" as meteorites were believed to be parts of the god Baitylos that had fallen to the Earth, and shrines were built around them.

According to the Book of Judges, the town of Bethel was known as Louza (Λουζα) / Lûz (לוּז) until the Late Bronze Age, when the Israelites settled in Canaan. According to *Cosmic Genesis* / *Bereshít* chapter 35, Abraham's grandson Jacob renamed Louza / Lûz to Bet El after having a dream in a field. This indicates that the name in this section of text was updated at some point in the Iron Age, likely when the text was standardized in the era of King Joash of Judah, between 836 and 796 BCE. There is a Samaritan village of Luza (قرية لوزة) located at the foot of Mount Gerizim, which suggests that Abraham's altar was on Mount Gerizim.

3 Codex Alexandrinus: Aŋgai (ⲁⲅⲅⲁⲓ)
- Septuagint manuscript 75: Aŋge (ⲁⲅⲅⲉ)
- Leningrad Codex: hā'ay (הָעַי)
- Peshitta: åy (ܐܝ)
- Targum Onkelos: 'ay (עַי)
- Targum Jerusalem: 'ay (עַי)
- Sahidic manuscript 2148: Akgai (ⲁⲕⲅⲁⲓ)
- Bohairic manuscripts: Agge (ⲁⲅⲅⲉ)

The Greek translators also transliterated this name as Gai (Γαι) in some of the later books of the Septuagint. The Hebrew term is often translated as "ruins" however, the place is inhabited during the era of Joshua, indicating "ruins" is an incorrect interpretation. If the

210

original book of Abraham was in Egyptian, the term used would have been kå (𓂓𓂝𓃀), the Egyptian word for "government office." As Sarai was later married to the King of Egypt, she would have needed to have been the daughter of a high-priest, and Abram's building an altar to his god between the Temple of El and the Egyptian government office would explain how he made contact with the Egyptian government. Marrying the daughters of the high priests was seen as a way for the king to legitimize his "godhood" by marrying into the families that represented the gods on Earth.

The practice of the king marrying the daughter(s) of the high priest(s) of the god(s) was later adopted by the kings of Israel, and continued until the Babylonian captivity. Several locations in Canaan were referred to as Gai, suggesting several regional administrative offices were active in Canaan at the time. If the Egyptians were already in control of Canaan at the time, it indicates that Abram traveled through Canaan while the Middle Kingdom still ruled the region, which is consistent with the later timeline of Jacob and Joseph settling in Egypt as the Middle Kingdom collapsed, and Moses leading the exodus 400 years later at the end of the Second Intermediate Period.

4 Codex Alexandrinus: arkontes faraō (ΑΡΧΟΝΤΕC ΦΑΡΑѠ). Translation: archons (or rulers) of pharaoh

- Leningrad Codex: śārê par'ōh (שָׂרֵי פַרְעֹה). Translation: officials (or princes, captains) of pharaoh

- Targum Onkelos: rabrəbê par'ōh (רַבְרְבֵי פַּרְעֹה). Translation: great masters (or great teachers) of pharaoh

- Targum Pseudo-Jonathan: rabrəbê par'ōh (רַבְרְבֵי פַּרְעֹה). Translation: great masters (or great teachers) of pharaoh

CHAPTER 12

• Sahidic manuscript 2037: arkōn mfaraō (ⲁⲣⲭⲱⲛ ⲙ̄ⲫⲁⲣⲁⲱ). Translation: ruler the pharaoh

The title "Pharaoh" (𓉐) was not in use in the era the text is set in, however, it was the word for "palace," at the time. It became a title for the king during the New Kingdom era, around 1550 BCE, and was the normal title of the king of Egypt by the era the Phoenician script version of *Cosmic Genesis* / *Bereshít* was composed in the early Iron Age. It is unclear if this was a translation of ḥqȧ (𓋾𓈎𓀁), meaning king, or a reference to the nobles in the palace, however, the verse now reads that she was then taken to the palace, suggesting that this was a reference to the officials working for the king.

The correlation of King Shulgi of Ur (c. 2094 BCE–2046 BCE) and King Khodollag / Kədārəlā'ōmer in chapter 14, suggests that this Egyptian king was Mentuhotep II (c. 2060–2009 BCE). Mentuhotep II was responsible for reunifying Egypt after the First Intermediate Period (Dark Age) and reestablishing Egyptian control over southern Egypt.

CHAPTER 13

Abram went up out of Egypt, he and his wife, and all that he had, and Lot with him, into the wilderness. Abram was very rich in livestock, and silver, and gold. He went back to the place from where he had come from, into the wilderness as far as the House of El, as far as the place where his tent was before, between the Temple of El and the government office, to the place of the altar, where he had pitched his tent, and Abram there called on the name of the Lord. Lot, who went out with Abram had sheep, and livestock, and tents. The land was not large enough for them to live together, because their possessions were great, and the land was not large enough for them to live together.

There was a struggle between the herders of Abram's livestock, and the herders of Lot's livestock, and the Canaanites and the Perizzites who then inhabited the land. Abram said to Lot, "Let there not be strife between me and you, and between my herders and your herders, for we are men. Look! Is not the whole land before you? Separate yourself from me. If you go to the left, I will go to the right, and if you go to the right, I will go to the left."

Lot, having lifted his eyes saw all the country around the Jordan, that it was all watered, (before God overthrew Sodom and Gomorrah), like the paradise of the Lord, and like the land of Egypt until you come to Zoar. Lot chose for himself all the country around Jordan, and Lot went to the east, and they were separated each from his brother. Abram lived in the land of Canaan. Lot lived in a city of the neighboring people and pitched his tent in Sodom. But the men of Sodom were evil, and exceedingly sinful before God. God said to Abram after Lot was separated from him, "Look up with your eyes, and Look from the place where you now are, northward and southward, and eastward and seaward, for all the land which you see, I will give it to you and your descendants forever. I will make your descendants like the sand of the land, if anyone could count the dust of the land, then your descendants will be counted. Arise and traverse the land, both in the length of it and in the breadth, for to you will I give it, and to your descendants forever."

Abram having lived at a distance, came and lived by the oak of Mamre, which was in Hebron, and he there built an altar to the Lord.[1]

CHAPTER 13 NOTES

1 Berlin Genesis: kuriō (ΚΥΡΙѠ). Translation: lord

• Septuagint manuscript 551: Kuriō tō Ṭeō (Κυβ̂ѳоо τоо Ѳ6оо). Translation: Lord the God

• Dead Sea Scroll 4QGen[b]: Yhwh (𐤉𐤄𐤅𐤉)

• Leningrad Codex: Yhōwâ (יְהֹוָה)

• Peshitta: mryå (ܡܪܝܐ). Translation: master (or lord)

• Targum Onkelos: Yəyā (??). Translation: Yahweh

• Targum Pseudo-Jonathan: Yəyā (??). Translation: Yahweh

• Sahidic manuscript 2037: joeis (ϫoєιc). Translation: master

CHAPTER 14

It happened in the kingdom of the Amorite shepherds,[1] the king of Sumer and Uruk,[2] Amar son of Shulgi,[3] King of Elam and Thargal,[4] and King of the Guti,[5] went to war with Barak, king of Sodom,[6] and with Barsa, King of Gomorrah,[7] and King Sennaar of Adama,[8] and King Shemaeber of Bet Rabim,[9] and King Balac of Shasziru.[10] All these agreed with one consent at the salt valley, (this is now the sea of salt). Twelve years they served Shulgi, and for thirteenth years[11] they revolted.

In the fourteenth year, Shulgi's representative returned, and the kings with him, and cut to pieces the Raphites in Astaroth Karnaim, and Shaszi[12] with them, and the Gomorrahns[13] in the city of Shaveh, and the Hurrians[14] in the mountains of Seir, to the turpentine tree of Paran which is in the desert. Having turned back they came to the well of judgment (this is Kadesh), and they cut in pieces all the princes[15] of rebelling Amorites,[16] and the Amorites dwelling in Hazezon-Tamar. The king of Sodom went out, and the king of Gomorrah, and the king of Adama, and the king of Bet Rabim, and the king of Shasziru, and they organized themselves into a formation against them, to battle in the Salt Valley, against Shulgi's representative, the King of Elam and Thargal, King of the Guti and the Amorite shepherds, King of Sumer and Uruk, King of the four lands,[17] against the five.

Now the Salt Valley consists of slime-pits, and the king of Sodom fled, and the king of Gomorrah, and they fell there,

215

CHAPTER 14

and those who were left, fled to the mountain country. They took all the cavalry of Sodom and Gomorrah, and all their provisions, and departed. They also took Lot the son of Abram's brother, and his property, and departed, as he lived in Sodom. One of those who had been rescued came and told Abram, then in the courthouse,[18] who governed for Elon the lord of the Amorites,[19] the brother of Eschol, and the brother of Onan, who were allied with Abram. Abram having heard that Lot his nephew had been taken captive, organized his three hundred and eighteen home-born slaves, and chased after them to Dan. He came on them in the night, he and his slaves, and he attacked them and chased them as far as Hobah, which is on the left of Damascus. He captured all the cavalry of Sodom, and he captured Lot his nephew, and all his possessions, and the women and the people. The king of Sodom went out to meet him after he returned from the slaughter of Shulgi's representative, and the kings with him, to the valley of Shaveh, (this was the plain of the kings).

King Melchizedek of Salem[20] brought out loaves and wine, as he was the priest of the Highest God.[21] He blessed Abram, and said, "Blessed, be Abram, by the Highest God, who made Shamayim and Eretz, and blessed is the Highest God who delivered your enemies into your hand." Abram gave him a tenth of everything.

The king of Sodom said to Abram, "Give me the men, and take the cavalry for yourself."

Abram said to the king of Sodom, "I will stretch out my hand to the Lord, the Highest God, who made Shamayim and

Eretz, that I will not take from all your goods, from a string to a shoe-lace, in case you should say, "I have made Abram rich." Except for the things the young men have eaten, and the portion for the men that went with me from Eschol, Onan, and Mamre. These will take a portion."

CHAPTER 14 NOTES

1 Berlin Genesis: -marabel (-ΜΑΡΑΒΕΛ). The papyrus is damaged at the beginning of the name, however, it is believed to have read "Amarabel."

- Septuagint manuscript 961: Amarfad (ΑΜΑΡΦΑΔ)
- Septuagint manuscript 64: Amarfal (Αμαρ$αλ)
- Septuagint manuscript 135: Armafaa (Αρμα$αλ)
- Septuagint manuscript 25: Armafal (Αρμα$αλ)
- Septuagint manuscript 120: Marfal (Μαρ$αλ)
- Septuagint manuscript 128: Marfar (Μαρ$αρ)
- Septuagint manuscript 426: Iamorfad (Ιαμορ$αλ)
- Septuagint manuscript 413: Amalfar (Αμαλ$αρ)
- Septuagint manuscript 799: Amardad (Αμαρδαλ)
- Septuagint manuscript 59: Armafan (Αρμα$αν)
- Leningrad Codex: 'Amrāpel (אַמְרָפֶל)
- Peshitta: Åmrpyl (ܐܡܪܦܝܠ)
- Targum Onkelos: 'Amrāpel (אַמְרָפֶל)
- Targum Jerusalem: 'Amrāpel (אַמְרָפֶל)
- Targum Pseudo-Jonathan: 'Amrāpel (אַמְרָפֶל)
- Sahidic manuscript 2020: Amarfal (ⲀⲘⲀⲢⲪⲀⲖ)
- Sahidic manuscript 2037: Amarfar (ⲀⲘⲀⲢⲪⲀⲢ)

- Bohairic manuscripts: Marfar (Uⲁⲣⲫⲁⲣ)

This term is generally read as the name of a king, however, later in the chapter is treated as the name of a kingdom. If the term originated in Old Akkadian, it would have been Amurru palu (𒈥𒌑 𒂍𒂖), meaning "Amorite shepherds." Amurru was generally viewed as the western-most region of Mesopotamian civilization, and one of the four regions of the Akkadian and Neo-Sumerian empires along with Elam in the east, Subartu (Assyria) in the north, and Akkad-Sumer in the south.

The king of this empire at the time, was almost certainly Amar-Sin of Ur, who is the only king of Sumer in the general era that fits the story. Amar-Sin was the king of Ur circa 2000 BCE, with different Assyriologists giving a range of dates between 2046 and 1973 BCE for his 9 year long reign. During his era, Ur established an empire across most of modern Iraq and Syria, as well as across southern and western Iran. His empire included Uruk and other ancient Sumerian and Akkadian cities, as well as the Assyrian city of Assur, although the exact extent is not clear. One of the subject peoples of his empire was the Guti of the Zagros mountains, whom many scholars believe are the Goyim listed among his subject nations. Another subject nation was Elam, which is also listed.

According to the scant surviving records of his campaigns, he defeated the Marhashi in southern modern Iran, as well as the Lullubi and Hamazi in west-central Iran, Irabel in northern Iraq, and suppressed a rebellion in Assur, appointing the Akkadian Zariqum as governor. Among his many conquests is a list of five cities that have yet to be identified, named Šasíru (𒂊𒐕𒈙𒌋), Šurudum (𒀀𒐊𒐡𒈬), Bitum-Rabium (𒊩 𒂍𒄷𒈬), Íabru (𒌓𒍢𒌋), and Úknuru (𒈾𒐕𒂠𒂖). Given the similarity of the names, they are probably the cities mentioned in this verse.

2 Septuagint manuscript 961: basileōs Sennaar Ariŏk (ΒΑϹΙΛΕΩϹ ϹΕΝΝΑΑΡΑΡΙΩΧ). Translation: king of Sennaar Ariokh

• Septuagint manuscript 509: basiléōs Senaar Ariŏk (μΑϹΙΛϬῶϹ Σαυλαρ Αβιοοχ). Translation: king of Senaar Ariokh

• Septuagint manuscript 135: basiléōs Sennaar Ariō (μΑϹΙΛϬῶϹ Σαυναρ Αβιοο). Translation: king of Sennaar Ario

• Septuagint manuscript 129: basiléōs Sennaar Ōriŏk (μΑϹΙΛϬῶϹ Σαυναρ ωβιοοχ). Translation: king of Sennaar Oriokh

• Septuagint manuscript 426: basiléōs Sennaar Ariōd (μΑϹΙΛϬῶϹ Σαυναρ Αβιοοδ). Translation: king of Sennaar Ariod

• Septuagint manuscript 82: basiléōs Sennaar kai Ariŏk (μΑϹΙΛϬῶϹ Σαυναρ ιϲαι Αβιοοχ). Translation: king of Sennaar and Ariokh

• Septuagint manuscript 458: basiléōs Ennaar Ariŏk (μΑϹΙΛϬῶϹ Εννλαρ Αβιοοχ). Translation: king of Ennaar Ariokh

• Septuagint manuscript 72: basiléōs Sanaar Ariŏk (μΑϹΙΛϬῶϹ Σδυλαρ Αβιοοχ). Translation: king of Sanaar Ariokh

• Septuagint manuscript 376: basiléōs Sennaar Argŏk (μΑϹΙΛϬῶϹ Σαυναρ Αβγοοχ). Translation: king of Sennaar Argokh

• Leningrad Codex: melek Šin'ār 'Aryôk (מֶלֶךְ שִׁנְעָר אַרְיוֹךְ). Translation: king of Shinar Aryok

• Peshitta: mlkå dSnȯr wÅrywk (ܡܠܟܐ ܕܣܢܥܪ ܘܐܪܝܘܟ). Translation: king of Snor and Aryok

• Targum Onkelos: malkā' dəBābel 'Aryôk (מַלְכָּא דְבָבֶל אַרְיוֹךְ). Translation: king of Babylon Aryok

• Targum Pseudo-Jonathan: malkā' dəpûnətôs 'aryôk (מַלְכָּא דְפוֹנְטוֹס אַרְיוֹךְ). Translation: king of Pontus Aryok

• Sahidic manuscript 2037: prro nte Senaar Ariŏk (ⲡⲣ̄ⲣⲟ ⲛ̄ⲧⲉ ⲥⲉⲛⲁⲁⲣ ⲁⲣⲓⲱⲭ). Translation: the king of Senaar Ariok

• Sahidic manuscript 2020: prro nSetenaar Ariŏk (ⲡⲣ̄ⲣⲟ ⲛⲥⲉⲧⲉⲛⲁⲁⲣ ⲁⲣⲓⲱⲭ). Translation: the king of Setenaar Ariok

CHAPTER 14

The text are largely divided into two interpretations, either this is "Sumer and Uruk," as found in Septuagint manuscript 82, the Peshitta, and Bohairic manuscripts, or it is just "Sumer," and the word Uruk is viewed as the name of the following king. In the Neo-Sumerian era, Uruk did maintain its autonomy within the empire. Amar-Sin held both the titles of "King of Sumer and Akkad," as well as "King of Uruk," therefore, this translation follows the "Sumer and Uruk" manuscripts.

3 Septuagint manuscript 961: basileōs Sellasaar Ǩodollag (ⲃⲁⲥⲓⲗⲉⲱⲥ ⲥⲉⲗⲗⲁⲥⲁⲁⲣ ⲭⲟⲇⲟⲗⲗⲁⲅ). Translation: king of Sellasaar Khodollag

- Codex Alexandrinus: basileus Sellasar o Ǩodollogomor (ⲃⲁⲥⲓⲗⲉⲩⲥ ⲥⲉⲗⲗⲁⲥⲁⲣ ⲟ ⲭⲟⲇⲟⲗⲗⲟⲅⲟⲙⲟⲣ). Translation: king of Sellasaar the Khodollogomor

- Cotton Genesis: -odolla- (-ⲟⲇⲟⲗⲗⲁ-). The Cotton Genesis was burned in 1731, and only part of the name "[Ǩ]odolla[g]" survives in this verse. Septuagint manuscript D also uses the variant Ǩodall (ⲭⲟⲇⲁⲗⲗ) twice later in the surviving sections of the chapter

- Septuagint manuscript 17: basileus Ellasar Ǩodolag (ⲩⲁⲥⲓⲗⲟⲩⲥ Ελλⲁⲥⲁⲣ χⲟⲇⲟⲗⲁγ). Translation: king of Ellasar Khodolag

- Septuagint manuscript 55: basileus Selasar Ǩodollag (ⲩⲁⲥⲓⲗⲟⲩⲥ Σℓⲇⲥⲁⲣ χⲟⲇⲟⲗⲗⲁγ). Translation: king of Selasar Khodollag

- Septuagint manuscript 64: basileus Ellasar kai Ǩodollogomor (ⲩⲁⲥⲓⲗⲟⲩⲥ Ελλⲇⲥⲁⲣ ⳑⲁⳗ χⲟⲇⲟⲗⳝⲟγⲟⲙⲟⲣ). Translation: king of Ellasar and Khodollogomor

- Septuagint manuscript 318: basileus Sellasar Ǩodall (ⲩⲁⲥⲓⲗⲟⲩⲥ Σℓ λⲇⲥⲁⲣ χⲟⲇⲁ λλ). Translation: king of Sellasar Khodall. Septuagint manuscript 318 also uses the variant Ǩodallogomōr (χⲟⲇⲁ λⳝⲟγⲟⲙⲟⲣ) for the rest of the chapter supporting the original text switching

CHAPTER 14

from "Shulgi" to "Shulgi's representative" after the first mention of his name.

• Septuagint manuscript 57: basileus Ellasar Ǩollodog (uλσιλόυc ελλᴧσαρ χολ/6λογ). Translation: king of Ellasar Khollodog. Septuagint manuscript 57 also uses the variant Ǩolodog (χο/6λογ) later in the chapter.

• Septuagint manuscript 343: basileōs Elassar Selaasar Ǩodologemor (uλσιλόⲱc ελλσσαρ Σℓλλσαρ χολο/6γ6μο/6). Translation: king of Elassar (Selaasar) Khodologemor. Septuagint manuscript 343 also uses the variants Ǩodollasomor (χολολλᴧσομο/6), Ǩolagomor (χολλγομο/6), Godollag (гολολλλγ), and Ǩodollag (χολολλλγ) later in the chapter.

• Septuagint manuscript 370: basileus Sallasar Ǩolodog (uλσιλόυc Σλλλᴧσαρ χο/6λογ). Translation: king of Sallasar Kholodog. Septuagint manuscript 370 also uses the variants Ǩollodog (χολ/6λογ) and Godollag (γολολλλγ) later in the chapter.

• Septuagint manuscript 426: basileus Ellasar Ǩōdollogomōr (uλσιλόυc ελλᴧσαρ χⲱλολ/6γομⲱ/6). Translation: king of Ellasar Khōdollogomōr. Septuagint manuscript 426 also uses the variants Ǩōdolagomōr (χⲱλολλγομⲱ/6) and Ǩodolagomōr (χολολλγομⲱ/6) later in the chapter.

• Septuagint manuscript 75: basileus Ellasar Khodollagomō (uλσιλόυc ελλᴧσαρ χολολλλγομⲱ). Translation: king of Ellasar Khodollagomō. Septuagint manuscript 75 also uses the variant Khologomōr (χο/6γομⲱ/6) later in the chapter.

• Septuagint manuscript 78: basileus Salasar Ǩodologobor (uλσιλόυc Σλλᴧσαρ χολο/6γουο/6). Translation: basileus Salasar Khodologobor. Septuagint manuscript 78 also uses the variants Ǩodolog (χολο/6γ) and Ǩolodog (χο/6λογ) later in the chapter.

• Septuagint manuscript 72: basileus Elasar kai Ǩodollag (uλσιλόυc ελλᴧσαρ lαℓ χολολλλγ). Translation: king of Elasar and Khodollag.

Septuagint manuscript 72 also uses the variants Ǩodollogomor (χοΔολόγομοβ), Ǩolag (χολΔγ), and Ǩollag (χολλΔγ) later in the chapter.

• Septuagint manuscript 107: basileus Ellasar kai Ǩodollogomor (uΔσιλόυc Ελλασαρ ιaι χοΔολόγομοβ). Translation: king of Ellasar and Khodollogomor. Septuagint manuscript 107 also uses the variants Todolog (ΤοΔολόγ) and Ǩolodog (χοιόΔογ) later in the chapter.

• Septuagint manuscript 414: basileus Elassar Ǩodollogomor (uΔσιλόυc ΕλΔσσαρ χοΔολόγομοβ). Translation: king of Elassar Khodollogomor. Septuagint manuscript 414 also uses the variant Ǩologodomor (χοιόγοΔομοβ) later in the chapter.

• Septuagint manuscript 664: basileus Elassar Ǩolodog (uΔσιλόυc ΕλΔσσαρ χοιόΔογ). Translation: king of Elassar Kholodog. Septuagint manuscript 664 also uses the variants Ǩodologomōr (χοΔολόγομωοβ) and Ǩodolog (χοΔολόγ) later in the chapter.

• Septuagint manuscript 122: basileus Ellasar Ǩolodog (uΔσιλόυc ΕλΔσσαρ χοιόΔογ). Translation: king of Ellasar Kholodog. Septuagint manuscript 664 also uses the variant Ǩollomor (χολόμοβ) later in the chapter.

• Leningrad Codex: melek 'Ellāsār Kədārəlā'ōmer (מֶלֶךְ אֶלָּסָר כְּדָרְלָעֹמֶר). Translation: king of Ellasar Kedarela'omer

• Peshitta: mlkå dDlsr wKrdlômr (ܡܠܟܐ ܕܕܠܣܪ ܘܟܪܕܠܥܡܪ). Translation: king of Dlsr and Krdlomr

• Targum Onkelos: malkā' də'Ellāsār Kədārəlā'ōmer (מַלְכָּא דְאֶלָּסָר כְּדָרְלָעֹמֶר). Translation: king of Ellasar Kedarelaomer

• Targum Pseudo-Jonathan: malkā' dəTalsar Kədārəlā'ōmer (מַלְכָּא דְתַלְסָר כְּדָרְלָעוֹמֶר). Translation: king of Talsar Kedarelaomer

• Sahidic manuscript 2037: prro of Sellasar Ǩōdologomor (ⲡ︦ⲣ︦ⲣⲟ ⲛ̄ⲧⲉ Ⲥⲉⲗⲗⲁⲥⲁⲣ Ⲭⲱⲇⲟⲗⲟⲅⲟⲙⲟⲣ). Translation: king of Sellasar Khoudologomor

• Sahidic manuscript 2020: prro of Sellaar Ǩodogllagomor (ⲡ︦ⲣ︦ⲣⲟ ⲛ̄ⲧⲉ Ⲥⲉⲗⲗⲁⲁⲣ Ⲭⲟⲇⲟⲩⲗⲗⲁⲅⲟⲙⲟⲣ). Translation: king of Sellasar Khoudologomor

The somewhat garbled string of words has been interrupted several ways. The most common interpretation is that "Sellasaar" and "Khodollag" are the name of two kings or city-states. "Sellasaar" is generally interpreted as a garbled translation of the name of the city of Larsaki (𒆜𒆳𒆠), while "Khodollag" is interpreted as the name of a king. The alternate common interpretation, as recorded in Septuagint manuscript 64 and 72, the Peshitta, and the Bohairic manuscripts, is that "king of Ellasar and Khodollogomor" is a continuation of the titles of the king. The Codex Alexandrinus includes a third variant, as "king of Sellasaar of Khodollogomor," which then suggests that "Sellassar" was either from, or the son of "Khodollogomor."

Based on the described events, this appears to be a reference to King Amar-Sin, and his father King Shulgi of the Neo-Sumerian empire's Ur III dynasty, with the original text reading Amar bīnum Shulgi (𒀫𒌇 𒀭𒊺𒌷 𒀭𒂄𒄀), meaning "Amar son of Shulgi." Shulgi (𒀭𒂄𒄀) was the king most responsible for the expansion of the Neo-Sumerian empire, conquering most of modern Iraq, and Syria, as well as most of southern Iran. His son Amar-Sin (𒀫𒀭𒂗𒍪) ruled at the height of the Neo-Sumerian empire, which began contracting after his death, and collapsed under his grandson's reign. Without the vowel markings added in the late-classical era, the name Ȧlsr (אלסר), found in the Masoretic text, is a direct transliteration of Amar (𒀫𒌇) using Canaanite phonetics: ȦL (𒀫) SUR (𒌇).

The Hebrew transliteration of Kədārəlā'ōmer (כְּדָרְלָעֹמֶר), and earliest Greek transliteration as Ǩodollag (Χοδολλαγ) do not appear directly related, however, the Greek translations are not consistent, with both variations of Khodollag and Khodollogomor being used. Some manuscripts use both in different verses, while others are consistent in the term used. This suggests that the Aramaic texts the Greeks translated included both a variant of the name "Khodollag," and a form of "Khodollag's âmr" (אֹמֵר), meaning "Khodollag's speaker" or "Khodollag's representative." In any event, the wars of Shulgi and Amar-Sin are being described in the text. In Shulgi's 37th regal year, the Amorites revolted, and he built the "Wall of the Land," to keep them from overrunning his entire empire. Shulgi's primary focus were his wars to conquer the Zagros mountains and Iranian plateau, and he never led an army to reconquer Amurru.

According to this verse, he sent his son Amar to reconquer the Amorties, and he failed. The verse suggests he returned in his 3rd year as king to reconquer the Amorites, however, settled for destroying the five cities in the Dead Sea region instead. Amar-Sin's chronicle omits mentioning what he did in his 3rd and 4th regal year, however, in his 5th year, he appointed a new high-priest at the temple of Inanna in Uruk, indicating whatever he was doing in his 3rd and 4th years was not successful. According to the chronicles from the Ur III dynasty, the Amorites would not be reconquered for another 29 years. Instead, Amar-Sin appears to have changed tactics in year 6 and 7 of his reign, and he destroyed the cities of Šaszíru (𒂊𒐏𒈨𒌋), Šurudum (𒋢𒊒𒁺𒌝), Bitum-Rabium (𒉈 𒂊𒊑𒌝), Íabru (𒅎𒄷𒌋), and Úknuru (𒌋𒉽𒌉𒌓), which appear to be the five cities mentioned as being allied to the Amorites. This was also recorded as the second time he destroyed Šaszíru (𒂊𒐏𒈨𒌋), indicating that he must have campaigned in the region during Shulgi's reign, as the city would not have been rebuilt in just a year or two.

CHAPTER 14

Based on this story in Cosmic Genesis, it appears that the Amorite rebellion was backed by the Egyptian government, as Terah's faction appears to have fled Ur early in Shulgi's reign, and Abram ultimately became the brother-in-law of the king of Egypt, and a judge among the Amorites. Terah and Abram are both recorded as leading armies that were apparently loyal to them, not Egypt or Amurru, suggesting they represented an alternate royal line or priestly line before leaving Ur. The Chronicle of the Early Kings, which was compiled centuries later in the Middle Babylonian era, records that Shulgi was punished by Marduk for stealing from the temple of Marduk in Babylon, however, Babylon had not been built yet, and Marduk does not appear to have been a god yet, so this must have been the temple of Nergal at nearby Kutha, where Shulgi was recorded as initiating religious reforms.

As the terms "Sellasaar," "Khodollag," and "Khodollogomor" appear to have originated with the names "Amar"(-Sin) and Shulgi, and the term "Shulgi's representative," those terms are restored in this translation.

4 Septuagint manuscript 961: basileōs Ailam Ṯargal (ΒΑСΙΛΕѠС ΑΙΛΑΜΘΑΡΓΑΛ). Translation: king of Ailam Thargal

• Codex Alexandrinus: basileus Ailam Ṯalga (ΒΑСΙΛΕΥС ΑΙΛΑΜ ΘΑΛΓΑ). Translation: king of Ailam Thalga

• Cotton Genesis: basileus Sailam Ṯalgal (ΒΑСΙΛΕΥС СΑΙΛΑΜ ΘΑΛΓΑΛ). Translation: king of Sailam Thalgal

• Septuagint manuscript 15: basileus Ailam Oargal (uλοτλόυς Αιλλμ Οαργαλ). Translation: king of Ailam Oargal

• Septuagint manuscript 55: basileus Ailam Oarǩal (uλοτλόυς Αιλλμ Οαρχλλ). Translation: king of Ailam Oarchal

• Septuagint manuscript 319: basileus Ailam Ṯarga (uλοτλόυς Αιλλμ Θαργα). Translation: land Ailam Tharga

225

CHAPTER 14

- Septuagint manuscript 120: basileus Aidam Ṭargal (uΔσιλθυc Διδὰμ Θαργαλ). Translation: king of Aidam Thargal

- Septuagint manuscript 128: basileus Aidam Ṭaragal (uΔσιλθυc Διδὰμ Θαρδγαλ). Translation: king of Aidam Tharagal

- Septuagint manuscript 129: basileus Ailam Ṭergal (uΔσιλθυc Διλὰμ Θδγαλ). Translation: king of Ailam Thergal

- Septuagint manuscript 343: basileōs Balaam de Ṭargal (uΔσιλσοοc βΔλλΔμ Δσ Θαργαλ). Translation: king of Balaam the Thargal

- Septuagint manuscript 426: basileus Elam Ṭargad (uΔσιλθυc Ελδμ Θαργαδ). Translation: king of Elam Thargad

- Septuagint manuscript 78: basileus Ailam Ṭelgar (uΔσιλθυc Διλδμ Θℓγℵ). Translation: king of Ailam Thelgar.

- Septuagint manuscript 71: basileus Ailam Ṭagal (uΔσιλθυc Διλδμ Θδγαλ). Translation: king of Ailam Thelgar

- Septuagint manuscript 72: basileus Elam Ṭargan (uΔσιλθυc Ελδμ Θαργαν). Translation: king of Elam Thargan.

- Septuagint manuscript 799: basileus Edam Ṭargal (uΔσιλθυc Εδὰμ Θαργαλ). Translation: king of Edam Thargal

- Septuagint manuscript 527: basileus Ailam Ṭagar (uΔσιλθυc Διλδμ Θδγℵ). Translation: king of Ailam Thagar

- Septuagint manuscript 53: basileus Ailam Ṭerǩal (uΔσιλθυc Διλδμ Θδχδλ). Translation: king of Ailam Therkhal

- Septuagint manuscript 59: basileus Selam Ṭargam (uΔσιλθυc Σℓδμ Θαργαμ). Translation: king of Selam Thargam

- Leningrad Codex: melek 'Êlām wəTid'āl (מֶלֶךְ עֵילָם וְתִדְעָל). Translation: king of Elam and Tidal

- Peshitta: mlkå dȮylm wTrȯyl (ܡܠܟܐ ܕܥܝܠܡ ܘܬܪܥܝܠ). Translation: king of Ȯylm and Trȯyl

- Targum Onkelos: malkā' də'Êlām wəTid'āl (מַלְכָּא דְעֵילָם וְתִדְעָל). Translation: king of Elam and Tidal

226

• Targum Pseudo-Jonathan: malkā' də'Êlām wəTid'āl (מַלְכָּא דְעֵילָם
וְתִדְעָל). Translation: king of Elam and Tidal

• Sahidic manuscript 2037: prro nElam mn Ṭargal (ⲡⲣ̄ⲣⲟ ⲛ̄ⲈⲗⲁⲘ
ⲙⲛ̄ ⲐⲀⲣⲅⲀⲗ). Translation: king of Elam and Thargal

• Sahidic manuscript 2020: prro nAilam mn Ṭarkad (ⲡⲣ̄ⲣⲟ ⲛ̄ⲀⲓⲗⲁⲘ
ⲙⲛ̄ ⲐⲀⲣⲕⲀⲗ). Translation: king of Ailam and Tharkad

Elam was the nation on the northern coast of the Persian in Gulf
at the time, while the variations of Ṭargal / Tid'āl were likely a
reference to Dilmun. The earliest recorded name of Dilmun was the
Sumerian pictogram 𒉌, which was spelled phonetically as Nituk^{ki}
(𒉌𒌇𒆠) by Sumerians, however, is believed to have been
pronounced as Dilmun or Telmun in Old Akkadian. The
pronunciation is unknown during the Neo-Sumerian era, however,
as the earlier Akkadian king Sargon had claimed to have conquered
Dilmun into his empire, and the later Sealand Dynasty, the last
Neo-Sumerian dynasty appears to have been based in Dilmun, it is
unlikely it was not also occupied by the Neo-Sumerian Empire.

While the local name of Dilmun is not known today, when the
Greeks ruled the region, they recorded the local name as Tharrō
(Θαρρώ), which is quite similar to the name found in the Greek and
Syriac translations, suggesting it was similar to the name in the
earlier Aramaic translation.

5 Codex Alexandrinus: basileus ethnōn (ⲃⲁⲥⲓⲗⲉⲨⲥ ⲉⲐⲛⲱⲛ).
Translation: king of nations (or tribes, peoples)

• Septuagint manuscript 135: basileōs ethnōn (ⲃⲁⲥⲓⲗⲉⲟⲥ ⲉⲐ$_{N}$ⲟⲟⲛ).
Translation: king of nations (or tribes)

• Leningrad Codex: melek gôyim (מֶלֶךְ גּוֹיִם). Translation: king of
Goys (or non-Semites)

• Peshitta: mlkå dGlyå (ܡܠܟܐ ܕܓܠܝܐ). Translation: king of Goys
(or non-Semites)

• Targum Onkelos: malkā' də'ammê (מַלְכָּא דְעַמְמֵי). Translation: king of people

• Targum Pseudo-Jonathan: ramā'â kəta'ălā' malkā' də'ammayā' mištam'în lêh (רְמָאה כְּתַעֲלָא מַלְכָּא דְעַמְמַיָא מִשְׁתַּתְמְעִין לֵיהּ). Translation: high ascended king of the peoples (or nations) inherited by (or allotted to) him

• Sahidic manuscript 2037: prro nnHetnos (ⲡⲣ̄ⲣⲟ ⲛ̄ⲛ̄ϩⲉⲑⲛⲟⲥ). Translation: king of the nations

The origin of the Hebrew word Gwy (גוי) is unclear, as the term does not appear to be Semitic. In Hebrew, the term traditionally meant Indo-European peoples, including Medes, Persians, Scythians, Greeks, and Romans. One proposal to explain the term is that it is an East Semitic loanword, as the Assyrians and Babylonians were using the word Guti (𒄖𒋾 / 𒄖𒋾) as a term to represent the Medes, Persian, and Scythians during the 1st millennium BCE.

The original Guti nation, that inhabited the Zagros mountains in the 3rd millennium BCE, are not believed to have been Indo-Europeans, however, the Medes settled in the same region during the early 1st millennium BCE, resulting the name being applied to the them as well. In the late 3rd millennium BCE, the Akkadians conquered the land of the Guti, known as Gutium[ki] (𒆰𒋾𒌝𒆠), however, the Guti rebelled and conquered the Akkadian empire late in the 3rd millennium BCE, and ruled Mesopotamia for almost a century. They were eventually driven out of Mesopotamia by Amar-Sin's great-grandfather, who then reunited the Sumero-Akkadian city-states and laid the foundations of the Empire of Ur. During the rule of Amar-Sin, the Guti were part of his empire, explaining why he held the title "King of the Guti."

6 Septuagint manuscript 961: Barak basileōs Sodomōn (ⲃⲁⲣⲁⲕ ⲃⲁⲥⲓⲗⲉⲱⲥⲥⲟⲇⲟⲙⲱⲛ). Translation: Barak king of Sodomon

CHAPTER 14

- Codex Alexandrinus: Balla basileōs Sodomōn (ΒΑΛΛΑ ΒΑϹΙΛΕѠϹ ϹΟΔΟΜѠΝ). Translation: Balla king of Sodomon

- Septuagint manuscript 17: Balak basileus Sodomōn (βαλαϰ υασιλϵυϲ Σοδομον). Translation: Balak king of Sodomon

- Septuagint manuscript 64: Bara basiléōs Sodomōn (βαρα υασιλϵѡϲ Σοδομον). Translation: Bara king of Sodomon

- Septuagint manuscript 392: Balba basiléōs Sodomōn (βαλυα υασιλϵѡϲ Σοδομον). Translation: Balba king of Sodomon

- Septuagint manuscript 75: Bara basiléōs Sodomōn (βαρα υασιλϵѡϲ Σοδομον) Translation: Bara king of Sodomon

- Septuagint manuscript 18: Marla basiléōs Sodomōn (Μαρλα υασιλϵѡϲ Σοδομον). Translation: Marla king of Sodomon

- Septuagint manuscript 120: Bara basiléōs Sodōmōn (βαρα υασιλϵѡϲ Σοδωμοον). Translation: Bara king of Sodomon

- Septuagint manuscript 500: Barlam basiléōs Sodomōn (βαρλαμ υασιλϵѡϲ Σοδομον). Translation: Barlam king of Sodomon

- Septuagint manuscript 370: Barlak basileus Sodomōn (βαρλαϰ υασιλϵυϲ Σοδομον). Translation: Barlak king of Sodomon

- Septuagint manuscript 246: Bara basileus Sodomon (βαρα υασιλϵυϲ Σοδομ℗). Translation: Bara king of Sodomon

- Septuagint manuscript 54: Malak basileus Sodomōn (Μαλαϰ υασιλϵυϲ Σοδομον). Translation: Malak king of Sodomon

- Septuagint manuscript 527: Bala basileus Sodomōn (βαλα υασιλϵυϲ Σοδομον). Translation: Bala king of Sodomon

- Leningrad Codex: Bera' Melek Sədōm (בֶּרַע מֶלֶךְ סְדֹם). Translation: Bera king of Sedom

- Peshitta: Brȯ mlkå dSdwm (ܒܪܥ ܡܠܟܐ ܕܣܕܘܡ). Translation: Brȯ king of Sdwm

- Targum Onkelos: Bera' malkā' diSdōm (בֶּרַע מַלְכָּא דְסְדֹם). Translation: Bera king of Sdom

• Targum Pseudo-Jonathan: bera' də'ôbədôy bəbîš malkā' diSdôm (בְּרַע דְעוֹבְדוֹי בְּבִישׁ מַלְכָּא דִסְדוֹם). Translation: Bera, the worker of evil, king of Sdom

• Sahidic manuscript 2037: Balak prro nSodoma (ⲂⲀⲖⲀⲔ ⲠϮ̄ⲢⲢⲞ Ⲛ̄ⲤⲞⲆⲞⲘⲀ). Translation: Balak king of Sodoma

This city is most likely the city called Šurudum (𒋗𒊒𒁺𒌝), which Amar-Sin claimed to have destroyed in year six of his reign. The 𒋗 logogram represented both the ŠUR and SUR sounds, however the Canaanites did not have a letter in either the Ugaritic or Phoenician scripts representing either ŠUR or SUR, and therefore the R sound was probably not recognized within the name, resulting in the transliteration of Sdm (𐤎𐤃𐤌). The common Greek and Coptic represents an Aramaic plural form, indicating the word was Sdwmn (𐤎𐤃𐤅𐤌𐤍) in Aramaic, meaning "Sodomites."

7 Septuagint manuscript 961: Barsa basileōs Gomorrạs (ΒΑΡϹΑ ΒΑϹΙΛΕⲰϹΓΟΜΟΡΡΑϹ). Translation: Barsa king of Gomorrahs

• Septuagint manuscript 707: Barsa basileōs Gomoras (Βαρσα υασιλέωϲ Γομορας). Translation: Barsa king of Gomoras

• Septuagint manuscript 730: Barsaba basileōs Gomorrạs (Βαρσαυα υασιλέωϲ Γομοβρας). Translation: Barsabaking of Gomorrahs

• Septuagint manuscript 370: Gabra basileōs Gomorrạs (Γαρυα υασιλέωϲ Γομοβρας). Translation: Gabra king of Gomorrahs

• Septuagint manuscript 799: Barga basileōs Gomorrạs (Βαρϳα υασιλέωϲ Γομοβρας). Translation: Bargaking of Gomorrahs

• Septuagint manuscript 53: Barsa basileōs Gomorrạs (Βαρσαϭ υασιλέωϲ Γομοβρας). Translation: Barsae king of Gomorrahs

• Leningrad Codex: Birša' melek 'Ămōrâ (בִּרְשַׁע מֶלֶךְ עֲמֹרָה). Translation: Birsha king Amora

• Peshitta: Bršȯ mlkå dȮmwrå (ܟ̇ܢܕ ܡܠܟܐ ܕܐܘܡܪܐ).
Translation: Brshȯ king of Omura

• Targum Onkelos: Birša' malkā' da'Ămōrâ (בִּרְשַׁע מַלְכָּא דַעֲמֹרָה).
Translation: Birsha king of Amora

• Targum Pseudo-Jonathan: Birša' də'ôbədôy biršî'ā' malkā'
da'Ămōrâ (בִּרְשַׁע דְעוֹבְדוֹי בִּרְשִׁיעָא מַלְכָּא דַעֲמוֹרָה). Translation: Birsha,
the worker of evil,

Based on the Hebrew, Aramaic, and Syriac spelling, this city is
most likely the city called Úk̆nuru (𒌷𒌦𒉡) in the list of cities
conquered by Amar-Sin, as a similar consonant shift between N and
M took place in the word Sumer, which is represented as Šin'ār /
Sennaar earlier in the verse.

8 Codex Alexandrinus: Sennaar basileōs Adama (ϹΕΝΝΑΑΡ
ΒΑϹΙΛΕⲰϹΑΔΑΜΑ). Translation: Sennaar king of Adama

Septuagint manuscript 509: Sennaar basileōs Sadama (Σαννααρ
υασιλῶος Σαδαμα). Translation: Sennaar king of Sadama

• Septuagint manuscript 15: Sennaab basileōs Adama (Σαννααυ
υασιλῶος Αδαμα). Translation: Sennaab king of Adama

• Septuagint manuscript 319: Sennaa basileōs Adama (Σανναα
υασιλῶος Αδαμα). Translation: Sennaa king of Adama

• Septuagint manuscript 314: Sennar basileōs Adama (Σανναρ
υασιλῶος Αδαμα). Translation: Sennar king of Adama

• Septuagint manuscript 14: Senaar basileōs Adama (Σαναρ
υασιλῶος Αδαμα). Translation: Senaar king of Adama

• Septuagint manuscript 426: Sennaar basileōs Adana (Σαννααρ
υασιλῶος Αδανα). Translation: Sennaar king of Adana

• Septuagint manuscript 54: Senagar basileōs Adama (Σαναγ
υασιλῶος Αδαμα). Translation: Senagar king of Adama

- Septuagint manuscript 376: Ennaab basileōs Adama (Εννααβ υλσιλόοος Λδαμα). Translation: Ennaab king of Adama

- Leningrad Codex: Šin.'āb. Melek 'Admâ (שִׁנְאָב ׀ מֶלֶךְ אַדְמָה). Translation: Shinaab king of Adma

- Peshitta: Šnåb mlkå dÅdmå (ܐܕܡܐ ܕ ܡܠܟܐ ܣܢܐܒ). Translation: Shnab king of Adma

- Targum Onkelos: Šin'āb malkā' də'Admâ (שִׁנְאָב מַלְכָּא דְאַדְמָה). Translation: Shinab king of Adma

- Targum Pseudo-Jonathan: Šin'āb da'ăpîlû lə'ābôy hăwâ šānê malkā' də'Admâ (שִׁנְאָב דְאַפִּילוּ לְאָבוֹי הֲוָה שָׁנֵי מַלְכָּא דְאַדְמָה). Translation: Shinab, who even rejected his ancestors, king of Adma

- Sahidic manuscript 2037: Balak prro nSodoma (Βαλακ πῬρο ῆСодома). Translation: Balak king of Sodoma

This city is not listed as one of the five cities destroyed by Amar-Sin in his 6th and 7th years, instead the name Íabru (𒄑𒆠) is used for the fifth city. The term ådmh (אדמה), is an unlikely name for a city, as it was the Amorite, Hurrian, and Edomite word for "land," and/or the "earth goddess," suggesting that either the name of the city was replaced with the word "land," or was never in the original Israelite version of the story, in which case Sennaar / Shinaab was being referred to as the king of "the land."

The city of Íabru (𒄑𒆠), which Amar-Sin destroyed circa 2000 BCE, may be the same place as the "ruin of the Hebrews" (בעיי העברים) that Moses led the Israelites to in Masoretic Numbers. This name was rendered as Akelgai (Αχελγαι) in the Septuagint's Numbers, and so it is not clear if the term was originally in Numbers and redacted by the Aramaic translator, or if an older term was replaced by the Hasmonean translators, however, it is unlikely the Hasmoneans would have added the "ruin of the Hebrews," as it seems incongruous with the rest of the narrative. Moreover the beginning of the Greek name does appear to be a transliteration of Hôy (הֹעִי), which was transliterated as Aŋgai (Αγγαι) when it was a separate word.

This suggests that the Aramaic text the Greeks translated used the name Hôy Ôlgy (ᴧᴧᴸ ᴧ�
ᴎ), meaning "ruins of Ôlgy." This appears to have resulted from a transcription error when translating the Phoenician script Hôy Ôbry (ᴢᴧ9ᴑ ᴢᴑᴧ), however it is difficult to imagine how the translator mistranscribed "Hebrew," suggesting it was an intentional alteration. However the name was spelled, the ruins were described as being in the desert to the east of Moab, in eastern modern Jordan, which is likely along Amar-Sin's route from Ur.

As the earliest records of the Ǩabiru (𒆙𒁁𒐼) were from around 300 years after Amar-Sin attacked Íabru (𒉿𒂅𒐼), it is plausible that Íabru was the ancestral homeland of the Ǩabiru, somewhere in the desert of eastern modern Jordan. It would have been impossible to translate Íabru (𒉿𒂅𒐼) into Egyptian without rendering the name Ôprw (𓇋𓊪𓂋𓅱), which was the Egyptian form of Habiru, however, referred to slaves from Edom, making the city's name the Egyptian equivalent of "Slave." As both the Greek and Hebrew translations used the name Adama, the original substitution of Adama for Íabru, probably took place in the Egyptian translation, with the name Îdwmȯ (𓇋𓂧𓅱𓐝𓂋𓈉) replacing Íabru (𒉿𒂅𒐼). This would have replaced the word "slave" with the name of the land the slaves were from in the Egyptian translation. As both the Septuagint and Masoretic text used the name Adama, that name is used in this translation, regardless of the name of the city in the records of Amur-Sin.

9 Codex Alexandrinus: Sumobor basileōs Seboim (ⲤⲨⲘⲞⲂⲞⲢ ⲂⲀⲤⲓⲗⲉⲱⲤⲤⲉⲂⲱⲓⲘ). Translation: Sumobor king of Seboim

• Septuagint manuscript 707: Sumbur basiléōs Sebōim (Συμμυϼ υλσιλϭϖc Σϭυοοιμ). Translation: Sumbur king of Seboim

• Septuagint manuscript 319: Sumōr basiléōs Seboein (Συμοοϼ υλσιλϭϖc Σϭυοϥν). Translation: Sumor king of Seboein

• Septuagint manuscript 343: Oumobor basiléōs Sebboim (Oυμουοϼ υλσιλϭϖc Σϭυυ℗μ). Translation: Oumobor king of Sebboim

• Septuagint manuscript 344: Sumor basiléōs Sebōim (Συμοϼ υλσιλϭϖc Σϭυοοιμ). Translation: Sumor king of Seboim

• Septuagint manuscript 426: Sumobor basiléōs Seboēm (Συμουοϼ υλσιλϭϖc Σϭυοℷμ). Translation: Sumobor king of Seboem

• Septuagint manuscript 75: Sumobor basiléōs Sebōneim (Συμουοϼ υλσιλϭϖc ΣϭυοοΝϥμ). Translation: Sumobor king of Seboneim

• Septuagint manuscript 422: Sumobōr basiléōs Sebōim (Συμουοοϼ υλσιλϭϖc Σϭυοοιμ). Translation: Sumobor king of Seboim

• Septuagint manuscript 458: Sumobor basiléōs Seboneim (Συμουοϼ υλσιλϭϖc Σϭυ℗ϥμ). Translation: Sumobor king of Seboneim

• Septuagint manuscript 71: Sumeōn basileus Seboeim (ΣυμϭϖοΝ υλσιλϭυc Σϭυοϥμ). Translation: Sumeon king of Seboeim

• Septuagint manuscript 72: Subōr basileus Seboēn (Συυοοϼ υλσιλϭυc Σϭυοℹω). Translation: Subor king of Seboen

• Septuagint manuscript 76: Sumobor basileus Seboim (Συμουοϼ υλσιλϭυc Σϭυ℗μ). Translation: Sumobor king of Seboin

• Septuagint manuscript 108: Simor basiléōs Sebōim (Σιμοϼ υλσιλϭϖc Σϭυοοιμ). Translation: Simor king of Seboim

• Septuagint manuscript 664: Summobor basiléōs Sebōim (Συμμουοϼ υλσιλϭϖc Σϭυοοιμ). Translation: Summobor king of Seboim

• Leningrad Codex: Šem'ēber melek Səbōyîm k [səbôyîm q] (שְׁמְאֵבֶר מֶלֶךְ צְבֹיִים כ [וְצְבֹויִים ק]). Translation: Shemeber king of Seboyim (k) [Seboyim (q)]

• Peshitta: Šmåyr mlkå dSbwåym (ܫܡܐܝܪ ܡܠܟܐ ܕܣܒܘܐܝܡ). Translation: Shmayr king of Sbuaym

• Targum Onkelos: Šem'ēber malkā' diSbôyim (שְׁמְאֵבֶר מַלְכָּא דְצְבוֹיִם). Translation: Shemeber king of Sboyim

• Targum Pseudo-Jonathan: Šem'ēber dimḥabbēl 'Êbərêh lîzənêh malkā' diSbôyim (שְׁמְאֵבֶר דִמְחַבֵּל אֵיבְרֵיה לִיזְנֵיה מַלְכָּא דְצְבוֹיִם). Translation: Shemeber, attacker (or terrorizer) of Eberêh (or crossers, Eberites, Hebrew, Habirus, Íabrus) who wandered, king of Sboyim

• Sahidic manuscript 2037: Semobor prro nSeboeim (Cемовор ⲡⲣ̄ⲣⲟ ⲛ̄Cевоеім). Translation: Semobor king of Seboeim

• Sahidic manuscript 2020: Sēmobor prro nSeboeim (Cнмовор ⲡⲣ̄ⲣⲟ ⲛ̄Cевоеім). Translation: Semobor king of Seboeim

If Sebōim / Səbōyîm was one of the five unknown cities attacked by Amar-Sin in his final two years, it was likely the city known as Bitum-Rabium (𒉺 𒂍𒂷). This name appears to be the Akkadian spelling of a Canaanite name Bt Rbm (𐤁𐤕 𐤓𐤁𐤌), meaning "Great House." Bitum (𒉺) was the Akkadian Cuneiform spelling of the Canaanite word bt (𐎁𐎚 / 𐤁𐤕), which meant "house," "temple," or "palace," depending on context, and continues to be the Hebrew word báyit (בַּיִת) and Arabic bayt (بَيْت). During the Egyptian rule of Canaan it was spelled as båyt (𓉐𓏤𓏏). Rbm (𐤓𐤁𐤌) was a Canaanite word, documented in the Ammonite and Phoenician dialects, but not in Eastern Semitic languages, where the parallel term was rapāšum (𒊏𒉺�), indicating that the city that Amar-Sin attacked was somewhere in Canaan east of the Jordan, as Egypt controlled west of the Jordan.

Multiple Egyptian-originating words in the Torah indicate that the Israelite scribe who adopted the words spoke the Fayyumic dialect of Egyptian, in which R sound was pronounced as an L sounds. It would have been impossible to translate Bitum-Rabium

(𓃾 𓏏 𓊪) into Egyptian without rendering the name as Båyt Rbw (𓉐𓏏𓃭𓏤 𓃭𓃭𓃭), meaning "House of the Libyans," a geographical impossibility. Therefore, it appears that the Egyptian translators substituted a term often used for Canaanites: Sbîw (𓍿𓃭𓃭𓃭), meaning "rebels," making the name Båyt Sbîw (𓉐𓏏𓏤𓃭𓃭 𓍿𓃭𓃭𓃭), meaning "House of the Rebels."

The term Båyt was probably also dropped before the name was translated back into cuneiform, as campaigns to suppress the Sbîw were common during the New Kingdom era. This would have left the Middle Babylonian cuneiform translator with the word Sbîw, the plural of Sbî to transliterate back into Canaanite, resulting in Szebiim (𒊺𒍢𒅎), which was later translated into Canaanite as Sbyym (𐤔𐤁𐤉𐤉𐤌) in the early iron age. Given the other parallels between the campaigns of the King of Ur Amar-Sin, and this king of Sumer Amarpel, the older name is restored from the records of Amar-Sin throughout *Cosmic Genesis* as Bet Rabim.

10 Berlin Genesis: basileōs Bala autē estin Sēgōr (ⲃⲁⲥⲓⲗⲉⲱⲥⲃⲁⲗⲁ ⲁⲩⲑⲏⲉⲥⲧⲓⲛⲥⲏⲅⲱⲣ). Translation: King Bala this is Segor

• Septuagint manuscript 15: basiléōs Bala aútē estin Sigōr (ⲙⲁⲥⲓⲗⲟⲥⲟⲥ ⲃⲁⲗⲁ ⲁⲟⲧⲏ ⲟⲥⲓⲛ Σιγοοβ). Translation: King Bala this is Sigor

• Septuagint manuscript 25: basiléōs Sala aútē estin Sēgōr (ⲙⲁⲥⲓⲗⲟⲥⲟⲥ Σαλα ⲁⲟⲧⲏ ⲟⲥⲓⲛ Σⲏγοοβ). Translation: King Sala this is Segor

• Septuagint manuscript 343: basiléōs Balaak aútē estin Sitōr (ⲙⲁⲥⲓⲗⲟⲥⲟⲥ ⲃⲁⲗⲁⲁⲕ ⲁⲟⲧⲏ ⲟⲥⲓⲛ Σιτοοβ). Translation: King Balaak this is Sitor

• Septuagint manuscript 79: basiléōs Bala aútē estin Sēgor (ⲙⲁⲥⲓⲗⲟⲥⲟⲥ ⲃⲁⲗⲁ ⲁⲟⲧⲏ ⲟⲥⲓⲛ Σⲏγοβ). Translation: King Bala this is Segor

- Septuagint manuscript 53: basiléōs Sabak aútē estin Ségōr (μλσιλόσος Σλυλι λϖτλ όςιν Σιγοοβ). Translation: King Sabak this is Segor

- Leningrad Codex: melek bela' hî'-Sō'ar (מֶלֶךְ בֶּלַע הִיא־צֹעַר). Translation: King Bela it Tzo'ar

- Peshitta: mlkå dBlŏ hy hy Sŏr (ܡܠܟܐ ܕܒܠܚ ܗܝ ܆ ܗܝ ܨܝܪ). Translation: king the Blo it is Tzor

- Targum Onkelos: malkā' dəBela' hî' Sō'ar (מַלְכָּא דְבֶלַע הִיא צֹעַר). Translation: king of Bela it's Tzoar

- Targum Pseudo-Jonathan: malkā' dəqartā' diBlā'at dayyrāhā' hî' Zô'ar (מַלְכָּא דְקַרְתָּא דְבָלְעַת דַּיְירָהָא הִיא זוֹעַר). Translation: king of the city of Blaat the archer (or shooter, thrower) it's Zoar

- Sahidic manuscript 2020: prro nBalak etetai te Ségōr (ⲡⲣ̅ⲣⲟ ⲛ̅Ⲃⲁⲗⲁⲕ ⲉⲧⲉⲧⲁⲓ̈ ⲧⲉ Ⲥⲏⲅⲱⲣ). Translation: king of Balak which is the Segor

This city appears to be the city called Šaszíru (𒂠𒍣𒊒), which Amar-Sin claimed to have destroyed in year six of his reign. The name appears to have been transliterated directly into Egyptian hieratic, and then transliterated incorrectly when the text was restored to Canaan during the New Kingdom era as Šŭszíru (𒂉𒍣𒊒), which was then transliterated into the confusing "it's Sor" (היא צער), as hyå (היא) was the Hebrew translation of the Middle Babylonian term šŭ (𒂉). Based on the Hebrew and Greek translations of "it's So'ar / Ségōr," the city is a generally accepted as being the Edomite city known as Sôr / Ségōr / Zoara, from the classical era.

Significant archaeological digs have been undertaken in at the ruins of the city since the 1970s, however, to date only iron age or more recent artifacts have been found, suggesting that Šasíru was not Sôr. Given the other parallels between the campaigns of the King of Ur Amar-Sin, and this king of Sumer Amarpel, the older name is restored from the records of Amar-Sin throughout Cosmic Genesis as Shasziru for both "it's Sēgōr" and Sēgōr, as Sēgōr / Ṣȯr would have to be an update to whatever was in the text in the interpretation were "it's Sēgōr" is a scribal note.

11 Codex Alexandrinus: tō triscaedecatō eti (ⲦⲰ ⲦⲢⲓⲤⲔⲀⲓⲆⲈⲔⲀⲦⲰ ⲈⲦⲈⲓ). Translation: the thirteenth year

• Leningrad Codex: ûšəlōš 'eśrēh šānâ (וּשְׁלֹשׁ עֶשְׂרֵה שָׁנָה). Translation: for thirteen years

• Samaritan Torah: wbšlš ȯšrh šgh (ⲀⲆ ⲀⲀⲰⲞ ⲰⳘⲀⲀ). Translation: and in thirteenth year

• Peshitta: wbdtlt ōšrå šnyn (ܘܒܕܬܠܬ ܥܣܪܐ ܫܢܝܢ). Translation: and in thirteenth year

• Targum Onkelos: ûtəlāt 'aśrê šənîn (וּתְלָת עַשְׂרֵי שְׁנִין). Translation: and for thirteen years

• Targum Pseudo-Jonathan: ûbitlasrê šənîn mārādû (וּבְתְלָסְרֵי שְׁנִין מְרָדוּ). Translation: and for thirteen years (or ages, eras)

• Sahidic manuscript 2020: mehmntšomte nrompe (ⲘⲈϨⲘⲚⲦϢⲞⲘⲦⲈ ⲚⲢⲞⲘⲠⲈ). Translation: thirteen or years

Amar-Sin, the King of the Four Regions, claimed he conquered or destroyed four similarly named cities in his sixth and seventh regal years, before dying in his ninth regal year. His successor Shu-Sin then ruled for nine years, meaning that the rebellion, if in the thirteenth year, would have been in the first year of the following king's reign: Ibbi-Sin, who was the last king of the Neo-Sumerian Empire. During Ibbi-Sin's reign, the Amorites revolted from his rule in Canaan, and after he was unable to reconquer them, Elam and other regions revolted, leading to the collapse of the Neo-Sumerian empire. According to *Cosmic Genesis / Bereshít*, the Amorites were ruling parts of Syria and Canaan at the time, north and east of the Egyptian controlled regions, and appear to have been allied to Egypt, based on Abram's position as a judge of the Amorites, and his being the Egyptian king's brother-in-law.

The difference between the Hebrew version, and the Greek, Syriac, and Samaritan versions is generally viewed by non-Jewish academics as a translation error within the Masoretic text, which must have happened after the Aramaic translation was made, presumably when the text was standardized in the Aramaic "Hebrew" script under the Hasmonean dynasty. An alternate interpretation is that the Hebrew version is older, and the alternate wording found in the Greek, Syriac, and Samaritan versions originated in Hezekiah's Aramaic translation of the Torah.

12 Codex Alexandrinus: ethnē iskhura ama autois (ⲈⲰⲚⲎⲒⲤⲬⲨⲢⲀ ⲀⲘⲀ ⲀⲨⲦⲞⲒⲤ). Translation: nation (or tribe) strong (or Ischyra) together with them

• Septuagint manuscript 392: ethnē iskhurotera ama autois (ἔθνη ἰσχυρότερα ἄμα αὐτοῖς). Translation: nation (or tribe) powerful together with them.

• Leningrad Codex: hazZûzîm bəhām (הַזּוּזִים בְּהָם). Translation: the Zuzes among

• Peshitta: wlŌšynā dbhyn (ܘܠܐܘܫܝܢܐ ܕܒܗܝܢ). Translation: and the Oshyna of them

• Targum Onkelos: wəyāt taqqîpayyā' dibhemtā' (וְיָת תַּקִּיפַיָּא דִּבְהֶמְתָּא). Translation: and the assaulters among them

• Targum Pseudo-Jonathan: wəyat taqîpayā' dibhemtā' (וְיָת תְּקִיפַיָא דְּבְהֶמְתָּא). Translation: and the assaulters among them

• Sahidic manuscript 2020: henhetnos eujoor (ϨⲈⲚϨⲈⲐⲚⲞⲤ ⲈⲨϪⲞⲞⲢ). Translation: the nations with the sons of strength

CHAPTER 14

The term in *Bereshít* appears to be a reference to the people from the town of Shasziru (目卌卄鑾Σ) which Amar-Sin reported destroying in his 6th year. The Greek translators or their Aramaic precursors appear to have not understood the reference, as the Greek phrase is not related. Based on the general usage for the word iskūrós (ἰσχῠρός) in the Septuagint, as a translation of the name El found in the Masoretic text, it appears that the Aramaic text read "nation of El," which probably seemed anachronistic to the Greek translators, resulting in the substitution.

As the Shaszi have already been mentioned in the text as one of the peoples involved in the war, the name Zûzîm is imported from the Masoretic text, and normalized to Shaszi based on the Akkadian spelling of the name.

13 Yale Genesis: Sommaious (ⲥⲟⲙⲙⲁⲓⲟⲩⲥ)

- Codex Alexandrinus: Somaious (ⲥⲟⲙⲁⲓⲟⲩⲥ)
- Septuagint manuscript 15: Sēmm (Σλμμ)
- Septuagint manuscript 55: Sonaious (ΣΘαιους)
- Septuagint manuscript 64: Ommaious (Oμμαιοσ)
- Septuagint manuscript 707: Sumeous (Συμ6σσ)
- Septuagint manuscript 319: Sōmaious (Σοομαισσ)
- Septuagint manuscript 343: Omoious (OμΘσσ)
- Septuagint manuscript 130: Amm (ⲁμμ)
- Septuagint manuscript 71: Someous (Σομ6σσ)
- Septuagint manuscript 314: Ommeous (Oμμ6σσ)
- Septuagint manuscript 551: Omsaious (Oμψαισσ)
- Septuagint manuscript 799: Ōmmeous (ωμμ6σσ)
- Septuagint manuscript 53: Oimm (Oιμμ)
- Septuagint manuscript 376: Sēmaious (Σλμαισσ)
- Septuagint manuscript 59: Sōmmaious (Σοομμαισσ)

CHAPTER 14

- Leningrad Codex: 'Êmîm (אֵימִים). Translation: terrors
- Peshitta: Åmnå (ܐܡܢܐ). Translation: evil
- Targum Onkelos: 'Êmətānê (אֵימְתָנֵי)
- Targum Jerusalem: 'Êmətānayā'n (אֵמְתָנַיָאן)
- Targum Pseudo-Jonathan: 'Êmətānê (אֵימְתָנֵי)
- Sahidic manuscript 2020: Omaios (ⲞⲘⲀⲒⲞⳙ)
- Bohairic manuscripts: Someos (ⳙⲞⲨⲉⲞⳙ)

As the Greek term was a transliteration of the term used in the Masoretic text, the Masoretic term is translated here. Based on the rest of the differences between the translations, the word Êmîm, may have originated in the name of the people from the town of Úǩnuru (𒌋𒈾𒊒) which Amar-Sin reported destroying in his 7th year. Uru (𒌋) meant "city," and therefore, the people from the city would have been the Úǩnim. As the name Úǩnuru ultimately became the Hebrew Ômrh (עמרה) and Greek Gomorrạs (Γομορρας), the English name of the people would be the Gomorrahns.

14 Codex Alexandrinus: Ǩordaious (ⲬⲞⲢⲆⲀⲒⲞⲨⳙ)
- Septuagint manuscript 55: Ǩōrrạious (Χοορραιοσυ)
- Septuagint manuscript 64: Ǩorrạíous (Χορραιοσυ)
- Septuagint manuscript 343: Ǩarrạious (Χαρραιοσυ)
- Septuagint manuscript 400: Ǩoraious (Χοραιοσυ)
- Septuagint manuscript 72: Ǩorrẹous (Χορρεοσυ)
- Septuagint manuscript 77: Orrạious (Ορραιοσυ)
- Septuagint manuscript 799: Ǩōreous (Χοορεοσυ)
- Septuagint manuscript 31: Ǩoraias (Χοραιας)
- Septuagint manuscript 59: Ǩōraious (Χοοραιοσυ)
- Leningrad Codex: Hōrî (חֹרִי)
- Peshitta Manuscript 5b1: Hwå (ܚܘ)

- Peshitta Manuscript 7a1: Hwrnå (ܚܘܪܢܐ)
- Targum Onkelos: Ḥôrā'ê (חוֹרָאֵי)
- Targum Jerusalem: Ḥôrāwā'ê (חוֹרְוָאֵי)
- Targum Pseudo-Jonathan: Ḥôrā'ê (חוֹרָאֵי)
- Sahidic manuscript 2020: Ǩorreos (Ⲭⲟⲣⲣⲉⲟⲥ)

These appear to be the people the Egyptians called the Ǩårw (𓎡𓄿𓂋𓘹𓅱), which are known as the Hurrians in modern history books. The Hurrians were an ancient people in the Middle East, known as Ǩarru (𒄷𒌨) in Akkadian Cuneiform, native to Northern Iraq, Syria, and eastern Turkey before the Semitic and Persian tribes migrated into the region. While they appear to have become a slave race for centuries under the rule of the Old Babylonian and Old Assyrian kingdoms, they became the dominant ethnic group of the Mitanni Empire between 1600 and 1300 BCE, after being freed by the Indo-Aryan Mitanni.

The variations found in Peshitta Manuscripts 5b1, from the 5th century, and 7a1, from the 7th century, are generally interpreted as part of the ongoing work to synchronize the Peshitta with the Masoretic text. The term Hwå (ܚܘܐ), used in 5b1, is the Syriac translation of "Mitanni" (Ευαιον / חֲוִילָה), while Hwrnå (ܚܘܪܢܐ), used in 7a1 is the Syriac translation of "Hurrian" (Χορραίους / חֹרִי). See note 44 in Chapter 10 for more information. Comparisons between the Septuagint and Masoretic text show the terms were used interchangeably in the Aramaic source text for the Septuagint, and the existence of the deviation from both the Greek and Hebrew in 5b1 suggests that the Peshitta was also based an older Aramaic text.

15 Codex Alexandrinus: arǩontas (ⲁⲣⲭⲟⲛⲧⲁⲥ). Translation: archons (or princes, rulers)

- Leningrad Codex: śədê (שָׂדֶה). Translation: field
- Peshitta: ršnå (ܪܫܢܐ). Translation: rulers (or chiefs)
- Targum Onkelos: ḥăqal (חֲקַל). Translation: field
- Targum Pseudo-Jonathan: ḥaqlê (חַקְלִי). Translation: field
- Sahidic manuscript 2020: aukotou (ⲁⲩⲕⲟⲧⲟⲩ)

16 Codex Alexandrinus: Amalēk (ⲀⲘⲀⲗⲎⲕ)
- Septuagint manuscript 17: Amalik (Ἀμαλικ)
- Septuagint manuscript 343: Amaleik (Ἀμαλἠκ)
- Septuagint manuscript 346: Amalēl (Ἀμαλᴧλ)
- Leningrad Codex: 'Ămālēq (עֲמָלֵק)
- Targum Onkelos: 'Ămālēq (עֲמָלֵק)
- Targum Jerusalem: 'Ămālēq (עֲמָלֵק)
- Targum Pseudo-Jonathan: 'Ămālēq (עֲמָלֵק)

In the Israelite books, the Amalek are periodically present in Canaan and the Sinai peninsula from the time of Abraham until the time of King David; however, there is no archaeological evidence of a tribe called "Amalek." The name is a transliteration of the Egyptian term åmw-rqî (𓄿𓄿𓂝𓏤 𓅱𓂝), which can be translated as "hostile Asiatics," "opposing Amorites," or "defiant fires."

The presence of the term supports this section of text having once been translated into Egyptian. The same word was pronounced as åmw-lqî in the Fayyumic dialect. The Fayyumic dialect was spoken in the Faiyum Oasis, as well as the region of the Nile where the canal that carried water into the Faiyum Oasis connected to the Nile. In this region was the Egyptian city of Nn-nswt (𓎛𓎛 𓎝𓈖), from which the dialect was likely derived. The name is commonly anglicized as Henen-Nesut, and was one of the capitals of Egypt during the First Intermediate Period, specifically during the 9th and 10th dynasties. The dialect is believed to have become dominant in the Faiyum Oasis during the 12th dynasty, when the Faiyum basin was flooded with Nile flood water diverted via a canal, turning the oasis into a lake the size of Lake Superior in North America. During this era, the Faiyum was colonized by Egyptians and refugees from the rebellion in Amorite-controlled Syria and Canaan. This suggests the inversion of the L and R sounds in this name was absorbed into written Canaanite during this era.

An Egyptian named Ahmose pen-Nekhbet reported fighting at Avaris and Sharuhen in the autobiography craved into his tomb. He also noted that the Egyptians fought the šåsw (𓈖𓄿𓊖), meaning "nomads," in the Sinai peninsula during these campaigns. These nomads do not appear to have been the Israelites, who, according to the Israelite texts, would have been deep in the wilderness east of Edom by that point. However, the *Book of Numbers* also places the "Amalek" north of the Negev, indicating these were the Amorite remnants of the Hyksos regime. In the time of Abraham, the Amorites began a rebellion against King Shulgi's Neo-Sumerian Empire, and therefore the term is translated literally.

17 Berlin Genesis: basilea Elasar oi Tesgar (ΒΑϹΙΛΕΑ ΕΛΑϹΑΡ ΟΙ ΤΕϹΓΑΡ). Translation: king Elasar the Tesgar

• Codex Alexandrinus: basilea Elasar oi tessares (ΒΑϹΙΛΕΑ ΕΛΑϹΑΡ ΟΙΤΕϹϹΑΡΕϹ). Translation: king Elasar the four

• Septuagint manuscript 64: basiléa Ellasar oi téssares (μασιλγὰ Ελλἀσαρ Θ τγσσαρὁϲ). Translation: king Ellasar the four

• Septuagint manuscript 318: basiléa Sellasar oi téssares (μασιλγὰ Σ⟨λλασαρ Θ τγσσαρὁϲ). Translation: king Sellasar the four

• Septuagint manuscript 707: basiléa Ellasas oi téssares (μασιλγὰ Ελλἀꝅαϲ Θ τγσσαρὁϲ). Translation: king Ellasar the four

CHAPTER 14

• Septuagint manuscript 343: basiléa Selasar oi téssares (ⲩⲁⲥⲓⲗⲧⲁ Ⲥⲉⲗⲁⲥⲁⲣ ⲑ ⲧⲧⲥⲥⲁⲣⲟⲥ). Translation: king Selasar the four

• Septuagint manuscript 426: basiléa Lasar oi téssares (ⲩⲁⲥⲓⲗⲧⲁ ⲗⲁⲥⲁⲣ ⲑ ⲧⲧⲥⲥⲁⲣⲟⲥ). Translation: king Lasar the four

• Septuagint manuscript 19: basiléa Ellasar kai oi téssares (ⲩⲁⲥⲓⲗⲧⲁ ⲉⲗⲗⲁⲥⲁⲣ ⲕⲁⲩ ⲑ ⲧⲧⲥⲥⲁⲣⲟⲥ). Translation: king Ellasar and the four

• Septuagint manuscript 799: basiléa Elasōr oi téssares (ⲩⲁⲥⲓⲗⲧⲁ ⲉⲗⲁⲟⲣ ⲑ ⲧⲧⲥⲥⲁⲣⲟⲥ). Translation: king Elasor the four

• Leningrad Codex: melek 'Ellāsār 'arbā'â (מֶלֶךְ אֶלְסָר אַרְבָּעָה). Translation: king Ellasar four

• Peshitta: mlkå dDlsr årbôå mlkyn (ܡܠܟܐ ܕܕܠܣܪ ܐܪܒܥܐ ܡܠܟܝܢ). Translation: king of Dlsr four kings

• Targum Onkelos: malkā' də'Ellāsār 'arbə'â (מַלְכָּא דְאֶלְסָר אַרְבְּעָה). Translation: king of Ellasar four

• Targum Jerusalem: malkā' də'Elāsār 'arba' (מַלְכָּא דְאֶלְסָר אַרְבַּע). Translation: king of Elasar four

• Targum Pseudo-Jonathan: malkā' ditlāsar 'arba'at (מַלְכָּא דְתְלָסַר אַרְבַּעַת). Translation: king of Tlasar four

This phrase appears to be a transliteration of the Neo-Sumerian title lugal an kišurra arbaim (𒈗 𒀭𒆠�19𒊏 𒐊𒄲𒆠𒀸), meaning "king of everything under the sky in the four (lands)." If this was the origin of the phrase, it would have to have been translated into Egyptian before being translated back into Canaanite in order to transition from kišurra to ellāsār. As the phrase fell out of common use after the fall of the Neo-Sumerian empire, it indicates the original text must have been written sometime between approximately 2330 and 2000 BCE.

CHAPTER 14

18 Codex Alexandrinus: Abram tō peratē (ΑΒΡΑΜ ΤѠ ΠΕΡΑΤΗ). Possible translations: Abram the end, Abram then at extremity, Abram then in the courthouse (via Egyptian)

- Leningrad Codex: 'Abrām hā'Ibrî (אַבְרָם הָעִבְרִי). Translation: Abram the Hebrew (or Eberite, crosser)

- Peshitta: Åbrm ôbryå (ܐܒܪܡ ܥܒܪܝܐ). Translation: Abram crosser (or Eberite)

- Targum Onkelos: 'Abrām 'ibrā'â (אַבְרָם עִבְרָאָה). Translation: Abram ferryman (or crosser, wrathful)

- Targum Pseudo-Jonathan: 'Abrām 'îbərā' (אַבְרָם עִיבְרָא). Translation: Abram ferryman (or crosser, wrathful)

The differences between the word Hebrew and Perate cannot be accounted for by a transliteration error. The term found in the Masoretic text is the word meaning "Hebrew," referring to either an individual Hebrew or the Hebrew language. The Aramaic version of the word is identical ôbry (^ץ͂Ꙩ), however, meant both "Hebrew" and "Aramean" or "Aramaic." The Greek term peratē is more obscure.

It could be interpreted as a variation on the Attican Greek dialect's perate (περατε), meaning "end," or "extremity," however, this interpretation does not fit the context, and like the Hebrew translation, the term is treated as a proper name. The term is a Middle Egyptian word per-ôåti (𓉐𓏤𓄿𓇯) for "courthouse" in the Heliopolite dialect, however, meant "house of lepers" or "hospital" in other Egyptian dialects. The two variations were based on the name of the goddess Ôåti (𓇯), whose name meant "leper" but was the judge of the dead in the Heliopolite theology.

The Heliopolite dialect was the official dialect of Egypt during the late Middle Kingdoms Canaanite dynasty, when the capital was in Îwnw (𓉺𓊖), as well as during the subsequent Canaanite dynasty, when the city was mentioned in Cosmic Genesis and Exodus as On

246

CHAPTER 14

($\Omega\nu$) and in Bereshít as 'Ôn (אֹן), and was later renamed Heliopolis (Ηλίου πόλις) by the Greeks. During the subsequent Hyksos dynasty, the capital was moved to Avaris, and then the New Kingdom's capital was in Thebes, meaning that the term has to be an artifact of a Middle Egyptian book of Abram or Israel, predating the Hyksos Dynasty. While the Heliopolite dialect's "courthouse" makes more sense than Abram judging from a hospital, it is likely that the Akkadian Cuneiform translators did not know the Heliopolite dialect, and did not want to write that Abram was living in a house of lepers, and so simply transliterated the word. The substitution of "the Hebrew" in the Masoretic text appears to be part of the Hasmonean redaction of circa 140 BCE, when the Judahite dialect of Canaanite became the "Hebrew" language.

19 Cotton Genesis: tē drui tē Mambrē o Amorrjs (ΤΗ ΔΡΥΙ ΤΗ ΜΑΜΒΡΗ Ο ΑΜΟΡΡΙC). Translation: the oak the Mambre the Amorrhis

• Septuagint manuscript 509: tē drui tē Mambrē o Amoris (τη Δρω τη Μαμμβρη ο Αμορις). Translation: the oak the Mambre the Amorite

• Septuagint manuscript 55: tē drui tē Mambrē o Olmoris (τη Δρω τη Μαμμβρη ο Ολμορις). Translation: the oak the Mambre the Olmoris

• Septuagint manuscript 127: tē drui tē Mabrē o Amoris (τη Δρω τη Μαυβρη ο Αμορις). Translation: the oak the Mabre the Amorite

• Septuagint manuscript 707: tē drui tē Mabri o Gauros (τη Δρω τη Μαυβρι ο Γαυρος). Translation: the oak the Mabri the Gauros

• Septuagint manuscript 313: tē drui tē Mambri o Amoris (τη Δρω τη Μαμμβρι ο Αμορις). Translation: the oak the Mambren the Amorite

CHAPTER 14

• Septuagint manuscript 426: tēn drun tēn mambrēn o Omoros (ﭏ ᲛᲚᲣ ﭏ ᲛᲒᲛᲛᲢᲚᲣ ο ᲝᲛᲝᲒᲝᲪ). Translation: the oak the Mambrēn the Omoros

• Septuagint manuscript 19: tē drui tē Mambē o Ammôr (ᲢᲚ ᲛᲚᲣ ᲢᲚ ᲛᲛᲛᲢᲚ ο ᲛᲛᲛᲝᲒ). Translation: the oak the Mambre the Ammor

• Septuagint manuscript 82: tē drui tē Maurē o Omoros (ᲢᲚ ᲛᲚᲣ ᲢᲚ ᲛᲛᲥᲢᲚ ο ᲝᲛᲝᲒᲪ). Translation: the oak the Maurethe Omoros

• Septuagint manuscript 458: tē drui tē Mambrē o Amōris (ᲢᲚ ᲛᲚᲣ ᲢᲚ ᲛᲛᲛᲛᲢᲚ ο ᲛᲛᲝᲒᲪ). Translation: the oak the Mambre the Amorite

• Septuagint manuscript 246: tē drui tē Mambē o Amoris (ᲢᲚ ᲛᲚᲣ ᲢᲚ ᲛᲛᲛᲢᲚ ο ᲛᲛᲝᲒᲪ). Translation: the oak the Mambre the Amorite

• Septuagint manuscript 46: tē drui tē Mambrē o Omōris (ᲢᲚ ᲛᲚᲣ ᲢᲚ ᲛᲛᲛᲛᲢᲚ ο ᲝᲛᲝᲒᲪ). Translation: the oak the Mambrethe Omoris

• Septuagint manuscript 72: tē drui tē Mambrē o Gambros (ᲢᲚ ᲛᲚᲣ ᲢᲚ ᲛᲛᲛᲛᲢᲚ ο ᲒᲛᲛᲛᲢᲝᲪ). Translation: the oak the Mambre the Gambros

• Septuagint manuscript 108: tē drui tē Mambrē o Amōr (ᲢᲚ ᲛᲚᲣ ᲢᲚ ᲛᲛᲛᲛᲢᲚ ο ᲛᲛᲝᲒ). Translation: the oak the Mambre the Amor

• Septuagint manuscript 314: tē drui tē Mambrē o Ammor (ᲢᲚ ᲛᲚᲣ ᲢᲚ ᲛᲛᲛᲛᲢᲚ ο ᲛᲛᲛᲛᲝᲒ). Translation: the oak the Mambre the Ammor

• Septuagint manuscript 799: tēn drun tēn Maurēn o Ammoris (ﭏ ᲛᲚᲣ ﭏ ᲛᲛᲥᲢᲚᲣ ο ᲛᲛᲛᲛᲝᲒᲪ). Translation: the oak the Maurēn the Amorite

• Leningrad Codex: bə'Ēlōnê Mamrē' hā'ĕmōrî (בְּאֵלֹנֵי מַמְרֵא הָאֱמֹרִי). Translation: at Elone for Mamre the speaker

• Peshitta: blwtå dMmrå åmwryå (ܒܠܘܛܐ ܕܡܡܪܐ ܐܡܘܪܝܐ). Translation: oak (or acorn) for Mmrå the speaker

248

CHAPTER 14

• Targum Onkelos: bəmêšərê Mamrē' 'Ĕmôrā'â (בְּמֵישְׁרֵי מַמְרֵא אֱמוֹרָאָה). Translation: plains of Mamre the Amorite

• Targum Pseudo-Jonathan: bəhezwê Mamrē' 'Ĕmôrā'â (בְּחֶזְוֵי מַמְרָא אֱמוֹרָאָה). Translation: insight of Mamre the Amorite

The Greek and Hebrew translations are noticeably different, however, both include Aramaic loanwords or transliterations. The word the Greeks translated as "oak" should have been åylnâ (אִילָנָא), however, that was neither translated nor transliterated into Hebrew, instead, the similar word ålny (אלני), was used. The Hebrew spelling of oak is ålwn (אלון), and therefore, the word in the Masoretic text is neither Hebrew nor Aramaic, suggesting a proper name in another dialect. The Greek term "Mambre the Amoris" appears to be a transliteration of the same terms found in the Masoretic text as mmrå håmry (ממרא האמרי), which is a transliteration of the Aramaic term "for the lord of the Amorites." Along with the rest of the sentence regarding "oak's" brothers, it indicates that the Aramaic text was about "Elon, Lord of the Amorites."

20 Codex Alexandrinus: Melǩisedek basileus Salēm (ΜΕΛΧΙϹΕΛΕΚ ΒΑϹΙΛΕΥϹϹΑΛΗΜ). Translation: Melkhisedek king of Salem

• Septuagint manuscript 961: -elkheise- (-ΕΛΧΕΙϹΕ-). Translation: -elkheise-. The section of text is damaged but appears to have listed the name as Melǩeisedek (ΜΕΛΧΕΙϹΕΛΕΚ).

• Septuagint manuscript 18: Melǩēsedek basileus Saleim (Μϡχισϐλϐμ uλσιλϐυc Σλλϕμ). Translation: Melkhisesek king of Saleim

• Septuagint manuscript 180: Melǩēsedek basileus Soluma (Μϡχισϐλϐμ uλσιλϐυc Σολυμϱ). Translation: Melkhisesek king of Soluma

249

CHAPTER 14

- Septuagint manuscript 318: Melǩēsedek basileus Salēm (Ⲙⲉⲭⲏⲥⲟⲥⲉⲕ ⲩⲁⲥⲓⲗⲉⲩⲥ Ⲥⲁⲗⲏⲙ). Translation: Melkhisesek king of Salem

- Septuagint manuscript 370: Melǩisesek basileus Salēm (Ⲙⲉⲭⲓⲥⲟⲥⲟⲥⲉⲕ ⲩⲁⲥⲓⲗⲉⲩⲥ Ⲥⲁⲗⲏⲙ). Translation: Melkhisesek king of Salem

- Septuagint manuscript 707: Melǩesedek basileus Salēm (Ⲙⲉⲭⲟⲥⲟⲥⲁⲟⲥⲉⲕ ⲩⲁⲥⲓⲗⲉⲩⲥ Ⲥⲁⲗⲏⲙ). Translation: Melkhesedek king of Salem

- Leningrad Codex: malkî-Sedeq melek Šālēm (מַלְכִּי־צֶדֶק מֶלֶךְ שָׁלֵם). Translation: king of justice (or right, Jupiter, Sydyk) king of Shalem

- Targum Onkelos: Malkîsedeq malkā' dÎrûšəlem (מַלְכִּי צֶדֶק מַלְכָּא דִירוּשְׁלֵם). Translation: Malki Sedeq of Jerusalem

- Targum Pseudo-Jonathan: Malkā' sadîqā' hû' Šēm bar Nah malkā' dÎrûšəlem (מַלְכָּא צַדִּיקָא הוּא שֵׁם בַּר נֹחַ מַלְכָּא דִירוּשְׁלֵם). Translation: king saintly (or righteous) who was of Shem son of Noah king of Jerusalem

- Sahidic manuscript 625: Melǩisedek de prro nSalēm (Ⲙⲉⲗⲭⲓⲥⲉⲇⲉⲕ ⲇⲉ ⲡⲣ̄ⲣⲟ ⲛ̄Ⲥⲁⲗⲏⲙ). Translation: Melkhisedek the king of Salem

- Sahidic manuscript 16L: Melǩis de prro nSalēm (Ⲙⲉⲗⲭⲓ̈ⲥ ⲇⲉ ⲡⲣ̄ⲣⲟ ⲛ̄Ⲥⲁⲗⲏⲙ). Translation: Melkhis the king of Salem

- Sahidic manuscript 2148: Mēlǩisedek de prro nSalēm (Ⲙⲏⲗⲭⲓ̈ⲥⲉⲇⲉⲕ ⲇⲉ ⲡⲣ̄ⲣⲟ ⲛ̄Ⲥⲁⲗⲏⲙ). Translation: Melkhisedek the king of Salem

In chapter 34, Jacob visits a town called "Salem a town by Shechem" (Σαλημ πολιν Σικιμων) in Septuagint manuscripts, however, which is mirrored by Šālēm 'îr Šəkem (שָׁלֵם עִיר שְׁכֶם) in the Leningrad Codex. While the Septuagint manuscripts have variances in the name, it is always a town by Shechem. The

CHAPTER 14

Hebrew text could be read as "Shalem town by Shechem," however, it is generally interpreted as "safely to the town of Shechem." There is a town named Salim (سالم) in the region of ancient Shechem, which Jeremiah called Salēm (Σαλημ / שלם) circa 584 BCE. Nevertheless, the traditional interpretation is that the city of Salem that Abraham visited was Jerusalem.

This is a common viewpoint from the Classical era, shared by Jews and Christians. The earliest reference to Jerusalem as Salem is found in the Psalms, where Salem is treated as another name for Zion. This interpretation of Salem as an older name of Jerusalem was implied in the Christian Letter to the Hebrews in the mid-1ˢᵗ century, and stated by the Judean historian Josephus in the late-1ˢᵗ century CE. It was repeated throughout the Medieval Period but started to be questioned when Egyptologists discovered the name Wrwšalim (𓂋𓊖𓈖𓅱𓈖𓂋𓅱) in the Middle Kingdom era execration texts. This is accepted as a hieratic transliteration of the Amorite name ᵘʳᵘÚrušalim (𒌷𒊑𒊭𒇴), which caused confusion for those using the Masoretic chronology.

Fortunately, the Old Kingdom era Autobiography of Weni confirms that there was a town called "Home of Peace" (𓉐𓊨) just south of the Jezreel Valley, ruled by someone called the "Lord of Justice" (𓂋𓊪 𓏏𓊨). This was around 200 hundred years before Abraham arrived in Salem, and therefore, this must have been the title of the ruler. A similar title was reported for the ruler of Jerusalem during Joshua's invasion 500 years after Abraham's time. When Joshua invaded Canaan, the defense of the southern Canaanite towns was led by Adoni-Zedek (אֲדֹנִי־צֶדֶק) in Masoretic Joshua, meaning "Lord of Justice," who was the ruler of Jerusalem.

21 Codex Alexandrinus: tēō tō usistō (ⲑⲉⲱ ⲧⲱ ⲩ϶ⲓⲥⲧⲱ). Translation: god the highest

251

CHAPTER 14

- Septuagint manuscript 458: ṭeō tou usistou (ⲑⲉ͞ⲱ ⲧⲱ ⲩⲯⲓϛⲟⲩ). Translation: god the highest

- Leningrad Codex: 'ēl 'elyôn (אֵל עֶלְיוֹן). Translation: god highest

- Peshitta: ålhå mrymå (ܐܠܗܐ ܡܪܝܡܐ). Translation: god of Miriam

- Targum Onkelos: 'ēl 'illā'â (אֵל עִלְאָה). Translation: god ascended

- Targum Pseudo-Jonathan: 'ĕlāhā' 'îlā'â (אֱלָהָא עִילָאָה). Translation: god highest

- Sahidic manuscript 625: noute etjose (ⲚⲞⲨⲦⲈ ⲈⲦⲜⲞⲤⲈ). Translation: god exulted

The Greek term Highest God (θεω τω υψιστω) shows up several Second Temple Era Jewish texts, including *1ˢᵗ Ezra, Judith, 3ʳᵈ Maccabees, Psalms,* and the *Wisdom of Joshua ben Sira.* Most of these texts were not redacted during the Hasmonean period and were not copied by the Masoretes, however, Psalms does appear to have been redacted, as the Masoretic version has the term Yahweh Elyom which strongly supports the Hasmonean redactors as having replaced El with Yahweh. The term El Elyon is known to have been a major god of the Canaanites, called ål wålyn in the Sefire Treaty from circa 750 BCE.

The quotes of Sanchuniathon's writing that have survived to the present, from circa 1200 BCE, referred to the god called Elioun as the primordial creator-god of the Canaanites. Jews, Christians, Muslims, and non-religious historians and archaeologists all consider Elyon (highest) to be an epithet and not a proper name.

CHAPTER 15

After these things the word of the Lord came to Abram in a vision, saying, "Don't be afraid Abram, I shield you, and your reward will be very great."

Abram said, "Master,[1] what will you give me? Whereas I am departing without a child, except the son of Masek my home-born female slave, this Eliezer of Damascus."

Abram said, "I am sad because you have given me no descendant, but my home-born will succeed me."

Immediately there was a voice of the Lord to him, saying, "This will not be your heir, but he that will come out of you will be your heir."

He took him out and said, "Look up to the sky, and count the stars, if you will be able to count them fully," and he said, "So will your descendants be."

Abram believed God,[2] and it was counted as righteousness for him. He said to him, "I am the god who led you out of the land of the Chaldeans, to give you this land to inherit."

He asked, "Despot, how will I know that I will inherit it?"

He answered him, "Take for me a heifer in her third year, and a female-goat in her third year, and a ram in his third year, a dove and a pigeon." So he took to him all these, and divided them in the middle, and set them opposite to each other, but the birds he did not divide. Birds came down on the bodies, even on the divided parts of them, and Abram drove them away. About sunset, a trance fell on Abram, and Look! A great gloomy terror fell on him.

It was said to Abram, "You will surely know that your descendants will be travelers in a land not their own, and they will enslave them, and afflict them, and humble them four hundred years. The nation whom they will serve, I will judge, and after this, they will come out here with much property. But you will depart to your fathers in peace, nourished in a good old age. In the fourth generation, they will return here, for the sins of the Amorites are not yet completed, even until now."

When the sun was about to set, there was a flame, and a smoking furnace and lamps of fire, which passed between these divided pieces. On that day, the Lord made a covenant with Abram, saying, "To your descendants, I will give this land, from the river of Egypt[3] to the great river Euphrates, from the Kenites, Kenizzites, Kadmonites, Cypriots, Perizzites, Raphites, Amorites, Canaanites, Mitanni, Girgashites, and the Jebusites."

CHAPTER 15 NOTES

1 Vienna Genesis: despota (ᴀᴇᴄʜᴏᴛᴀ). Translation: despot (or tyrant, lord, master)

• Septuagint manuscript 319: despota kurie (ΔϭοϭοτΔ ʟυβιϭ). Translation: despot (or tyrant, lord, master) lord

- Septuagint manuscript 57: K$_x$^{e} (אָ). Translation: Lord
- Leningrad Codex: ădônāy Yĕhōwih (אֲדֹנָי יֱהוִֹה). Translation: lord Yahweh
- Peshitta: mryå ålhå (ܡܪܝܐ ܐܠܗܐ). Translation: master (or lord) god
- Targum Onkelos: 'ēl 'illā'â (אֵל עִלָּאָה). Translation: god ascended
- Targum Jerusalem: Yəyā 'ĕllōhîm (יְיָ אֱלֹהִים). Translation: Yahweh gods (or god via Neo-Assyrian)
- Targum Pseudo-Jonathan: Yəyā 'ĕllōhîm (יְיָ אֱלֹהִים). Translation: Yahweh gods (or god via Neo-Assyrian)
- Sahidic manuscript 625: joeis (ϫⲟⲉⲓⲥ). Translation: master

2 Septuagint manuscript 961: kai episteusen abram eis T̄N̄ (ⲕⲁⲓ ⲉⲡⲓⲥⲧⲉⲩⲥⲉⲛ ⲁⲃⲣⲁⲙ ⲉⲓⲥ ⲑ̄ⲛ̄). Translation: and believed Abram of god
- Septuagint manuscript 509: kai epísteusen Abram tō teō (και ϭπιϛϭυϭσαν Αϱϱαμ τοο θϭοω). Translation: and believed Abram the god
- Septuagint manuscript 108: kai epísteusai Abram tō teō (και ϭπιϛϭυϭσαι Αϱϱαμ τοο θϭοω). Translation: and believed Abram the god
- Septuagint manuscript 344: kai epísteusen Abraam tō teō (και ϭπιϛϭυϭσαν Αϱϱαλμ τοο θϭοω). Translation: and believed Abraham the god
- Leningrad Codex: wəhe'ĕmin baYhōwâ (וְהֶאֱמִן בַּיהוָֹה). Translation: and he believed in Yhōwâ
- Peshitta: whymn åbrm bålhå (ܘܗܝܡܢ ܐܒܪܡ ܒܐܠܗܐ). Translation: and believed Abram the god
- Targum Onkelos: wəhêmîn bəmêmərā' daYyā (וְהֵימִין בְּמֵימְרָא דַיְיָ). Translation: and believed in the name of Yahweh
- Sahidic manuscript 625: afticteye (ⲁϥⲡⲓⲥⲧⲉⲩⲉ). Translation: he believed

CHAPTER 15

3 Berlin Genesis: potamou Aiguptou (ΠΟΤΑΜΟΥ ΑΙΓΥΠΤΟΥ). Translation: river Egyptian

• Septuagint manuscript 75: potamou tou Aigúptou (ποτΑμου τω Αιγυπ]ου). Translation: river the Egyptian

• Leningrad Codex: nəhar Miṣrayim (נְהַר מִצְרִים). Translation: river Egyptians

• Peshitta Manuscript 5b1: årôå dMṣryn (ܕܡܨܪܝܢ ܐܪܥܐ). Translation: land the Egyptians

• Peshitta Manuscript 7a1: nhrå dMṣryn (ܕܡܨܪܝܢ ܢܗܪܐ). Translation: river the Egyptians

• Targum Onkelos: nahărā' dəMiṣrayim (נַהֲרָא דְמִצְרִים). Translation: river of Egypt

• Targum Pseudo-Jonathan: nîlôs dəMiṣrayim (נִילוֹס דְמִצְרִים). Translation: Nile of Egypt

• Sahidic manuscript 625: mpiero nKēme (ⲙⲡⲓⲉⲣⲟ ⲛ̄ⲕⲏⲙⲉ). Translation: of the river (or canal) in Egypt (or black)

• Sahidic manuscript 2037: peiero nKēme (ⲡⲉⲓⲉⲣⲟ ⲛ̄ⲕⲏⲙⲉ). Translation: the river in Egypt (or black)

• Sahidic manuscript 2042: epierro nKume (ⲉⲡⲓⲉⲣⲣⲟ ⲛ̄ⲕ ⲩⲙⲉ). Translation: at the river in Kume

The variations found in Peshitta Manuscripts 5b1, from the 5th century, and 7a1, from the 7th century, are generally interpreted as part of the ongoing work to synchronize the Peshitta with the Masoretic text. As few early copies of the Septuagint's Cosmic Genesis survive, and those that do show signs of massive rewriting in the early Christian era, it is unclear if the original Septuagint and Aramaic source text referred to the "land of Egypt," or "river of Egypt."

CHAPTER 16

Sarai the wife of Abram carried him no children, and she had an Egyptian maid whose name was Hagar. So Sarai said to Abram, "Look, the Lord has restrained me from bearing, therefore, go into my maid, that I may get children for myself through her."

Abram listened to the voice of Sarai. So Abram had lived ten years in the land of Canaan when Sarai the wife of Abram having taken Hagar the Egyptian, her handmaid, gave her to Abram her husband as a wife to him. He went into Hagar and she conceived and learned that she was with child, and her mistress was ashamed before her.

Sarai said to Abram, "I am injured by you. I gave my handmaid into you, and when I saw that she was with child, I was embarrassed before her. The Lord judge between me and you."

Abram said to Sarai, "Look your handmaid is in your hands, use her as it may seem good to you."

Sarai chastised her, and she fled from her presence. The messenger of the lord[1] found her by the fountain of water in the wilderness, by the fountain in the way to Zur. The messenger of the lord asked her, "Hagar, Sarai's maid, where are you coming from, and where are you going?"

CHAPTER 16

She answered, "I am fleeing from the presence of my mistress Sarai."

The messenger of the lord said to her," Return to your mistress, and submit yourself under her hands."

The messenger of the lord said to her, "I will surely multiply your descendants, and it will not be numbered for multitude."

The messenger of the lord said to her, "Look you are with child, and will carry a son, and will call his name Ishmael, for the Lord has listened to your humiliation. He will be a wild man, his hands against all, and the hands of all against him, and he will live in the presence of all his brothers."

She called the name of the Lord the god who spoke to her, you are God who sees me," for she said, "I have openly seen him that appeared to me."

Therefore she called the well, "The well of him whom I have openly seen." (Look, it is between Kadesh and Bered.) Hagar carried a son for Abram, and Abram called the name of his son which Hagar carried to him, Ishmael. Abram was eighty-six years old when Hagar carried Ishmael for Abram.

CHAPTER 16 NOTES

1 Codex Alexandrinus: aŋgelos KU tou TU (ⲀⲄⲄⲈⲖⲞⲤⲔⲨⲦⲞⲨⲐⲨ). Translation: messenger lord the god

CHAPTER 16

• Septuagint manuscript 707: aŋgelon Kuríou tou ţeou (ΔγβⱯ Ⱪυβιου τꙍ θϭου). Translation: messenger lord the god

• Leningrad Codex: mal'ak Yəhōwâ (מַלְאַךְ יְהֹוָה). Translation: messenger Yahweh

• Peshitta: mlåkh dmryå (ܡܠܐܟܗ ܕܡܪܝܐ). Translation: messenger the master (or lord)

• Targum Onkelos: mal'ākā' daYyā (מַלְאָכָא דַיְיָ). Translation: messenger the Yahweh

• Targum Pseudo-Jonathan: mal'ākā' daYyā (מַלְאָכָא דַיְיָ). Translation: messenger of Yahweh

• Sahidic manuscript 2042: aŋgelos mpjoeis (ⲁⲅⲅⲉⲗⲟⲥ ⲙ̅ⲡϫⲟⲉⲓⲥ). Translation: angel of the master

CHAPTER 17

Abram was ninety-nine years old, and the Lord appeared to Abram and said to him, "I am the god Shaddai.[1] Be very pleasing before me, and be blameless. I will establish my covenant between me and you, and I will multiply you greatly."

Abram fell on his face, and God said to him, "Look! My covenant is with you, and you will be the father of many nations. Your name will no longer be Abram, but your name will be Abraham, for I have made you a father of many nations. I will increase you very greatly, and I will make nations from you, and kings will come out of you. I will establish my covenant between you and your descendants after you, for all their generations, as an eternal covenant, to be your god, and a god of your descendants after you. I will give you and your descendants after you, the land in which you stay, including all the land of Canaan as an eternal possession, and I will be a god to them."

God said to Abraham, "You will also fully follow my covenant, you and your descendants after you, for all their generations. This is the covenant, that you will fully keep between me and you, and between your descendants after you for all their generations, every male among you will be circumcised. You will be circumcised in the flesh of your foreskin, and it will be as a sign of a covenant between me and you. The child will be circumcised by you at eight days

261

old, every male throughout your generations, and the slave born in the house, and he that is bought with silver, of every son of a stranger, who is not of your descendants. He who is born in your house, and he that is bought with silver will surely be circumcised, and my covenant will be on your flesh as an eternal covenant. The uncircumcised male, who will not be circumcised in the flesh of his foreskin on the eighth day, that mind will be utterly destroyed from its family, for he has broken my covenant."

God said to Abraham, "Sarai your wife, her name will not be called Sarai, Sarah will be her name. I will bless her and give you a son through her, and I will bless him and he will become nations, and kings of nations will come from him."

Abraham fell on his face and laughed, and asked in his heart, "Will there be a child to one who is a hundred years old? Will Sarah who is ninety years old, become pregnant?"

Abraham said to God, "Let this Ishmael live before you."

God said to Abraham, "Yes, watch, Sarah your wife will carry a son for you, and you will call his name Isaac,[2] and I will establish my covenant with him, as an eternal covenant, to be a god to him and his descendants after him. Concerning Ishmael, see, I have heard you, and, watch, I have blessed him, and will increase him and multiply him greatly. He will father twelve nations, and I will make him a great nation. But I will establish my covenant with Isaac, whom Sarah will carry for you at this time, in the next year."

CHAPTER 17

He stopped speaking with him, and God went up from Abraham. Abraham took Ishmael his son, and all his home-born slaves, and all those bought with silver, and every male of the men in the house of Abraham, and he circumcised their foreskins immediately that day, following what God had told him. Abraham was ninety-nine years old when his foreskin was circumcised. Ishmael his son was thirteen years old when his foreskin was circumcised. At that time, Abraham was circumcised, and Ishmael his son, and all the men of his house, both those born in the house and those bought with silver from alien nations.

CHAPTER 17 NOTES

1 Codex Alexandrinus: Egō eimi o ṮS sou (ⲉⲅⲱ ⲉⲓⲙⲓ ⲟ ⲑⲥ̄ ⲥⲟⲩ). Translation: I am the god of you

• LXX 17: Egō eimi Kurios o teós sou (ϭγⲟⲟ ϥⲙ Ⲕⲩβⲓⲟⲥ ⲟ θ϶ⲟⲥ ⲥⲟⲩ). Translation: I am Lord the god of you

• Leningrad Codex: Ănî-ēl Šadday (אֲנִי־אֵל שַׁדַּי). Translation: I'm god Shaddai

• Peshitta: Ånå ånå Åylšdy ålhå (ܐܢܐ ܐܢܐ ܐܠܫܕܝ, ܐܠܗܐ). Translation: I am Åylšdy god

• Targum Onkelos: 'ănā' 'ēl Šadday (אֲנָא אֵל שַׁדַּי). Translation: I'm god Shaddai

• Targum Pseudo-Jonathan: 'ănā' 'ēl Šaday (אֲנָא אֵל שַׁדַי). Translation: I'm god Shaddai

The Greek, Hebrew, Hebrew and Aramaic translations often differ in regards to the name or title Shaddai, suggesting that the early Aramaic and Canaanite (Judahite or Samaritan) source texts they worked from differed in regards to this word. The term was

263

omitted throughout Cosmic Genesis, indicating the Aramaic translator had omitted it, however, it was almost certainly in the Canaanite version the Hebrew translator worked from, as it is used consistently in the other Masoretic books, and is mentioned again when Moses god's name Ōn is introduced in *Exodus*.

In the Peshitta, the term is interpreted as the proper name of the god speaking, while in the Targums and Masoretic text, it could either be a name or a description. El Shaddai was the supreme god of the Amorites, who they called Bel Šadi (🜛 ⬧🜏). There are many references to the Amorites in *Cosmic Genesis*, and the Israelites later believed the Amorites had worshiped their god according to the books of *Exodus / Names*, *Numbers*, and *Deuteronomy*.

The cause of the confusion over the term Shaddai, is likely due to the difference between the meaning of the word in Canaanite versus Aramaic. In Akkadian cuneiform, which was adopted as the written script by many cultures, the term was ^{deity}šēdu (🜛🜏), however, it referred to a "protective spirit" or "lesser god." In the later Aramaic language, the word became šydå (𐎐𐎚𐎃), meaning "demon" in the classical sense, as a type of muse or nymph. Whereas in Canaanite, šd (𐎌𐎄) took on a different meaning, generally interpreted as "powerful" by the Early Classical Era, which is likely where the Greeks ultimately derived the term "omnipotent" (παντοκράτορος), which was used later in the Septuagint where the Masoretic text generally uses the term Shaddai.

This alternate interpretation of the šd (𐎌𐎄) in Canaanite is likely due to the Egyptian New Kingdom era rule over Canaan, when Šd (𓂡𓈖𓏛), was worshiped in the region. Shed, who was often referred to as "the savior," was virtually identical to the earlier Canaanite god Resheph who was largely suppressed after the fall of the Hyksos dynasty.

CHAPTER 17

In the Masoretic *Book of Job*, Eliphaz referred to humanity as the "sons of Resheph" (בני-רשף) instead of the "sons of Adam," and then refers god as Shaddai (שדי). This usage is consistent throughout Masoretic Job, indicating that at some point the name Resheph was updated to Shaddai, likely during the New Kingdom era, when Resheph worship was suppressed due to his associated with the earlier Hyksos dynasty.

In this particular verse, the term ^{deity}Šadi (✳𒂥𒄿𒀭) is transliterated directly into Hebrew as âl Šdy (אל שדי), which has to have been in the Akkadian Cuneiform version of the text, and is therefore imported to this translation.

2 Berlin Genesis: Eisak (ΕΙϹΑΚ)
* Septuagint manuscript 961: Isak (ΙϹΑΚ)
* Codex Alexandrinus: Isaak (ΙϹΑΑΚ)
* Leningrad Codex: Yiṣḥāq (יִצְחָק)
* Targum Onkelos: Yiṣḥāq (יִצְחָק)
* Targum Pseudo-Jonathan: Yiṣḥāq (יִצְחָק)

This is a transliteration of the East Semitic word išši'ak (𒂗𒊺𒀝), meaning "representative" in Babylonian and Assyrian. The term was used in a religious context, as the išši'ak of a god; however, beginning around 2025 BCE, the Assyrians declared independence from the Neo-Sumerian empire, and the kings of Assyria adopted the title of išši'ak. Given that the king of Ur in the time of Abraham had to have been King Shulgi, who ruled between 2094 BCE and 2046 BCE, the Egyptian king would have been Mentuhotep II, who ruled between 2060 and 2009 BCE. The emergence of the Assyrian kingdom circa 2025 BCE, using the title išši'ak, suggests that King Mentuhotep II would have believed Abraham was also trying to declare a kingship over Samaria, explaining why his messenger would have demanded Abraham execute Isaac.

CHAPTER 17

Isaac was also known as "Israel" in Egypto-Israelite texts, although the Jewish texts claim that this name or title originated at the time of Jacob. If Isaac's full name was Išši'ak 'usa-ra-ilu (𒂍𒀭𒌓 𒄩𒈨𒉿𒌉𒆠) in Amorite, then the name would have meant "Representative named who struck god," which is similar to the Hebrew interpretation of the name. However, if the name "Israel" originated in an Old Sumerian title, the same phase would have been 'usa-ra-Ān (𒀭𒂵𒋛𒊭𒆠), meaning "speaker of the seal of god," suggesting Terah had held a sacred seal in Ur before fleeing, and may have carried it with him.

CHAPTER 18

God appeared to him by the oak of Mamre, as he sat by the door of his tent at noon. He lifted his eyes and saw, and saw three men stood before him, and having seen them he ran to meet them from the door of his tent and bowed to the ground.

He said, "Lord, if I have found favor in your sight, do not overlook your servant. Let water now be brought and let them wash your feet, and refresh yourselves under the tree. I will bring bread, and you will eat, and after this, you will depart on your journey, on account of which refreshment you have turned aside."

He said, "So do as you have said."

Abraham hurried to the tent to Sarah, and said to her, "Hurry, and knead three measures of fine flour, and make cakes."

Abraham ran to the cows, and took a young calf, tender and good, and gave it to his servant, and he hurried to dress it. He took butter and milk, and the calf which he had prepared, and he set them before them, and they did eat, and he stood by them under the tree.

He asked him, "Where is Sarah your wife?"

He answered and said, "Look! In the tent."

He answered, "I will return and visit you in the same season, and Sarah your wife will have a son."

CHAPTER 18

Sarah heard at the door of the tent, being behind him. Abraham and Sarah were old, advanced in days, and the custom of women ceased with Sarah. Sarah laughed in herself, saying, "The thing has not as yet happened to me, even until now, and my lord is old."

The Lord said to Abraham, "Why is it that Sarah has laughed to herself, saying, 'Will I really become pregnant? I am already old.' Will anything be impossible for God? At this time I will return to you in the season, and Sarah will have a son."

But Sarah denied it, saying, "I did not laugh," because she was afraid.

He answered her, "No, but you did laugh."

The men having risen from there looked towards Sodom and Gomorrah. Abraham went with them, attending them on their journey. The Lord said, "Will I hide from Abraham my servant the things I intend to do? But Abraham will become a great and populous nation, and in him will all the nations of the land be blessed. For I know that he will command his sons, and his house after him, that they will keep the ways of the Lord, to do justice and judgment, that the Lord may bring on Abraham all things whatever he has spoken to him."

The Lord said, "The cries from Sodom and Gomorrah have been increasingly reported to me, and their sins are very great. So I will go down and see if they correspond with the cry which is reported to me, and if not, that I may know."

CHAPTER 18

The men having departed from there came to Sodom, and Abraham was still standing before the Lord. Abraham approached and asked, "Would you destroy the righteous with the wicked, and will the righteous be like the wicked? If there are fifty righteous in the city, will you destroy them? Won't you spare the whole place for the sake of the fifty righteous if they are in it? By no means will you do this thing, to destroy the righteous with the wicked so the righteous will be like the wicked. By no means. You who judges the whole earth, will you not do right?"

The Lord answered, "If there are in Sodom fifty righteous in the city, I will spare the whole city and the whole region for their sake."

Abraham asked, "Now I have begun to speak to my Lord, and I am dirt and ashes. But if the fifty righteous should be only forty-five, will you destroy the whole city because of the five missing?"

He answered, "I will not destroy it if I find forty-five there."

He continued to question him still, "But if there are forty found there?"

He answered, "I will not destroy it for the sake of forty."

He asked, "Will there be anything against me, Lord, if I speak? But if there are thirty found there?"

He answered, "I will not destroy it for the sake of thirty."

CHAPTER 18

He asked, "Since I am able to speak to the Lord, what if there are twenty found there?"

He answered, "I will not destroy it if I find twenty there."

He asked, "Will there be anything against me, Lord, if I speak once more? But if there are ten found there?"

He answered, "I will not destroy it for the sake of the ten."

The Lord departed when he ended speaking with Abraham, and Abraham returned to his home.

CHAPTER 19

The two messengers came to Sodom in the evening. Lot sat by the gate of Sodom, and Lot having seen them, rose up to meet them, and he worshiped with his face to the ground, and said, "Look! My lords turn aside into the house of your servant. Rest from your journey and powder your feet. When you rise early in the morning, you can depart on your journey."

They answered, "No, we will stay in the street."

He constrained them, and they turned aside to him, and they entered into his house, and he made a feast for them, and baked unleavened cakes for them, and they ate. But before they went to sleep, the men of the city, the Sodomites, surrounded the house, both young and old, all the people together. They called out Lot, and said to him, "Where are the men that came to you tonight? Bring them out to us, so we can be with them."

Lot went out to them to the porch, and he shut the door behind him, and said to them, "By no means, brothers! Do not act wickedly! Instead, I have two daughters who have not yet known a man. I will bring them out to you, and you can use them however you please. Only, do not injure these men, who came under the shelter of my roof to avoid this."

CHAPTER 19

They replied to him, "Stand back! You came to reside here, and now you judge? Now then, we will harm you even more than them!"

They pushed hard against Lot, and they were close to breaking the door. The men reached out their hands and pulled Lot to them inside the house, and shut the door of the house. They struck the men that were at the door of the house with blindness, both small and great, and they grew tired of searching for the door. The men asked Lot, "Have you sons-in-law here, or sons, or daughters, or if you have any other friend in the city, bring them out of this place. For we are going to destroy this place, for their cry has been raised before the Lord, and the Lord has sent us here to destroy."

Lot went out, and spoke to his sons-in-law, who had married his daughters, and said, "Rise, and depart out of this place, for the Lord is about to destroy the city!"

But what he said seemed absurd to his sons-in-law. When it was morning, the messengers rushed Lot, saying, "Rise and take your wife, and your two daughters that you have, and go out, in case you are also destroyed with the iniquities of the city."

They were troubled, and the messengers[1] grabbed his hand, and the hand of his wife, and the hands of his two daughters, because the Lord had spared him. When they brought them out, they said, "Save your life by any means. Don't look around to that which is behind, or stay in any of the country around it, escape to the mountain, in case, perhaps you are overtaken together with them."

Lot said to them, "I beg, Lord, since your servant has found mercy before you, and you have magnified your right-eousness in what you do towards me, in that my mind may live, but, I will not be able to escape to the mountain, in case perhaps the destruction overtakes me and I die. Look, this city is near for me to escape to, it is a small one, and there I will be safe. Is it not small? My mind will survive because of you."

He answered him, "Look, I have respected your opinion also about this thing, that I should not overthrow the city which you have spoken of. Hurry and escape to there, for I will not be able to do anything until you have arrived there."

(Therefore he called the name of that city, Zoar.)[1]

The sun had risen above the land when Lot entered into Zoar. The Lord rained brimstone and fire out of the sky, from the Lord, on Sodom and Gomorrah.[3] He overthrew those cities, and all the country around it, and all that lived in the cities, and the plants growing out of the ground.

His wife turned back, and she became a pillar of salt. Abraham rose up early to go to the place where he had stood before the Lord. He looked towards Sodom and Gomorrah, and the surrounding country, and saw that a flame went up from the land like the smoke of a furnace.

It happened that when God destroyed all the cities and the region around them, God remembered Abraham, and sent Lot out of the middle of the destruction, when the Lord destroyed

CHAPTER 19

those cities in which Lot lived. Lot left Zoar and lived in the mountain with his two daughters, for he was afraid to live in Zoar. He lived in a cave with his two daughters.

The elder said to the younger, "Our father is old, and there is no one on the land who will come into us, as it is done in all the land. Come, and let us make our father drink wine, and let us sleep with him, and let us raise children from our father."

They made their father drink wine that night, and the elder went in and lay with her father that night, and he did not know when he slept and when he rose up. It happened in the morning, that the elder said to the younger, "Look, I slept last night with our father, let us make him drink wine in tonight also, and you go in and sleep with him, and let us raise descendants from our father."

They made their father drink wine that night also, and the younger went in and slept with her father, and he did not know when he slept, nor when he arose. The two daughters of Lot conceived by their father. The elder carried a son and called his name Moab, saying, "He is of my father."

This is the father of the Moabites to this present day. The younger also carried a son, and called his name Benammi, saying, "The son of my family." This is the father of the Ammonites to this present day.

CHAPTER 19

CHAPTER 19 NOTES

1 Codex Alexandrinus: aŋgeloi (ⲀⲄⲄⲈⲖⲞⲓ). Translation: messengers (or angels)

• Leningrad Codex: 'ănāšîm (אֲנָשִׁים). Translation: men (or husbands)

• Peshitta Manuscript 5b1: gbrå (ܓܒܪܐ). Translation: heroes

• Peshitta Manuscript 7a1: mlåôå (ܡܠܐܟܐ). Translation: messengers (or angels)

• Targum Onkelos: gūbrayyā' (גֻבְרַיָּא). Translation: heroes

• Targum Pseudo-Jonathan: mal'ăkayā' dahăwô mədamyāyn ləgabrayā' (מַלְאָכַיָּא דַהֲווֹ מְדַמְיִין לְגַבְרַיָּא). Translation: messengers who were disguised as hero

• Sahidic manuscript 2042: rōme (ⲣⲱⲙⲉ). Translation: men

This variation found in Peshitta Manuscripts 5b1, from the 5th century, and 7a1, from the 7th century, is generally interpreted as part of the ongoing work to synchronize the Peshitta with the Septuagint.

2 This scribal note appears to confirm that the name was recorded as Šūszíru (𒂍𒈬𒌑𒊺) before being transcribed into the Phoenician Canaanite script, as šū szíru (𒂍𒈬 𒌑𒊺) translates as "it is seed (or semen, offspring, descendants)." This note was probably added by the Akkadian cuneiform translator in the late New Kingdom era who first interpreted the name this way. For more information on Shasziru, see the note in chapter 14.

3 Septuagint manuscript 64: Sodoma kai Gomorrạ (ⲤⲞⲆⲞⲘⲀ ⲕⲀⲓ ⲅⲞⲘⲞⲣⲣⲀ). Translation: Sodoma and Gomorrah

• Septuagint manuscript 131: Sodoma kai Gomora (Σοδομὰ μαἰ Γομορα). Translation: Sodoma and Gomora

CHAPTER 19

- Septuagint manuscript 319: Sodōma kai Gomora (Σολοομα και Γομορα). Translation: Sodoma and Gomora
- Septuagint manuscript 75: Sōdomōn kai Gomorra (Σωδομοον και Γομοβρα). Translation: Sodomon and Gomorrah
- Septuagint manuscript 500: Sōdoma kai Gomorra (Σωδομα και Γομοβρα). Translation: Sodoma and Gomorrah
- Leningrad Codex: Sədōm wə'al-'Ămōrâ (סְדֹם וְעַל־עֲמֹרָה). Translation: Sedom and the Amora
- Peshitta: Sdwm wôl Ômwrâ (ܣܕܘܡ ܘܥܠ ܥܡܘܪܐ). Translation: Sdwm and the Omwra
- Targum Onkelos: Sədôm wə'al 'Ămôrâ (סְדוֹם וְעַל עֲמוֹרָה). Translation: Sedom and the Amora
- Targum Jerusalem: Sədôm wa'Ămôrâ (סְדוֹם וַעֲמוֹרָה). Translation: Sedom and Amora
- Targum Pseudo-Jonathan: Sədôm wə'al 'Ămôrâ (סְדוֹם וְעַל עֲמוֹרָה). Translation: Sedom and the Amora
- Vetus Latina manuscripts: Sodoma et Gomoram (Soδomλ ετ Comoraω). Translation: Sodoma and Gomoram
- Sahidic manuscript 2037: Sodoma mn Gomorra (Coλoma ϩn Γomoppλ). Translation: Sodoma and Gomorra

The Tall el-Hammam archaeological site at the foot of Mount Sodom, in Jordan, dates back to circa 1700 BCE and shows widespread damage caused by intense heat. It is theorized that the meteor impacted and burst in the atmosphere, leveling towns across a 200 square mile (500 km²) area. While the damage is evident from the archaeological record, the cause is unclear, and no impact site has been found. Some scholars believe this destruction may have been the source of the story of Sodom and Gomorrah.

CHAPTER 20

Abraham left there for the southern country, and lived between Kadesh and Zoar, and stayed in Gerar. Abraham said concerning Sarah his wife, "She is my sister," as he was afraid to say, "She is my wife," in case at any time the men of the city should kill him for her sake. So Abimelech king of Gerar sent and took Sarah.

God came to Abimelech by night in sleep, and said, "Look, you die for the woman, whom you have taken, has lived with a husband."

However Abimelech had not touched her, and he begged, "Lord, will you destroy an ignorant sinner and just nation? Didn't he tell me, 'She is my sister,' and didn't she say to me, 'He is my brother?' With a pure heart and in with clean hands have I done this."

God said to him in sleep, "Yes, I knew that you did this with a pure heart, and I spared you, so that you should not sin against me, therefore I did not allow you to touch her. But now return the man his wife, for he is a prophet and will pray for you, and you will live. But if you don't restore her, know that you and all yours will die."

Abimelech rose early in the morning and called all his servants, and he told them these words, and all the men were terrified. Abimelech called Abraham and demanded of him, "What is this that you have done to us? Have we sinned against you? You have brought on me and my kingdom a great sin! You have done to me something no one should do."

Abimelech asked Abraham, "What have you seen in me that you have done this?"

Abraham answered, "Well I thought, 'Surely God is not worshiped in this place, and they will kill me for my wife.' For truly she is my sister by my father, but not by my mother, and she became my wife. It happened when God brought me out of the house of my father, that I said to her, 'This righteousness you will perform for me, in every place into which we enter, say about me, "He is my brother."'"

Abimelech took a thousand didrachmas, and sheep, and calves, and servants, and maidservants, and gave them to Abraham, and he returned him Sarah his wife. Abimelech said to Abraham, "Look, my land is before you, live wherever it may please you."

To Sarah, he said, "Look, I have given your brother a thousand didrachmas, those will be for you, the price of your discretion. To all the women you speak with, tell the truth in all things."

Abraham prayed to God, and God healed Abimelech, and his wife, and his women servants, and they carried children. Because the Lord had sealed every womb in the house of Abimelech, because of Sarah Abraham's wife.

CHAPTER 21

The Lord visited Sarah, as he said, and the Lord did to Sarah, as he spoke. She conceived and carried for Abraham a son in old age, at the set time the Lord had told to him. Abraham called the name of his son that was born to him, who Sarah gave birth to, Isaac. Abraham circumcised Isaac on the eighth day, as God commanded him. Abraham was a hundred years old when Isaac his son was born to him. Sarah said, "The Lord has made laughter for me, for whoever will hear will rejoice with me."

She asked, "Who will tell Abraham that Sarah suckles a child? I have born a child in my old age!"

The child grew and was weaned, and Abraham made a great feast the day that his son Isaac was weaned. When Sarah saw the son of Hagar the Egyptian, who was born to Abraham, playing with Isaac her son, she said to Abraham, "Throw out this slave-woman and her son, for the son of this slave-woman will not inherit along with my son Isaac."

But the matter appeared very difficult before Abraham, concerning his son. But God said to Abraham, "Let it not be hard for you concerning the child and concerning the slave-woman. In all things whatever Sarah will say to you, listen to her voice, as from Isaac will your descendants come. Moreover, I will make the son of this slave-woman a great nation because he is your descendant."

CHAPTER 21

Abraham rose up in the morning and took loaves and a skin of water, and gave them to Hagar, and he put the child on her shoulder and sent her away, and after she departed, she wandered in the wilderness near Beersheba. The water was emptied from the skin, and she placed the child under a fir tree. She departed and sat down opposite him at the distance of a bow-shot, as she said, "I can't see the death of my child."

She sat opposite him, and the child cried out loud, and wept. God heard the voice of the child from the place where he was, and The messenger of the lord called down to Hagar, out of the sky, and said to her, "What is it Hagar? Don't be afraid, for God has heard the voice of the child from the place where he is. Rise up, and take the child, and hold him in your hand, for I will make him a great nation."

God opened her eyes, and she saw a well of living water, and she went and filled the skin with water, and gave the child drink. God was with the child, and he grew and lived in the wilderness, and became an archer. He lived in the wilderness, and his mother chose him a wife from Paran in Egypt.

It happened at that time that Abimelech spoke to Abraham, along with Ochozath his friend, and Phichol the chief captain of his army, saying, "God is with you in all things, whatever you may do. Now, therefore, swear to me by God that you will not injure me, nor my descendants, nor my name, but according to the righteousness which I have performed with you you will deal with me, and with the land in which you have stayed."

CHAPTER 21

Abraham answered, "I will swear."

Abraham reproved Abimelech because of the wells of water, which the servants of Abimelech took away. Abimelech said to him, "I don't know who has done this thing to you. You did not tell it to me, and I didn't hear of it before today."

Abraham took sheep and calves and gave them to Abimelech, and both made a covenant. Abraham set seven ewe lambs by themselves. Abimelech asked Abraham, "What are these seven ewe lambs that you have set alone?"

Abraham said, "You will receive the seven ewe lambs from me, that they may be for me as a witness, that I dug this well."

Therefore he named the name of that place, "The Well of the Oath," as they both swore there. They made a covenant at the Well of the Oath, and then Abimelech rose up, and Ochozath his friend, and Phichol the commander-in-chief of his army, and they returned to the land of the Pelesets.[1] Abraham planted a field at Beersheba[2] and called there on the name of the Lord the god Eternal.[3] Abraham stayed in the land of the Pelesets many days.

CHAPTER 21 NOTES

1 Codex Alexandrinus: Fulistieim (ϷΥΛΙϹΤΙΕΙΜ)
- Septuagint manuscript 131: Fulēst (Ϸυλλς)
- Septuagint manuscript 392: Fil (Ϸιλ)

- Septuagint manuscript 108: Filust (Φιλυστ)
- Septuagint manuscript 799: Filēstēeim (Φιλησληϊμ)
- Septuagint manuscript 376: Filulist (Φιλυλις)
- Leningrad Codex: Pəlištîm (פְּרִשְׁתִּים)
- Peshitta: Plštyå (ܦܠܫܬܝܐ)
- Targum Onkelos: Pəlištā'ê (פְּלִשְׁתָּאֵי)
- Targum Pseudo-Jonathan: Pəlîšəta'ê (פְּלִישְׁתָּאֵי)
- Sahidic manuscript 2211: Filistiem (ⲫⲓⲗⲓⲥⲧⲓⲉⲓⲙ)
- Sahidic manuscript 2002: Fulistieim (ϥⲩⲗⲓⲥⲧⲓⲉⲓⲙ)

The Peleseti were an ancient people based in the region of the modern Gaza Strip of the Palestinian Territories. The earliest surviving mention of them is from the reliefs of the Temple of Ramses III at Medinet Habu in Egypt that dates back to some time between 1186 and 1155 BCE, in which they were called Pwlåsåtî (𓂋𓇋𓏏𓈖𓍿𓀀). They were also known in cuneiform as the ᵏᵘʳPalastu (𒆳𒆪𒊬𒋫𒀸𒌈).

It is unclear where they came from, however, one theory is that they were the Pala, a Luwian people from the Black Sea coast of Anatolia. The region was an independent country called Palaa (𒆳𒉺𒆷𒀀) in the Hittite records from the 1600s BCE, however, have become part of the Neshite Empire by the 1500s BCE. Around the time the Pelesets invaded Canaan, the Pala were driven from their homeland by the neighboring Kaskians from northeast Anatolia, which supports the connection between the groups, however, it has yet to be proven conclusively.

The presence of the Pelesets in Southern Canaan during the time of Abraham and Isaac is anachronistic, and therefore this section of text, describing the origin of the Semitic tribes, found in both the Septuagint and the Masoretic text, likely dates to the original Phoenician translation in the early Iron Age.

2 Septuagint manuscript 961: freati tou orkismou (ⲫⲣⲉⲁⲧⲓ ⲧⲟⲩ ⲟⲣⲕⲓⲥⲙⲟⲩ). Translation: well of the administration of the oath

• Codex Alexandrinus: freati tou orkou (ⲫⲣⲉⲁⲧⲓ ⲧⲟⲩ ⲟⲣⲕⲟⲩ). Translation: well of the oath

• Septuagint manuscript 19: frear tou orkismou (ϕϵⲁⲣ τω οϱμισμου). Translation: well of the oath

• Septuagint manuscript 56: frea tou orkismou (ϕϵⲁ τω οϱμισμου). Translation: well of the oath

• Septuagint manuscript 610: freatos tou orkismou (ϕϵⲁτος τω οϱμισμου). Translation: well of the oath

• Leningrad Codex: bə'ēr šāba' (בְּאֵר שָׁבַע). Translation: well of the oath (or Beersheba)

• Peshitta: br šbå (ܟܪ ܫܒܥ). Translation: well of the oath (or Beersheba)

• Targum Onkelos: bə'ēr šāba' (בְּאֵר שְׁבַע). Translation: well of the oath (or Beersheba)

• Targum Jerusalem: bə'ēr šāba' (בְּאֵר שְׁבַע). Translation: well of the oath (or Beersheba)

• Targum Pseudo-Jonathan: bêrā' dəšeba' hûrəpan (בֵּירָא דְשָׁבַע חוּרְפַן). Translation: well of seven lambs

• Sahidic manuscript 2211: tšōte mpanaš (ⲧϣⲱⲧⲉ ⲙ̄ⲡⲁⲛⲁϣ). Translation: the well (or cistern) of oath

As the Greek term was a translation of the Hebrew name, the name of the town is restored in this translation. The region around the modern Beersheba has been inhabited since before 3000 BCE.

3 Septuagint manuscript 961: onoma tou K̄Ū T̄S̄ aiōnios (ⲟⲛⲟⲙⲁ ⲧⲟⲩ ⲕ̄ⲩ̄ ⲑ̄ⲥ̄ ⲁⲓⲱⲛⲓⲟⲥ). Translation: name of the Lord god of centuries (or eons, time)

• Septuagint manuscript 509: onoma Kuríou teos aiōnios (Θομα Κυϱιου θϵος αϳωνιος). Translation: name of Lord god of centuries (or eons, time)

• Septuagint manuscript 121: onomati Kuríou teos aiōnios (ⲪⲟⲙⲅⲁⱠⲓ Ⲕⲩⲫⲓⲟⲩ ⲑⲋ̄ⲟⲥ ⲁⲓⲟⲱⲛⲓⲟⲥ). Translation: name of Lord god of centuries (or eons, time)

• Septuagint manuscript 130: onoma Kuríou teos aiōnoss (Ⲫⲟⲙⲅⲁ Ⲕⲩⲫⲓⲟⲩ ⲑⲋ̄ⲟⲥ ⲁⲓⲟⲱⲛⲟⲥ). Translation: name lord god of centuries (or eons)

• Leningrad Codex: šēm Yəhōwâ 'ēl 'ôlām (שֵׁם יְהֹוָה אֵל עוֹלָם). Translation: name Yahweh God of the World (or universe, eternity)

• Peshitta: šmh dmrå ålhå dôlmå (ܫܡܗ ܕܡܪܐ ܐܠܗܐ ܕܥܠܡܐ). Translation: name of the master god of the age (or world)

• Targum Onkelos: šəmā' dayyā 'ĕlāhā' də'almā' (שְׁמָא דַּיְיָ אֱלָהָא דְּעָלְמָא). Translation: name of the Yahweh god of the age (or world)

• Targum Jerusalem: šēm mêmərā' dayyā 'ĕlāhā' də'almā' (שֵׁם מֵימְרָא דַּיְיָ אֱלָהָא דְעָלְמָא). Translation: name command (or word) of Yahweh god of the age (or world)

• Targum Pseudo-Jonathan: šēm mêmərā' dayyā 'ŏlāhā' 'almā' (שֵׁם מֵימְרָא דַּיְיָ אֱלָהָא עָלְמָא). Translation: name command (or word) of Yahweh god forever

• Sahidic manuscript 2211: mpran mpjoeis pnoute pšaeneh (Ⲙ̄ⲡⲢⲁⲛ Ⲙ̄ⲡⲭⲟⲉⲓⲥ ⲡⲛⲟⲩⲧⲉ ⲡϣⲁⲉⲛⲉϩ). Translation: my name is the master the god for eternity

This verse does not survive in any of the Dead Sea Scrolls, however, the Greek word aiōnios (αἰώνιος) does appear to be a translation of the Hebrew word ôwlm (עולם), indicating the word was present in the text the Greeks translated.

CHAPTER 22

It happened after these things that God tempted Abraham, and called to him, "Abraham! Abraham?"

He answered, "Look! I am here."

He said, "Take your son, the beloved one, whom you love, Isaac, and go into the highland,[1] and offer him there as a whole burnt offering, on one of the mountains which I will tell you."

Abraham got up in the morning and saddled his donkey, and he took with him two servants, and Isaac his son, and took split wood for a whole burnt offering, he arose and departed, and came to the place that God told him. On the third day, Abraham looked with his eyes, saw the place far away. Abraham told his servants, "Sit here with the donkey, and I and the boy, will go further, and after we worship, we will return to you."

Abraham took the wood of the whole burnt offering and laid it on Isaac his son, and he took in his hands both the fire and the dagger, and the two traveled together. Isaac said to Abraham his father, "Father?"

He replied, "What is it, son?"

He asked, "Look, the fire and the wood, where is the sheep for a whole burnt offering?"

CHAPTER 22

Abraham answered, "God will provide himself a sheep for a whole burnt offering, my son."

Both traveled together and came to the place where God told him. There Abraham built the altar, and laid the wood on it, and having bound the feet of Isaac his son together, he laid him on the altar, on the wood. Abraham stretched out his hand to take the dagger to kill his son.

The messenger of the lord called him out of the sky saying, "Abraham! Abraham?"

He answered, "Look, I am here."

He ordered, "Don't lay your hand on the child or do anything to him. Now I know that you fear God and for my sake, you have not spared your beloved son."

Abraham lifted up his eyes and saw a ram caught by his horns in a thicket of Sabec, and Abraham went and took the ram, and offered him up for a whole burnt offering in the place of Isaac his son. Abraham called the name of that place, "The Lord has seen," that they might say today, "In the mountain, the Lord was seen."

The messenger of the lord visited Abraham a second time out of the sky, saying, "I have sworn by myself," the Lord says, "because you have done this thing on my account, and have not spared your beloved son, surely I will bless you, and I will multiply your descendants like the stars of the sky, and like the sand of the seashore, and your descendants will inherit the cities of their enemies. In your descendants will all the nations of the land be blessed, because you have listened to my voice."

Abraham returned to his servants, and they arose and went together to the well of the oath, and Abraham lived at the well of the oath. It happened after these things, that it was reported to Abraham, Men saying, Look, Milcah herself too has born sons to Nahor your brother, Huz the firstborn, and Baux his brother, and Kemuel the father of the Syrians, Chesed, Hazo, Phaldes, Jidlaph, and Bethuel, and Bethuel fathered Rebekah. These are eight sons which Milcah carried for Nahor the brother of Abraham. His concubine whose name was Reumah, who also carried Tebah, Gaham, Tochos, and Mocha.

CHAPTER 22 NOTES

1 Codex Alexandrinus: gēn tēn uselēn (ⲅⲏⲛ ⲧⲏⲛ ⲩⲋⲏⲗⲏⲛ). Translation: land that is high

• Leningrad Codex: 'el-'Eres hammōriyyâ (אֶל־אֶרֶץ הַמֹּרִיָּה). Translation: the land that's rebellious (or disobedient)

• Peshitta: årôå dåmwryå (ܐܪܥܐ ܕܐܡܘܪܝܐ). Translation: land is rebelling (or disobedient)

• Targum Onkelos: 'ar'ā' pûləhānā' (אַרְעָא פּוּלְחָנָא). Translation: land of ritual (or rite, or cult)

• Targum Jerusalem: tûr môriyâ (טוּר מוֹרִיָה). Translation: mount Morriya

• Targum Pseudo-Jonathan: 'ara' pûləhānā' (אֲרַע פּוּלְחָנָא). Translation: land of ritual (or rite, or cult)

CHAPTER 22

• Sahidic manuscript 16L: ejn oua nntoou (ⲉⲭⲛ̄ ⲟⲩⲁ ⲛ̄ⲛ̄ⲧⲟⲟⲩ). Translation: upon (or against) one (or blasphemy) mountain (or necropolis)

The Greek translation does not reflect the meaning of the Hebrew text, as the meaning of hammōriyyâ (הַמֹּרִיֶּה) is disobedience, rebelliousness, or defiance.

CHAPTER 23

The life of Sarah was a hundred and twenty-seven years.
Sarah died in the city of Arboc, which is in the valley. This is
Hebron in the land of Canaan. Abraham came to lament for
Sarah and to mourn. Abraham stood up from before his dead,
and Abraham spoke to the sons of the Cypriots, saying, "I am a
traveler and a stranger among you, therefore, give me
ownership of a burying-place among you, so I can bury my
dead away from me."

The sons of the Cypriots answered Abraham, saying, "Not
so, lord, but hear us. You are among us, a king from God.
Bury your dead in our best sepulchers, for none of us will by
any means withhold his sepulcher from you so that you
should not bury your dead there."

Abraham got up and bowed to the people of the land, to the
sons of the Cypriots. Abraham spoke to them, saying, "If you
have it in your mind that I should bury my dead out of my
sight, listen to me, and speak for me to Ephron the son of
Zohar. And let him give me the double cave which he has,
which is in a part of his field, let him give it to me for the
silver it is worth, to possess a burying-place among you."

Now Ephron was sitting in the middle of the children of
the Cypriots, and Ephron the Cypriot answered Abraham and
spoke in front of the sons of the Cypriots, and of all who
entered the city, saying, "Be with me, my lord, and hear me,

I give to you the field and the cave which is in it. I have given it to you before all my countrymen. Bury your dead."

Abraham bowed before the people of the land. He said to Ephron before the people of the land, "Since you are on my side, hear me. Take the price of the field from me, so I can bury my dead there."

But Ephron answered Abraham, saying, "No, my Lord. I have heard, the land is worth four hundred silver shekels,[1] but what can this be between me and you? No, go bury your dead."

Abraham listened to Ephron, and Abraham gave to Ephron the silver, which he mentioned in front of the sons of the Cypriot, four hundred shekels of silver approved with merchants. The field of Ephron, which was in Double Cave, which is opposite Mamre, the field and the cave, which was in it, and every tree which was in the field, and whatever is in its borders around it, were made sure to Abraham for a possession, before the sons of the Cypriots, and all that entered into the city. After this, Abraham buried Sarah his wife in the double cave in the field, which is opposite Mamre, (this is Hebron in the land of Canaan). So the field and the cave which was in it were secured as Abraham's possession, as a burial place, by the sons of the Cypriot.

CHAPTER 23 NOTES

1 Codex Alexandrinus: didrakmōn (ⲇⲓⲇⲣⲁⲭⲙⲱⲛ)

- Septuagint manuscript 318: didragmōn (ⲇⲓⲇⲣⲁⲅⲙⲟⲟⲛ)
- Septuagint manuscript 707: didragma (ⲇⲓⲇⲣⲁⲅⲙⲁ)
- Septuagint manuscript 16: dēnariōn (ⲇⲓⲩⲁⲣⲓⲟⲟⲛ)
- Septuagint manuscript 128: dragmōn (ⲇⲣⲁⲅⲙⲟⲟⲛ)
- Septuagint manuscript 246: ditragma (ⲇⲓⲧⲣⲁⲅⲙⲁ)
- Septuagint manuscript 129 didragma (ⲇⲓⲇⲣⲁⲅⲙⲁ)
- Septuagint manuscript 108: didrakmon (ⲇⲓⲇⲣⲁⲭⲙ®)
- Septuagint manuscript 799: didragma (ⲇⲓⲇⲣⲁⲅⲙⲁ)
- Septuagint manuscript 664: didrakma (ⲇⲓⲇⲣⲁⲭⲙⲁ)
- Leningrad Codex: šeqel-kesep (שֶׁקֶל־כֶּסֶף). Translation: shekel of silver
- Peshitta: tql (ܬܩܠ). Translation: weight (or shekel)
- Targum Onkelos: kaspå (כַּסְפָּא). Translation: silver
- Sahidic manuscript 16L: sateere nhat (ⲥⲁⲧⲉⲉⲣⲉ ⲛ̄ϩⲁⲧ). Translation: stater of silver

The shekel was a unit of weight used throughout the Middle East for thousands of years, weighing approximately 8.6 grams of silver. The Greek drachma was a coin weighing approximately half a shekel, and therefore under Greek rule of the Middle East, a two-drachma coin was used. The stater mentioned in the Coptic translation was a Greek coin valued at 2 or 3 drachma, depending on where it was minted. The Corinthian stater was also 8.6 grams, like the Athenian didrachma and the older Egyptian Shekel. As the Greeks clearly translated shekel into didrachma, the term shekel is restored in this translation.

CHAPTER 24

Abraham was old, advanced in days, and the Lord blessed Abraham in all things. Abraham said to his slave, the elder of his house, who had command over all his possessions, "Put your hand under my thigh, and I will have you swear an oath by the Lord, the god of the sky and the god of the land,[1] that you don't take a wife for my son Isaac from the daughters of the Canaanites, among whom I live. But you will go instead to my country, where I was born, and to my tribe, and you will take from there, a wife for my son Isaac."

The slave asked him, "Should I take back your son to the land you came from, if the woman is not willing to return with me to this land?"

Abraham answered him, "Make sure that you don't take my son back there. The Lord, the god Shamayim, and the god Eretz, who brought me out of my father's house, and out of the land from where I sprang, who spoke to me, and who swore to me, saying, 'I will give this land to you and to your descendants,' he will send his messenger before you, and you will take a wife for my son from there. If the woman should not be willing to come with you into this land, you will be clear from my oath, only don't take my son back there."

The slave put his hand under the thigh of his master Abraham and swore to him about this. The slave took ten camels from among his master's camels, and he took some of all the goods of his master with him, and he arose and went into Mesopotamia to the city of Nahor. He let his camels sleep outside the city, by the well of water in the evening, when girls go out to draw water.

He said, "Lord the god of my master Abraham, bring success to my travels today, and deal mercifully with my master Abraham. See I stand by the well of water, and the daughters of those that live in the city come out to collect water. It will be, the young girl to which I will ask, "Lower your pitcher, that I may drink," and she will reply, "Drink and I will give your camels water, until they are finished drinking," this is the one you have prepared for your slave Isaac, and so I will know that you have thought mercifully with my master Abraham."

It happened before he had done speaking in his mind, that Rebekah the daughter of Bethuel, the son of Milcah, the wife of Nahor, the brother of Abraham, came out with a pitcher on her shoulders. The young girl was very beautiful in appearance. She was a virgin and a man had not known her, and she went down to the well, and filled her pitcher, and came up. The slave ran up to meet her, and said, "Give me a little water to drink out of your pitcher."

She replied, "Drink Sir," and she hurried to lower the pitcher on her arm, and gave it to him, to drink from, until his thirst was sated. She said, "I will also collect water for your camels until they have all drank."

CHAPTER 24

She hurried, and emptied the pitcher into the trough, and ran to the well to draw again, and drew water for all the camels. The man paid close attention to her but remained silent to know whether the Lord had made his way prosperous or not. When all the camels had finished drinking, the man took golden earrings, each a beka[2] in weight, and he put two bracelets on her hands, their weight was ten pieces of gold. He asked her, "Whose daughter are you? Tell me if there is room for us to lodge with your father."

She told him, "I am the daughter of Bethuel the son of Milcah, whom she carried for Nahor," and she told him, "We have both straw and much provisions, and a place for resting."

The man was very pleased, and worshiped the Lord, saying, "Blessed is the Lord the god of my master Abraham, who has not allowed his righteousness to fail, nor held his truth from my master, and the Lord has brought me successfully to the house of my lord's brother."

The girl ran and reported these words in the house of her mother. Rebekah had a brother whose name was Laban, and Laban ran out to meet the man at the well. It happened when he saw the earrings and the bracelets in the hands of his sister, and when he heard the words of Rebekah his sister, saying, "The man spoke to me like this," that he went to the man, as he stood by the camels at the well. He said to him, "Come in here, you blessed of the Lord, why do you stand outside, when I have prepared the house and a place for the camels?"

CHAPTER 24

The man entered into the house, and unloaded the camels, and gave the camels straw and provisions, and water to wash his feet, and the feet of the men that were with him. He placed before them loaves to eat, but he said, "I will not eat until I have said my words."

He answered, "So speak."

He said, "I am a slave of Abraham, and the Lord has blessed my master greatly, and he is exalted, and he has given him sheep and calves, silver and gold, men-slaves and slave-women, camels and donkeys. Sarah my master's wife carried one son for my master after he had grown old, and he gave him whatever he had. And my master made me swear, 'You will not take a wife for my son from the daughters of the Canaanites, among whose land I live. But you will go to the house of my father, and to my tribe, and you will take a wife for my son from there.'"

"I asked my master, 'What if the woman will not go with me.' He said to me, 'Lord the god, to whom I have been acceptable in his presence, will send out his messenger with you and will bless your journey, and you will take a wife for my son, from my tribe, and from the house of my father. Then you will be clear from my curse, for if you have gone to my tribe, and they did not give her to you, then you will be clear from my oath.'"

"When I arrived at the well today, I said, 'Lord the god of my master Abraham, if you bless my journey that I am now on, look, I stand by the well of water, and the daughters of the men of the city come out to draw water, and it will be that the girl to whom I will say, 'Give me a little water to drink out of your pitcher,' and she will say to me, 'Drink and I will also draw water for your camels,' this will be the wife whom the Lord has prepared for his own slave Isaac, and hereby will I know that you have worked mercy with my master Abraham. It happened before I had done speaking in my mind, immediately Rebekah came out, having her pitcher on her shoulders, and she went down to the well and drew water, and I asked her, 'Give me something to drink.' She rushed to let down her pitcher on her arm from herself, and said, 'Drink and I will give your camels water,' and I drank, and she gave the camels water."

"I asked her, 'Whose daughter are you? Tell me,' and she answered, 'I am the daughter of Bethuel, the son of Nahor, whom Milcah carried for him,' and I put on her the earrings and the bracelets on her hands. Being very happy I worshiped the Lords, and I blessed the Lord the god of my master Abraham, who has helped me succeed in finding the correct road so that I should take the daughter of my master's brother for his son. If you will then deal mercifully and justly with my lord, tell me, and if not, tell me if I should turn to the right or to the left."

Laban and Bethuel answered and said, "This matter has come from the Lord, we will not be able to answer you bad or good. Look, Rebekah is before you, take her and leave, and let her be wife to the son of your master, as the Lord has said."

CHAPTER 24

When the slave of Abraham heard these words, he bowed himself to the Earth before the Lord.[3] The slave had brought out jewels of silver and gold and clothing and gave them to Rebekah and gave gifts to her brother and her mother. Then he and the men traveling with him ate and drank and went to sleep. He rose in the morning and asked, "Send me away, so I may return to my master."

Her brothers and her mother said, "Let the young girl remain with us for ten days,[4] and after that, she will depart."

But he said to them, "Don't delay me, for the Lord has blessed the journey for me. Send me away, that I may return to my master."

They replied, "Let's call the girl, and ask her."

They called Rebekah, and asked her, "Will you go with this man?"

She answered, "I will go."

So, they sent out Rebekah their sister, and her goods, with the slave of Abraham, and his attendants. They blessed Rebekah, and said to her, "You are our sister. Become tens of millions and let your descendants possess the cities of their enemies."

Rebekah rose up with her women, and they mounted the camels and went with the man, and the slave took Rebekah and departed. Isaac went through the wilderness to the well of the vision, and he lived in the land towards the south. Isaac went out into the plain in the evening to meditate, and having lifted up his eyes, he saw camels coming. And Rebekah lifted up her eyes and saw Isaac, and she quickly climbed down from the camel, and said to the slave, "Who is that man that walks in the plain to meet us?"

The slave answered, "This is my master, and she took her veil and covered herself."

The slave told Isaac all the things that he had done. Isaac went into the house of his mother and took Rebekah, and she became his wife, and he loved her, and Isaac was comforted by Sarah his mother.

CHAPTER 24 NOTES

1 Codex Alexandrinus: K̄N̄ ton T̄N̄ tou ŌŪNŌŪ kai ton T̄N̄ tēs gēs (K̄N̄ ΤΟΝ Θ̄N̄ ΤΟΥ Ō̄YNO̅Y̅ ΚΑΙ ΤΟΝ Θ̄N̄ ΤΗCΓΗC). Translation: Lord the god the sky and the god earth

• Leningrad Codex: Yhōwâ 'ĕlōhê haššāmayim wē'lōhê hā'āres (יְהוָה אֱלֹהֵי הַשָּׁמַיִם וֵאלֹהֵי הָאָרֶץ). Translation: Yahweh god the skies (or Shamayim) and god the land (or Eretz)

• Peshitta: mryå ålhå dšmyå wålhå dårôå (ܡܪܝܐ ܐܠܗܐ ܕܫܡܝܐ ܘܐܠܗܐ ܕܐܪܥܐ). Translation: master god the sky and god the land

• Targum Onkelos: mêmərā' daYyā 'ĕlāhā' dišmayyā' wē'lāhā' də'ar'ā' (מֵימְרָא דַיְיָ אֱלָהָא דִשְׁמַיָּא וֵאלָהָא דְאַרְעָא). Translation: command (or word) the Yahweh god the sky and god the land

• Targum Pseudo-Jonathan: mêmərā' dayyā 'ĕlāhā' dəmôtəbêh bišmê mərômā' hû' 'ĕlāhā' dəšûlətānêh 'al 'ar'ā' (מֵימְרָא דַיְיָ אֱלָהָא דְמוֹתְבֵיה בִּשְׁמֵי מְרוֹמָא הוּא אֱלָהָא דְשׁוּלְטָנֵיה עַל אַרְעָא). Translation:

command (or word) of the Yahweh god of sky above also the dominator of the earth

• Sahidic manuscript 2020: mpran mpjoeis pnoute pšaeneh (Ṁⲡⲣⲁⲛ Ṁⲡⲭⲟⲉⲓⲥ ⲡⲛⲟⲩⲧⲉ ⲡϣⲁⲉⲛⲉϩ). Translation: my name is the master the god for eternity

Based on the Masoretic reading, these were probably originally three different gods. Both the Canaanite god of the skies Shamayim (שָׁמַיִם), and the Canaanite god of the earth Eretz (אֶרֶץ), were called on separately in other sections of the Torah and Tanakh, including as witnesses of the oaths between the Lord and humanity. By the beginning of the Christian era, the verse appears to been interpreted as a long title of the Lord.

2 Septuagint manuscript 961: drakmēn (ⲆⲣⲀⲔⲘⲎⲚ)

• Codex Alexandrinus: drakmēs (ⲆⲣⲀⲬⲘⲎⲤ)

• Septuagint manuscript 509: drakmēn (Δεαχμlω)

• Septuagint manuscript 630: dragmēn (Δεαγμlω)

• Septuagint manuscript 318: drakmē (Δεαχμλ)

• Septuagint manuscript 730: didrakmone-dak (ΔιΔεαχμ℗б-δαχ)

• Septuagint manuscript 30: dragmon (Δεαγμ℗)

• Septuagint manuscript 129: didragmēnedeid (ΔιΔεαγμlωбΔϥΔ)

• Septuagint manuscript 246: didragmēs (ΔιΔεαγμλc)

• Septuagint manuscript 54: didrakmōn (ΔιΔεαχμοον)

• Septuagint manuscript 569: didragmon (ΔιΔεαγμ℗)

• Septuagint manuscript 107: drakmon (Δεαχμ℗)

• Septuagint manuscript 664: drakmōn (Δεαχμοον)

• Septuagint manuscript 59: didrakmēn (ΔιΔεαχμlω)

• Leningrad Codex: beqa' (בֶּקַע). Translation: half-shekel

• Peshitta: mtqlå (ܡܬܩܠܐ). Translation: weight (or shekel, beka)

• Targum Onkelos: sil'în (סִלְעִין). Translation: selas

- Targum Jerusalem: sal'în (סַלְעִין). Translation: selas
- Targum Pseudo-Jonathan: sal'în (סַלְעִין). Translation: selas
- Sahidic manuscript 2069: ḥiskite (ϩⲓⲥⲕⲓⲧⲉ). Translation: half-qite

The drachma was a Greek coin used from around 1100 BCE, worth approximately 4.3 grams of silver. The beka was the half-shekel measurement used in ancient Canaan. The half-qite mentioned in the Coptic translation was an ancient Egyptian unit of measurement equal to a drachma. A qite was equal to a didrachma, meaning "double-dramcha." The measurement was in use in the New Kingdom era, as the qdt (𓈎𓂧𓏏), and in the early Iron Age as the qt (𐤒𐤕).

The Egyptian term was antiquated by the time the Coptic translation was made, yet it is used consistently in Sahidic manuscripts, such as 2069, 2002, and 2020, ranging from the 6th century to the 11th century CE. This could indicate that Sahidic translation was partially based on a demotic Egyptian translation. There were some Israelite texts translated into demotic in the 7th and 6th centuries BCE; however, translations of the Torah have not been found. References to Abraham, Isaac, and Jacob are common in Egypto-Israelite texts, suggesting that a version of *Cosmic Genesis* did exist in Demotic. As "drachma" was the Greek translation of beka, the term beka is restored in this translation.

3 Berlin Genesis: gēn tō $\overline{\text{KŌ}}$ (ⲅⲏⲛ ⲧⲱ ⲕ̄ⲱ̄). Translation: Earth the lord

- Septuagint manuscript 961: gēn $\overline{\text{KŌ}}$ (ⲅⲏⲛ ⲕ̄ⲱ̄). Translation: Earth lord
- Septuagint manuscript 31: pēgēn Kuriō (πηγην Κυριω). Translation: well (or fountain) lord
- Leningrad Codex: 'arsâ laYhōwâ (אֶרְצָה לַיהֹוָה). Translation: Earth to (or for) Yahweh

• Peshitta: årôå qdm mryå (ܐܪܥܐ ܩܕܡ ܡܪܝܐ). Translation: land before lord

• Targum Onkelos: 'ar'ā' qŏdām Yəyā (אַרְעָא קֳדָם יְיָ). Translation: land before Yahweh

• Targum Pseudo-Jonathan: 'ar'ā' qŏdām Yəyā (אַרְעָא קֳדָם יְיָ). Translation: land before Yahweh

4 Codex Alexandrinus: ēmeras ōsei deka (ΗΜΕΡΑC ѠCEI ΔΕΚΑ). Translation: days until ten

• Septuagint manuscript 56: ēmeras ōs ēmeras deka (ἡμέρας ὡς ἡμέρας δέκα). Translation: days as days ten

• Leningrad Codex: yāmîm 'ô 'āśôr (יָמִים אֹו עָשֹׂור). Translation: days or ten

• Peshitta Manuscript 5b1: ymn ôrn bôrn åw ôhrå yrk̆n (ܝܡܢ ܐܘܪܢ ܒܐܘܪܢ ܐܘ ܐܚܪܐ ܝܪ̈ܚܝܢ). Translation: days season (or time) until season (or time) or ten months (or moons)

• Peshitta Manuscript 7a1: ôrn yrk̆ ywmyn (ܐܘܪܢ ܝܪܚ ܝܘܡܝܢ). Translation: time (or season) month (or moon) days

• Targum Onkelos: 'immānā' 'iddan bə'iddan 'ô 'aśrā' yarhîn (עִמְנָא עִדָּן בְּעִדָּן אֹו עַשְׂרָא יַרְחִין). Translation: day eon (or age, time) in (or with) eon (or age, time) or for ten months (or moons)

• Targum Pseudo-Jonathan: šattā' hădā' 'ô 'āśar yarhîn (שַׁתָּא חֲדָא אֹו עָשַׂר יַרְחִין). Translation: year or for ten months (or moons)

This verse has been unclear since before the Greek and Hebrew translations were made. The similarity of the Targum Onkelos from the 2nd century CE, and Peshitta Manuscript 5b1 from the 5th century indicates that the Aramaic text was different from both the Greek and Hebrew translations. The surviving Greek copies of Cosmic Genesis, including the Berlin Genesis papyrus from the 2nd century CE, all show signs of being reworked to synchronize with the Hebrew translation of Bereshít the Jews were using at the time. The Targum Onkelos, which is generally dated to sometime between 100 and 120 CE, is according to the Megillah tractate in the Talmud, a restoration of an Aramaic language version of the Torah in circulation before the time of Ezra the Scribe, circa 350 BCE.

The Targum Onkelos is attributed to Onkelos, a convert to Judaism, who, based on the interchangeable usage of the names in the *Megillah* tractates of the Jerusalem and Babylonian Talmuds, appears to have been Aquila of Sinope, a disciple of Rabbi Akiva. According to Epiphanius' *De Ponderibus et Mensuris*, Aquila was a Christian relative of the Roman emperor Hadrian, who was sent to Jerusalem to rebuild the city after the First Jewish-Roman War. In Jerusalem he was rejected by the Christians for practicing astrology, as so converted to Judaism.

The similarities between the Targum Onkelos and the Peshitta Manuscript 5b1 suggest that both manuscripts drew from an older Aramaic text of Bereshít which was different from the surviving Hebrew and Greek translations. If the Aramaic source contained the original text, then the confusing surviving Hebrew translation would have been a simplification of the original text. Based on the verse found in Onkelos and 5b1, the original text probably read, "until the new year, in ten months." This reading would be based a precursor to the Aramaic translation using the Egyptian term mswt-rỏ where Onkelos uses the term "day eon" (עידן עימנא). Mswt-rỏ was the name of the Egyptian New Years festival, which translates as "birth (or expected time) of Ra (or day)."

By the New Kingdom it had also become the name of the last month of the Egyptian Civil Calendar, however, in this usage it appears to been a reference to the new year, not the month. If the original text did read "the new year, in ten months," then the earliest Aramaic translation must have been made before the simplified Hebrew translation that survives in the Masoretic text.

CHAPTER 24

The origin of "day eon" as a translation for Mswt-rȯ, likely dates to the New Kingdom era cuneiform translation of Cosmic Genesis, when the term would have probably been rendered as úmuum adunum (𒐬𒐬𒐬 𒐬𒐬𒐬), meaning "sun (or days) appointed time (or period)."

CHAPTER 25

Abraham took another wife, whose name was Chettura. She carried for him Zimran, Jokshan, Medan, Midian, Ishbak, and Shuah.

Jokshan fathered Sheba and Dedan.

The sons of Dedan were the Assyrians, the Latusians, and the Leums.

The sons of Midian were Gephar, Epher, Enoch, Abida, and Eldaah, and all these were sons of Chettura.

Nevertheless, Abraham gave all his possessions to Isaac his son.

To the sons of his concubines, Abraham gave gifts, and while he was still living, he sent them east, into the country of the east, away from his son Isaac.

These were the years of the days of the life of Abraham as many as he lived, a hundred and seventy-five years, and Abraham died at a good old age, an old man full of days, and was added to his people. Isaac and Ishmael his sons, buried him in the double cave, in the field of Ephron, the son of Zohar the Cypriot, which is near Mamre, the field and the cave that Abraham bought from the sons of the Cypriot, and there they buried Abraham and Sarah his wife.

After Abraham was dead, God blessed Isaac his son, and Isaac lived by the "well of the vision."

CHAPTER 25

These are the generations of Ishmael, the son of Abraham, whom Hagar the Egyptian, the woman-slave of Sarah carried for Abraham. These are the names of the sons of Ishmael, and the names of their generations. The firstborn of Ishmael were Nebajoth, Kedar, Adbeel, Mibsam, Masma, Duma, Mesha, Hadar, Teman, Jetur, Naphish, and Kedemah.

These are the sons of Ishmael, and these are their names, in their tents and in their dwellings, twelve princes according to their nations. These are the years of the life of Ishmael, a hundred and thirty-seven years, and he died and was added to his family. He lived from Havilah to Zur, which is opposite Egypt until one comes to the Assyrians, and he lived in the presence of all his brothers.

These are the generations of Isaac the son of Abraham. Abraham fathered Isaac. Isaac was forty years old when he took Rebekah as a wife, the daughter of Bethuel the Syrian, from Syrian Mesopotamia, the sister of Laban the Syrian.

Isaac prayed to the Lord concerning Rebekah, his wife, because she was barren, and the Lord heard him, and his wife Rebekah conceived in her womb. The babies moved within her, and she said, "If it is so for me, why is this happening to me?"

She went to inquire of the Lord, and the Lord said to her, "There are two nations in your womb, and two peoples will be separated from your belly, and one people will excel the other, and the greater will serve the less."

CHAPTER 25

The days were fulfilled that she should deliver, and she had twins in her womb. The first came out red, and hairy all over like an animal skin, and she called his name Esau. After this, his brother came out, and his hand grabbed the heel of Esau, and she called his name Jacob. Isaac was sixty years old when Rebekah carried them. The boys grew, and Esau was a man skilled in hunting and living in the country, while Jacob was a simple man living in a house. Isaac loved Esau because his food was venison, but Rebekah loved Jacob. Jacob cooked a stew, and Esau came in from the plain collapsing.

Esau said to Jacob, "Let me eat that red stew because I am collapsing," and so his name was called Edom.

Jacob said to Esau, "Sell me your birthright today."

Esau replied, "Look, I am going to die, and what good is this birthright that belongs to me?"

Jacob said to him, "Swear to me today," and he swore to him, and Esau sold his birthright to Jacob. Jacob gave bread to Esau, and lentil stew and he ate and drank, and he arose and departed, and so Esau slighted his birthright.

CHAPTER 26

There was a famine in the land, besides the earlier famine which was during the time of Abraham, and Isaac went to Abimelech the king of the Pelesets to Gerar. The Lord appeared to him and said, "Don't go down to Egypt but stay in the land that I will tell you. Stay in this land and I will be with you, and bless you. I will give you and your descendants all this land, and I will establish my oath which I swore to your father Abraham. I will multiply your descendants like the stars of the sky, and I will give to your descendants all this land, and all the nations of the land will be blessed in your descendants. Because Abraham your father listened to my voice and kept my injunctions, and my commandments, and my ordinances, and my statutes."

Isaac lived in Gerar, and when the men of the place questioned him about Rebekah his wife, he said, "She is my sister," as he was afraid to say, "She is my wife," in case the men of the land should kill him because of Rebekah, because she was beautiful. He remained there a long time, and Abimelech the king of Gerar leaned to look through the window and saw Isaac playing with Rebekah his wife. Abimelech called Isaac, and asked, "Is she your wife? Why have you said, 'She is my sister?'"

Isaac answered him, "I did so because I thought, 'At some point, I may die because of her.'"

CHAPTER 26

Abimelech said to him, "Why have you done this to us? One of my family may have laid with your wife in the near future, and you would have brought a sin of ignorance on us."

Abimelech commanded all his people, "Every man that touches this man and his wife will die."

Isaac sowed in that land, and he found in that year the barley grew a hundred-fold, and the Lord blessed him. The man was praised and increased until he became very famous. He had flocks of sheep, and herds of oxen, and many tilled fields, and the Pelesets envied him. All the wells, which the servants of his father had dug in the time of his father, the Pelesets filled up with dirt. Abimelech said to Isaac, "Leave from among us, as you have become much stronger than we are."

Isaac departed from there, and traveled to the valley of Gerar, and lived there. Isaac re-dug the wells of water, which the servants of his father Abraham had dug, which the Pelesets had filled in after the death of his father Abraham, and he called them by the names that his father had named them. The servants of Isaac dug in the valley of Gerar, and they found there a well of living water. The shepherds from Gerar fought with the shepherds of Isaac, saying that the water was theirs, and they called the name of the well, "Injury," for they had injured him. After departing there, he dug another well, and they fought also for that one, and he named it "Enmity."

CHAPTER 26

After leaving there they dug another well, and they did not fight over that one so he named it "Room," saying, "Because now the Lord has made room for us, and has increased us on the land."

He traveled from there to the "Well of the Oath." The Lord appeared to him that night, and said, "I am the god of Abraham your father. Don't be afraid, for I am with you, and I will bless you, and multiply your descendants for the sake of Abraham your father."

He built an altar there and called on the name of the Lord. He pitched his tent there, and the servants of Isaac dug a well there, in the valley of Gerar. Abimelech came to him from Gerar, and so did Ochozath his friend, and Phichol the commander-in-chief of his army. Isaac asked them, "Why have you come to me? Before you hated me and sent me away from you."

They replied, "We have certainly seen that the Lord was with you, and we said, "Let there be an oath between us and you," and we will make a covenant with you, so you will do no wrong to us, as we have not hated you, and as we have treated you well, and have sent you away peacefully, now you are blessed by the Lord."

He made a feast for them, and they ate and drank. They rose in the morning and swore to each other, and Isaac sent them away, and they departed from him in safety. It happened on that day, that the servants of Isaac came and told him of the well which they had dug, and they said, "We have not found water."

He called it, "Oath." Therefore he called the name of that city, the "Well of Oath," until today. Esau was forty years old, and he took as wife a Djahite,[1] the daughter of Beeri the Cypriot,[2] and one from Al-Sharat,[3] the daughter of Elon the Cypriot,[4] and they were provoking to Isaac and Rebekah.

CHAPTER 26 NOTES

1 Berlin Genesis: Ioudein (ιΟΥΔΕΙΝ)

- LXX 15: Ioudit̲ (ιουΔϥθ)
- LXX 18: Ioudēn (ιουΔιω)
- LXX 64: Ioudin (ιουΔιν)
- LXX 135: Ioudit̲ (ιουΔιθ)
- LXX 55: Ioudēt̲ (ιουΔιλθ)
- LXX 370: Oudēn (ΟυΔιω)
- LXX 56: Adan (Αδαν)
- LXX 569: Ioud (ιουΔ)
- LXX 53: Addan (Ααδαν)
- Leningrad Codex: Yəhûdît (יְהוּדִית). Translation: Judahitess
- Peshitta: Yhwdyt (ܝܗܘܕܝܬ)
- Targum Onkelos: Yəhûdît (יְהוּדִית). Translation: Judahitess
- Targum Pseudo-Jonathan: Yəhûdît (יְהוּדִית). Translation: Judahitess
- Bohairic manuscripts: Ioudim (ιοῦΔιμ)

The Hebrew and Aramaic Yehudit (יְהוּדִית) is the name generally transliterated as Judith in English, however, the earliest surviving

CHAPTER 26

Greek and Coptic manuscripts used the name Ioudin / Ioudim (Ἰουδειν / ⲒⲞⲨⲀⲒⲘ), indicating the early Aramaic translation likely used a different name. This alternate name likely originated in a misreading of the name Yhwdyt (𐤕𐤉𐤃𐤅𐤄𐤉) as Yhwdyn (𐤍𐤃𐤅𐤄𐤉) during an early translation from Canaanite into Aramaic.

As the name Yhwdyt was the Canaanite name for a Judahite woman, and the Kingdom of Judah did not exist in the time of Esau, it likely started as a reference to a Djahite woman, as the Djâhî (𒁹𒌅𒀀) people lived in southern Canaan before the Judahites are reported to have migrated into the era in the *Book of Judges*.

2 LXX 911: Baiēr tou Ḱettaíou (ⲃⲀⲒⲎⲢ ⲦⲞⲨ ⲭⲉⲦⲦⲀⲒⲞⲨ). Translation: Baier of Khettaiou

• LXX 961: Baiēl tou Ḱettaíou (ⲃⲀⲒⲎⲗ ⲦⲞⲨ ⲭⲉⲦⲦⲀⲒⲞⲨ). Translation: Baiel of Khettaiou

• Codex Alexandrinus: Beēr tou Ḱettaíou (ⲃⲉⲎⲢ ⲦⲞⲨ ⲭⲉⲦⲦⲀⲒⲞⲨ). Translation: Beer of Khettaiou

• LXX 15: Beēa tou Ḱettaíou (ⲃⲟⲗⲀ ⲧⲱ ⲭⲟⲧⲗⲓⲟⲩ). Translation: Beaa of Khettaiou

• LXX 19: Beōr tou Ḱettaíou (ⲃⲟⲱⲣ ⲧⲱ ⲭⲟⲧⲗⲓⲟⲩ). Translation: Beor of Khettaiou

• LXX 53: Alon tou Ḱettaíou (ⲁⲗⲟⲟⲛ ⲧⲱ ⲭⲟⲧⲗⲓⲟⲩ). Translation: Alon of Khettaiou

• LXX 56: Ailōn tou Ḱettaíou (ⲁⲓⲗⲟⲟⲛ ⲧⲱ ⲭⲟⲧⲗⲓⲟⲩ). Translation: Ailon of Khettaiou

• LXX 82: Beēl tou Ḱettaíou (ⲃⲟⲗⲗ ⲧⲱ ⲭⲟⲧⲗⲓⲟⲩ). Translation: Beel of Khettaiou

• LXX 246: Aibeēr tou Ḱettaíou (ⲁⲓⲩⲟⲗⲣ ⲧⲱ ⲭⲟⲧⲗⲓⲟⲩ). Translation: Aibeer of Khettaiou

• LXX 319: Bathouēl tou Ḱettaíou (ⲃⲁⲑⲟⲩⲗⲗ ⲧⲱ ⲭⲟⲧⲗⲓⲟⲩ). Translation: Bathouel of Khettaiou

CHAPTER 26

- LXX 370: Beēr tou Ǩetteou (ц6ь.β το х6ꝓ6ου). Translation: Beer of Khetteou
- LXX 426: Beērei tou Ǩettaíou (β6ь.β̣ το х6ꝓ̣λιου). Translation: Beerei of Khettaiou
- Leningrad Codex: Bəērî haHittî (בְּאֵרִי הַחִתִּי). Translation: Beeri the Cypriot
- Peshitta: Brta dbry Ǩytya (ܟ̈ܬ݂ܐ ܕܒܪ݂, ܣܘܬ݂ܟ). Translation: Brta the child of Ǩytya
- Targum Onkelos: Bə'ērî Hittā'â (בְּאֵרִי חִתָּאָה). Translation: Beeri Hittaa
- Bohairic manuscripts: Beēl piǨettaiou (ⲂⲉⲎⲗ ⲡⲓⲬⲉⲧⲧⲁⲓⲟⲧ). Translation: Beel of Khettaiou

3 Berlin Genesis: Basemmaṯ (ⲂⲀⲤⲉⲘⲘⲀⲐ)
- Cotton Genesis: Basenamaṯ (ⲂⲀⲤⲉⲚⲀⲘⲀⲐ)
- Codex Alexandrinus: Masemmaṯ (ⲘⲀⲤⲉⲘⲘⲀⲐ)
- LXX 14: Masemma (Μασόμμα)
- LXX 15: Bessemaṯ (Β6σσόμαθ)
- LXX 16: Basemma (Βλσόμμα)
- LXX 17: Basemaṯ (Βλσόμμα)
- LXX 18: Masemman (Μασόμμαν)
- LXX 19: Masetham (Μασόθλμ)
- LXX 44: Asemat (Ασόματ)
- LXX 52: Masemam (Μασόμαμ)
- LXX 53: Elibema (Ελιμόμα)
- LXX 55: Besemaṯ (Β6σόμαθ)
- LXX 57: Massema (Μασσόμα)
- LXX 71: Masema (Μασόμα)
- LXX 72: Bassemaṯ (Βλσσόμαθ)
- LXX 73: Maasema (Μαλσόμα)
- LXX 107: Asemmat (Ασόμματ)
- LXX 246: Bathemma (Βλθόμμα)

314

- LXX 265: Alibamē (ⲁⲗⲓⲩⲁⲙⲏ)
- LXX 319: Mesemaṯ (Μόσόμαθ)
- LXX 381: Bessema (βόσόμα)
- LXX 424: Massemma (Μασόμμα)
- LXX 618: Besema (βόσόμα)
- LXX 619: Basemēkaṯ (βⲗⲟⲥⲙⲏⲕⲁθ)
- LXX 761: Massemman (Μασόμμαν)
- LXX 799: Basaimaṯ (βⲗⲟⲥⲁⲓⲙⲁθ)
- Leningrad Codex: Bāśəmat (בְּשְׂמַת)
- Peshitta: Bsmt (ܒܣܡܬ)
- Targum Onkelos: Bāśəmāt (בְּשְׂמָת). Translation: Judahitess
- Bohairic manuscripts: Besemaṯ (Ⲃⲉⲥⲉⲙⲁⲑ)
- Old Armenian manuscripts: Masemat' (Մասեմաթ)

If Yəhûdît (יְהוּדִית) is interpreted as being a reference to a woman from Djâhî (𓂧𓏭𓈉), then Bāśəmāt (בְּשְׂמָת) is likely a reference to på-Småt (𓂧 𓇋𓈖𓄿), a land the Egyptians recorded as being somewhere in southern Canaan or northern Arabia in the middle Bronze Age. It is theorized to have been a reference to the highlands of Al-Sharat in southern Jordan.

4 Berlin Genesis: Ailōn tou Euaiou (ⲁⲓⲗⲱⲛ ⲧⲟⲩ ⲉⲩⲁⲓⲟⲩ). Translation: Ailon of Euaiou

- Cotton Genesis: Aidōm tou Euaiou (ⲁⲓⲇⲱⲙ ⲧⲟⲩ ⲉⲩⲁⲓⲟⲩ). Translation: Aidom of Euaiou
- Codex Alexandrinus: Ailōm tou Euaiou (ⲁⲓⲗⲱⲙ ⲧⲟⲩ ⲉⲩⲁⲓⲟⲩ). Translation: Ailom of Euaiou
- LXX 15: Elōn tou Euaiou (Ελων τω Ευαιου). Translation: Elon of Euaiou
- LXX 16: Edōn tou Euaiou (Εδων τω Ευαιου). Translation: Edon of Euaiou
- LXX 17: Elōm tou Euaiou (Ελωμ τω Ευαιου). Translation: Elom of Euaiou

CHAPTER 26

- LXX 31: Ailōn tou Eueou (ܐܝܠܘܢ ܛܘ ܐܘܕܘ). Translation: Ailon of Eueou

- LXX 53: Ana tugátera Sebegōn tou Euaiou (ܐܢܐ ܬܘܓܐܢܬܪܐ ܣܘܓܝܘܢ ܛܘ ܐܘܐܝܘ). Translation: Ana daughter of Sebegon the Euaiou

- LXX 54: Ailōm tou Eaiou (ܐܝܠܘܡ ܛܘ ܐܝܘ). Translation: Ailom of Eaiou

- LXX 56: Ana tugátēr Sebegōn tou Euaiou (ܐܢܐܬܘܓܐܢܬܗܒ ܣܘܓܝܘܢ ܛܘ ܐܘܐܝܘ). Translation: Ana daughter Sebegon the Euaiou

- LXX 59: Ailōn tou Seuaiou (ܐܝܠܘܢ ܛܘ ܣܘܐܝܘ). Translation: Ailon of Seuaiou

- LXX 71: Ailōn tou Ebaiou (ܐܝܠܘܢ ܛܘ ܐܘܐܝܘ). Translation: Ailon of Ebaiou

- LXX 79: Elam tou Ebraiou (ܐܠܡ ܛܘ ܐܘܒܝܘ). Translation: Ailon the Hebrew (or crosser, Habiru)

- LXX 319: Aiōn tou Eueou (ܐܝܘܢ ܛܘ ܐܘܕܘ). Translation: Aion of Eueou

- LXX 426: Ailōm tou Ǩettaiou (ܐܝܠܘܡ ܛܘ ܟܘܛܝܘ). Translation: Ailon the Cypriot

- LXX 551: Edōm tou Euaiou (ܐܕܘܡ ܛܘ ܐܘܐܝܘ). Translation: Edom of Euaiou

- LXX 708: Aulōn tou Euaiou (ܐܘܠܘܢ ܛܘ ܐܘܐܝܘ). Translation: Aulon of Euaiou

- Leningrad Codex: Êlōn haHittî (אֵילֹן הַחִתִּי). Translation: Elon the Cypriot

- Peshitta: Ǎylwn Ǩytyå (ܐܝܠܘܢ ܟܬܝܐ). Translation: Aylun the Ǩytyå

- Targum Onkelos: Êlōn Hittāâ (אֵילוֹן חִתָּאָה). Translation: Elon the Cypriot

- Bohairic manuscripts: Elōm piEuaiou (Ⲉⲗⲱⲙ ⲡⲓⲈⲧⲁⲓⲟⲩ). Translation: Elom the Euaiou

CHAPTER 27

After Isaac was old, his eyes were blinded and he could not see, and he called Esau, his elder son, and said to him, "My son?"

He answered, "Know that I am here."

He said, "Know that I have grown old, and don't know the day of my death. Now then take the weapons, both your quiver and your bow, and go into the plain, and get me venison, and make me meats as I like them, and bring them to me so I can eat, that my mind will bless you before I die."

Rebekah heard Isaac speaking to Esau his son, and Esau went to the plain to procure venison for his father. Rebekah said to Jacob, her younger son, "Know that I heard your father speaking to Esau your brother, saying, 'Bring me venison, and prepare me meats, that I may eat and bless you before the Lord before I die.' Now then my son, listen to me, as I command you. And go to the livestock and take for me there two kids, tender and good, and I will make them meats for your father, as he likes. And you will bring them to your father, and he will eat, that your father may bless you before he dies."

Jacob said to his mother Rebekah, "Esau, my brother, is a hairy man while I am a smooth man. Suppose my father feels me, and he will know that I am a liar, and I will bring on a curse on myself, and not a blessing."

CHAPTER 27

His mother said to him, "Your curse is on me son. Only listen to my voice, and go and bring them to me."

So he went and brought them to his mother, and his mother made meats as his father liked them. And Rebekah took the fine clothing of her elder son Esau which was with her in the house, put it on Jacob her younger son. She put on his arms the skins of the sheep, and on the bare parts of his neck. She gave the meats, and the loaves which she had prepared, into the hands of Jacob her son.

He brought them to his father, and said, "Father?"

He replied, "Look I am here. Who are you son?"

Jacob said to his father, "I am Esau, your firstborn, and have done as you told me. Rise and sit, and eat of my venison, so your mind may bless me."

Isaac asked his son, "What is this, that you have found so quickly?"

He answered, "That which the Lord, your god brought to me."

Isaac told Jacob, "Come near to me, so I can feel you son, if you are my son Esau."

Jacob approached his father Isaac, and he felt him, and said, "The voice is Jacob's voice, but the hands are the hands of Esau."

He did not know him, as his hands were hairy like the hands of his brother Esau, and he blessed him, asking, "Are you my son Esau?"

He answered, "I am."

He said, "Bring it here, and I will eat of your venison son, so my mind may bless you," and he brought it to him, and he ate, and he brought him wine, and he drank.

Isaac his father, said to him, "Approach me and kiss me son."

He approached and kissed him, and smelled the odor of his garments, and blessed him, and said, "I know the smell of my son is like the smell of an abundant field, which the Lord has blessed. May God give to you of the dew of the sky, and the oil of the land, and an abundance of grain and wine. Let nations serve you, and princes bow down to you, and may you be the lord of your brother, and may the sons of your father do reverence to you, and accursed is he who curses you and blessed is he who blesses you."

After Isaac had finished blessing his son Jacob, right after Jacob had left the presence of Isaac his father, it happened that Esau his brother returned from hunting. He also prepared meats and brought them to his father, and he asked his father, "Let my father get up, and eat his son's venison, so that your mind may bless me."

Isaac his father asked him, "Who are you?"

He answered, "I am your firstborn son Esau."

CHAPTER 27

Isaac was bewildered, and asked, "Who then is it that has procured venison for me and brought it to me? I already ate it before you came, and I have blessed him, and he will be blessed."

When Esau heard the words of his father Isaac, he cried out greatly and bitterly, saying, "I beg you, bless me also father!"

He answered him, "Your brother has come with subterfuge, and stolen your blessing."

He said, "He was named Jacob rightly! Know that this is the second time he has supplanted me. He has taken both my birthright and now he has taken my blessing!"

Esau asked his father, "Have you no blessing left for me father?"

Isaac answered Esau, "If I have made him your lord, and have made all his brothers his servants, and have strengthened him with grain and wine, then what will I do for you, son?"

Esau said to his father, "Have you only one blessing father? I beg you, bless me also father."

Isaac was troubled, and Esau cried aloud and wept. Isaac his father answered and said to him, "Know that your life will be of the oil of land, and of the dew of the sky from above. You will live by your sword and will serve your brother, and there will be a time when you will break and loosen his shackle from off your neck."

CHAPTER 27

Esau was angry with Jacob because of the blessing, that his father blessed him, and Esau thought, "Let the days of my father's mourning draw near, that I may kill my brother Jacob."

The words of Esau her elder son were reported to Rebekah, and she sent and called Jacob her younger son, and said to him, "Know that Esau, your brother, threatens to kill you. Now then my son, listen to my voice, and get up and leave quickly into Mesopotamia, to Laban my brother in Harran. Live with him some days, until your brother's anger and rage against you subsides, and he forgets what you have done to him, and I will send and fetch you there, in case at any time I should be bereaved of you both in one day."

Rebekah said to Isaac, "I am tired of my life, because of the daughters of the sons of the Cypriots. If Jacob takes a wife of the daughters of this land, why should I live?"

CHAPTER 28

Isaac called Jacob, and he blessed him, and commanded him, "You will not take a wife from the daughters of the Canaanites. Rise and leave quickly to Mesopotamia, to the house of Bethuel the father of your mother, and take for yourself from there a wife from the daughters of Laban your mother's brother. May the god Shaddai[1] bless you, and increase you, and multiply you, and you will become a number of nations. May he give you the blessing of my father Abraham, both you and your descendants after you, to inherit the land of your travels, which God gave to Abraham.

So Isaac sent Jacob away, and he went into Mesopotamia, to Laban the son of Bethuel the Syrian, the brother of Rebekah the mother of Jacob and Esau. Esau saw that Isaac had blessed Jacob, and sent him away to Syrian Mesopotamia as he blessed him, to fetch a wife for himself from there, when he ordered him, "You will not take a wife of the daughters of the Canaanites," and Jacob listened to his father and his mother, and went to Syrian Mesopotamia. When Esau realized that the daughters of Canaan were evil in the eyes of Isaac, Esau went to Ishmael and took Mahalath the daughter of Ishmael, the son of Abraham, the sister of Nebajoth, as a wife in addition to his other wives.

Jacob left the Well of the Oath and traveled to Harran, and came to a certain place and slept there, as the sun had gone down, and he took one of the stones of the place, and put it at his head, and lay down to sleep in that place. He dreamed and saw a ladder fixed on the land whose top reached to the sky, and the messengers of God ascended and descended on it.[2]

The Lord stood on it, and said, "I am the god of your father Abraham, and the god of Isaac. Don't be afraid. I will give you and your descendants the land on which you lie. Your descendants will be like the sand of the land, and it will spread out to the sea, and the south, and the north, and to the east, and through you and your descendants will all the tribes of the land be blessed. Understand that I am with you to protect you forever in all the paths that you will travel, and I will bring you back to this land. I will not desert you until I have done all that I have told you."

Jacob awoke from his sleep, and said, "The Lord is in this place, and I did not know it."

He was afraid, and said, "How terrible is this place! This is none other than the house of God, and this is the gateway to the sky."

Jacob rose up in the morning and took the stone that had laid there by his head, and he set it up as a pillar and poured oil on the top of it. He named that place: Beth El. (The name of the town had previously been Luz.) Jacob vowed a vow, "If the Lord the god will be with me, and guard me throughout this journey which I am going on, and give me bread to eat, and clothing to put on, and bring me back in safety to the house of my father, then the Lord will be my god. This stone, which I have set as a pillar for you, will be the Temple of God

CHAPTER 28

for me, and of everyone, whatever you will give me, I will tithe a tenth for you."

CHAPTER 28 NOTES

1 Codex Alexandrinus: T̅S̅ K̅S̅ mou (ⲐⲤ ⲔⲤ ⲘⲞⲨ). Translation: god lord of mine

- LXX 64: ṯeos mou (θεός μου). Translation: god of mine
- Leningrad Codex: 'ēl šadday (אֵל שַׁדַּי). Translation: god Shaddai
- Peshitta: åylšdy (ܐܝܠܫܕܝ)
- Targum Onkelos: 'ēl šadday (אֵל שַׁדַּי). Translation: god Shaddai
- Targum Pseudo-Jonathan: 'ēl šadday (אֵל שַׁדַּי). Translation: god Shaddai

This is the second deviation between Cosmic Genesis and Bereshít regarding the god Shaddai, and the second time the name or title Shaddai is missing entirely from the Septuagint's translation. The name Shaddai is imported from *Bereshít*. For more information on the god Shaddai, see the note in chapter 17.

2 This story of a ladder reaching up into the sky was also found in the creation mythology of Heliopolis, in which Osiris climbed a ladder up into Nut (Night-sky). As a result, Egyptian tombs often included a ladder, and had the ceiling of the crypt, or interior or the lid of the sarcophagus painted blue with stars, representing Nut. The story involving Osiris appeared in the fifth dynasty, supplanting the an older version of the story in which Horus the Elder was assisted to climb the ladder into the sky by his four sons. As the Egyptian story is much older than the Israelite version, it seems likely that the story, of Jacob's dream itself, was based on the story from the creation mythology of Heliopolis.

CHAPTER 29

Jacob having lifted up his feet went to the land of the east to Laban, the son of Bethuel the Syrian, and the brother of Rebekah, mother of Jacob and Esau. He looked and found a well in the plain. There were three flocks of sheep resting at it, as out of that well they watered the flocks, but there was a great stone at the mouth of the well. There were all the flocks gathered, and they used to roll away the stone from the mouth of the well, and water the flocks, and set the stone again in its place on the mouth of the well.

Jacob asked them, "Brothers, where are you from?" They answered, "We are from Harran."

He asked them, "Do you know Laban the son of Nahor?"

They answered, "We do know him."

He asked them, "Is he well?"

They answered, "He is well. Look Rachel his daughter came with the sheep."

Jacob said, "It is still midday, it is not yet time for the flocks to be gathered together. Water your flocks, and leave and feed them."

They replied, "We will not be able to until all the shepherds are gathered together, and they roll away the stone from the mouth of the well. Then we will water the flocks."

CHAPTER 29

While he was still speaking to them, Rachel the daughter of Laban came with her father's sheep, as she fed the sheep of her father. When Jacob saw Rachel the daughter of Laban, his mother's brother, and the sheep of Laban, his mother's brother, he came and rolled the stone away from the mouth of the well, and watered the sheep of Laban, his mother's brother. Jacob kissed Rachel, and cried with a loud voice, and wept. He told Rachel that he was the close relative of her father and the son of Rebekah, and she ran and reported to her father according to these words. It happened when Laban heard the name of Jacob, his sister's son, he ran to meet him, and embraced and kissed him, and brought him into his house, and he told Laban all these things.

Laban said to him, "You are of my bones and of my flesh," and he was with him a month.

Laban said to Jacob, "Surely you will not serve me for nothing, because you are my brother. Tell me what your reward is to be."

Now Laban had two daughters, the name of the elder was Leah, and the name of the younger, Rachel. The eyes of Leah were weak. But Rachel was beautiful in appearance, and very beautiful in attitude. Jacob loved Rachel, and offered, "I will serve you seven years for your younger daughter Rachel."

Laban replied to him, "It is better that I should give her to you, than that I should give her to another man. Live with me."

CHAPTER 29

Jacob served for Rachel seven years, and they seemed to him like just a few days, because of his love of her. Jacob said to Laban, "Give me my wife, for my days are completed, that I may go into her."

Laban gathered together all the men of the land and held a marriage feast. However, he took his daughter Leah and brought her to Jacob, and Jacob went into her. Laban gave his daughter Leah, Zilpah his woman-slave, to be her woman-slave. In the morning Jacob realized it was Leah, and Jacob demanded from Laban, "What is this that you have done to me? Did I not serve you for Rachel? Why have you deceived me!"

Laban answered, "In our country, we do not give the younger before the elder! Work another seven years, and I will give her to you also, in return for your labor."

Jacob did so, and worked another seven, and Laban gave him his daughter Rachel as a wife. Laban gave to his daughter his woman-slave Bilhah, as a woman-slave for her.

He went into Rachel, and he loved Rachel more than Leah, and he served him another seven years. When the Lord the god saw that Leah was hated, he opened her womb, but Rachel was barren. Leah conceived and carried a son for Jacob, and she called his name, "Reuben," saying, "Because the Lord has looked on my humiliation, and has given me a son, now my husband will love me."

Chapter 29

She conceived again and carried a second son for Jacob, and she said, "Because the Lord has heard that I am hated, he has given to me this one also," and she called his name, "Simeon."

She conceived yet again, and carried a son, and said, "Now my husband will be with me, for I have born him three sons." Therefore she called his name, "Levi."

Having conceived yet again, she carried a son, and said, "Now yet again I will give thanks to the Lord."

Therefore she called his name, "Judah," and stopped becoming pregnant.

CHAPTER 30

When Rachel saw that she carried no children for Jacob, she was jealous of her sister, and said to Jacob, "Give me children, or I will kill myself!"

Jacob was angry with Rachel, and said to her, "Am I in the place of the god who has deprived you of the fruit of the womb?"

Rachel said to Jacob, "See my woman-slave Bilhah, go into her, and she will bear on my knees, and I also will have children through her."

She gave him Bilhah her slave, as a wife for him, and Jacob went into her. Bilhah, Rachel's slave, conceived and carried Jacob a son, and Rachel said, "God has given judgment for me, and listened to my voice, and has given me a son," therefore she called his name, "Dan."

Bilhah, Rachel's slave, conceived again and carried a second son for Jacob, and Rachel said, "God has helped me. I competed with my sister and won," and she called his name, "Naphtali."

Leah saw that she stopped becoming pregnant, and she took Zilpah her slave, and gave her to Jacob as a wife, and he went into her. Zilpah the slave of Leah conceived and carried Jacob a son, and Leah said, "It is joyous," and she called his name, "Gad."

CHAPTER 30

Zilpah, the slave of Leah conceived again and carried Jacob a second son, Leah said, "I am blessed, and the women will pronounce me blessed," and she called his name, "Asher."

Reuben went out on the day of the barley harvest, and found apples of mandrakes in the field, and brought them to his mother Leah, and Rachel said to Leah her sister, "Give me from your son's mandrakes."

Leah asked, "Is it not enough for you that you have taken my husband, will you also take my son's mandrakes?"

Rachel answered, "Not so. Let him lie with you tonight, in trade for your son's mandrakes."

Jacob came in out of the field at even, and Leah went out to meet him, and said, "You will come to me today, for I have hired you for my son's mandrakes," and he lay with her that night.

God listened to Leah, and she conceived and carried Jacob a fifth son. Leah said, "God has given me my reward because I gave my slave to my husband," and she called his name "Issachar," which means "Reward."

Leah conceived again and carried Jacob a sixth son, and Leah said, "God has given me a good gift at this time. My husband will prefer me, for I have carried him six sons," and she called his name, "Zebulun."

After this, she carried a daughter, and she called her name, "Dinah." God remembered Rachel, and God listened to her, and he opened her womb. She conceived and carried Jacob a son, and Rachel said, "God has taken away my shame."

She called his name Joseph, saying, "Let God add to me another son."

It happened after Rachel had born Joseph, Jacob said to Laban, "Send me away, that I may go to my place and to my land. Give my wives and my children, for whom I have served you, that I may depart, for you know the service which I have done for you."

Laban said to him, "If I have found favor in your sight, stay, perhaps understood well, for the Lord has blessed me at your coming in. State your wages to me, and I will give them."

Jacob replied, "You know in what ways I have served you, and how much of your livestock is with me. You had little before my time, and it has increased to a great multitude, and the Lord the god has blessed you at my feet. Now then, when will I set up also my own house?"

Laban asked him, "What will I give you?"

Jacob answered him, "You will not give me anything. If you will do this for me, I will again tend your flocks and look after them. Let all your sheep pass by today, and separate out every gray sheep from the rams, and everyone speckled and spotted goat, and this will be my reward. And my right-eousness will listen to me in the morning, for it is my reward before you. Whatever will not be spotted and speckled among the goats, and gray among the rams will be taken with me."

CHAPTER 30

Laban said to him, "Let it be as you"ve said." He separated in that day the spotted and speckled male-goats, and all the spotted and speckled female-goats, and all that was gray among the rams, and everyone that was white among them, and he gave them into the hand of his sons. He set a distance of a three days' journey between them and between Jacob. Jacob tended the livestock of Laban that were left behind.

Jacob took for himself green sticks of styrax trees and walnut and other trees, and Jacob peeled in them white stripes, and as he drew off the green, the white stripe which he had made appeared alternate on the sticks. He laid the sticks which he had peeled, in the hollows of the watering-troughs, that whenever the livestock should come to drink, as they should have come to drink before the sticks, the livestock might conceive at the sticks. So the livestock conceived at the sticks, and the livestock brought out young speckled and streaked and spotted with ash-colored spots. Jacob separated the lambs and set before the sheep a speckled ram, and every variegated one among the lambs, and he separated flocks for himself alone and did not mingle them with the sheep of Laban. It happened in the time in which the livestock became pregnant, conceiving in the belly, Jacob put the sticks before the livestock in the troughs, that they might conceive by the sticks. But he did not put them in indiscriminately whenever the livestock happened to bring out, but the unmarked ones were Laban's, and the marked ones were Jacob's. The man became very rich, and he had many livestock, and oxen, and servants, and woman-slaves, and camels, and donkeys.

CHAPTER 31

Jacob heard the words of the sons of Laban, saying, "Jacob has taken all that was our father's, and from our father's property he has received all this glory."

Jacob saw the attitude of Laban, and saw it was not towards him as it had been before. The Lord said to Jacob, "Return to the land of your father, and to your family, and I will be with you."

Jacob sent, and called Leah and Rachel to the plain where the flocks were. He said to them, "I see the face of your father, that it is not towards me as before, but the god of my father is with me. You too know, that with all my might I have served your father. But your father deceived me and changed my wages for the ten lambs, yet God gave him no power to hurt me. If he should say, 'The speckled will be your reward, then all the livestock would carry speckled,' and if he should say, 'The white will be your reward, then all would the livestock carry white.' So God has taken away all the livestock of your father, and given them to me. It happened when the livestock conceived and were with young, that I saw with my eyes while sleeping, and I saw the male-goats and the rams leaping on the sheep and the female-goats, speckled and variegated and spotted with ash-colored spots. The messenger of God said to me while I slept, 'Jacob,' and I asked, 'What is it?' He said, 'Look with your eyes, and see the male-goats and the rams leaping on the sheep and the female-goats, speckled and variegated and spotted with ash-colored spots, for I have seen all things that Laban does to you. I am the God who appeared to you in the house of God, where you anointed a pillar to me, and vowed to me. Now then arise and depart out of this land, return to the land of your birth, and I will be with you.'"

Rachel and Leah answered, "Have we still a part or inheritance in the house of our father? Are we not considered strangers to him? He sold us and consumed our silver. All the wealth and the glory which God has taken from our father, it will be ours' and our childrens'. Now then do whatever God has told you."

Jacob rose and placed his wives and his children up on the camels. He took away all his possessions and all his stores, which he had received in Mesopotamia, and all that belonged to him, to depart to Isaac his father in the land of Canaan. Laban went to shear his sheep, and Rachel stole her father's icons. Jacob hid the matter from Laban the Syrian, so as not to tell him that he ran away. He departed with all that belonged to him, and passed over the river, and went into the mountains of Gilead.

But it was told to Laban the Syrian on the third day, that Jacob had fled, and he took his brothers with him, and chased after him a journey of seven days, and caught up to him in the mountains of Gilead. God came to Laban the Syrian in sleep at night, and said to him, "Pay attention that you don't at any time speak evilly to Jacob."

CHAPTER 31

Laban caught up with Jacob, where Jacob pitched his tent in the mountains, and Laban stationed his brothers in the mountains of Gilead. Laban asked Jacob, "What have you done? Why did you run away secretly, and rob me and lead away my daughters like captive slaves? If you had told me, I would have sent you away with joy, and with songs, and timbrels, and harp. Was I not considered worthy to embrace my children and my daughters? Now then, you have worked foolishly. Now my hand has the power to hurt you, but the god of your father spoke to me yesterday, saying, "Pay attention that you don't at any time speak evilly to Jacob." Now then go on your way, for you have earnestly desired to depart to the house of your father. But why have you stolen my gods?"

Jacob answered Laban, "I was afraid, as I thought that at any point you might take away your daughters from me, and all my property."

Jacob continued, "With whoever you will find your gods, he will not live in the presence of our brothers. Take note of whatever I have of your property and take it," and he found nothing with him, but Jacob did not know that his wife Rachel had stolen them.

Laban went in and searched in the house of Leah, and did not find them, and he went out of the house of Leah, and searched in the house of Jacob, and in the house of the two woman-slaves, and did not find them, and he went also into the house of Rachel. Rachel took the icons, and placed them among the camel's packs, and sat on them. She said to her father, "do not be angry lord. I can't rise up before you, for it is with me according to the manner of women."

Laban searched in all the house and did not find his icons. Jacob was angry and argued with Laban, and Jacob answered and said to Laban, "What is my injustice, and what is my sin, that you have chased after me, and that you have searched all the furniture of my house? What have you found of all the furniture from your house? Set it here between your relations and my relations, and let them decide between us. For twenty years I have been with you, your sheep and your female-goats have not failed in carrying, and I did not eat the rams from your livestock. That which was stolen from your animals I did not report to you, and I made good from my own, both the thefts of the day and the thefts of the night. I was parched with heat by day and chilled with frost by night, and my sleep departed from my eyes. For twenty years have I been in your house. I served you fourteen years for your two daughters, and six years as a shepherd, and you falsely rated my pay for ten lambs. Unless I had the god of my father Abraham, and the fear of Isaac, now you would have sent me away empty. God saw my humiliation, and the labor of my hands, and rebuked you yesterday."

Laban answered Jacob, "The daughters are my daughters, and the sons my sons, and the livestock are my livestock, and all things which you see are mine, and the property of my daughters. What will I do to them today, or their children which they carried? Now then come, let me make a covenant, both I and you, and it will be as a witness between me and you."

He said to him, "Understand, there is no one with us. See God is a witness between me and you."

Jacob took a stone and set it up for a pillar. Jacob said to his brothers, "Gather stones," and they gathered stones and made a stack, and ate there on the stack.

Laban said to him, "This stack witnesses between me and you today."

Laban called it, the "Stack of Testimony," and Jacob called it, the "Witness Stack."

Laban said to Jacob, "See this stack and the pillar which I have set between me and you. This stack witnesses, and this pillar witnesses."

Therefore its name was called, the "Stack Witnesses."

The witness of which he spoke was, "Let God see it between me and you, because we are about to depart from each other. If you will humiliate my daughters, if you should take wives in addition to my daughters, see, there is no one with us watching, but God is witness between me and you."

Laban said to Jacob, "Know this stack and this pillar are a witness. For if I should not cross over to you, neither should you cross over to me, for mischief beyond this stack and this pillar. The god of Abraham and the god of Nahor judge between us," and Jacob swore by the fear of his father Isaac.

CHAPTER 31

He offered a sacrifice in the mountain and called his brothers, and they ate and drank, and slept in the mountain. Laban rose up in the morning, and kissed his sons and his daughters, and blessed them, and Laban having turned back, departed to his place.

CHAPTER 32

Jacob left for his journey, and looking up, he saw the camp of the army of God, and the messengers of God met him. When he saw them Jacob said, "This is the Camp of God, and he called the name of that place, "Encampments."

Jacob sent messengers before him to Esau his brother to the land of Seir, in the country of Edom. He ordered them, saying, "Say this to my Lord Esau. So says your servant Jacob, 'I have stayed with Laban and waited until now. There were born to me oxen, and donkeys, and sheep, and men-slaves and women-slaves, and I sent word to my Lord Esau, that your servant might find favor in your sight.'"

The messengers returned to Jacob and reported, "We came to your brother Esau, and he comes to meet you with four hundred men."

Jacob was greatly terrified and was confused, and he divided the people that were with him, and the cows, and the camels, and the sheep, into two camps. Jacob said, "If Esau should come to one camp, and attack it, the other camp will be safe."

Jacob said, "God of my father Abraham, and god of my father Isaac, Lord, you are he who said to me, 'Depart quickly to the land of your birth, and I will do good for you.' Let there be for me a sufficiency of all the justice and all the truth which you have worked with your servant. For with this, my wand, I passed over this Jordan. Now I have become two camps. Save me from the hand of my brother, from the hand of Esau, for I am afraid of him, in case he should come and slaughter me, and the mothers of the children. But you said, "I will do you good, and will make your descendants like the sand of the sea, which will not be a countable number."'

He slept there that night, and took of the gifts which he carried with him, and sent out to Esau his brother, two hundred female-goats, twenty male-goats, two hundred sheep, twenty rams, thirty camels milking their foals, forty cows, ten bulls, twenty donkeys, and ten colts. He gave them to his servants and separated the groups, and he said to his servants, "Go out ahead of me, and put a space between the two groups."

He ordered the first, "If Esau my brother meets you, and asks you, 'Who are you? Where do you go, and whose are these possessions advancing before you?' You will answer, 'Your servant Jacob. He has sent gifts to my lord Esau, and he follows behind us."

He ordered the first and the second and the third, and all that went before him after these flocks, saying, 'You will speak to your master Esau when you find him, and you will say, "See, your servant Jacob follows us."'

As he thought, "I will reduce his anger with the gifts going to his presence, and afterward I will see his face, and perhaps he will accept me."

CHAPTER 32

So, the presents went on before him, but he himself stayed that night in the camp. He rose up in that night, and took his two wives and his two servant-maids, and his eleven children, and crossed over the ford of Jabbok. He took them, and passed over the torrent, and brought over all his possessions. Jacob was left alone, and a man wrestled with him until the morning. He saw that he could not prevail against him, and he touched the broad part of his thigh, and the broad part of Jacob's thigh was numbed during his wrestling with him.

He said to him, "Let me go, the day has dawned."

But he said, "I will not let you go, unless you bless me."

He asked him, "What is your name?"

He answered, "Jacob."

He said to him, "Your name will no longer be called Jacob. Your name will be Israel. You have prevailed with God, and will be mighty among men."

Jacob asked, "Tell me your name."

He replied, "Why do you ask my name?" and he blessed him there.

Jacob called the name of that place, "Face of God," as, he said, "I have seen God, face to face, and my life was saved."

The sun rose on him when he passed the Face of God, and he halted on his thigh. Therefore, the children of Israel will not eat the sinew which was benumbed, which is on the broad part of the thigh, until today, because the messenger had touched the broad part of the thigh of Jacob, the sinew which was numbed.

CHAPTER 33

Jacob looked up with his eyes and saw Esau his brother coming with four hundred men with him, and Jacob divided the children with Leah and Rachel, and the two slave-women. He put the two slave-women and their children first, and Leah and her children behind, and Rachel and Joseph last. He approached them and bowed to the ground seven times until he drew near to his brother. Esau ran on to meet him, and embraced him, and fell on his neck, and kissed him, and they both wept. Esau looked up and saw the women and the children, and asked, "Who are these to you?"

He answered, "The children with which God has mercifully blessed your servant."

The woman-slaves and their children approached and did reverence. Leah and her children approached and did reverence, and after this Rachel and Joseph approached and did reverence.

He asked, "What are these companies that I have met?"

He answered, "Gifts that your servant might find favor in your sight, my Lord."

Esau stated, "I have much my brother. Keep your own."

Jacob offered, "If I have found favor in your sight, receive the gifts through my hands. As I have seen your face, I have seen the face of God, and you will be very pleased with me.

CHAPTER 33

Receive my blessings, which I have brought you because God has had mercy on me, and I have all things," and he constrained him, and he took them.

He said, "Let us leave, and proceed right now."

He replied to him, "My Lord knows, that the children are very young, and the flocks and the herds with me are young. If I will drive them hard one day, all the livestock will die. Let my Lord go on before his servant, and I will have strength on the road according to the ease of the journey before me, and according to the speed of the children until I come to my lord at Seir."

Esau offered, "I will leave some of my people with you."

He asked, "Why? It is enough that I have found favor before you my lord."

Esau left that day on his journey to Seir. Jacob departed to his tents, and he made houses for himself there, and for his livestock he made stalls, therefore he called the name of that place, "Booths." Jacob came to Salem, a city of Shechem, which is in the land of Canaan when he departed out of Mesopotamia in Syria, and pitched his tent in front of the city. He bought the portion of the field, where he pitched his tent, from Hamor the father of Shechem, for a hundred lambs. He set up there an altar and called on God of Israel.

CHAPTER 34

Dinah, the daughter of Leah, whom she carried for Jacob, went out to see the daughters of the inhabitants. Shechem the son of Hamor the Mitannian, the ruler of the land, saw her, and took her and lay with her, and embarrassed her. He was attached to the mind of Dinah the daughter of Jacob, and he loved the girl, and he spoke to her according to the heart of the girl. Shechem spoke to Hamor his father, saying, "Take for me this girl as a wife."

Jacob heard that the son of Hamor had defiled Dinah his daughter while his sons were with his livestock in the plain. Jacob was silent until they came. Hamor the father of Shechem went out to Jacob, to speak to him. The sons of Jacob came from the plain, and when they heard, the men were deeply pained, and it was very grievous to them, because the man worked folly in Israel, having lain with the daughter of Jacob, which was not to be. Hamor spoke to them, saying, "Shechem my son has chosen in his heart your daughter. Give her therefore to him for a wife, and intermarry with us. Give us your daughters, and take our daughters for your sons. And live among us. And, Look, the land is spacious before you, live in it, and trade, and get possessions in it."

Shechem said to her father and to her brothers, "I would find favor with you, and we will give whatever you will name. Demand a large of dowry, and I will give accordingly as you ask me, only give me this girl for a wife."

CHAPTER 34

The sons of Jacob answered Shechem and Hamor his father dishonestly and spoke to them because they had defiled Dinah their sister. Simeon and Levi, the brothers of Dinah, said to them, "We will not be able to do this thing, to give our sister to a man who is uncircumcised, for it is a reproach to us. Only on these terms will we conform to you, and live among you, if you also will be as we are, in that every male of you be circumcised. And we will give our daughters to you, and we will take of your daughters for wives to us, and we will live with you, and we will be as one race. But if you will not listen to us to be circumcised, we will take our daughter and depart."

The words pleased Hamor, and Shechem the son of Hamor. The young man did not delay to follow this instruction, for he was much attached to Jacob's daughter, and he was the most honorable of all in his father's house. Hamor and Shechem his son came to the gate of their city, and spoke to the men of their city, saying, "These men are peaceful, let them live with us on the land, and let them trade in it, and Look the land is extensive before them. We will take their daughters for us as wives, and we will give them our daughters. Only on these terms will the men conform to us to live with us to be one people, if every male among us is circumcised, as they also are circumcised. And will not their livestock and their quadrupeds, and their possessions, be ours? Only in this let us conform to them, and they will live with us."

All that went in at the gate of their city listened to Hamor and Shechem his son, and they were circumcised in the flesh of their foreskin every male. It happened on the third day, when they were in pain, the two sons of Jacob, Simeon and Levi, Dinah's brothers, took each man his sword, and came on the city safely, and killed every male. They killed Hamor and Shechem his son with the edge of the sword, and took Dinah out of the house of Shechem, and left. The sons of Jacob came and slaughtered and ravaged the city in which they had defiled Dinah their sister. They took their sheep, oxen, and donkeys, and all things whatever were in the city, and whatever were in the plain. They took as slaves all the people from there, and all their goods, and their wives, and plundered both whatever was in the city, and whatever was in the houses.

Jacob said to Simeon and Levi, "You have made me villainous, and I will be hated by all the people in the land, both among the Canaanites and the Perizzites, and I am few in number. They will gather themselves against me and cut me in pieces, and I will be utterly destroyed, and my house."

They replied, "They will not treat our sister like a whore!"

CHAPTER 35

God said to Jacob, "Rise, go up to Bethel and live there, and build an altar there to the god that appeared to you when you fled from the face of Esau your brother."

Jacob said to his house, and to all that were with him, "Remove the strange gods[1] from among you, and purify yourselves, and change your clothes. Let us rise and go up to Bethel, and let us there make an altar to God who hears me in the day of trouble, who was with me, and saved me throughout in the journey on which I went."

They gave to Jacob the gods of the foreigners, which were in their hands, and the earrings which were in their ears, and Jacob hid them under the turpentine tree which is in Shechem and destroyed them to today. So Israel departed from Shechem, and the fear of God was on the cities around them, and they did not chase after the children of Israel. Jacob came to Luz, which is in the land of Canaan, (which is Beth El), he and all the people that were with him. He built there an altar and called the name of the place the House of God, for there God appeared to him when he fled from the face of his brother Esau.

Deborah, Rebekah's nurse, died and was buried below Bethel under the oak, and Jacob named it, "The Oak of Mourning."

CHAPTER 35

God appeared to Jacob once more in Luz, when he came out of Mesopotamia in Syria, and God blessed him. God said to him, "Your name will not be called Jacob, but Israel will be your name," and he renamed him Israel.

God said to him, "I am the god Shaddai.[2] Increase and multiply, for nations and gatherings of nations will be of you, and kings will come out of your loins. The land which I gave to Abraham and Isaac, I have given it to you, and it will come to pass that I will give this land also to your descendants after you."

God went up from him, from the place where he spoke with him. Jacob set up a pillar in the place where God spoke with him, even a pillar of stone, and offered a libation on it, and poured oil on it. Jacob called the name of the place in which God spoke with him, Bethel.

Jacob moved from Bethel and pitched his tent beyond the Tower of Gader, and it happened when he drew near to Chabratha, to enter into Ephrath, Rachel gave birth, and her birthing was hard labor. It was such a difficult labor that the midwife said to her, "Be of good courage, for you will also have this son."

It happened during her giving up the spirit, for she was dying, that she called his name, Ben-Anu,[3] but his father called his name Benjamin. So Rachel died and was buried on the road to Ephrath (this is Bethlehem).[4] Jacob set up a pillar on her tomb, and this is the pillar on the tomb of Rachel, until today.

CHAPTER 35

It happened when Israel lived in that land, that Reuben went and lay with Bilhah, the concubine of his father Jacob, and Israel heard, and the thing appeared grievous before him.

The sons of Jacob were twelve. The sons of Leah were the firstborn of Jacob: Reuben, Simeon, Levi, Judah, Issachar, Zebulun. The sons of Rachel were Joseph and Benjamin. The sons of Bilhah, the woman-slave of Rachel, were Dan and Naphtali. The sons of Zilpah, the woman-slave of Leah, were Gad and Asher. These are the sons of Jacob, which were born to him in Mesopotamia in Syria.

Jacob came to Isaac his father to Mamre, to a city of the plain, (this is Hebron in the land of Canaan), where Abraham and Isaac stayed. The days of Isaac which he lived were a hundred and eighty years. Isaac gave up the spirit and died, and was laid to his family, old and full of days, and Esau and Jacob his sons buried him.

CHAPTER 35 NOTES

1 Codex Alexandrinus: ṭeous tous allotrious (ⲐⲈⲞⲨⲤ ⲦⲞⲨⲤ ⲀⲰⲰⲞⲦⲢⲒⲞⲨⲤ). Translation: gods of strangers (or foreigners, aliens)
• Leningrad Codex: 'ĕlōhê hannēkār (אֱלֹהֵי הַנֵּכָר). Translation: god strange (or foreign, alien)
• Peshitta: ålhå mn byntkwn (ܐܠܗܐ ܡܢ ܒܝܢܬܟܘܢ). Translation: god of the foreigners
• Targum Onkelos: ṭa'ăwat 'ammayyā' (טַעֲוַת עַמְמַיָּא). Translation: error (or mistaken) of nations (or peoples)

CHAPTER 35

• Targum Pseudo-Jonathan: ṭa'ăwat 'ammayā' (טַעֲוַת עַמְמַיָא). Translation: error (or mistaken) of nations (or peoples)

2 Codex Colberto-Sarravianus: egō o T̄S̄ sou ikanos (ⲉⲅⲱⲟⲑ̄ⲥ̄ⲥⲟⲩ ⲓⲕⲁⲛⲟⲥ). Translation: I'm the god of your skill
• Vienna Genesis: egō o T̄S̄ sou (ⲉⲅⲱⲟⲑ̄ⲥ̄ⲥⲟⲩ). Translation: I'm the god of you
• LXX 135: egō o ṭeos sou ikanōs (ἐγὼ ο θεός σου ικἀνῶος). Translation: I'm the god of your skill
• LXX 82: egō o ṭeos sou ikanoustō (ἐγὼ ο θεός σου ικἀνουαῖο). Translation: I'm the god of your sufficiency
• Leningrad Codex: ănî ēl šadday (אֲנִי אֵל שַׁדַּי). Translation: I'm god Shaddai
• Peshitta: ånå ånå åylšdy ålhå (ܐܢܐ ܐܢܐ ,ܐܝܠܫܕܝ ܐܠܗܐ). Translation: I am Åylšdy god
• Targum Onkelos: 'ănā' 'ēl šadday (אֲנָא אֵל שַׁדַּי). Translation: I'm god Shaddai
• Targum Pseudo-Jonathan: 'ănā' 'ēl šaday (אֲנָא אֵל שַׁדַּי). Translation: I'm god Shaddai

This is the third deviation between *Cosmic Genesis* and *Bereshít* regarding the god Shaddai, and the third time the name or title Shaddai is missing entirely from the Septuagint's translation. The name Shaddai is imported from *Bereshít*. For more information on the god Shaddai, see the note in chapter 17.

3 Codex Alexandrinus: uios odunēs mou (ⲩⲓⲟⲥ ⲟⲇⲩⲛⲏⲥ ⲙⲟⲩ). Translation: son of pain of mine.
• Leningrad Codex: ben-'ônî (בֶּן־אוֹנִי). Translation: son of power
• Peshitta: br kåby (ܒܪ ܟܐܒܝ). Translation: son of pain (or wound, disease)
• Targum Onkelos: bar dəwāy (בַּר דְּוָי). Translation: son of the woe

354

• Targum Pseudo-Jonathan: bar dəwûyî (בַּר דְּווּיִי). Translation: son of the woe

The Greek translation appears to be partially an interpretation of ånå (אֲנָא), meaning "I," however, it is not clear where the term "pain" came from. The Hebrew term åwny (אוֹנִי) is not a proper term, however, is considered to be a decedent of the older Ugaritic Canaanite word ån (𐎀𐎐) meaning power, and closely related to the Akkadian word ān (𒀭), meaning "god" or "star."

The differences between the names that Rachel and Jacob gave the child represent the difference between the Akkadian Ān and Egyptian Amen (𓇋𓏠𓈖, transliteration: îmn) names, indicating that when the text was written, Ān and Amen were considered the same god. As the Greeks appear to have mistranslated the name, the older name is restored from *Bereshít*.

4 LXX 961: Efrata autē estin Baethēleem (ΕΦΡΑΘΑ ΑΥΤΗ ΕϹΤΙΝ ΒΑΙΘΗΛΕΕΜ). Translation: Ephratha this is Bethlehem.

• Codex Alexandrinus: Efrata autē estin Bēthleem (ΕΦΡΑΘΑ ΑΥΤΗ ΕϹΤΙΝ ΒΗΘΛΕΕΜ). Translation: Ephratha this is Bethlehem.

• Vienna Genesis: Efrata autē estin Bētēle- (ΕΦΡΑΘΑ ΑΥΤΗ ΕϹΤΙΝ ΒΗΘΗΛΕ-). The name Bethlehem is damaged, however, is believe to have originally read Bētēleem (ΒΗΘΗΛΕΕΜ).

• LXX 131: Efrata hautē estin Bētlem (Εφρα θά λᴅτλ ϭϛιν βλ̃λϭϻ). Translation: Ephratha this is Bēthlem.

• LXX 346: Eufrata hautē estin Baetēl (Ευφρα θά λᴅτλ ϭϛιν βαθλλ). Translation: Euphtatha this is Bethel.

• LXX 25: Eufrata hautē estin Bitleem (Ευφρα θά λᴅτλ ϭϛιν βιλϭϭϻ). Translation: Euphtatha this is Bethlehem.

• LXX 57: Eftara hautē estin Bētleem (Εφθαρλ λᴅτλ ϭϛιν βλ̃λϭϻ). Translation: Ephthara this is Bethlehem.

• LXX 128: Eufrata hautē estin Bētleem (Ευφρα θά λᴅτλ ϭϛιν βλ̃λϭϻ). Translation: Euphtatha this is Bethlehem

CHAPTER 35

- LXX 370: Efranṯa hautē estin Biṯleem (Ε𝔣ϱαℕθλ λ𝖆̄тℏ 𝔤ςιℕ β𝔡𝔜λ𝔤𝔤μ). Translation: Ephrantha this is Bethlehem.

- LXX 56: Efraṯ hautē estin Bēṯleem (Ε𝔣ϱαθ λ𝖆̄тℏ 𝔤ςιℕ βℏ𝔜λ𝔤𝔤μ). Translation: Ephrath this is Bethlehem.

- LXX 79: Eufranṯa hautē estin Bēṯleem (Ευ𝔣ϱαℕθλ λ𝖆̄тℏ 𝔤ςιℕ βℏ𝔜λ𝔤𝔤μ). Translation: Eyphrantha this is Bethlehem.

- LXX 346: Efraṯa hautē estin Baeṯēl (Ε𝔣ϱαθλ λ𝖆̄тℏ 𝔤ςιℕ βα𝔣θℏ λ). Translation: Ephratha this is Bethel.

- LXX 107: Efranṯa hautē estin Bēṯleem (Ε𝔣ϱαℕθλ λ𝖆̄тℏ 𝔤ςιℕ βℏ𝔜λ𝔤𝔤μ). Translation: Ephrantha this is Bethlehem

- Leningrad Codex: 'eprātâ hiw' bêt lāhem (אֶפְרָ֫תָה ה֥וֹא בֵּ֣ית לָֽחֶם). Translation: Eprata it's Bethlehem (or "house of bread," Temple of Lehem)

- Peshitta: Ȧprt. hy hy byt lǩm (ܐܦܪܬ: ܗܝ, ܗܝ, ܒܝܬ ܠܚܡ). Translation: Aprt: it is Bethlehem (or house of bread, Temple of Lehem)

- Targum Onkelos: 'eprāt hî' bêt lāhem (אֶפְרָת הִיא בֵּית לְחֶם). Translation: Eprat it's Bethlehem (or "house of bread," Temple of Lehem)

- Targum Jerusalem: 'eprāt (אֶפְרָת)

- Targum Pseudo-Jonathan: 'eprāt (אֶפְרָת)

The Hebrew and Aramaic name of Eprātâ appears to be a corrupted Canaanite transliteration of the Egyptian name r-pr-t (𓂋𓉐𓏏), which translates as "temple of bread," one meaning of the Canaanite name Byt Lhm (𐤁𐤉𐤕 𐤋𐤇𐤌). This suggests this section of text was a written in, or translated into Egyptian, and later translated into Canaanite, when the scribal note was added.

CHAPTER 36

These are the generations of Esau; this is Edom. Esau took to himself wives of the daughters of the Canaanites; Adah, the daughter of Helon the Cypriot, and Aholibamah, daughter of Anah the son of Zibeon, the Mitannian, and Bashemath, daughter of Ishmael, sister of Nebajoth. Adah carried to him Eliphaz, and Bashemath carried Deuel. Aholibamah carried Jeush, and Jaalam, and Korah; these are the sons of Esau, which were born to him in the land of Canaan.

Esau took his wives, and his sons, and his daughters, and all the persons of his house, and all his possessions, and all his livestock, and all that he had got, and all things whatever he had acquired in the land of Canaan, and Esau went out from the land of Canaan, from the face of his brother Jacob. For their substance was too great for them to live together, and the land of their residence could not bear them, because of the abundance of their possessions. Esau lived in mount Seir; Esau, he is Edom.

These are the generations of Esau, the father of Edom in Mount Seir. These are the names of the sons of Esau. Eliphaz, the son of Adah, the wife of Esau, and Deuel, the son of Bashemath, wife of Esau.

The sons of Eliphaz were Teman, Onam, Shophan, Gatam, and Kenez. And Timnath was a concubine of Eliphaz, the son of Esau, and she carried Amalek to Eliphaz. These are the sons of Adah, the wife of Esau.

These are the sons of Deuel; Nahath, Zerah, Shammah, and Mizzah. These were the sons of Bashemath, wife of Esau. These are the sons of Aholibamah, the daughter of Anah, the son of Zibeon, the wife of Esau, and she carried to Esau, Jeush, and Jaalam, and Korah.

These are the chiefs of the son of Esau, even the sons of Eliphaz, the firstborn of Esau; chief Teman, chief Onam, chief Shophan, chief Kenez, chief Korah, chief Gatam, and chief Amalek. These are the chiefs of Eliphaz, in the land of Edom, the sons of Adah. These are the sons of Deuel, the son of Esau; chief Nahath, chief Zerah, chief Shammah, and chief Mizzah. These are the chiefs of Deuel, in the land of Edom; these are the sons of Bashemath, wife of Esau.

These are the sons of Aholibamah, wife of Esau; chief Jeush, chief Jaalam, chief Korah. These are the chiefs of Aholibamah, daughter of Anah, wife of Esau.

These are the sons of Esau, and these are the chiefs; these are the sons of Edom.

These are the sons of Seir, the Hurrians, who inhabited the land; Lotan, Shobal, Zibeon, Anah, and Dishon, and Ezer, and Rison. These are the chiefs of the Hurrians, the son of Seir, in the land of Edom.

The sons of Lotan were Hori and Hemam, and the sister of Lotan, Timnath.

CHAPTER 36

These are the sons of Shobal: Golam, and Manahath, and Ebal, and Shophan, and Onam.

These are the sons of Zibeon: Ajah and Anah. This is the Anah who found Jimna in the wilderness when he tended the animals of his father Zibeon.

These are the sons of Anah: Dishon and Aholibamah was the daughter of Anah.

These are the sons of Dishon: Hemdan, and Eshban, and Ithran, and Harran.

These are the sons of Ezer: Balaam, and Zaavan, and Akan.

These are the sons of Rison: Huz, and Aran.

These are the chiefs of Hurrians: chief Lotan, chief Shobal, chief Zibeon, chief Anah, chief Dishon, chief Ezer, chief Rison. These are the chiefs of the Hurrians, in their principalities in the land of Edom.

These are the kings which reigned in Edom before a king reigned in Israel. And Riblah, son of Beor, reigned in Edom, and the name of his city was Dinhabah. And Riblah died, and Jobab, son of Zerah, from Bosorrha reigned in his place.

Jobab died, and Hushim, from the land of the Temanites, reigned in his place.

Hushim died, and Hadad son of Bered, who cut off Midian in the plain of Moab, ruled in his place, and the name of his city was Getthaim.

Hadad died, and Samlah of Masrekah reigned in his place.

CHAPTER 36

Samlah died, and Saul of Rehoboth by the river reigned in his place.

Saul died, and Baalhanan the son of Achbor reigned in his place.

And Baalhanan the son of Achbor died, and Arad the son of Bered reigned in his place, and the name of his city was Peor, and the name of his wife was Mehetabel, daughter of Matred, son of Mezahab.

These are the names of the chiefs of Esau, in their tribes, according to their place, in their countries, and in their nations: chief Timnath, chief Gola, chief Jetheth, chief Aholibamah, chief Elah, chief Pinon, chief Kenez, chief Teman, chief Mazar, chief Magediel, and chief Zaphoin. These are the chiefs of Edom in their dwelling-places in the land of their possession; this is Esau, the father of Edom. Jacob lived in the land where his father stayed, in the land of Canaan.

CHAPTER 37

These are the generations of Jacob. Joseph was seventeen years old, feeding the sheep of his father with his brothers. He was young compared to the sons of Bilhah, or the sons of Zilpah, the wives of his father, and Joseph brought to Israel, their father, the hateful reproach of his brothers. Jacob loved Joseph more than all his sons because he was to him the son of old age, and he made a coat for him of many colors. His brothers had seen that his father loved him more than all his sons, and hated him, and could not say anything nice to him.

Joseph had a dream and reported it to his brothers. He told them, "Hear this dream which I have had. I thought you were binding sheaves in the middle of the field, and my sheaf stood up and was erect, and your sheaves turned around and bowed to my sheaf."

His brothers said to him, "Will you indeed reign over us, or will you be Lord over us?" They hated him even more for his dreams and for telling them.

He had another dream, and related it to his father and his brothers, saying, "Look, I have had another dream, and in it, the sun, the moon, and the eleven stars bowed to me."

His father rebuked him, and said to him, "What is this dream that you have dreamed? Will both I and your mother and your brothers come and bow before you to the ground?"

CHAPTER 37

His brothers envied him, but his father observed it. His brothers went to feed the sheep of their father at Shechem. Israel said to Joseph, "Don't your brothers feed their flock in Shechem? I will send you to them."

He replied to him, "Look, I am here."

Israel said to him, "Go and see if your brothers and the sheep are well, and bring me word," and he sent him out of the Valley of Hebron, and he came to Shechem.

A man found him wandering in the field, and the man asked him, "What do you seek?" He answered, "I am seeking my brothers. Tell me where they feed their flocks."

The man said to him, "They have departed here. I heard them saying, 'Let us go to Dothan,'" and Joseph went after his brothers, and found them in Dothan.

They spied him from a distance before he drew near to them, and they wickedly took counsel to kill him. And each said to his brother, "Look, the dreamer comes. Now then, come and let's kill him, and throw him into one of the pits, and we will say, 'An evil wild animal has devoured him, and we will see what his dreams will be.'"

When Reuben heard it, he rescued him out of their hands by saying, "Let us not strike the life from him." Reuben said to them, "Don't shed blood. Throw him into one of these pits in the wilderness but do not lay your hands on him," that he might rescue him out of their hands, and return him to his father.

CHAPTER 37

It happened, when Joseph came to his brothers, that they stripped Joseph of his many-colored coat that was on him. They took him and cast him into the pit, and the pit was empty, it had no water. They sat down to eat bread and having lifted up their eyes they saw Ishmaelite travelers coming from Gilead, and their camels were heavily loaded with spices, and resin, and stacte, and they went to bring them to Egypt.

Judah said to his brothers, "What profit is it if we kill our brother, and hide his blood? Come, let's sell him to these Ishmaelites, but let's not turn our hands against him, because he is our brother and our flesh, and his brothers listened."

The men, the merchants of Madian, went by, and they drew and lifted Joseph out of the pit, and the Ishmaelites sold Joseph to for twenty pieces of gold, and they brought Joseph down into Egypt.

And Reuben returned to the pit and didn't see Joseph in the pit, and he tore his garments. He returned to his brothers and said, "The boy is gone, and where am I to go?"

Having taken the coat of Joseph, they killed a goat kid and stained the coat with its blood. They took the coat of many colors, and brought it to their father, and said, "We have found this. Know if it is your son's coat or not."

He recognized it, and said, "It is my son's coat, an evil wild animal has eaten him. A wild animal has carried off Joseph!"

Jacob tore his clothes, and put sackcloth on his loins, and mourned for his son many days. All his sons and his daughters

CHAPTER 37

gathered themselves together and came to comfort him, but he would not be comforted, saying, "I will go down to my son mourning to Sheol,[1] and his father wept for him."

The Midianites sold Joseph in Egypt to Pehtiefra,[1] the emissary[2] of Pharaoh,[3] captain of the guard.

CHAPTER 37 NOTES

1 Codex Alexandrinus: Adou (ⲀⲆⲞⲨ). Translation: Hades (or the underworld, to one's fill)

• LXX 458: adēn pros ton uion mou penthōn auton (ⲀⲆⲎⲚ ⲡⲣⲟⲥ ⲧⲱ ⲱⲟⲛ ⲙⲟⲩ ⲡⲉⲛⲑⲟⲟⲛ ⲀⲨⲧⲱ). Translation: Hades (or gland) besides (or in addition to) the son (or child) my grief (or sorrow) myself

• Leningrad Codex: Šə'ōlā (שְׁאֹלָה). Translation: grave (or underworld)

• Peshitta: Šywl (ܫܝܘܠ). Translation: underworld

• Targum Onkelos: Šə'ôl (שְׁאוֹל). Translation: underworld

• Targum Pseudo-Jonathan: bê qəbûrətā' (בֵּי קְבוּרְתָּא). Translation: funeral house

2 Codex Alexandrinus: Petrefē (ⲡⲉⲧⲣⲉⲫⲏ)

• LXX 84: Petefrē (ⲡⲉⲧⲉⲫⲣⲏ)
• LXX 127: Pentefrē (ⲡⲁⲛⲧⲉⲫⲣⲏ)
• LXX 16: Pettefrē (ⲡⲉⲧⲧⲉⲫⲣⲏ)
• LXX 75: Pentefris (ⲡⲁⲛⲧⲉⲫⲣⲓⲥ)
• LXX 408: Pettefri (ⲡⲉⲧⲧⲉⲫⲣⲓ)
• Leningrad Codex: Pôtîpar (פּוֹטִיפַר)
• Peshitta: Pwṭypr (ܦܘܛܝܦܪ)
• Targum Onkelos: Pôtîpar (פּוֹטִיפַר)

364

CHAPTER 37

- Targum Jerusalem: Pôtîpar (פּוֹטִיפַר)
- Targum Pseudo-Jonathan: Pôtîpar (פּוֹטִיפַר)
- Bohairic manuscripts: Petefrē (Ⲡⲉⲧⲉⲫⲣⲏ)

This appears to be a transliteration of the Egyptian name Pehti-ef-rŏ (𓄖𓏏𓏏𓇌𓄂𓇳𓇌), meaning "he has the strength of the sun." See the note on Pehtiefra in chapter 39 for alternate transliterations.

3 Codex Alexandrinus: sparonti (ⲥⲧⲁⲣⲟⲛⲧⲓ)
- LXX 84: spadonti (ⲥⲡⲁⲇⲟⲛⲧⲓ)
- LXX 135: eunoukhō (ⲉⲩⲛⲟⲩⲭⲱ). Translation: eunuch.
- LXX 392: epadonti (ⲉⲡⲁⲇⲟⲛⲧⲓ). Translation: sing.
- LXX 75: adonti (ⲁⲇⲟⲛⲧⲓ). Translation: please.
- LXX 72: paidonti (ⲡⲁⲓⲇⲟⲛⲧⲓ)
- LXX 799: speudonti (ⲥⲡⲉⲩⲇⲟⲛⲧⲓ). Translation: set going
- LXX 664: spendonti (ⲥⲡⲉⲛⲇⲟⲛⲧⲓ). Translation: make a drink offering
  - Leningrad Codex: sərîs (סָרִיס). Translation: eunuch
  - Peshitta: dkšå (ܕܟܫܐ). Translation: attendant
  - Targum Onkelos: rabbā' (רַבָּא). Translation: great
  - Targum Jerusalem: šalîṭā' (שְׁלִיטָא)
  - Targum Pseudo-Jonathan: rabbā' (רַבָּא). Translation: greats

None of the source texts agree on the word, with most of the Greek manuscripts including a transliteration of a word that Greeks found in the Aramaic text they translated. Some Greek, Hebrew, and Aramaic manuscripts include translations of the term as "eunuch" or "singer," however, only the Masoretic text and LXX 135 use the same term as later in chapter 37, which confirms that the early Aramaic translation used a different term. The original title was probably wpwtî (�daⲁ), the Middle Egyptian word for "messenger," and the title of the king's personal emissary.

The phonetic spelling of the Middle Egyptian pronunciation of the word in cuneiform would have been úapùàtiti

CHAPTER 37

(▦⊏◁⊢▤⊬⊢◁⟨◁⟨), however, ▦ can be transliterated as either Ú or SAM, ⊬ can be transliterated as Å or ǨUD, and ◁⟨ can be transliterated as TI or TENG. As the Canaanite script did not include letters representing the SAM, ǨUD, or TENG sounds, the ▦ would have been transliterated as ś (𐤥), ⊬ would have been transliterated as D (𐤀), and ◁⟨◁⟨ could have been transliterated as NT (𐤕𐤍), resulting in the Canaanite spelling as spdnt (𐤕𐤍𐤃𐤐𐤎), which appears to be the origin of Greek transliterations.

4 Codex Alexandrinus: faraō (ΦΑΡΑѠ). Translation: pharaoh
- Leningrad Codex: parōh (פַּרְעֹה). Translation: pharaoh
- Peshitta: prōwn (ܦܪܥܘܢ). Translation: pharaoh
- Targum Onkelos: parōh (פַּרְעֹה). Translation: pharaoh
- Bohairic manuscripts: faraō (ⲫⲁⲣⲁⲱ). Translation: pharaoh

Both the Greek and Hebrew terms were the equivalent of the modern term Pharaoh, a title of the King of Egypt, however, this translation is anachronistic to the era the story is set in. Both the Greek and Hebrew terms are ultimately derived from the Egyptian word pr-åȯ (𓉐𓂧), meaning "big house," or "palace."

During the New Kingdom era, the term became the title of the king of Egypt, which was adopted into Akkadian Cuneiform as Pirāú (𒉿𒊏𒌋), Canaanite as Prȯh (𐤄𐤏𐤓𐤐), Aramaic as Prȯw (פרעו), Greek as Pharaō (Φαραω), and Hebrew as Par'oh (פַּרְעֹה). The story is set during the Middle Kingdom era, when the king of Egypt's title was Nesut (transliterated hieroglyphs: nswt. Spelled variously as 𓇓𓏏𓈖, 𓇓𓏏, or 𓇓𓏏𓀀 depending on context). As the term "Pharaoh" is found in all copies of Cosmic Genesis and Bereshít, it likely originated with a reference to the palace, not the king himself.

Based on the Exodus' (Masoretic Names') claims that the Israelites were in Egypt for 400 years, and the Septuagint's dating for the exodus events as correlating with the collapse of the Hyksos

366

dynasty circa 1550 BCE, this would indicate that the Israelites entered Egypt circa 1950 BCE, during the reign of Senusret I the second king of the Middle Kingdom era. In year 25 of his reign, circa 1946 BCE, Egypt was devastated by a famine caused by a low Nile flood, which mirrors the famine in Egypt that Joseph prophesied later in the book. Senusret I also oversaw many construction projects, as confirmed by archaeology. He oversaw the rebuilding of the temples of the sun gods in Iwnw, later known as Åwn (און) in Hebrew and Heliopolis (Ἡλίου πόλις) in Greek. Senusret I also oversaw the building of the White Chapel in Karnak, which served as the capital building of Egypt during the Middle Kingdom. The name White Chapel is unusual for Egypt, however, it is the translation of the name É-Babbara (𒂍𒌓𒌓𒁀 / 𒂍𒌓𒌓𒁀), suggesting there were also members of the cult of Sippar influencing the court of Senusret I, which is likely who had the Hieratic transcription of the Book of Job at the time.

CHAPTER 38

It happened at that time, that Judah went down from his brothers and came as far as to a certain man of Adullamite, whose name was Hirah. Judah saw there the daughter of a Canaanite man, whose name was Shuah, and he took her and went into her. She conceived and carried a son, and called his name, Ur. She conceived and carried a son again, and called his name, Onan. She again carried a son and called his name Shelah. She was in Cozbi when she carried them. Judah took a wife for Ur his firstborn, whose name was Tamar. Ur, the firstborn of Judah, was wicked before the Lord, and God killed him. Judah said to Onan, "Go into your brother's wife, and marry her as her brother-in-law, and bring up descendants for your brother."

Onan, knowing that the descendants would not be his, pulled out when he went into his brother's wife, that he spilled it on the ground so that he should not give seed to his brother's wife. This appeared evil before God, and he killed him also.

Judah said to Tamar, his daughter-in-law, "You sit a widow in the house of your father-in-law until Shelah my son is grown. He said, "In case he also dies like his brothers," and Tamar departed and sat in the house of her father.

The days were fulfilled, and Shuah the wife of Judah died, and Judah, being comforted, went to them that sheared his sheep, himself and Hirah his shepherd the Adullamite, to Timnath. It was told to Tamar his daughter-in-law, saying, "Look, your father-in-law goes up to Timnath, to shear his sheep."

Having taken off the garments of her widowhood from her, she put on a veil, and ornamented her face, and sat by the gates of Enan, which is along the road to Timnath, for she saw that Shelah was grown, but he gave her not to him for a wife. And when Judah saw her, he thought her to be a whore for she covered her face, and he did not know her. He went out of his way to her, and said to her, "Let me come into you," for he did not know that she was his daughter-in-law.

She asked, "What will you give me if you come into me?"

He answered, "I will send you a goat kid from my flock."

She asked, "Well, will you give me collateral until you send it?"

He inquired, "What collateral will I give you?"

She answered, "Your ring, and your bracelet, and the wand in your hand," and he gave them to her and went into her, and she conceived by him. She arose and departed, and took her veil off her, and put on the garments of her widowhood.

Judah sent the goat kid by the hand of his shepherd the Adullamite, to receive the pledge from the woman, and he did not find her. He asked the men of the place, "Where is the whore who was in Enan by the roadside?"

CHAPTER 38

They said, "There was no whore here."

He returned to Judah, and said, "I have not found her, and the men of the place say, 'There is no whore here.'"

Judah said, "Let them have her, but let's not be insulted! I sent this kid, and you have not found her." After three months, it was told to Judah, "Tamar your daughter-in-law has grievously played the whore, and look, she is pregnant from prostitution."

Judah ordered, "Bring her out, and let her be burnt."

As they were bringing her, she sent a message to her father-in-law, saying, "I am with child by the man who owns these things," and she said, "Find out who owns this ring, bracelet, and wand."

Judah knew them, and said, "Tamar is cleared rather than I, inasmuch as I gave her not to Shelah my son," and he was not with her again.

It happened when she was in labor, that she also had twins in her womb. It happened as she was giving birth, one thrust out his hand, and the midwife having taken hold of it, tied on his hand a scarlet thread, saying, "This one will come out first."

He drew back his hand, then immediately his brother came out, and she asked, "Why has the barrier been cut through because of you?" and she called his name, Pharez. After this came out his brother, on whose hand was the scarlet thread, and she called his name, Zerah.

CHAPTER 39

Joseph was brought down to Egypt, and Pehtiefra[1] the official[2] of Pharaoh, the captain of the guard, an Egyptian, bought him from the hands of the Ishmaelites, who brought him down there. The Lord was with Joseph, and he was a prosperous man, and he was in the house with his lord, the Egyptian. His master knew that the Lord was with him, and the Lord blessed his hands at whatever he happened to do.

Joseph found favor in the presence of his master and was very pleasing to him, and he set him over his house and all that he had he gave into the hand of Joseph. It happened after that he was set over his house, and over all that he had, that the Lord blessed the house of the Egyptian for Joseph's sake, and the blessing of the Lord was on all his possessions in the house, and in his field. He committed all that he had into the hands of Joseph, and he did not know of anything that belonged to him, except the bread which he himself ate. Joseph was handsome in form and exceedingly beautiful in attitude. It happened after these things, that his master's wife cast her eyes on Joseph, and said, "Lie with me."

But he would not, and said to his master's wife, "If because of me, my master knows nothing in his house and has given into my hands all things that belong to him, and in this house, there is nothing above me, nor has anything been kept back from me, except you, because you are his wife, how then will I do this wicked thing, and sin against God?"

CHAPTER 39

She talked with Joseph each day, but he didn't listen and sleep with her, or be with her. It happened one day, when Joseph went into the house to do his business, there was no one from the household there, and she caught hold of him by his clothes, and said, "Lie with me," and he fled leaving his clothes in her hands. When she saw that he had left his clothes in her hands, and fled, and gone away, that she called those that were in the house, and said, "See, he has brought to us a Habiru slave[3] to mock us. He came into me, saying, "Lie with me," and I cried with a loud voice, and when he heard I raised my voice and cried, he fled and left his clothes with me."

She left the clothes by her until the master came to his house, and then told him, "The Habiru slave, whom you brought to us, came to me and mocked me, and said, "I will lie with you." When he heard me raised my voice and cry, he fled leaving his clothes with me."

When his master heard what his wife said, when she said, "Your servant did this to me," he was very angry. His master took Joseph, and threw him into the prison, into the place where the king's prisoners are kept.

The Lord was with Joseph and poured down mercy on him, and he gave him favor in the sight of the chief prison guard. The chief prison guard gave the prison into the hand of Joseph, and all the men led away to prison, and all things whatever they did there, he did them. Because of him, the chief prison guard knew nothing, for all things were in the hand of Joseph, because the Lord was with him, and whatever things he did, the Lord made them prosper in his hands.

CHAPTER 39 NOTES

1 Codex Alexandrinus: Petefrē (ⲠⲈⲦⲈⲪⲣⲏ)

• LXX 630: Petefrēs (ⲡ6ⲧ6ϐⲗⲥ)

• LXX 730: Patronōsieim (ⲡⲀⲧⲣⲫⲱⲟⲥⲓⲇⲙ)

• LXX 56: Pettefrē (ⲡ6ⲧⲕ6ϐⲗ)

• LXX 121: Pentefrē (ⲡⲁⲧ6ϐⲗ)

• LXX 16: Pettefrēs (ⲡ6ⲧⲕ6ϐⲗⲥ)

• LXX 75: Pentefris (ⲡⲁⲧ6ϐⲓⲥ)

• LXX 19: Petefris (ⲡ6ⲧ6ϐⲓⲥ)

• Leningrad Codex: Pôtîpar (פּֽוֹטִיפַר).

• Peshitta: Pwṭypr (ܦܘܛܝܦܪ)

• Targum Onkelos: Pôtîpar (פּוֹטִיפַר)

• Targum Pseudo-Jonathan: Pôtîpar (פּוֹטִיפַר)

• Bohairic manuscripts: Petefrē (Ⲡⲉⲧⲉⲫⲣⲏ)

This appears to be a transliteration of the Egyptian name Pehti-ef-rô (𓄊𓏏𓇳), meaning "he has the strength of the sun." See the note on Pehtiefra in chapter 37 for alternate transliterations.

2 Codex Alexandrinus: eunoŭkos (ⲈⲨⲚⲞⲨⲭⲞⲤ)

• Leningrad Codex: sərîs (סָרִיס). Translation: eunuch

• Peshitta: dkšå (ܕܟܫܐ). Translation: attendant

• Targum Onkelos: rabba (רַבָּא). Translation: great

Both the Greek and Hebrew terms appear to be mistranslations based on the shifting meaning of the Aramaic term xâje (خواجه) during the Persian-era. The term originally meant "lord" or "vizier," however, after the dynastic revolution of Darius the Great, the government began to promote homosexuals and eunuchs over married men as they were viewed as less likely to attempt to overthrow the government, meaning that xâje meant "eunuch," or "gentlemen" by the end of the Persian era. This shift in the meaning of the Persian term caused a similar shift in the cuneiform title šu rēšu (𒊭𒊕), meaning "the head" in Akkadian cuneiform, but meaning "eunuch," or "nobleman" by the end of the Persian era. The Aramaic and Canaanite transliterations of Akkadian cuneiform term also shifted, resulting in the mistranslations found in the Greek and Hebrew texts. As the term would have meant "official" originally, that term is used in this translation.

3 Codex Alexandrinus: paida ebrai (ΠΑΙΔΑ ΕΒΡΑΙ). Translation: slave (or child, son, daughter, servant) ŏbryå (transliteration of the Aramaic ܥܒܪܝܐ meaning "crosser")

• LXX 400: paida Ebraion (παιδα Εϥραϕ). Translation: slave (or child, son, daughter, servant) Hebrew (or Israelite, Aramean, Eberite)

• Leningrad Codex: 'îš 'ibrî (אִישׁ עִבְרִי). Translation: man (or husband) Hebrew (or Eberite)

• Peshitta: ŏbdå ŏbryå (ܥܒܕܐ ܕܥܒܪܝܐ). Translation: servant (or slave) crosser

• Targum Onkelos: gabrā' 'ibrā'â (גַּבְרָא עִבְרָאָה). Translation: man (or husband) crosser

If the Aramaic text of Genesis was based on an Akkadian Cuneiform source text, then this term must have been in the Cuneiform version as it is in both the Hebrew and Greek translations. The likely term would have been ḫabiru (𒄩𒁉𒊒), meaning "dusky," which was a word used to describe groups of marauders in the Middle East in the era. The term was in use from approximately 1800 to 1200 BCE, however, does not appear to have been an ethnic term, but was generally used to describe rebels, mercenaries, outlaws, raiders, servants, and slaves. The people in question were also known as Middle Egyptian as Ȯprw (𓏏𓃀𓂋𓅱), meaning the term could have been in an Egyptian precursor to the Cuneiform book of Genesis.

CHAPTER 40

It happened after these things, that the chief cupbearer of the king of Egypt and the chief baker trespassed against their lord, the king of Egypt. Pharaoh was angry with his two officials, with his chief cupbearer, and with his chief baker. He put them into the prison, into the place where Joseph had been led to. The chief prison guard committed them to Joseph, and he stood by them, and they were some days in the prison. They both had a dream in one night, and the vision of the dream of the chief cupbearer and chief baker, who belonged to the king of Egypt, who were in the prison, was this. Joseph went to them in the morning and saw them, and they had been troubled. He asked the officials of Pharaoh who were with him in the prison with his master, saying, "Why is it that your moods are sad today?"

They said to him, "We have seen a dream, and there is no interpreter of it."

Joseph said to them, "Is not the interpretation of them through God? Tell them than to me."

The chief cupbearer related his dream to Joseph, and said, "In my sleep, a vine was before me. In the vine were three stems, and it budding shot forth blossoms; the clusters of grapes were ripe. The cup of Pharaoh was in my hand, and I took the bunch of grapes, and squeezed it into the cup, and gave the cup into Pharaoh's hand."

Joseph said to him, "This is the interpretation of it. The three stems are three days. In three days, Pharaoh will remember your office, and he will restore you to your place of chief cupbearer, and you will give the cup of Pharaoh into his hand, according to your former high place, as you were used to be cupbearer. But remember me when it is good with you, and deal mercifully with me, and mention me to Pharaoh, and bring me out of this dungeon. I was stolen away out of the land of the Habirus, and here I have done nothing, but they have thrown me into this pit."

The chief baker saw that he interpreted correctly, and he said to Joseph, "I also saw a dream, and I thought I put up on my head three baskets of mealy food. In the upper basket, there was the work of the baker of every kind which Pharaoh eats, and the fowls of the air ate them out of the basket that was on my head."

Joseph answered him, "This is the interpretation of it. The three baskets are three days. In three days, and Pharaoh will take away your head from off you, and will hang you on a tree, and the birds of the sky will eat your flesh from off you."

It happened on the third day that it was Pharaoh's birthday, and he made a banquet for all his servants, and he remembered the office of the cupbearer and the office of the baker in the middle of his servants. He restored the chief cupbearer to his office, and he gave the cup into Pharaoh's hand. He hanged the chief baker, as Joseph had interpreted to them. Yet the chief cupbearer did not remember Joseph, but forgot him.

CHAPTER 41

After two years, Pharaoh had a dream, and he thought he stood on the bank of the river and as watched there came up, as it were, out of the river, seven cows, beautiful in appearance, and choice of flesh, and they fed on the sedge. Another seven cows came up after these, out of the river, ill-favored and lean-fleshed, and fed by the other cows on the bank of the river. The seven ill-favored and lean cows devoured the seven greatly favored and choice of flesh cows, and Pharaoh woke up.

He dreamed again, and saw seven ears came up on one stalk, choice and good. And then saw seven thin ears, blasted with wind, grew up after them. The seven thin ears, blasted with the wind, devoured the seven choice and full ears, and Pharaoh woke up, and it was a dream. In the morning his mind was troubled, and he sent and called all the interpreters in Egypt, and all her wise men, and Pharaoh told them his dream, and there was no one to explain it to Pharaoh.

The chief cupbearer said to Pharaoh, "I remember today my mistake. When Pharaoh was angry with his servants, and put us in prison in the house of the captain of the guard, both me and the chief baker. And we saw a dream, both in one night, I and he, and we saw each his own dream. There was there with us a young man, a Habiru slave of the captain of the guard, and we told him our dreams, and he interpreted them for us. It happened as he interpreted them to us, exactly so it happened, both that I was restored to my office, and that he was hanged."

Pharaoh called for Joseph, and they brought him out from the prison, and shaved him, and changed his clothes, and he came to Pharaoh. Pharaoh said to Joseph, "I have seen a vision, and there is no one to interpret it. But, I have heard men say that you can hear dreams and interpret them."

Joseph answered Pharaoh, "Without God, a true answer will not be given to Pharaoh."

Pharaoh spoke to Joseph, saying, "In my dream, I thought I stood by the bank of the river, and there came up, as it were, out of the river, seven cows greatly favored and choicest flesh, and they fed on the sedge. Then seven other cows came up after them, out of the river, evil and ill-favored and lean-fleshed, so terrible that I have never seen any like them in all the land of Egypt. The seven ill-favored and thin cows ate up the seven first good and choice cows. They went into their bellies, and they were not perceptible that they had gone into their bellies, and their appearance was as terrible looking as they had been before, and after I awoke, I fell asleep and dreamed again, and in my sleep seven ears grew up on one stem, full and good. Another seven thin ears, and blasted with the wind, grew up close to them. The seven thin and blasted ears devoured the seven fine and full ears. So I told the inter-preters, and there was no one to explain it to me."

Joseph said to Pharaoh, "The dreams of Pharaoh are the same. Whatever God does, he has shown to Pharaoh. The seven good cows are seven years, and the seven good ears are seven years. The dreams of Pharaoh are the same. The seven thin cows that came up after them are seven years, and the seven thin and blasted ears are seven years, there will be seven years of famine. As for the word which I have told Pharaoh, whatever God intends to do, he has shown to Pharaoh. Watch, for seven years there will be plenty in all the land of Egypt. But there will come seven years of famine after these, and they will forget the plenty that will be in all Egypt, and the famine will consume the land."

"The plenty will not be remembered in the land because of the famine that will come after this, for it will be very terrible. Concerning the repetition of the dream, coming to Pharaoh twice, it is because God is saying it will come true, and God will rush to accomplish it. Now then, search out a wise and prudent man, and set him over the land of Egypt. Let Pharaoh appoint local governors over the land, and let them take up the fifth part of all the produce of the land of Egypt for the seven years of the plenty. Let them gather all the food of these seven good years that are coming, and let the grain be gathered under the hand of Pharaoh, and let food be kept in the cities. The stored food will be for the land against the seven years of famine, which will be in the land of Egypt and the land will not be utterly destroyed by the famine."

The words were pleasing in the sight of Pharaoh, and in the sight of all his servants. Pharaoh said to all his servants, "Will we find such a man as this, who has the spirit of God in him?"

CHAPTER 41

Pharaoh said to Joseph, "Since God has shown you all these things, there is not a wiser or more prudent man than you. You will be over my house, and all my people will be obedient to your mouth. I will only be greater than you when it comes to the throne."

Pharaoh said to Joseph, "Understand, I set you today over all the land of Egypt."

Pharaoh took his ring off his hand, and put it on the hand of Joseph, and put a robe of fine linen on him, and put a necklace of gold around his neck. He mounted him on the second of his chariots, and a herald made a proclamation before him, and he set him over all the land of Egypt, and made him his cupbearer.

Pharaoh said to Joseph, "I am Pharaoh, without you, no one will lift up his hand in all the land of Egypt."

Pharaoh called the name of Joseph, Psonthom Phanech,[1] and he gave him Aseneth, the daughter of Pehtiefra, priest of Heliopolis,[2] to marry.

Joseph was thirty years old when he stood before Pharaoh, king of Egypt.[3] Joseph left the presence of Pharaoh and traveled through the land of Egypt. The land produced, in the seven years of plenty, whole handfuls of grain. He gathered all the food of the seven years during which was plenty in the land of Egypt, and he stored up the food in the cities, and the food of the fields of a city around it he stored up in it. Joseph gathered a great deal of grain. like the sand of the sea

CHAPTER 41

until it could not be counted, as there was no way of counting it.

To Joseph were born two sons, before the seven years of famine came, which Aseneth, the daughter of Pehtiefra, priest of Heliopolis, carried for him. Joseph called the name of the firstborn Manasseh. "For God," he said, "has made me forget all my difficulties, and all things belong to my father."

He called the name of the second Ephraim. "For God," he said, "has increased me in the land of my humiliation."

The seven years of plenty passed away, which were in the land of Egypt. The seven years of famine began to come, as Joseph said, "and there was a famine in all the land, but in all the land of Egypt there was bread."

All the land of Egypt was hungry, and the people cried to Pharaoh for bread. Pharaoh said to all the Egyptians, "Go to Joseph, and do whatever he tells you."

The famine was on the face of all Eretz, and Joseph opened all the granaries and sold to all the Egyptians. All countries came to Egypt to buy of Joseph, for the famine prevailed in all the land.

CHAPTER 41 NOTES

1 Codex Alexandrinus: Sonoomfanēk (ⲧⲟⲛⲟⲟⲙⲫⲁⲛⲏⲭ)
• LXX 15: Somtomfanēk (Ⲩⲟⲙⲑⲟⲙⳃⲇⲡⲗⲓ)
• LXX 17: Somtomfanēk (Ⲩⲟⲙⲑⲟⲙⳃⲇⲡⲗⲭ)
• LXX 135: Asomtomfanēk (Ⲁⲩⲟⲙⲑⲟⲙⳃⲇⲡⲗⲭ)

- LXX 318: Sonṭofanēǩ (Ⲩⲫⲑⲟ𝟅ⲇ𝔭ⲗⲭ)
- LXX 319: Sonṭomfanēk (Ⲩⲫⲑⲟⲙ𝟅ⲇ𝔭ⲗⳃ)
- LXX 73: Ṡomfṭomfanēǩ (Ⲩⲟⲙ𝟅ⲑⲟⲙ𝟅ⲇ𝔭ⲗⲭ)
- LXX 121: Ṡonṭōmfanēǩ (Ⲩⲫⲑⲱⲙ𝟅ⲇ𝔭ⲗⲭ)
- LXX 343: Sonṭomfanēǩ (Ⲩⲫⲑⲟⲙ𝟅ⲇ𝔭ⲗⲭ)
- LXX 426: Somfṭomfanē (Ⲩⲟⲙ𝟅ⲑⲟⲙ𝟅ⲇ𝔭ⲗ)
- LXX 79: Ṡomṭoumfanēǩ (Ⲩⲟⲙⲑⲟⲩⲙ𝟅ⲇ𝔭ⲗⲭ)
- LXX 413: Ṡomṭofanēk (Ⲩⲟⲙⲑⲟ𝟅ⲇ𝔭ⲗⳃ)
- LXX 458: Sonṭomfanik (Ⲩⲫⲑⲟⲙ𝟅ⲇ𝔭ⲓⳃ)
- LXX 72: Sonṭonfaniēl (Ⲩⲫⲑⲫ𝟅ⲇ𝔭ⲓⲗλ)
- LXX 618: Sonṭomfanēm (Ⲩⲫⲑⲟⲙ𝟅ⲇ𝔭ⲗμ)
- LXX 527: Somṭomfanek (Ⲩⲟⲙⲑⲟⲙ𝟅ⲇ𝔭ⳝⳃ)
- LXX 59: Sonṭōmfanēǩ (Ⲩⲫⲑⲱⲙ𝟅ⲇ𝔭ⲗⲭ)
- Leningrad Codex: Sāpənat Pa'nēaḥ (צָפְנַת פַּעְנֵחַ)
- Peshitta: Spnt Pȯnǩ (ܨܦܢܬ ܦܥܢܚ)
- Targum Onkelos: gabrā' dəmittamrān golyān lêh (גֻּבְרָא דְּמִטַּמְרָן גָּלְין לֵיהּ). Translation: man to whom hidden things are revealed
- Targum Pseudo-Jonathan: gabrā' ditmîrān məparsēm (גֻּבְרָא דְּטְמִירָן מְפַרְסֵם). Translation: man of famous secrets
- Sahidic manuscripts.: Psoṭomfanēǩ (Ⲡⲥⲟⲑⲟⲙⲫⲁⲛⲏⲭ)
- Bohairic manuscripts: Psonṭōmfanēǩ (Ⲡⲥⲟⲛⲑⲱⲙⲫⲁⲛⲏⲭ)

The meaning of this name was lost until Egyptologists deciphered Ancient Egyptian. The 1st century CE Jewish historian Josephus believed it meant "a finder of mysteries," which was later adopted by Protestant Christian translators. In the 4th century, Jerome translated it as "savior of the world" when he translated the first official Latin Bible. Since hieroglyphics were deciphered, the name had been reconstructed as "the god speaks [and] he lives" (transliterated hieratic: ȯḏd pȯ nṯr iw.f ȧnǩȧ) by Georg Steindorff in 1889, which is now widely accepted.

2 Codex Alexandrinus: Iou poleōs (ιογποϩεωc)
- LXX 15: Iliou póleōs (ιϩιου πολϭϫϫc)
- LXX 343: Ēlíou póleōs (Hϩιου πολϭϫϫc)
- Leningrad Codex: 'Ôn (אֹן)
- Peshitta: Åwn (ܐܘܢ)
- Targum Onkelos: 'Ôn (אוֹן)
- Targum Pseudo-Jonathan: Tānîs (טָנִיס)
- Bohairic manuscripts: On (ⲞⲚ)

The city of Iwnw (𓉺𓊖) was the northern major religious center of Egypt. During the Second Intermediate era it became known by the shortened form Iwn (𓉺), which served as the basis of the Canaanite Åwn (און), which was later adopted as the classical Hebrew Åwn (און), and then medieval Hebrew 'Ôn (אֹן). The city was called Heliopolis by the Greeks, meaning "Sun-City," as most of the gods worshiped there were Solar gods, including the creator-god Atum, the solar-disk Aten, the sun Ra, and the scarab-beetle god Khepri. The major exception was the lunar-god Iȯhw. Joseph having been given the daughter of a high-priest to wed would become a priest as well, although the text does not clarify which god he was the priest of. Nevertheless, he is never connected to the Sun in any way, and as an interpreter of dreams, the moon makes more sense as Joseph's god, implying he was the priest of Iȯhw.

3 The famine started in regal year 25 of King Senusret I, caused by the Nile floods stopping for several years. There is a range of dates indicated for his reign. Depending on the Egyptologists, Senusret I's reign could have begun anytime between 1971 and 1920 BCE. The verse indicates that Joseph would have been five when Senusret I assumed the throne, meaning Joseph would have been born sometime between 1976 and 1925 BCE. This dating parallels the later claim in Exodus that the Israelites were in Egypt for 400 years before the Exodus in the mid-1500s BCE.

CHAPTER 42

Jacob heard that there was grain for sale in Egypt, and said to his sons, "Why are you indolent? Understand that I have heard that there is grain in Egypt. Go down there, and buy us some food so we may survive, and not starve."

The ten brothers of Joseph went down to buy grain out of Egypt. But Jacob did not send Benjamin, the brother of Joseph with his brothers. As he thought, "Perhaps disease might infect him."

The sons of Israel traveled to buy with those that traveled, for the famine was in the land of Canaan. Joseph was the ruler of the land and sold to all the people of the land. After arriving, the brothers of Joseph did reverence to him, bowing with their faces to the ground. When Joseph saw his brothers, he recognized them, but acted like a stranger to them, and spoke hard words to them, asking, "Where have you come from?"

They answered, "From the land of Canaan, to buy food."

Joseph recognized his brothers, but they did not recognize him. Joseph remembered his dream, that he saw, and he said to them, "You are spies. You have come to spy out the boundaries of the land."

CHAPTER 42

But they replied, "No lord, we are your servants, and have come to buy food. We are all sons of one man. We are peaceful. Your servants are not spies."

He said to them, "No! You have come to see the boundaries of the land."

They said, "We are your servants, and are twelve brothers, from the land of Canaan. The youngest is with our father today, and the other one no longer exists."

Joseph said to them, "It is like I said to you, when I said, 'You are spies,' and here you will be known as such. By the health of Pharaoh, you will not leave here unless your younger brother comes here. Send one of you to get your brother, while you go into prison until it is clear if you are speaking the truth or not. But, if not, by the health of Pharaoh, you are proven to be spies."

He put them in prison for three days, and on the third day, he said to them, "Do this, and you will live, for I fear God. If you are peaceful, leave one of your brothers in prison, but you go and take back grain you"ve purchased. Bring your younger brother to me, and your words will be believed. But if not, you will die," and they did so.

Each said to his brother, "Yes, we are at fault concerning our brother, when we disregarded the anguish of his mind when he implored us, and we did not listen to him, and therefore this punishment has come on us."

CHAPTER 42

Reuben said to them, "Didn't I tell you, 'Don't hurt the boy?' Yet you didn't listen to me! Now see, his blood is required."

They did not know that Joseph understood them, for there had been an interpreter between them. Joseph left them and cried, then returned and spoke to them, and he took Simeon from them and chained him before their eyes. Joseph gave orders to fill their sacks with grain, and to return their silver, to each into his sack, and to give them provision for the road, and it was done for them. After putting the grain on the donkeys, they departed there.

One opened his sack to feed his donkeys when they stopped to rest, and saw also his bundle of silver, as it was in the mouth of his sack. He said to his brothers, "My silver has been returned to me, and look, it is in my sack."

Their hearts were amazed, yet they were troubled, saying to each other, "What is this that God has done to us?"

They returned to their father Jacob, in the land of Canaan, and reported to him all that had happened to them, saying, "The man, the lord of the land, spoke harshly to us, and put us in prison, like spies in the land. We said to him, 'We are men of peace. We are not spies. We are twelve brothers, sons of our father. One no longer exists, and the youngest is with his father today in the land of Canaan.' The man, the lord of the land, said to us, 'So I will know that you are peaceful, leave one brother here with me, and take the grain you have purchased for your family, and leave. Bring to me your younger brother, and then I will know that you are not spies, but that you are men of peace, and I will return your brother to you, and you may trade in the land.'"

It followed as they were emptying their sacks, there was each man's bundle of silver in his sack, and they and their father saw their bundles of silver and were afraid. Their father Jacob said to them, "You have saddened me. Joseph is gone, Simeon is gone, and you will take Benjamin? All these things have come on me."

And Reuben said to his father, "Murder my two sons if I don't bring him back to you! Give him to me, and I will bring him back to you!"

But he said, "My son will not go down with you, because his brother is dead, and only he is left, and suppose it will happen that he is afflicted on the way when you travel, then you will bring down my old age with sorrow to Sheol."

CHAPTER 43

The famine continued in the land, and when they had finished eating the grain that they had brought out of Egypt, their father said to them, "Go back, and buy us a little food."

Judah said to him, "The man, the lord of the country, swore to us, 'You will not see my face unless your younger brother is with you.' If then, you send our brother with us, we will go down and buy food for you, but if you don't send our brother with us, we will not go, for the man said to us, 'You will not see my face unless your younger brother is with you.'"

Israel asked, "Why did you harm me when you told the man that you had a brother?"

They answered, "The man intensely interrogated us about our family, asking, 'Does your father still live?' and 'Do you have a brother?' We answered his questions, and did not know that he would tell us, 'Bring your brother.'"

Judah said to his father Israel, "Send the boy with me, and we will rise and leave, so we may live and not die, both we and you and our property. I swore by my hand before him, 'If I don't bring him to you, and place him before you, I will be guilty before you forever.' If we had not delayed, we should have already returned twice by now."

CHAPTER 43

Israel, their father, said to them, "If it is so, do this, and take the fruits of Eretz in your packs and carry down to the man presents of gum and honey, and frankincense, and stacte, and turpentine, and walnuts. Take twice the silver in your hands, and also the silver that was returned in your packs take back with you, in case, perhaps, it is a mistake. Take your brother, and rise and return to the man. May the god Shaddai[1] give you favor in the sight of the man, and may he send away your other brother, and also Benjamin, as I have been bereaved, and am bereaved."

The men took these presents, and double the silver, and took in their hands also Benjamin, and they rose up and went down to Egypt, and stood before Joseph. Joseph saw them and his brother Benjamin, born of the same mother, and he said to the steward of his household, "Bring the men into the house, and kill animals and prepare them, for the men are to eat bread with me at noon."

The man did as Joseph had said, and he brought the men into the house of Joseph. The men, when they had realized that they were brought into the house of Joseph, said, "We are brought in because of the silver that was returned in our packs before. So they can organize charges against us, and take us as slaves, and also our donkeys."

After approaching the man who was over the house of Joseph, they asked him on the porch of the house, "We beg you, lord. We came down before to buy food. It happened, when we went to unpack and opened our packs, there was also the silver of each of us in his pack. We have now brought back in our hands, the weight of the silver, and we have brought more silver with us to buy food. We don't know who put the silver into our packs."

He said to them, "God dealt mercifully with you. Don't be afraid. Your god, and god of your fathers, has given you treasures in your packs, and I have enough of your good silver."

He brought Simeon out to them, and he brought water to wash their feet and fed their donkeys. They prepared their gifts until Joseph came at noon, for they heard that he was going to dine there. Joseph entered the house, and they brought him the gifts which they had in their hands, into the house, and they did him reverence with their face to the ground. He asked them, "How are you?" and he asked them, "Is your father, the old man of whom you spoke, healthy? Is he still alive?"

They answered, "Your servant, our father is well. He is still alive."

He said, "Blessed be that man by God," and they bowed, and did him reverence.

Joseph looked up with his eyes and saw his brother Benjamin, born of the same mother, and he asked, "Is this your younger brother, whom you spoke of bringing to me?" and he said, "God have mercy on you, my son."

Joseph was troubled, for his bowels yearned over his brother, and he wanted to cry, and he went into his room and cried. He washed his face and came out, and held back himself, and said, "Set out bread."

They set out bread before him alone, and for them by themselves, for the Egyptians eating with him, ate by themselves, for the Egyptians could not eat bread with the Hebrews. It is an abomination to the Egyptians. They sat down before him, the firstborn according to his seniority, and the younger according to his youth, and the men were amazed, everyone looking at his brother. They took their portions from him for themselves. But Benjamin's portion was five times the size of the others' portions. They drank their fill with him.

CHAPTER 43 NOTES

1 Codex Alexandrinus: T̄S K̄S (өскс). Translation: god lord
- Leningrad Codex: ēl šadday (אֵל שַׁדָּי). Translation: god Shaddai
- Peshitta: åylšdy (ܐܠܫܕܝ)
- Targum Onkelos: ēl šadday (אֵל שַׁדַּי). Translation: god Shaddai
- Targum Pseudo-Jonathan: ēl šaday (אֵל שַׁדַּי). Translation: god Shaddai

This is the fourth deviation between Cosmic Genesis and Bereshít regarding the god Shaddai, and the fourth time the name or title Shaddai is missing entirely from the Septuagint's translation. The name Shaddai is imported from *Bereshít*. For more information on the god Shaddai, see the note in chapter 17.

CHAPTER 44

Joseph ordered the steward of his house, "Fill the men's packs with food, as much as they can carry, and put the silver of each in the opening of his pack. Put my silver cup into the pack of the youngest, along with the price of his grain."

It was done according to the words of Joseph, as he had ordered.

The morning dawned, and the men were sent away, along with their donkeys. When they had left the city, and were not far away, Joseph said to his steward, "Rise, and chase after the men, and you will capture them, and demand of them, 'Why have you repaid evil for good? Why have you stolen my silver cup? Is it not this, in which my lord drinks? He divines omens with it! You have accomplished evil in doing this.'"

He found them and said these words. They asked him, "Why does our lord say these words? Your servants would never do this! If we brought back from the land of Canaan, the silver which we found in our packs, why would we steal silver or gold out of the house of your lord? With whoever of your servants you find this cup, let him die! Moreover, we will be slaves to our lord."

He replied, "Now then, it will be as you say. With whoever the cup will be found, he will be my slave, but you will be clear."

CHAPTER 44

They hurried, and each man took down his pack and placed them on the ground, and they opened their packs. He searched, beginning with the oldest until he came to the youngest, and he found the cup in Benjamin's pack. They tore their garments, and each man laid his pack on his donkey and returned to the city. Judah and his brothers came to Joseph, while he was still there, and fell on the ground before him.

Joseph said to them, "What is this, that you have done? Don't you know that a man like me can divine the truth?"

Judah said, "What will we say to our lord? What will we say that could be justified when God has discovered the unrighteousness of your servants! See, we are slaves to our lord, both we and he with whom the cup has been found."

Joseph said, "Far be it from me to do this! The man with whom the cup has been found will be my slave. But you may return in safety to your father."

Judah approached him, and said, "I beg, lord, let your servant say a few words before you, and do not be angry with your servant, for you are next to Pharaoh. Lord, you asked your servants, asking, 'Do you have a father or a brother?' We answered my lord, 'We have a father, an old man, and he had a son in his old age, a young one, and his brother is dead, and he alone has been left behind to his mother, and his father loves him.' You said to your servants, 'Bring him down to me, and I will take care of him.' and we said to my lord, 'The child will not be able to leave his father, but if he should leave his father, he will die.' But you said to your servants, 'Only if

398

your younger brother comes down with you, will you see my face again.'"

"When we went up to your servant, our father, we reported to him the words of our lord, and our father said, 'Go back and buy us a little food.' We replied, 'We will not be able to go down unless our younger brother goes down with us, we will go down. We will not be able to see the man's face if our younger brother is not with us.' Your servant, our father, said to us, 'You know that my wife carried me two sons, and one has departed from me, and you said that he was eaten by wild animals, and I have not seen him until now. If you take this one also from my presence, and an affliction happens to him on the road, then you will bring down my old age with sorrow to Sheol.'"

"Now then, if I should go to your servant, our father, and the boy should not be with us, and his life depends on this boy's life, it will happen that when he sees the boy is not with us, he will die, and your servants will bring down the old age of your servant, our father, with sorrow to Sheol. Your servant has received the boy, in charge from his father, saying, 'If I don't return him to you, and place him before you, I will be guilty to my father forever.' Now then, I will remain a slave with you, instead of the boy, a domestic slave of my lord. Just let the boy return with his brothers. How will I return to my father, and say, 'The boy is not with us?' What evil will I see befall my father?"

CHAPTER 45

Joseph could not contain himself when all were standing by him, but said, "Dismiss all from me," and no one stood near Joseph when he made himself known to his brothers. He spoke with sobbing in his voice and all the Egyptians heard, and it was reported to the house of Pharaoh. Joseph said to his brothers, "I am Joseph. Does my father still live?"

His brothers could not answer him, as they were troubled. Joseph said to his brothers, "Come close to me," and when they drew near he said, "I am your brother Joseph, whom you sold into Egypt. Now then, don't be sad, and don't let it be difficult for you, in that you sold me here, for God sent me before you, for life. This is the second year that there is famine in the land, and there are still five more years remaining in which there is going to be neither plowing nor harvesting. God sent me before you, that there might be left among you a remnant in the land, to feed a great remnant of you. Now then, you did not send me here, but God did, and he has made me like a father to Pharaoh, and lord of all his house, and ruler of all the land of Egypt. Rise, therefore, and return to my father, and say to him, 'Your son Joseph says the following, "God has made me lord of all the land of Egypt. Therefore, come down to me, and don't delay, and you will live in the land of Goshen of Arabia, and you will be near me, you and your sons, and your grandsons, your sheep, oxen, and whatever things are yours. I will feed you there as the famine will continue for five more years. Otherwise, you be consumed, and your sons, and all your possessions. See with your eyes, and the eyes of my brother Benjamin, that it is my mouth that speaks to you.'" Report to my father all my glory in Egypt, and all things that you have seen, and rush to bring my father down here."

He fell on his brother Benjamin's neck and cried on him, and Benjamin cried on his neck. He kissed all his brothers and cried on them, and after these things, his brothers said to him. The report was carried into the house of Pharaoh, saying, "Joseph's brothers have come," and Pharaoh was glad, and also his household.

Pharaoh said to Joseph, "Tell your brothers, 'Fill your wagons, and depart to the land of Canaan. Pick up your father, and your possessions, and come to me, and I will give you some of all the goods of Egypt, and you will eat the marrow of the land.' Order them also, that they should take for themselves wagons out of the land of Egypt, 'for your little ones, and for your wives, and carry your father,' and then return. Do not be sparing, regarding your property, as all the wealth of Egypt will be yours."

The children of Israel did so, and Joseph gave them wagons, as per the words spoken by King Pharaoh, and he gave them provisions for the journey. He gave them each two sets of clothing, but for Benjamin, he gave three hundred pieces of gold, and five changes of clothing. For his father, he sent the same amount of present, and ten donkeys carrying some of all the good things of Egypt, and ten mules, carrying bread, for his father's journey. He sent away his brothers, and they left, and he said to them, "Don't be angry on the road."

They left Egypt, and traveled into the land of Canaan, to Jacob their father. They reported to him, "Your son Joseph is alive, and he is ruler over all the land of Egypt," and Jacob was amazed, and he did not believe them. They told him all the words said by Joseph, everything he had said to them, and having seen the wagons which Joseph sent to take him up, the spirit of Jacob their father revived.

Israel said, "It is a wonderful thing for me if Joseph my son is still alive. I will go see him before I die."

CHAPTER 46

Israel departed, he and all that he had, and traveled to the Well of the Oath, and he offered a sacrifice to the god of his father Isaac. God spoke to Israel in a night vision, "Jacob! Jacob?"

He asked, "What is it?"

He answered him, "I am the god of your fathers. Don't be afraid to go down to Egypt, for I will make you a great nation there. I will go down with you into Egypt, and I will bring you up at the end, and Joseph will put his hands on your eyes."

Jacob rose up from the well of the oath, and the sons of Israel carried their father, and the property, and their wives, on the wagons that Joseph had sent to carry them. They carried their goods and all their property which they had gotten in the land of Canaan, and they came into the land of Egypt, Jacob, and all his descendants with him. The sons, and the sons of his sons with him, his daughters, and the daughters of his daughters, and he brought all his descendants into Egypt.

These are the names of the sons of Israel that went into Egypt with their father Jacob; Jacob and his sons.

The firstborn of Jacob was Reuben.

CHAPTER 46

The sons of Reuben were Enoch, Phallu, Hezron, and Carmi.

The sons of Simeon were Jemuel, Jimna, Ohad, Jachin, Zohar, and Saul, the sons of a Canaanite woman.

The sons of Levi were Gershon, Kohath, and Merari.

The sons of Judah were Er, Onan, Shelah, Pharez, and Zerah, however, Er and Onan had died in the land of Canaan.

The sons of Pharez were Hezron and Hamul.

The sons of Issachar were Tola, Pua, Asum, and Shimron.

The sons of Zebulun were Sered, Elon, and Achoel.

These are the sons of Leah, which she carried for Jacob in Mesopotamia in Syria, and Dinah his daughter. All the minds, sons and daughters, thirty-three.

The sons of Gad were Zephon, Haggi, Shuni, Ezbon, Aedis, Arodi, and Areli.

The sons of Asher were Jimnah, Ishuah, Isui, Beriah, and Serah their sister.

The sons of Beriah were Chobor and Malchiel.

These are the sons of Zilpah, which Laban gave to his daughter Leah, who carried these for Jacob, sixteen minds.

The sons of Rachel, the wife of Jacob, were Joseph and Benjamin.

CHAPTER 46

There were sons born to Joseph in the land of Egypt, who Aseneth, the daughter of Pehtiefra, priest of Heliopolis, carried for him, including Manasseh and Ephraim.

There were sons born to Manasseh, which the Syrian concubine carried for him, including Machir.

Machir fathered Gilead.

The sons of Ephraim, the brother of Manasseh were Sutalaam and Gaham.

The sons of Sutalaam were Edom.

The sons of Benjamin were Belah, Becher, and Asbel.

The sons of Belah were Gera, Naaman, Ehi, Rosh, and Muppim, and Gera fathered Arad.

These are the sons of Rachel, which she carried for Jacob; all the minds were eighteen.

The son of Dan was Hushim.

The sons of Naphtali were Jahzeel, Guni, Izhar, and Shillem.

These are the sons of Bilhah, who Laban gave to his daughter Rachel, who carried these for Jacob; all the minds were seven.

All the minds that came with Jacob into Egypt, who came out of his thighs, besides the wives of the sons of Jacob, including all the minds were sixty-six.

CHAPTER 46

The sons of Joseph, who were born for him in the land of Egypt, were nine minds; all the minds of the house of Jacob who came with Joseph into Egypt were seventy-five minds. He sent Judah before him to Joseph, to meet him face to face at the Temple of Atum in Pi-Ramesses.[1]

Joseph harnessed his chariots and went up to meet Israel his father, in Per-Atum, and after appearing before him, fell on his neck, and wept with abundant weeping.

Israel said to Joseph, "After this, I will die happily as I have seen your face, and you are still alive!"

Joseph said to his brothers, "I will go and tell Pharaoh, 'My brothers, and my father's house, who were in the land of Canaan, have come to me. The men are shepherds, and they have been herders of livestock, and they have brought with them their livestock, and their cows, and all their property.' If then Pharaoh calls you, and asks you, 'What is your occupation?' You will say, 'We, your servants, are herdsmen from our youth until now, both we and our fathers,' so that you may live in the land of Goshen of Arabia, for every shepherd is an abomination to the Egyptians."

CHAPTER 46 NOTES

1 Cotton Genesis: Ērōōn polin eis gēn Ramessē (ⲎⲢⲰⲰⲚⲠⲞⲖⲒⲚ ⲈⲒⲤ ⲄⲎⲚ ⲢⲀⲘⲈⲤⲤⲎ). Translation: Heroöpolis (or Pithom, Per-Atum, Heroes' city) in land Ramesse

CHAPTER 46

- LXX 509: Ērōōn polin eis gēn Ramessē (Ηβοοοον πολιν ϟc ϥⲱ Pⲁⲙⲥⲥⲟⲗ). Translation: Heroöpolis (or Pithom, Per-Atum, Heroes' city) in land Ramesse
- LXX 392: Ērōōn polin eis gēn Ramessē (Ηⲣοοον πολιν ϟc ϥⲱ Pⲁⲙⲥⲥⲟⲗ). Translation: Heroöpolis (or Pithom, Per-Atum, Heroes' city) in land Ramesse
- LXX 346: Ērōōn polin pros gēn Rakessē (Ηβοοοον πολιν πⲣⲟc ϥⲱ Pⲁⲗⲥⲥⲟⲗ). Translation: Heroöpolis (or Pithom, Per-Atum, Heroes' city) towards land Rakesse
- LXX 17: Ērōōn polin eis tēn Ramesē (Ηβοοοον πολιν ϟc ⲧ̂ⲏ Pⲁⲙⲥⲟⲗ). Translation: Heroöpolis (or Pithom, Per-Atum, Heroes' city) inthe Ramesē
- LXX 25: Ērōōn polin eis gēn Rem (Ηβοοοον πολιν ϟc ϥⲱ Pⲥⲙ). Translation: Heroöpolis (or Pithom, Per-Atum, Heroes' city) in land Rem
- LXX 75: Ērōōn polin eis gēn Ramaisi (Ηβοοοον πολιν ϟc ϥⲱ Pⲁⲙⲁ/ⲥⲓ). Translation: Heroöpolis (or Pithom, Per-Atum, Heroes' city) in land Ramaisi
- LXX 408: Ērōōn polin eis gēn Ramesoi (Ηβοοοον πολιν ϟc ϥⲱ Pⲁⲙⲥⲟ⊕). Translation: Heroes' city in land Ramesoi
- LXX 76: Iroōn polin eis gēn Ramesē (ιⲣοⲟⲛ πολιν ϟc ϥⲱ Pⲁⲙⲥⲟⲗ). Translation: Heroöpolis (or Pithom, Per-Atum, Heroes' city) in land Ramese
- LXX 527: Ērōōn palin en gē Ramesē (Ηβοοοον πⲁλιν ⲟⲩ ϥⲗ Pⲁⲙⲥⲟⲗ). Translation: Heroes' city in land Ramese
- LXX 44: Ērōōn polin eis gēn Ramesēn (Ηβοοοον πολιν ϟc ϥⲱ Pⲁⲙⲥⲟ⳽). Translation: Heroöpolis (or Pithom, Per-Atum, Heroes' city) in land Ramesen
- LXX 376: Ērōōn polin eis gēn Ramesai (Ηβοοοον πολιν ϟc ϥⲱ Pⲁⲙⲥⲥⲁ/). Translation: Heroöpolis (or Pithom, Per-Atum, Heroes' city) in land Ramesai

CHAPTER 46

- LXX 610: Ērōōn palin eis gēn Ramesē (Ηρ́ωοον πλλιν ις γιω Ρλμ6σ7.). Translation: Heroes' city backin land Ramesē
- Leningrad Codex: gōšənâ wayyābō'û 'arṣâ gōšen (גֹּשְׁנָה וַיָּבֹאוּ אַרְצָה גֹּשֶׁן). Translation: goshenah and will come (or import) land Goshen
- Peshitta: gšn wåtw lårȯå dgšn (ܓܫܢ ܘܐܬܘ ܠܐܪܥܐ ܕܓܫܢ). Translation: Gšn and will come to the land the Gšn
- Targum Onkelos: ləpannā'â qȯdāmôhî ləgšen wa'ătô lə'ar'ā' dəGšen (לְפַנָּאָה קֳדָמוֹהִי לְגֹשֶׁן וְאָתוֹ לְאַרְעָא דְגֹשֶׁן). Translation: clear a place before him in Goshen. They then came to the land of Goshen.
- Targum Jerusalem: Gȯšənā' (גּוֹשְׁנָא)
- Targum Pseudo-Jonathan: gȯšənā' wə'ătô lə'ar'ā' dəGšen (גּוֹשְׁנָא וְאָתוֹ לְאַרְעָא דְגֹשֶׁן). Translation: goshena and traveled to (or in the proximity of) Gshen

The terms found in the Septuagint and Masoretic text do not correlate, suggesting the Aramaic version of Genesis read differently than the Paleo-Hebrew version. The meaning of gōšen (גֹּשֶׁן), the term found in Bereshít, has been debated for thousands of years. If the word was based on an Egyptian term, it was probably the Egyptian word gesen (𓂝𓈖), meaning "oil of." In 1885, the Egyptologist Édouard Naville identified this as the name of the Egyptian district that encompassed the region of Wadi Tumilat, Pithom, and the city of Ramesses, during the 26th Dynasty, between 672 and 525 BCE, suggesting the name was updated to Goshen when the Judahite version of Bereshít was compiled for King Josiah's Torah circa 625 BCE.

The Aramaic version of Genesis could not have included the words goshenah / goshen as the Greeks did not transliterate the terms, instead, translating the terms they found as Êrōōn polin and Ramesses. Êrōōn polin (Ηρωων πολιν), meaning "Hero's city" in Greek, was the Greek name of the city known as Per-Atum (𓉐�)

410

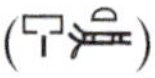

in Egyptian, meaning the "Temple of Atum." The other term found in the Septuagint is unusual, as the Greeks should have translated the term as "land of Ramesses" (χωρα των Ραμεσση) if that was the intent.

The Greek translation indicates the Aramaic text they worked from read ârq rômsîs (𐤑𐤏𐤑𐤏𐤅𐤉 𐤐𐤉𐤍), meaning "land Ramesses." This is one possible direct Aramaic translation of the Egyptian name Pi-Ramesses (𓉐 𓂝𓏤𓏲𓏏), meaning "House," "Palace," "Temple;" or "Domain" of Ramesses. Pi-Ramesses was the name of a major city in northern Egypt during the New Kingdom Era, founded by King Ramesses II (1279–1213 BCE), near the site of the older Hyksos capital of Ḥwt-wôrt (𓉐𓂋𓏤𓊖), meaning "mansion of the region," more commonly transliterated as Avaris from the later Greek transliteration of Αυαρις.

As Pi-Ramesses was only known as Pi-Ramesses during the New Kingdom Era, this means the Aramaic version had to have been translated from a Cuneiform version of Abraham / Cosmic Genesis translated sometime before the 12th century BCE. As this book of Abraham appears to have been written in Egyptian, the original local was likely Ḥwt-wôrt / Avaris. As the original text could not have been referring to the city of Per-Atum within the city of Pi-Ramesses (or Avaris), the alternate translation of Temple of Atum in Pi-Ramesses is used.

CHAPTER 47

Joseph went to Pharaoh and said, "My father and my brothers, and their livestock, oxen, and all their possessions, have come out of the land of Canaan, and see, they are in the land of Goshen."

He took from among his brothers, five men and brought them before Pharaoh.

Pharaoh asked the brothers of Joseph, "What is your occupation?"

They answered Pharaoh, "Your servants are herders, both we and our father," and they said to Pharaoh, "We have come to stay in the land, for there is no pasture for the flocks of your servants, for the famine has prevailed in the land of Canaan. So now, let us live in the land of Goshen."

Pharaoh said to Joseph, "Let them live in the land of Goshen, and if you know that there are able men among them, make them overseers of my livestock."

So Jacob and his sons came into Egypt, to Joseph, and Pharaoh the king of Egypt heard of it.

Pharaoh spoke to Joseph, saying, "Your father, and your brothers, have come to you. See, the land of Egypt is before you. Settle your father and your brothers in the best land."

CHAPTER 47

Joseph brought Jacob his father and set him before Pharaoh, and Jacob blessed Pharaoh. Pharaoh asked Jacob, "How many years have you lived?"

Jacob answered Pharaoh, "I have lived a hundred and thirty years. Few and evil have been the days of the years of my life. They have not attained the length of days of my fathers, that they lived."

Jacob blessed Pharaoh and departed from him. Joseph settled his father and his brothers, and gave them a possession in the land of Egypt, in the best land, in the land of Ramesses, as Pharaoh commanded.

Joseph gave provisions to his father, and his brothers, and to all the house of his father, enough grain for each person. There was no grain in all the land, for the famine was great. Both the land of Egypt and the land of Canaan fainted from the famine. Joseph gathered all the silver that was found in the lands of Egypt and Canaan, in return for the grain which they bought, and he distributed grain to them, and Joseph brought all the silver into the house of Pharaoh. The economy in the land of Egypt failed, and in the land of Canaan, and all the Egyptians came to Joseph, saying, "Give us bread, and why do we die in your presence? For our silver is spent."

Joseph said to them, "Bring your livestock, and I will give you bread for your livestock if your silver is spent."

They brought their livestock to Joseph, and Joseph gave them bread in return for their horses, and for their sheep, and for their oxen, and for their donkeys, and Joseph provided

CHAPTER 47

them with bread, for all their livestock in that year. That year ended and they came to him in the second year, and said to him, "Must we then be consumed before our lord? If our silver has failed, and our possessions, and our livestock, was brought to you, our lord, and there has not been left to us, before our lord, more than our own bodies, and our land, we are indeed destitute. In order, then, that we don't die before you, and the land is made desolate, buy us, and our land, for bread, and we and our land will be slaves to Pharaoh. Give seed that we may sow, and live and not die, and so our land will not be made desolate."

Joseph bought all the land of the Egyptians for Pharaoh, as the Egyptians sold their land to Pharaoh, for the famine prevailed against them, and the land became Pharaoh's. He brought the people into slavery to him, as slaves, from one frontier of Egypt to the other, excepting only the land of the priests, Joseph did not buy this, for Pharaoh gave a portion as a gift to the priests, and they ate their portion which Pharaoh gave them, and therefore, they did not sell their land. Joseph said to all the Egyptians, "Understand, I have bought you and your land today for Pharaoh. Take seed with you, and sow the land. There will be fruits from it, and you will give a fifth part to Pharaoh, and the four remaining parts will be for yourselves, as seed for the land, and as food for you, and all that are in your houses."

They answered, "You have saved us, and we have found favor before our lord, and we will be slaves to Pharaoh."

CHAPTER 47

Joseph appointed it to them as an ordinance until today, to reserve the fifth part for Pharaoh, on the land of Egypt, excepting only the land of the priests, that was not Pharaoh's. Israel lived in Egypt, in the land of Goshen, and they gained an inheritance on it, and they increased and multiplied greatly. Jacob survived seventeen years in the land of Egypt, and Jacob's days of the years of his life were a hundred and forty-seven years.

The days of Israel drew near for him to die, and he called his son Joseph, and said to him, "If I have found favor before you, put your hand under my thigh, and you will execute mercy and truth towards me, so as not to bury me in Egypt. But I will sleep with my fathers, and you will carry me up out of Egypt, and bury me in their sepulcher."

He answered, "I will do according to your word."

He continued, "Swear to me," and he swore to him. Israel worshiped the highest with the wand.

CHAPTER 48

After this, that it was reported to Joseph, "See, your father is ill." and he took his two sons, Manasseh and Ephraim, to Jacob.

It was reported to Jacob, "Look, your son Joseph comes to you," and Israel strengthened himself and sat up on the bed.

Jacob said to Joseph, "The god Shaddai[1] appeared to me in Luz, in the land of Canaan, and blessed me, and said to me, 'Look, I will increase you, and multiply you, and will make of you multitudes of nations, and I will give this land to you, and to your descendants after you, as an eternal possession.' Now then your two sons, who were born to you in the land of Egypt, before I came to you in Egypt, are mine. Ephraim and Manasseh, like Reuben and Simeon, they will be mine. The children which you will father from now on will be in the name of their brothers. They will be named after their inheritances. As for me, when I came out of Mesopotamia in Syria, Rachel, your mother, died in the land of Canaan, as I approached the horse-track of Chabratha, in the land of Canaan, in route to Ephrath, and I buried her in the road of the track." (This is Bethlehem.)

And when Israel saw the sons of Joseph, he asked, "Who are these to you?"

Joseph answered his father, "They are my sons, whom God gave me here."

Jacob said, "Bring me them, that I may bless them."

Now the eyes of Israel were dim through age, and he could not see, and he brought them near to him, and he kissed them and embraced them. Israel said to Joseph, "I have not been deprived of seeing your face, and God has shown me your descendants also."

Joseph brought them out from between his knees, and they did reverence to him, with their face to the ground. Joseph took his two sons, both Ephraim in his right hand, but on the left of Israel, and Manasseh on his left hand, but on the right of Israel, and brought them near to him. But Israel stretched out his right hand, laid it on the head of Ephraim who was the younger, and his left hand on the head of Manasseh, crossing his arms. He blessed them and said, "God, in whose sight my fathers were very pleasing, including Abraham and Isaac, God who continues to feed me from my youth until today. The messenger who delivers me from all evils, bless these boys, and my name will be called on them, and the name of my fathers, Abraham and Isaac, and let them be increased to a great multitude on the land."

Joseph having seen that his father put his right hand on the head of Ephraim, it seemed grievous to him, and Joseph took hold of the hand of his father, to remove it from the head of Ephraim to the head of Manasseh. Joseph said to his father, "Not so, father. This is the firstborn, lay your right hand on his head."

CHAPTER 48

He would not, and said, "I know it, son, I know it. He also will be a people, and he will be exalted, but his younger brother will be greater than he, and his seed will become a multitude of nations."

He blessed them on that day, saying, "Through you, Israel will be blessed. God will make you like Ephraim and Manasseh," and he set Ephraim before Manasseh.

Israel said to Joseph, "See, I die, and God will be with you, and restore you to the land of your fathers. I give you Shechem, a select portion above your brothers, which I took out from the hands of the Amorites with my sword and bow."

CHAPTER 48 NOTES

1 Codex Alexandrinus: T͞S mou (ΘΣ ΜΟΥ). Translation: god of mine

- Leningrad Codex: ēl Šadday (אֵל שַׁדַּי). Translation: god Shaddai
- Peshitta: åylšdy (ܐܠܫܕܝ)
- Targum Onkelos: ēl Šadday (אֵל שַׁדַּי). Translation: god Shaddai
- Targum Pseudo-Jonathan: ēl Šaday (אֵל שַׁדַּי). Translation: god Shaddai

This is the fifth deviation between *Cosmic Genesis* and *Bereshít* regarding the god Shaddai, and the fifth time the name or title Shaddai is missing entirely from the Septuagint's translation. The name Shaddai is imported from *Bereshít*. For more information on the god Shaddai, see the note in chapter 17.

CHAPTER 49

Jacob called his sons, and said to them, "Assemble yourselves, so I may tell you what will happen to you in future days. Gather around, and hear me, sons of Jacob. Listen to Israel; listen to your father."

"Reuben, my firstborn. You are my strength and the first of my children. Hard to put up with. Hard and self-willed. You were insolent like water. Don't explode with violence, for you went up to the bed of your father, and then you defiled the couch, where you went."

"Simeon and Levi, brothers. Accomplished the injustice of their cutting off. Don't let my mind come into their counsel and don't let my inward parts contend in their conspiracy, for in their anger they killed men, and in their passion, they ham-stringed a bull. Cursed be their anger, for it was willful, and their anger, for it was aggravated. I will divide them from Jacob, and scatter them from Israel."

"Judah, your brothers have praised you, and your hands will be on the back of your enemies. Your father's sons will do you reverence. Judah, is a lion's cub, from the tender plant, my son, you are gone up, having couched you lie like a lion, and like a cub, who will stir him up? A ruler will not fail from Judah, nor a prince from his thighs, until there come the things stored up for him, and he is the expectation of nations. Binding his foal to the vine, and the foal of his donkey to the branch of it, he will wash his robe in wine, and his garment in the blood of the grape. His eyes will be more cheering than wine, and his teeth whiter than milk."

"Zebulun will live on the coast, and he will be a haven of ships and will extend to Sidon."

"Issachar has desired that which is good, resting between the inheritances. Having seen the resting place that it was good, and the land that it was fertile, he subjected his shoulder to labor, and became a farmer."

"Dan will judge his people, and Israel too, like one tribe. Let Dan be a serpent on the road, besetting the road, biting the heel of the horse, and the rider will fall backward, waiting for the salvation of the Lord."

"Gad, a plundering army will plunder him, but he will plunder them, chasing closely after them."

"Asher, fat will be his bread, and he will surrender the weak to princes."

"Naphtali is a spreading stem, bestowing beauty on its fruit."

"Joseph is a son increased. My dearly loved son is increased, my youngest son, return to me. Against whom men taking evil counsel reproached him, and the archers pressed hard on him. But their bow and arrows were mightily consumed, and the sinews of their arms were slackened by the hand of the mighty one of Jacob, and there is he, that strengthened Israel from the god of your father, and with Shaddai[1] helped you and he blessed you with the blessing of Shamayim above, and the blessing of Eretz possessing all things, because of the blessing of the breasts and of the womb, the blessings of your father and your mother; it has prevailed above the blessing of the lasting mountains, and beyond the blessings of the eternal hills, and they will be on the head of Joseph and on the head of the brothers of whom he took the lead."

"Benjamin, like a ravenous wolf will still eat in the morning, and at evening he gives food."

All these are the twelve sons of Jacob, and their father spoke these words to them, and he blessed them. He blessed each of them according to his blessing. He said to them, "I am added to my people, you will bury me with my fathers in the cave, which is in the field of Ephron the Cypriot, in the double cave which is opposite Mamre, in the land of Canaan, the cave which Abraham bought of Ephron the Cypriot, for a possession of a sepulcher."

There, they buried Abraham and Sarah his wife. There, they buried Isaac and Rebekah his wife, and there they buried Leah in the portion of the field, and of the cave that was in it, purchased from the sons of the Cypriots. Jacob finished giving orders to his sons and lifted up his feet onto the bed, and he died and was gathered to his people.

CHAPTER 49

CHAPTER 49 NOTES

1 Codex Alexandrinus: T̄S̄ mou (ѲC̄ мОY). Translation: god of mine

- Leningrad Codex: ēl Šadday (אֵל שַׁדָּי). Translation: god Shaddai
- Peshitta: åylšdy (ܐܝܠܫܕܝ)
- Targum Onkelos: ēl Šadday (אֵל שַׁדַּי). Translation: god Shaddai
- Targum Pseudo-Jonathan: ēl Šaday (אֵל שַׁדַּי). Translation: god Shad

This is the sixth deviation between *Cosmic Genesis* and *Bereshít* regarding the god Shaddai, and the sixth time the name or title Shaddai is missing entirely from the Septuagint's translation. The name Shaddai is imported from *Bereshít*. For more information on the god Shaddai, see the note in chapter 17.

In this verse, the word åt (את) appears to be a translation of itti (𐎛𐎚𐎚𐎛), meaning "with," which is one of åt's more archaic interpretations. In most cases, the Masoretic text uses åt (את) the same way as the Phoenician åyt (𐤀𐤉𐤕) and Aramaic yt (𐡉𐡕), both meaning "you," however, that interpretation is not valid in this verse.

CHAPTER 50

Joseph fell on his father's face, and wept and kissed him. Joseph commanded his servants, the embalmers, to embalm his father, and they embalmed Israel. They waited the forty days for him, which are the days that embalming takes, and Egypt mourned for him seventy days. And when the days of mourning were past, Joseph said to the princes of Pharaoh, "If I have found favor in your sight, speak concerning me to Pharaoh, saying, 'My father commanded me,' saying, 'In the sepulcher which I dug for myself in the land of Canaan you will bury me.' Now then I will go up and bury my father, and return again."

Pharaoh replied to Joseph, "Go up and bury your father, as he forced you to swear," and so Joseph went up to bury his father, and all the servants of Pharaoh went up with him, and the elders of his house, and all the elders of the land of Egypt, and all the household of Joseph, and his brothers, and all the house of his father, and his families, but they left behind the sheep and oxen in the land of Goshen. There went up with him also chariots and cavalry, and there was a very great company. They came to the threshing floor of Atad, which is beyond Jordan, and they mourned him with great lamentation, and he sat shiva for his father seven days. The inhabitants of the land of Canaan saw the mourning at the floor of Atad, and said, "This is a great mourning for the Egyptians," therefore he called its name, "The mourning of Egypt," which is beyond Jordan.

His sons did this for him. His sons carried him up into the land of Canaan and buried him in the double cave, which cave Abraham bought for possession of a burying place from Ephrom the Cypriot, near Mamre. Then Joseph returned to Egypt, he and his brothers, and those that had gone up with him to bury his father. When the brothers of Joseph saw that their father was dead, they said, "Let's keep watch, in case at any time Joseph remembers our the evil against him and pays us back all the evils which we have done against him."

They came to Joseph, and said, "Your father commanded us before his death, saying, 'Tell Joseph, "Forgive them their injustice and their sin, in all the evil they have done to you."' Now accept the injustice of the servants of the god of your father.'"

Joseph wept while they spoke to him, then they came to him and said, "We, these persons, are your servants."

Joseph consoled them, "Don't be afraid, for I am God's. You took counsel against me for evil, but God took counsel for me for good, that the matter might be as it is today, and many people might be fed." He said to them, "Don't be afraid, I will maintain you, and your families," and he comforted them and spoke kindly to them.

Joseph lived in Egypt, he and his brothers and all the family of his father, and Joseph lived a hundred and ten years. Joseph saw the children of Ephraim to the third generation, and the sons of Machir, the son of Manasseh, were borne on the thigh of Joseph. Joseph spoke to his brothers, saying, "I die, but God will surely visit you and will bring you out of this land to the land that God swore to our fathers, Abraham, Isaac, and Jacob."

Joseph commanded the sons of Israel, saying, "When God visits you, then you will carry my bones up with you."

Joseph died at a hundred and ten years, and they buried him in a coffin in Egypt.

MAPS

Sumer between 6500 and 2900 BCE:

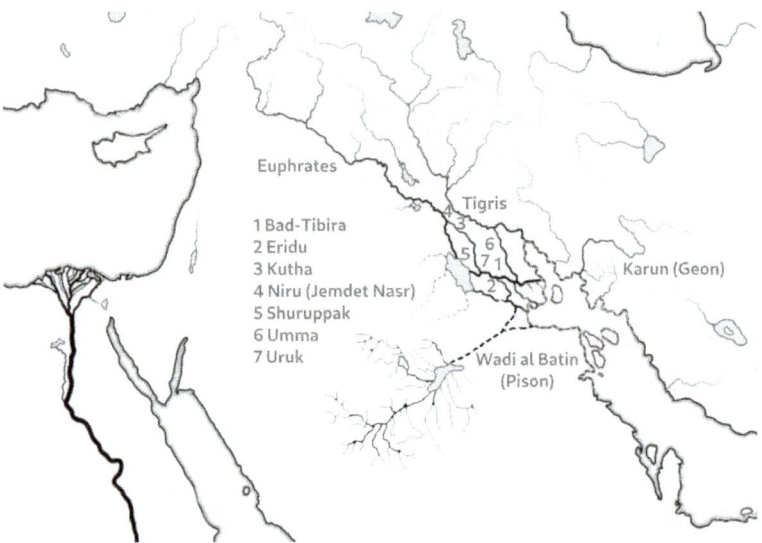

Neo-Sumerian Empire (Ur III) and Egypt circa 2000 BCE:

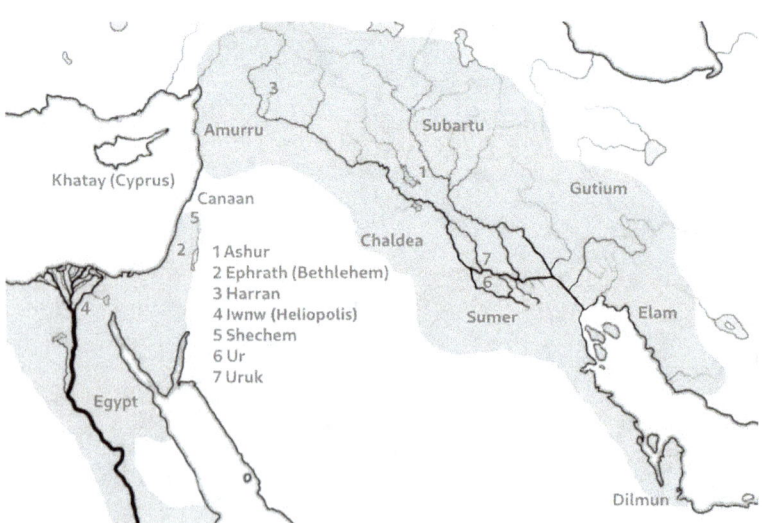

Septuagint Manuscripts

The following is a list of the Septuagint manuscripts referenced in the notes for this book.

LXX A (Codex Alexandrinus) is dated to the 5th century. It is currently located at the British Library (Royal 1 D. VIII) in London.

LXX B (Codex Vaticanus) is dated to the 4th century. It is currently located at the Vatican Library (Gr. 1209) in Vatican City.

LXX D (Cotton Genesis) is dated to the 4th through 6th centuries. It is currently located at the British Library (Otto B VI) in London.

LXX G (Codex Colberto-Sarravianus) is dated to the 4th or 5th century. Sections are currently located at the University Library (Voss. Graec. in qu. 8) in Leiden, National Library of France (Coisl. Gr. 17) in Paris, and the National Library of Russia (Gr. 3) in St. Petersburg.

LXX L (Vienna Genesis) is dated to the 5th or 6th century. It is currently located at the Austrian National Library (Theol. Gr. 31) in Vienna.

LXX 14 is dated to the 11th century. It is currently located at the Vatican Library (Vat. Palat. Gr. 203) in Vatican City.

LXX 15 is dated to the 10th century. It is currently located at the National Library of France (Coisl. Gr. 2) in Paris.

LXX 16 is dated to the 11th century. It is currently located at the Laurentian Library (v. 38) in Florence.

LXX 17 is dated to the 10th century. It is currently located at the State Historical Museum (Gr. 385) in Moscow.

LXX 18 is dated to the 11th century. It is currently located at the Laurentian Library (Pal. 242) in Florence.

LXX 19 is dated to the 12th century. It is currently located at the Chigi Palace (R. VI. 38) in Rome.

LXX 25 is dated to the 11th century. It is currently located at the Bavarian State Library (Gr. 9) in Munich.

LXX 31 is dated to the 15th century. It is currently located at the Austrian National Library (Theol. Gr. 7) in Vienna.

LXX 44 is dated to the 15th century. It is currently located at the Stadtbibliothek (A 1) in Zittau.

LXX 46 is dated to the 15th century. It is currently located at the National Library of France (Coisl. Gr. 4) in Paris.

LXX 53 is dated to 1439. It is currently located at the National Library of France (Gr. 17 A) in Paris.

LXX 54 is dated to the 13th or 14th century. It is currently located at the National Library of France (Gr. 5) in Paris.

LXX 55 is dated to the 10th century. It is currently located at the Vatican Library (Regin. Gr. 1) in Vatican City.

LXX 56 is dated to 1093. It is currently located at the National Library of France (Gr. 3) in Paris.

LXX 57 is dated to the 11th century. It is currently located at the Vatican Library (Gr. 747) in Vatican City.

LXX 58 is dated to the 11th century. It is currently located at the Vatican Library (Regin. gr. 10) in Vatican City.

LXX 59 is dated to the 15th century. It is currently located at the University Library (BE 7b. 10) in Glasgow.

LXX 64 is dated to the 10th century. It is currently located at the National Library of France (Gr. 2) in Paris.

LXX 71 is dated to the 13th century. It is currently located at the National Library of France (Coisl. Gr. 1) in Paris.

LXX 72 is dated to the 13th century. It is currently located at the Bodleian Library (Canonic. Gr. 35) in Oxford.

Septuagint Manuscripts

LXX 74 is dated to the 13th century. It is currently located at the Laurentian Library (S. Marco 700) in Florence.

LXX 75 is dated to 1125. It is currently located at University College (52) in Oxford.

LXX 76 is dated to the 13th century. It is currently located at National Library of France (Coisl. Gr. 4) in Paris.

LXX 77 is dated to the 13th or 14th centuries. It is currently located at the Vatican Library (Gr. 748) in Vatican City.

LXX 78 is dated to the 12th century. It is currently located at the Vatican Library (Gr. 383) in Vatican City.

LXX 79 is dated to the 12th or 13th centuries. It is currently located at the Vatican Library (Gr. 1668) in Vatican City.

LXX 82 is dated to the 12th century. It is currently located at the National Library of France (Coisl. Gr. 3) in Paris.

LXX 84 is dated to the 10th or 11th centuries. It is currently located at the Vatican Library (Gr. 1901) in Vatican City.

LXX 106 is dated to the 14th century. It is currently located at the Biblioteca Comunale Ariostea (187 I-III) in Ferrara.

LXX 107 is dated to 1334. It is currently located at the Biblioteca Comunale Ariostea (188 I) in Ferrara.

LXX 108 is dated to the 13th century. It is currently located at the Vatican Library (Gr. 330) in Vatican City.

LXX 120 is dated to the 12th or 13th centuries. It is currently located at the Biblioteca Marciana (Gr. 23) in Venice.

LXX 121 is dated to the 10th century. It is currently located at the Biblioteca Marciana (Gr. 3) in Venice.

LXX 122 is dated to the 15th century. It is currently located at the Biblioteca Marciana (Gr. 6) in Venice.

LXX 125 is dated to the 14th century. It is currently located at the State Historical Museum (Gr. 30) in Moscow.

LXX 127 is dated to the 10th century. It is currently located at the State Historical Museum (Gr. 31) in Moscow.

LXX 128 is dated to the 11th century. It is currently located at the Vatican Library (Gr. 1657) in Vatican City.

LXX 129 is dated to the 11th or 12th centuries. It is currently located at the Vatican Library (Gr. 1252) in Vatican City.

LXX 130 is dated to the 12th or 13th centuries. It is currently located at the Austrian National Library (Theol. Gr. 23) in Vienna.

LXX 131 is dated to the 10th century. It is currently located at the Austrian National Library (Theol. Gr. 57) in Vienna.

LXX 134 is dated to the 11th centuries. It is currently located at the Biblioteca Marciana (Plut. 5.1) in Venice.

LXX 135 is dated to the 10th centuries. It is currently located at the University Library (A. N. III. 13) in Basel.

LXX 246 is dated to 1195 CE. It is currently located at the Vatican Library (Gr. 1238) in Vatican City

LXX 313 is dated to the 11th century. It is currently located at the National Library of Greece (43) in Athens.

LXX 314 is dated to the 13th century. It is currently located at the National Library of Greece (44) in Athens.

LXX 318 is dated to the 10th or 11th centuries. It is currently located at the Vatopedi (598) on Mount Athos.

LXX 319 is dated to 1021. It is currently located at the Vatopedi (600) on Mount Athos.

LXX 343 is dated to the 11th century. It is currently located at the Great Lavra (352) on Mount Athos.

LXX 344 is dated to the 10th century. Sections are currently located at the Pantokratoros Monastery (24) on Mount Athos, and the Patriarchal Library (Τάφου 510 β) in Jerusalem.

LXX 346 is dated to 1326. It is currently located at the Protaton (53) on Mount Athos.

LXX 370 is dated to the 11th through 14th centuries. It is currently located at the Vatican Library (Chis. R VIII 61) in Vatican City.

LXX 376 is dated to the 15th century. It is currently located at the Royal Library (Y-II-5) in El Escorial.

LXX 392 is dated to the 10th century. It is currently located at the Abbey of Saint Mary of Grottaferrata (A. γ. I) in Grottaferrata.

LXX 400 is dated to the 11th century. It is currently located at the National Library of Greece (Μετ. Τάφου, 224) in Athens.

LXX 407 is dated to the 9th century. It is currently located at the Patriarchal Library (Τάφου 2) in Jerusalem.

LXX 408 is dated to the 12th or 13th centuries. It is currently located at the Patriarchal Library (Τάφου 3) in Jerusalem.

LXX 413 is dated to the 13th century. It is currently located at the Library of the Topkapı Palace (8) in Istanbul.

LXX 414 is dated to the 14th century. It is currently located at the University Library (Voss. Graec. in fol. 13) in Leiden.

LXX 422 is dated to the 12th century. It is currently located at the British Library (Add. 35123) in London.

LXX 426 is dated to the 11th century. It is currently located at the British Library (Add. 39585) in London.

LXX 458 is dated to the 12th century. It is currently located at the University Library (62) in Messina.

LXX 500 is dated to the 11th or 12th centuries. It is currently located at the Austrian National Library (Suppl. Gr. 176) in Vienna.

Septuagint Manuscripts

LXX 509 is dated to the 9th or 10th centuries. Sections are currently located at the Bodleian Library (Auct. T. inf. 2. 1) in Oxford, University Library (Add. 1879. 7) in Cambridge, British Library (Add. 20002) in London, and the National Library of Russia (Gr. 62) in St. Petersburg.

LXX 527 is dated to the 14th century. It is currently located at the Bibliothèque de l"Arsenal (Gr. 8415) in Paris.

LXX 550 is dated to the 12th century. It is currently located at the National Library of France (Gr. 128) in Paris.

LXX 551 is dated to the 13th century. It is currently located at the National Library of France (Gr. 129) in Paris.

LXX 569 is dated to the 13th century. It is currently located at the National Library of France (Gr. 161) in Paris.

LXX 610 is dated to the 14th century. It is currently located at the National Library of France (Suppl. gr. 609) in Paris.

LXX 615 is dated to the 11th century. It is currently located at the Pelekete monastery (216) on Patmos Island.

LXX 618 is dated to the 13th century. It is currently located at the Pelekete monastery (410) on Patmos Island.

LXX 664 is dated to the 14th century. It is currently located at the Vatican Library (Pii. II. gr. 20) in Vatican City.

LXX 707 is dated to the 10th or 11th centuries. Sections are currently located at Saint Catherine's Monastery (Codex Gr. 1) in the Sinai, and the National Library of Russia (Gr. 260) in St. Petersburg.

LXX 730 is dated to the 10th century. It is currently located at the Biblioteca Marciana (Gr. 15) in Venice.

LXX 739 is dated to the 10th century. It is currently located at the Biblioteca Marciana (Gr. 534) in Venice.

LXX 761 is dated to the 13th century. It is currently located at the Zentralbibliothek (C 11) in Zürich.

SEPTUAGINT MANUSCRIPTS

LXX 799 is dated to 1280. It is currently located at the National Library of Greece (2491) in Athens.

LXX 814 (Yale Genesis) is dated to the 1st through 3rd centuries. It is currently located at Yale University (P. CtYBR Inv. 419) in New Haven.

LXX 833 is dated to the 8th or 9th centuries. It is currently located at the University Library (S. Salv. 140+126) in Messina.

LXX 903 is dated to the 3rd or 4th centuries. It is currently located at the Ägyptisches Museum (P. 9778) in Berlin.

LXX 907 (Papyrus Oxyrhynchus 1007) is dated to the 3rd century. It is currently located at the British Library (Inv. 2047) in London.

LXX 911 (Berlin Genesis) is dated to the 3rd century. It is currently located at the Institute of Archaeology at the University of Warsaw (P. Berlin G 2a-17b, u 46-61) in Warsaw.

LXX 912 (Papyrus 12) is dated to the 3rd century. It is currently located at the Morgan Library & Museum (Pap. Gr. 3; P. Amherst 3b) in New York.

LXX 961 is dated to the 4th century. It is currently located at the Chester Beatty Library (P. Ch. Beatty IV) in Dublin.

ALTERNATIVE SOURCES

The following is a list of alternative ancient translations that were used for comparative analysis. Both the Peshitta and Coptic translations are believed to have been heavily based on the Septuagint, although do inherit relics of older Imperial Aramaic translations, or imports from the Hebrew translation.

The Leningrad Codex is dated to 1008 (or 1009) CE. It is currently located at the National Library of Russia (Firkovich B 19 A) in St. Petersburg. The Leningrad Codex is the oldest complete copy of the Hebrew scriptures used within Judaism.

The Peshitta is the Classical Syriac Aramaic translation of the Christian bible. The Old Testament was translated from older Aramaic and Hebrew sources during the late 2nd century CE.

Peshitta manuscript 5b1 is dated to the 5th century. It is currently located at the British Library (Add. 14,425) in London.

Peshitta manuscript 7a1 is dated to the 6th or 7th centuries. It is currently located at the Ambrosian Library (B. 21 Inf.) in Milan.

The Targum Onkelos is generally accepted as having been compiled by Aquila (Onkelos) of Sinope between 100 and 120 CE, although the surviving copies are all in Babylonian Aramaic, and the text appears to have been updated linguistically in Babylon in the 4th or 5th centuries CE. Some scholars believe Aquila was reworking a now lost, older Judean-Aramaic targum from the 1st century. The Megillah (3a) tractate of the Babylonian Torah claims that the Onkelos Targum is a restoration of a version of the Torah in use before the time of Ezra the scribe in the 4th century BCE. While the idea that Aquila and Onkelos were the same person, the Talmuds mention both of them doing the same thing, creating a targum in the same era, but do not confirm they are the same person. Therefore, the Onkelos is sometimes viewed as being a continuation of an older Babylonian Aramaic translation from the Neo-Babylonian, Persian, or Greek eras.

The Targum Pseudo-Jonathan has historically been misidentified as the Targum Jonathan, and is also called the Targum Jerusalem in some literature, although this is not the same document as the Targum Jerusalem listed below. It is written in Palestinian-Aramaic, and generally dated to sometime between the 4th and 11th centuries. Some scholars believe it originated in the 4th century and was modified after the Islamic conquest of Palestine, as it includes some Arabic names generally found in Islamic sources. It existed before the crusades, as it was documented at the time.

The Targum Jerusalem, sometimes called the Targum Jerusalem II or the Fragments Targum, is a collection of fragments from one or more targums written in Judean Aramaic that surfaced in Italy during the medieval era. It contains a number of heretical concepts, such as Judean-polytheism, suggesting some are a relic of a polytheist Israelite sect from before the Maccabean Revolt. The oldest Targum Jerusalem fragments date to the medieval period or later, and are copies of a manuscript reworked in the 5th century CE. However, the Targum is written in a form of Judeo-Aramaic that supports its origin in the Persian, Hellenistic, or Hasmonean eras.

The Vetus Latina manuscripts are Old Latin manuscripts translated from Aramaic and Greek sources between the 3rd century BCE and 4th century CE. Surviving manuscripts are copies that were made much later. The earliest surviving manuscripts that include Cosmic Genesis date to the 5th century CE.

Bohairic manuscripts are translations of the Septuagint into Bohairic (also known as Memphitic), one of the six dialects of Coptic, the classical era form of the Egyptian language. These dialects were written slightly differently, and therefore words transliterated into Coptic retain slightly different pronunciations, reflecting the different source texts used. Bohairic originated in the western Nile Delta of northern Egypt. The earliest Bohairic manuscripts date to the 4th century, however, the majority of texts come from the 9th century or later. Bohairic is the dialect used today as the liturgical language of the Coptic Orthodox Church, although Sahidic was used before the 11th century. Translations of the Septuagint were made into at least five of the Coptic dialects, however, complete copies only survive in Bohairic and Sahidic.

Papyrus Bohairic 2 is a fragmentary early Christian Bohairic manuscript dated to the 4th century.

Lycopolitan manuscripts are translations of the Septuagint into Lycopolitan (also known as Subakhmimic and Assiutic), one of the three minor of Coptic, the classical era form of the Egyptian language. The dialect was closely related to Akhmimic, which was more common. The surviving Lycopolitan manuscripts are mostly Gnostic and Manichaean works, which date to between the 4th and 7th centuries.

Lycopolitan manuscript 200 is dated to the 4th through 7th centuries.

Oxyrhynchite manuscripts are translations of the Septuagint into Oxyrhynchite (also known as Middle Egyptian or Mesokemic), one of the minor of Coptic, the classical era form of the Egyptian language. The dialect was closely related to Fayyumic, and was spoken in the region around Oxyrhynchus, known today as el-Bahnasa (البهنسا). Oxyrhynchite manuscripts date to the 4th and 5th centuries.

Oxyrhynchite manuscript 201 is dated to the 4th or 5th centuries.

Sahidic manuscripts are translations of the Septuagint into Sahidic (also known as Thebaic), one of the six dialects of Coptic, the classical era form of the Egyptian language. Sahidic was the dominant form of Coptic used before the 11th century, and is believed to have originated in the region around Hermopolis, at the boundary between Upper and Lower Egypt. Translations of the Septuagint into Sahidic are known to have existed by the 4th century, however, early non-dialect specific translations are generally accepted as having been made as early as the 1st century CE, with some scholars suggesting the 1st century BCE. The early non-dialect specific forms of Coptic are generally grouped with Sahidic, as Sahidic did not have a standardized spelling until the 6th century.

Sahidic manuscript 16L is a Sahidic Coptic and Arabic parallel text dated to earlier than 1443. It is currently located at the Biblioteca Apostolica Vaticana (Borg. copt. 109, cass. XXIII, fasc. 99) in Vatican City.

Sahidic manuscript 299L is a Sahidic manuscript dated to earlier than 1131. It is currently located at the Coptic Museum (Inv. n° 3948) in Cairo, Bibliothèque nationale de France (Copte 129 and Copte 133) in Paris, the British Library (Or. 6954 and Or. 3579 A) in London, Österreichische Nationalbibliothek (K 9618, K 9683, K 9684, K 9698, K 9704, K 9721) in Vienna, and the Biblioteca Apostolica Vaticana (Borg. copt. 109, cass. XXII, fasc. 87) in Vatican City.

Sahidic manuscript 625L is a Sahidic manuscript dated to the 7th century. It is currently located at the Bibliothèque nationale de France (Copte 129 and Copte 132) in Paris, the British Library (Or. 6954) in London, Bodleian Library (Copt. d. 246) in Oxford, the Biblioteca Nazionale (I.B. 13) in Naples, and the Universitätsbibliothek (Frag. 40, pieces 2-3) in Oslo.

Sahidic manuscript 2002 is a late Sahidic manuscript dated to the 9th century. It is currently located at the Universitätsbibliothek Leuven (Copt. Lov. 2) in Leuven.

Sahidic manuscript 2020 is a late Sahidic manuscript dated to the 11th century. It is currently located at the Staatsbibliothek zu Berlin

ALTERNATIVE TRANSLATIONS

Preußischer Kulturbesitz (Ms. or. fol. 1605, Blatt 1) in Berlin, the Bibliothèque nationale de France (Copte 129 and Copte 102) in Paris, the British Library (Or. 6954 and Or. 6701) in London, the Österreichische Nationalbibliothek (K 9375) in Vienna, and the Biblioteca Apostolica Vaticana (Borg. copt. 109, cass. I, fasc. 2 and Vat. Copto 111, fol. 96-97) in Vatican City.

Sahidic manuscript 2037 is dated to the 9th or 10th century. It is currently located at the Coptic Museum (Inv. N° 2698) in Cairo, the Bibliothèque nationale de France (Copte 129 and Copte 133) in Paris, the University Library (Or. 16.1699 Π I) in Cambridge, the Österreichische Nationalbibliothek (K 9431, K9376, K 9377, K 9379, K 9432, K 9433, K 9434, and K 9435) in Vienna, the University Library (P. Mich. Inv. No. 158,1) in Ann Arbor, and Biblioteca Apostolica Vaticana (Borg. copt. 109, cass. I, fasc. 1) in Vatican City.

Sahidic manuscript 2042 is dated to the 10th century. It is currently located at the Bibliothèque nationale de France (Copte 129) in Paris, the British Library (Or. 6782 and Or. 6954) in London, the Biblioteca Nazionale (I.B. 13) in Naples, the Österreichische Nationalbibliothek (K 9380 and K 9381) in Vienna, the Pushkin State Museum of Fine Arts (I.1.b.650) in Moscow, and Biblioteca Apostolica Vaticana (Borg. copt. 109, cass. I, fasc. 3) in Vatican City.

Sahidic manuscript 2069 is dated to the 7th or 8th century. It is currently located at the Coptic Museum (Inv. n° 3853) in Cairo, the Bibliothèque nationale de France (Copte 129 and Copte 133) in Paris, and the British Library (Or. 3579 A) in London.

Sahidic manuscript 2148 is dated to the 11th century. It is currently located at the Bibliothèque nationale de France (Copte 129) in Paris, the British Library (Or. 3579 A) in London, and the Österreichische Nationalbibliothek (K 9879, K 9875, K 9876, K 9877, K 9878) in Vienna, and the Biblioteca Apostolica Vaticana (Borg. copt. 109, cass. X, fasc. 32) in Vatican City.

ALTERNATIVE TRANSLATIONS

Sahidic manuscript 2210 is dated to the 6th century. It is currently located at the British Library (Or. 5287) in London.

Sahidic manuscript 2211 is dated to the 6th century. It is currently located at the Bodleian Library (Copt. c. 20) in Oxford.

Sahidic manuscript 2212 is dated to the 7th century. It is currently located at the Corpus Christi College (Hoskyns MS 541) in Cambridge.

The Armenian bible was translated from the Septuagint in the 5th century, replacing the older Armenian bible that had been translated from Aramaic texts, however, includes some of the older names.

DEAD SEA SCROLLS

The following is a list of the Dead Sea Scrolls mentioned in the notes for this book. Most are held by the Israel Museum in Jerusalem.

DSS 1Q1 (1QGen) is dated to the Herodian Dynasty in Judea (37 BCE to 6 CE)

DSS 4Q2 (4QGen[b]) is dated to the Roman era in Judea and Palestine (6 to 390 CE).

DSS 4Q4 (4QGen[d]) is dated to the Hasmonean Dynasty in Judea (140 to 37 BCE)

DSS 4Q5 (4QGen[e]) is dated to the Herodian Dynasty in Judea (37 BCE to 6 CE)

DSS 4Q6 (4QGen[f]) is dated to the Hasmonean Dynasty in Judea (140 to 37 BCE)

DSS 4Q7 (4QGen[g]) is dated to the Hasmonean Dynasty in Judea (140 to 37 BCE).

DSS 4Q9 (4QGen[j]) is dated to the Hasmonean Dynasty in Judea (140 to 37 BCE)

DSS 4Q11 (4QpaleoGen-Exod[l]) is dated to the Hasmonean Dynasty in Judea (140 to 37 BCE)

DSS Mur1 is dated to the Roman era in Judea and Palestine (6 to 390 CE).

ALSO AVAILABLE

ALSO AVAILABLE